WILLIAMS & ROGERS SERIES

COMMERCIAL LAW

BY

D. CURTIS GANO, LL.M.

OF THE ROCHESTER, N.Y., BAR

ASSISTED BY

SAMUEL C. WILLIAMS

TEACHER OF COMMERCIAL LAW IN THE
ROCHESTER BUSINESS INSTITUTE

REVISED BY

RALPH E. ROGERS

OF THE NEW YORK BAR

AMERICAN BOOK COMPANY

NEW YORK   CINCINNATI   CHICAGO

PREFACE

THE author of this work has aimed to select from the extensive field of the law those fundamental principles, a knowledge of which the business man will most frequently find of value to him, and which the teacher of Commercial Law will regard most useful to his classes.

It is not the purpose of this volume to make lawyers of its readers, but to teach them to discern the ways that lead from litigation, and to enable them to conduct their business dealings with an intelligent idea of their legal rights and limitations.

Technical terms have been avoided as far as possible, and when it has been thought advisable to use them they have been fully defined either in the text or in the glossary. The latter contains a most complete list of the legal terms ordinarily employed, with concise yet sufficient definition.

The subjects discussed have been arranged i. the order in which it is deemed advisable for the teacher to present them. It is believed that all of the subjects with which the business man should become familiar have been included in the present volume, and are explained with sufficient detail to give the reader a correct knowledge of the law concerning them. In many instances different conclusions that have been arrived at by the courts in the several states have been pointed out in detail, that the student may understand the conflicts in the laws of the different jurisdictions.

Believing that in the illustration of legal principles, actual cases decided by the courts furnish material much more valuable for the student than purely hypothetical cases, careful selection has been made throughout the text from the reports of cases in the different American and English courts.

3

The tabulations at the end of the volume give in a general way the statutes of the different states on several important topics, and may be consulted by the student in determining the law in his own state.

Full sets of forms have been given in appropriate connection with the text, and they will be found a valuable guide to the student not only while using this work as a text, but also as a reference when occasion may require his use of such forms in business transactions.

D. CURTIS GANO.

CONTENTS

5

COMMERCIAL LAW

LAW IN GENERAL

Definition. — Law in its broadest sense is a rule of action. Every plant grows and every animal lives, develops, and dies according to a law; the movements of the heavenly bodies as well as the changes of the seasons are also under a like control. It follows, therefore, that law in a general sense is a very comprehensive subject and includes all of the sciences.

In a narrower sense law is the system of principles and rules which relate to the actions of men in their dealings and relations with one another.

Law Classified. — Law may be classified as moral, international, and municipal.

Moral Law. — The code of ethics which prescribes the right and wrong in the conduct of one toward another, is called the moral law. Its rules are enforced by the sentiment of the people derived from their belief in, and understanding of, right and wrong. The study of this subject belongs to the science of ethics rather than to law. It is moral laws that tell us to deal honestly, to speak truthfully, and not to take advantage of the weak.

International Law. — The law which regulates the intercourse of nations is international law. It consists of rules and principles founded on customs, treaties, the weight of opinion as to justice, and the mutual obligations which civilized nations recognize as binding upon them in their dealings with other nations, each being supreme and independent. The conduct of the vessels of different nations toward one another on the high seas, which are open to all, is a question of international law, as

7

are the rights and protection of representatives of one country within the boundary of another.

Municipal Law. — The rules of action prescribed by the supreme power in a state, commanding what is to be done and prohibiting what is not to be done, constitute municipal law.

Every state or nation must have some head or supreme power, and in a republic like ours this power rests in the people and is administered by the officers whom they elect. The laws are made by the legislators, administered by the executive department of the government, and interpreted by the courts who apply these laws to the cases that are brought before them.

It is necessary in civilized nations that the conduct of man in relation with his brother man be regulated and restricted. Otherwise a resort to arms would be the only redress for a wrong. So it is that municipal law is required in order to insure justice and harmony. Because of this branch of the law contracts can be enforced, possession of real property acquired by its true owner, and crimes punished.

Municipal Law Classified. — Again, municipal law can be classified as constitutional law, ecclesiastical law, statute law, common law, and equity.

Constitutional Law. — Every nation or state has a constitution, either written or unwritten, under which the nation exists and which as the basis of its power regulates, distributes, and limits its different functions and departments. The law applying to these constitutions and to the establishment, powers, and limitations of the government as applicable thereto is known as constitutional law. The United States Constitution provides that no person shall be deprived of life, liberty, or property without due process of law. The law applicable to such a case is constitutional law.

Ecclesiastical Law. — This is the law administered in the English ecclesiastical courts and is a system restricted mainly to the affairs of the church and matters pertaining thereto. This court is not known in America. In England, among other things, the ecclesiastical law had control of questions affecting the marriage relation.

Statute Law. — Statute law is made up of legislative enactments duly sanctioned and authenticated.

Common Law and Equity. — The great body of municipal law in early English practice was known as the common law and consisted originally only of customs. These, however, because of long usage came in time to have the force of laws. As the affairs of a growing commercial country became more intricate, the hard and fast rules of common law which were firmly bound down by precedent were found inadequate for all the needs of the people, and there sprang up the chancery courts which decided controversies from an equitable standpoint and gave relief independent of precedent. This chancery or equity court still exists in a modified form, but the distinction between common law and equity has in a great measure disappeared. The distinction of to-day consists in the relief sought; if it be merely money damages, then it is a common law case; if some extraordinary relief, as prohibiting a man from erecting a powder factory on his land which would endanger his neighbor's dwelling, or correcting a deed of land which was improperly drawn, then the case is in equity.

Division of Common Law. — Common law can be divided into criminal and civil law.

Criminal Law. — The preservation of society demands that certain rules be laid down regulating the acts of its members toward the community in general. A violation of these laws is an offense against the state and is called a crime. The law which treats of crimes and their punishment is called criminal law. It forbids one man to steal from another, making it a crime, because such acts endanger the security of property and the safety of society, and a punishment of imprisonment for such an offense is therefore provided.

Civil Law. — As distinguished from the criminal law, that branch of law which looks to the establishment and recovery of private rights is called civil law. It controls the private rights and remedies of men in their relations with each other, in contrast with those that are public and affect the community in general.

Commercial Law. — The subject which we are about to pursue, commercial law, is a branch of the civil law, and includes the laws regulating the rights and relations of persons engaged in trade or commercial pursuits, as the law of contracts, of partnership, or of agency.

Sources of Laws. — Our laws may be considered as derived from three sources, the common law, the statutes, and the Constitution. The common law, which was derived primarily from the English law, was established in this country by the early English settlers. It is made up of the rules and customs which were in use from time immemorial and came to be recognized as laws. It is also termed the unwritten law, because in the early times it consisted merely of the customs of the people. Now it is embodied in the decisions of our courts, the great mass of our reports of these decisions being the common law in this way reduced to writing.

The United States and also each of the several states have their law-making bodies. In the United States it is Congress, and in the states, the legislatures. These bodies from time to time pass certain laws, which are known as the statute laws, also called the written laws. These statutes may expressly change the common law, as is often the case, when the condition of the nation or the progress of the people requires it. For instance, by the common law a wife could hold no property, as at her marriage it reverted to her husband, but by the statute law in all of the states this is changed, and now in most of them she can hold property to the same extent as though unmarried. In other cases the statutes declare and put in express terms a part of what formerly existed in the common law; as, under the common law persons meeting on the highway were to turn to the right, and the same rule is now laid down in the statutes.

The constitutions of the United States and of the several states are another form of the written law.

In the United States the Constitution is paramount in importance, and, in so far as it applies, all other laws must give way. It provides that certain subjects that come within the province of the general government shall be under the exclusive authority of Congress, and that the constitutions and legislatures of the several states can not provide or make laws to the contrary. On the other hand, all subjects not expressly confided to Congress are left to the state authorities, and are under the control of the constitution and statutes of the state. Every state statute must be in conformity with the constitution of the state, as well as with the Constitution and laws of the United States. The common or unwritten laws also must be in conformity with the statutes of the state, as well as with the state constitutions and the Constitution and laws of the United States.

QUESTIONS ON LAW IN GENERAL

1. Define law in its broadest sense.
2. Name and define the classifications of law in a narrower sense.
3. Name and define the classifications of municipal law.
4. Name and define the classifications of common law.
5. What are the three sources of our laws?
6. When the laws from these different sources conflict, which is paramount?

CONTRACTS

1. IN GENERAL

Definition. — A contract is an agreement between two or more persons, based upon legal consideration, or in writing under seal, to do or not to do some particular thing.

Necessary Conditions. — There are many elements necessary to make a legal and binding contract, but there are four elements at the foundation of all contracts. These are:

1. Competent parties.
2. Legal subject-matter.
3. Agreement.
4. Consideration.

Or, in the case of some written contracts, a seal, which is said to import consideration.

Executed and Executory Contracts. — Contracts may be considered under the classification of executed and executory contracts.

An executed contract is one in which the transaction has been performed and the terms of the agreement fulfilled. It is a contract which has been carried out.

An executory contract is one in which the thing agreed upon has not been done.

In some cases the contract may be executed on one side and executory on the other; that is, one party may have performed his part of the contract, while the other party has not.

An illustration of this class of contracts is found in *Andreas* v. *Holcombe*, 22 Minn. 339,[1] which was an action upon the following agreement : —

_____

[1] The cases cited throughout this book arose in the state or country indicated in the title. Thus the case of *Andreas* v. *Holcombe*, 22 Minn. 339, given above, arose in the state of Minnesota and will be found in volume 22 of the reports of the

$140.   St. Paul, Minn., 17 June, 1874.

" In consideration for causing a 12-inch view of Park Place Hotel to be
printed in his atlas of the state of Minnesota, I promise to pay A. T. Andreas,
or his order, the sum of one hundred forty dollars ; payments to be made, one
half on completion of design, draft, or sketch ; remainder when atlas is complete.   One hundred extra views given on delivery of atlas.
                                              " E. V. Holcombe."

Andreas had got out the book, including the view as above specified.   The
defense claimed that the agreement was not binding upon both parties.   It
was held that while the writing did not show any consideration on the part of
Andreas, it was in the nature of a request to do the things specified, and
became a binding and valid contract when performed on the one side, as the
performance was but complying with the request.

Miller v. *McKenzie*, 95 N.Y. 575, was an action upon a promissory note
given by McKenzie.   The consideration was for board and care during illness
and for future services to be rendered by plaintiff when required.   Such services
were rendered by plaintiff until McKenzie died.   It was held that a promissory
note given in consideration of future services to be rendered, becomes valid
upon the performance of such services in reliance thereon, even though there
was no agreement on the part of the payee at the time of receiving the note to
render them.

Formal and Simple Contracts. — Contracts are again classi-
fied as formal and simple.

Supreme Court of that state at page 339.   Andreas was the plaintiff in this case and
Holcombe the defendant.

In most of the states the plaintiff's name is given first, followed by the abbreviation " v.," standing for the Latin word versus, meaning against, and this is followed
by the name of the defendant.   The title of the above case should be read, Andreas
against Holcombe, 22 Minnesota 339.

In some states the title of the case is changed when it is appealed to a higher
court, and the name of the person appealing from the decision of the lower court
is placed first, so if the appeal should be taken by the defendant, the title would be
exactly reversed.   If that were the rule in Minnesota and the defendant had been
taking the appeal, the title in the above case would have been *Holcombe* v. *Andreas,*
but this is not the practice in a majority of the states.

Some of the reports of the courts are not known by the name of the state, but by
the name of the reporter who compiled and edited the decision.   In such cases the
name of the state has been inserted in parenthesis.   On page 22 the case of *Arnold*
v. Richmond Iron Works, 1 Gray (Mass.) 434, arose in the state of Massachusetts
and is reported in volume one of Gray's reports, Gray being the name of the reporter,
and when he was succeeded by another, the reports then took the name of the new
reporter.   The practice of naming the reports after the reporter is now almost uni-
formly abandoned.

Formal contracts are also known as contracts under seal, an are required to be executed in a certain way ; that is, with a sea attached. Contracts executed in this way do not require an consideration. The seal is said to import a consideration.

In *Van Valkenburgh* v. *Smith*, 60 Me. 97, the defendant, to obtain th discharge of a suit pending against a railway company and in favor of plaintif gave a bond to plaintiff conditioned upon allowing a given time within whic defendant would give certain notes indorsed to plaintiff as specified. This wa not done, and the defense set up was that there was no consideration for th agreement. The court held that the bond being under seal, the law implies . consideration from the solemnity of its execution.

Rutherford v. *Baptist Convention*, 9 Ga. 54, was an action on a writte instrument given to the Baptist Convention, and recited the consideration t be "the importance of literary and religious institutions to the wellbeing of society." The instrument was sealed. The defense was, no consideration The court said, "The seal imports a consideration, and no other consideratio is necessary to give it validity."

Under the English law the form of the seal was definitel prescribed. In early times the seal was an impression on wax but statutes have relaxed the rigor of the rule, and now the im pression may be on a wafer or on the document itself, and ir some states a scroll or mark made with the pen, or the wor "seal," printed or written, if employed as a seal, is sufficient.

L.S. are letters commonly used to designate a seal. The are the initial letters of the Latin words *locus sigilli*, meaning the place of the seal.

In *Norvell* v. *Walker*, 9 W. Va. 447, the parties entered into a writte agreement which concluded with the words, "Witness the following signature and seals." Then followed W's signature followed by the scroll, and directl under it N's signature. It was held that the one scroll was adopted as th seal of both parties and was sufficient.

Farmers and Manufacturers Bank v. *Haight*, 3 Hill (N.Y.) 493, is a cas decided in New York in 1842. It was held that the seal of a private individua or of a religious corporation impressed directly upon paper without the use o wax or other tenacious substance is a nullity. [But this does not express th law in New York State at the present time.]

The principal requisite to the validity of the seal is that i must be the intent of the parties to use the scroll or mark as uch, and this is usually expressed by the words, "In witness hereof we have hereunto set our hands and seals the day and ear first above written," or some form analogous thereto.

A seal is not now given the prominence it formerly had, and some jurisdictions it is regarded as merely presumption of onsideration. The contracts usually required to be sealed are eeds, bonds and mortgages, and some other instruments of an nportant nature.

A simple contract, known also as a parol contract, is one that epends for its validity upon the presence of consideration. It ay be a contract required by law to be in some particular form ther than under seal, as contracts which by law are required be in writing. It may also be a contract of which no particu- r form is required by law; as one that is valid whether written oral, for instance a contract of employment.

Oral and Written Contracts. — As just indicated, contracts may e either oral or written. All contracts under seal must be in riting, and some simple contracts as well, but the majority of e contracts in business relations are oral. You hire a man to a day's work for you. He agrees. This is an oral contract.

Express and Implied Contracts. — There are also express and plied contracts, the former being those in which the agree- ent on each side is expressly stated, and the latter those in hich the terms are understood from acts or words.

Blackstone, Vol. II., p. 443, says: "When the terms of the agreement are enly uttered and avowed at the time of the making, as to deliver an ox, or loads of timber, or to pay a stated price for certain goods, it is an express ntract. Implied are such as reason and justice dictate and which therefore e law presumes that every man undertakes to perform; as, if I employ a rson to do any business for me or perform any work, the law implies that I dertake, or contract, to pay him as much as his labor deserves."

2. PARTIES

Two or more Persons Necessary. — We have learned that a ntract is an agreement between two or more persons. The estion arises as to what persons can be parties to a contract.

Our definition says that there must be two or more person
A man can not contract with himself ; that is, a man, as truste
or agent, can not in such capacity deal with himself in his ind
vidual capacity.

In *Bain* v. *Brown*, 56 N.Y. 285, Brown was the agent for Bain and w
authorized to sell certain real estate for $17,000. He contracted to sell
this figure and so advised Bain. Next day he negotiated to sell the proper
to other parties for $26,000 and signed a contract in his own name. He th
secured an assignment of the first contract and had Bain deed direct to tl
second purchasers. An action was brought to recover the difference betwe(
$17,000 and $26,000, and it was held that, assuming the first sale to be ma(
in good faith, the agent could not appropriate the advances, but the princip
was entitled to the benefit.

In *White* v. *Ward*, 26 Ark. 445, it was held that the purchase by a truste
or agent, of the property of which he has the sale, carries fraud on the face of
It is an abuse of confidence and any title or benefit derived therefrom inures
the benefit of the principal.

There are disqualifying circumstances or conditions, necessai
for us to consider, which render a person incompetent to ente
into a contract with another.

3. INFANCY

Infancy Defined. — By the common law, all persons under th
age of twenty-one years are infants, and this is the law in a
of the states, excepting a few in which by statute females ar
declared of age at eighteen, and either males or females upo
marriage at any age.

There is a period in the life of every person during whicl
because of his tender years, he is incapable of doing busines
for himself, when he is not of sufficient maturity to bind himse
by agreement. But as the child increases in age, his ment;
capacity grows and strengthens, and he arrives at a time whe
he is fully qualified to care for himself and to make agreemen
that will bind him.

The exact age when this condition begins differs with differer
persons, but the law decides that twenty-one is an average ag

and it is then that the person, in the eyes of the law, attains full mental capacity.

Law Protects Infants. — Until this age arrives, the law puts many safeguards around the infant, so that he shall not be imposed upon. In general it may be said that any contract made by an infant is, in law, voidable; that is, the infant upon becoming of age can repudiate it and demand that any consideration he may have paid be returned to him.

In *Spencer* v. *Carr*, 45 N.Y. 406, the parents of an infant six years of age deeded real estate to her. Subsequently, the parents deeded the same property in trust to another, and the infant, at the mother's request, signed the mother's name to the deed. It was held that the infant could claim title under the original deed to her.

In *Carpenter* v. *Carpenter*, 45 Ind. 142, plaintiff, an infant, had traded horses. He tired of his bargain and, having tendered back the horse he received, demanded his original horse. It was refused. The court held that he could recover his horse, even though he could not tender back the horse he got in the trade, and even if the horse he got was injured or dead. It is not necessary for the disaffirmance that the other party be put *in statu quo*, unless it is possible for the infant to do so. This case also holds that the fact that the infant falsely represented himself to be of age did not prevent his avoiding the contract.

The Contract of an Infant is Voidable and not Void. — No one but himself, his legal representative after his death, or those entitled to his estate, if the contract is avoided, can disaffirm it. The contract is said to be held in abeyance during the infancy, and upon the infant's becoming of age he may either affirm or disaffirm the contract. When a contract with an infant is made by a person of full age, the infant alone has the right to disaffirm; the other party can not repudiate it. The privilege is also personal to the infant; neither his guardian during his minority nor his creditors after he has become of age can disaffirm his contracts.

In *Kendall* v. *Lawrence*, 22 Pick. (Mass.) 540, an infant deeded certain land to another and after becoming of age neither avoided nor confirmed the deed. After he became of age creditors of the infant tried to set aside the sale or take the land on attachment. It was held that the deed was valid as to third parties. The deed of a minor is voidable and the right to avoid it is personal privilege to the minor and his heirs.

Affirmance of Executed Contracts. — The question at once arises, must the infant, upon becoming of age, disaffirm to avoid the contract, or will it be considered to be avoided unless he actually affirms it? The answer depends entirely upon the nature of the contract. The rule varies in its application to executed and executory contracts. In the case of an executed contract the benefit which the infant seeks to bestow has been given to the other party and is good until it is disaffirmed, and the disaffirmance must be by express words or by some distinct and positive act which leaves no doubt of the intent.

In *Towle* v. *Dresser*, 73 Me. 252, plaintiff, an infant, sold a horse to defendant and took two notes in payment. Later he tendered back the notes, rescinded the contract, and sued for possession of the horse. It was held that he could recover the horse. This, it will be seen, is a case in which express disaffirmance is necessary. This case also holds that the disaffirmance can be made during the infancy, and this suit was brought by plaintiff, through his father while he was yet an infant.

Silence for a reasonable time after majority will be construed in many cases of this kind, as an affirmance, if it is coupled with a retention of the benefits.

Affirmance of Executory Contracts. — On the other hand, if the contract is executory, it is necessary for the infant to affirm upon becoming of age, or the contract is avoided. In such an agreement infancy is a defense if sued upon, unless it can be shown that the contract was affirmed after maturity.

Eureka Co. v. *Edwards*, 71 Ala. 248, was an action to cancel a deed executed by minors. It was held that if an infant execute a deed to lands, binding ratification of the contract after he becomes of age requires that there be some positive act on his part either affirming the conveyance or making it inconsistent with the right to repudiate it.

An infant can generally disaffirm his contracts before as well as after becoming of age.

In *Childs* v. *Dobbins*, 55 Iowa 205, plaintiff, a minor, entered into a contract with defendant for the purchase of some trees and shrubbery amounting to $500, which he paid. About five days thereafter and while still a minor he tendered back the stock and demanded the consideration paid. It was held that an infant can disaffirm a contract at any time during minority or within reasonable time thereafter.

The rule is well established that the infant can not avoid a part and affirm the rest. He can not affirm as to part and disaffirm as to the balance.

Heath v. *West*, 28 N.H. 101, was a case in which plaintiff purchased a horse, paying $75 in cash and giving his note secured by a mortgage on the horse for the balance. Plaintiff refused to pay the mortgage, and when the horse was sold to satisfy the same, brought an action to recover it. Held, that he could not repudiate the mortgage and hold the horse. It was all one transaction and he could not avoid a part and affirm the rest. He must take the benefits with the detriments.

In rescinding an executed contract the infant must restore what he has received if he has the property and he is liable to an action at law for its recovery; still the right of an infant to disaffirm is superior to this right, and although the consideration the infant has received may have disappeared, yet the infant may disaffirm, even if he can not return the thing received or its equivalent.

In *Green* v. *Green*, 69 N.Y. 553, defendant being a minor sold certain land to his father for $400. After arriving at his majority he reëntered upon said land and disaffirmed his contract. An action for trespass was brought by the father. The son did not offer to restore the $400 and it was shown that he had used up, lost, or squandered the money, and had no part of it when he became of age. Held that he had the right to disaffirm the deed without restoring the consideration. The right to rescind is a protection for the infant and is not contingent upon an impossibility, and it might be impossible for him to restore the consideration if he did not have it.

There is a particular class of infant's contracts that are always void and therefore of no effect. This class is the infant's power of attorney under seal, which is in no case valid. Many jurisdictions extend the rule to every appointment of an agent in any case, except where such appointment is necessary. When, however, the welfare of the infant requires the employment by him of others to perform services in his behalf, an appointment of an agent under such circumstances will be valid as for necessaries.

In *Trueblood* v. *Trueblood*, 8 Ind. 195, a bond was given by an infant and his father that the infant would, upon becoming of age, convey a certain piece of property, and an action was brought to compel the transfer. It was proved that after becoming of age he ratified the act of his father in giving the bond as his agent. He later repudiated it and sold to another. The court held that an infant could not appoint an agent. Such an act is void and a ratification after becoming of age can not make it of any effect.

Contracts for Necessaries. — But there exist a number of cases in which an infant will be absolutely bound by his contracts, the principal illustration being his contracts for necessaries.

If the law did not give protection to parties furnishing the necessaries of life to an infant, we can see that many cases would arise in which the infant might suffer. Therefore the law says that when an infant is not supplied with necessaries by his parents or guardian or others to whom he may look, he may contract for them himself. The law creates a promise on the part of the infant to pay what they are reasonably worth, but this does not mean that the tradesman can charge what he pleases, so it will be seen that the infant is still protected.

In *Hyman* v. *Cain*, 48 N.C. 111, defendant, who was an orphan about nine years of age, boarded with the plaintiff for about two years. An action was brought for his board. The court held that the law will imply a promise on the part of an infant to pay a reasonable price for necessaries furnished to him.

Morton v. *Steward*, 5 Bradwell (Ill.) 533, was an action on a note given by an infant, and it was proved that the consideration was necessaries furnished the infant. But the court held that an infant is incapable of stating an account or binding himself by a note to pay a particular price or sum for necessaries, although he is liable for the reasonable value of the necessaries furnished. It is required for the protection of the infant that the price charged should be inquired into.

Necessaries Defined. — The question is often in dispute as to what are necessaries, and the rule generally laid down is that they are anything required by the particular person for his reasonable comfort, subsistence, and education, regard being had to his means, occupation, and standing in society.

Peters v. *Fleming*, 6 M. & W. 41, was an action in an English court for a bill of goods sold defendant. They consisted of four finger rings, a watch chain, some pins, etc., amounting to over £8. The plaintiff sought to hold defendant for necessaries. It appeared that the defendant was a student at the University of Cambridge, that his father was a gentleman of fortune and a member of parliament. The court held that it was a question for the jury whether the articles were such as a person in his station in life would reasonably require, and that necessaries included articles useful and suitable to the state and condition of the party.

In *Strong* v. *Foote*, 42 Conn. 203, the defendant, a minor fifteen years of age and the owner of a large fortune, had his teeth filled by the plaintiff, a dentist. The bill rendered amounted to $93. It was proved that the teeth were decayed and pained the defendant. Held, that the work was for necessaries.

In *Werner's Appeal*, 10 Norris (Pa.) 222, it was held that a bill of $45 for nursing an infant through his last illness and preparing his body for burial was a necessary and proper charge against his estate.

An infant is liable for necessaries supplied to his wife the same as if he were an adult.

A tradesman who furnishes an infant with supplies is bound to show that they are necessaries, and if the infant already has a sufficient supply, he can not recover.

Barnes v. *Toye*, 13 Q. B. D. (Eng.) 410, was an action for the price of necessaries furnished an infant. The defense was that the infant was already sufficiently supplied with goods of the same class and was not in want of these. The court held that the defendant could show that the goods were not necessaries as he was already supplied with sufficient goods of a similar description, and it was immaterial whether the plaintiff did or did not know of the existing supply.

4. INSANITY

General Rule. — Since a contract requires a meeting of the minds of the contracting parties, it is evident that a person lacking the mental capacity can not make a valid contract. Some insane persons appear perfectly rational and others have rational periods. It is difficult, therefore, to determine the mental condition of the party, and one may deal with an insane person and be in ignorance of his insanity.

The rule as generally adopted in this country is that if the insanity of an individual has not been decreed by the courts, and a party dealing with him is ignorant of the insanity, and the contract has been so far executed that the parties can not be put in their original condition, the insane party is held.

Gribben v. *Maxwell*, 34 Kan. 8, was an action to set aside a conveyance of real property executed by one Olive Gribben, a lunatic. The purchaser did not know of her insanity, and paid a fair price for the property. The cour held that where the purchase of the real estate was made and the conveyanc obtained in good faith prior to an inquisition and finding of lunacy, and for a fair and reasonable price, without knowledge of the insanity, no advantag being taken of the insane person, the conveyance can not be avoided, if th consideration has not been returned to the purchaser and no offer has been made to return it.

But if the lunatic has been declared by the courts to be insane or the party dealing with him knew of his insanity, the contrac is void.

In *Carter* v. *Beckwith*, 128 N.Y. 312, plaintiff, an attorney, upon the reques of B, who had been legally declared insane, instituted proceedings to have him adjudged sane, and to have the control of his property restored to him. In this proceeding it was determined that he was still insane, and the application was refused. After B's death, plaintiff presented his claim for services. I was held that he could not recover on the ground of a contract with B, as any contract entered into with a person judicially declared insane is absolutely void The court, however, in its discretion allowed reasonable costs.

If the lunatic afterwards becomes sane, he may then ratify or disaffirm all of his voidable contracts, the same as an infant upon attaining his majority.

In *Arnold* v. *Richmond Iron Works*, 1 Gray (Mass.) 434, an insane person deeded away some land, and after becoming of sound mind and knowing that the grantees were in possession, did not reënter or disaffirm the conveyance but received payments on the notes given for the purchase price. Held, tha from this act his intention to ratify the deed may be inferred, although he di not know at the time that he had the power to avoid the deed. The deed wa not void, but voidable, and in order to avoid such a deed before affirmance, the consideration for it must be restored.

A lunatic, like an infant, is liable for necessaries.

Sawyer v. *Lufkin*, 56 Me. 308, was an action for services in caring for de fendant, who was an insane person and incapable of caring for herself. The court held that if necessaries are furnished an insane person in good faith and under justifiable circumstances, the person furnishing them may recover of th insane person. The judge said, "If the law were not so, the insane migh perish if guardians having means should neglect or refuse to furnish the sup plies needed. They stand in the same position as a minor, and are liable fo necessaries."

During a lucid interval, the lunatic being sane, his contract are binding on him unless he has been declared legally insane.

Drunkenness may render a Contract Voidable. — If a man enters into a contract while drunk, he may afterwards affirm or disaffirm it, unless he has been judicially declared a habitual drunkard, in which case his contracts are void.

In *Carpenter* v. *Rodgers*, 61 Mich. 384, the plaintiff traded a good team of horses, worth $150 to $200, with defendant, a horse dealer, for a team worth about $75. It was shown that plaintiff was of feeble mind and scarcely able to do business, and that when the deal was made he was intoxicated to such degree that he did not know what he was doing. There was, however, no rescission on the part of plaintiff, nor offer to return the team. Held, that a contract entered into by a party so drunk as not to know what he is doing is voidable only and not void, and may therefore be ratified or rescinded when he becomes sober. Not having been rescinded the contract was binding.

In *Bush* v. *Breinig*, 113 Pa. St. 310, Breinig attended a public sale of real property, and having made the highest bid, the property was struck off to him. Afterwards, while so drunk as to be deprived of reason and understanding, he executed a written contract of purchase and paid part of the purchase price. Thereafter he sought to avoid the contract and brought action to recover the money paid. The court allowed him to rescind the contract and to recover his money.

To affect his contract it is necessary that his reason be so impaired by intoxication for the time being as to render him incompetent to comprehend the consequences of his acts.

In *Johns* v. *Fritchey*, 39 Md. 258, a party sought to avoid a power of attorney given by him, on the ground that he was intoxicated. The court held that to avoid the contract on such grounds it was incumbent on him to produce clear and satisfactory proof that he was in such a state of drunkenness at the time as to be unable to know what he was doing, or to judge of the consequence of his own acts.

Cummings v. *Henry*, 10 Ind. 109, was an action to recover on a note given for the purchase price of a horse. It was proved that defendant was intoxicated at the time and had afterwards offered to return the horse and asked for rescission of the contract. Held, that the party might rescind if he was so far intoxicated as to render him incompetent to contract.

5. MARRIED WOMEN

Under the common law, from the earliest times, the husband was the head of the family. At marriage a life interest in his wife's real estate and the absolute title to her personal property vested in him. She could not sue or be sued without his joining, or being joined as a party; her earnings became his, and in fact the identity of the married woman was lost and she could no in her own name make a contract.

This is now so completely changed by statute throughout our own country and in England that it is scarcely worth our notic except as an illustration of the changes which our laws underg during the progress of time. Now we find that by statute th married woman can conduct her own separate business, ca contract independently of her husband, and in fact in most o the states she has the same legal rights and powers as a unmarried woman.

6. OFFER AND ACCEPTANCE

The Foundation of a Contract. — Traced back to its origin a contract amounts to this : The first party says, " I will take certain sum for this article ; " to which the second party answers " I will accept your offer and give you the specified sum."

You enter a furniture store. The tradesman by exhibiting his wares virtually says he will take the stated price for such articles. You say you will take a certain chair, marked $10 Here we have an offer and acceptance.

The offer must be explicit. If A says, " I may take $100 for this horse when I get ready to sell him," this is not an offer which B can accept and thereby create a contract.

The acceptance must be absolute and on the exact terms con tained in the offer. If A offers to sell a load of hay for $10 and B says he will give him $9 for it, no contract is made be cause there is no acceptance of the offer.

In *Minneapolis & St. Louis Railway* v. *Columbus Rolling Mill*, 11 U.S. 149, plaintiff asked defendant's price on iron rails. On December defendant offered to sell plaintiff from 2000 to 5000 tons of iron rails at certain price, and added, " If accepted, we shall expect to be notified prior t December 20." On December 16 plaintiff wired, " Please enter our orde for 1200 tons as per your favor of the 8th." December 18 defendant wired "We can not book your order at that price." On December 19 plaintiff wired, "Enter our order for 2000 tons as per your letter of the 8th." The defendant refused to furnish the rails; and in an action brought for breach of contract, the court held that the telegram of the 16th was not an acceptance, as it was different in terms from the offer, and that this order amounted to a rejection of the offer and left it no longer open, so the telegram of the 19th was of no effect.

There must be no Qualification in the Acceptance.— If A offers to sell his automobile to B for $600, and B accepts if A will take $300 down and his note for the balance at 30 days, the acceptance is qualified and does not constitute a contract.

In *Baker* v. *Holt*, 56 Wis. 100, defendant in Connecticut wrote to plaintiff in Wisconsin, offering to sell him certain land at a stated price payable at a specified time, but said nothing about the place of payment or delivery of the deed. Plaintiff replied that he would take the land upon the terms mentioned, and added, "You may make out the deed, leaving the name of the grantee blank, and forward the same to I. L. Mosher at Grand Rapids, Wis., or to your agent, if you have one here, to hand to me on the payment of $200 and the delivery of necessary security." Held, that the acceptance was not good, as it was based upon the conditions that the deed be executed in blank and that payment be made in Wisconsin.

In *Honeyman* v. *Marryatt*, 6 H. L. C. (Eng.) 112, an estate was advertised for sale on certain terms. A authorized his solicitor to make an offer. B's agent in reply wrote, "Mr. B has authorized me to accept the offer subject to the terms of a contract being arranged between his solicitor and yourself. Mr. B requires a deposit of from £1200 to £1500 and the completion of the purchase at midsummer day next." There was no reply to this letter. Held, that the acceptance was conditional and so formed no complete contract.

The Offer and Acceptance must pertain to the Same Object. — A may offer to sell his bay horse for $100. B says, "I will give you that amount for your gray." There is no contract because the minds of the parties have not met.

The Offer must be communicated to the Party accepting it.— If the offer is not communicated, it can not be said that the minds of the parties met. If A says to B, "I will sell my horse to X for $100, if he will give that amount," it does not constitute an offer to X, even though B, without authority, tells X about it, as it cannot be said to have been communicated by A.

In some states it is held that one who gives the information concerning the parties to a crime without any knowledge of the reward which has been offered, cannot claim the reward as the offer has not really been communicated to him. Other states hold that he can recover, as the reward is a public offer and when acted upon binds the offerer. The weight of authority seems to be in favor of denying the right of the plaintiff to recover when he had no knowledge of the reward prior to the time of the giving of the information.

When a man works for another without his request or knowledge, there is no contract and he can not recover.

In *Bartholomew* v. *Jackson*, 20 Johns. (N.Y.) 28, Jackson owned a field in which Bartholomew had a stack of wheat and which he had promised to move in time for plowing. Notice having been given, he promised that it would be moved at 10 A.M. Relying on this promise, Jackson, shortly after 10 A.M. set fire to the stubble in a distant part of the field, but later found the stack was not removed, so did it himself to save the grain, and then sued Bartholomew for the work. Held, the services were rendered without request and with no promise express or implied to pay for them, and there can be no recovery. The judge said, "If a man humanely bestows his labor, and even risks his life in voluntarily aiding to preserve his neighbor's house from destruction by fire, the law considers the services rendered as gratuitous."

The Acceptance must be Communicated. — Not only must the offer be communicated, as we have seen, but the acceptance must also be communicated, and whether it reaches the offerer or not, it must be something more than a mere mental assent.

Stensgaard v. *Smith*, 43 Minn. 11, was a case in which the plaintiff received from the defendant a letter or statement setting forth that in consideration of plaintiff's agreement to act as agent for the sale of certain land, defendant gave to plaintiff the exclusive right of sale of same for three months, and promised to pay a stated commission on said sales. Plaintiff, who was a real estate broker, took immediate steps to advertise and to post notices for the sale of said premises, but one month thereafter defendant sold to another. Action was brought for damages for breach of contract. Held, that there was no contract. The instrument conferred authority on plaintiff to sell, and if he did sell, promised a commission. There was no mutuality of obligation. The plaintiff did not bind himself to do anything. If plaintiff, acting under this authority, had sold before revocation, the sale would have completed the contract, and the commission would have been earned.

An Acceptance is binding as soon as Made. — As we have seen, the offer must be communicated to the party before it is effectual, while an acceptance is binding as soon as made, even though it has not come to the knowledge of the offerer. The acceptance must be made in the way prescribed or in the way that would naturally be expected. If the offerer requires or suggests a mode of acceptance, he takes the risk of the acceptance reaching him. A common illustration of this is the case of an offer made through the post office, for in such a case it may be assumed that the acceptance is to be made in the same way unless otherwise expressly stated. When made in the required way, it is held that as soon as the acceptance is sent the contract is made. And the completion of the agreement dates from the time of mailing the letter or sending the telegram, and not from the time of receiving it.

Taylor v. *Merchants Fire Insurance Co.*, 9 How. (U.S.) 390, was a case in which, after some correspondence, the defendant insurance company wrote that they would insure plaintiff's house for $57. This letter was received on December 21, and on that day plaintiff accepted the offer and sent his letter of acceptance with check inclosed. On December 22, and before plaintiff's letter of acceptance and check reached defendant, the house was burned down. Held, that the contract was complete when the letter of acceptance was mailed, and therefore the company was liable.

In *Trevor* v. *Wood*, 36 N.Y. 307, plaintiff living in New York telegraphed defendant in New Orleans, asking the price of Mexican dollars delivered. On January 31 defendant answered by telegraph, giving price on 50,000, and on the same day plaintiff telegraphed and accepted the offer. The telegraph lines became disabled and the message was not received until defendant had wired that the dollars had been sold to other parties. Held, that the contract was closed as soon as the acceptance was sent. As the offer was by telegraph, it was sufficient to accept in the same manner, and the offerer was bound irrespective of the time the acceptance was actually received.

Acceptance must be made as Prescribed. — But the preceding rule does not hold good if the offerer prescribes a particular way in which the acceptance must be made. For example, if the offer is made by mail and expressly requires that the acceptance shall be telegraphed back, it will not be sufficient to send the acceptance by mail.

The offer may be withdrawn any time before acceptance
but the notice of withdrawal dates from the time it reaches the
party to whom it is sent. The offer is made irrevocable only by
acceptance.

In *White* v. *Corlies*, 46 N.Y. 467, plaintiff, who was a builder, received a note
from the defendant which said, "Upon an agreement to finish the fitting up
of offices at 57 Broadway in two weeks from date you can commence at once."
No reply was sent, but plaintiff bought lumber and prepared to begin work.
Next day defendant withdrew the offer. Held, that there was no agreement.
The mere buying of lumber was not an act sufficient to notify defendant of
the acceptance. A mere mental determination to accept is not sufficient; the
manifestation of assent must be sufficient to give notice to the defendant.

In *Boston & Maine Ry.* v. *Bartlett*, 3 Cush. (Mass.) 224, defendant made
a proposition in writing to plaintiff to accept a certain price for some land,
taken within thirty days. Plaintiff accepted the proposition before the thirty
days expired. Held, it was a continuous offer that might be withdrawn at any
time before acceptance, but its acceptance within the given time, and before
being withdrawn, constituted a valid contract that could be enforced.

An Offer may Lapse. — The lapse of an offer may be caused
by the death of either party before acceptance.

Pratt v. *Trustees*, 93 Ill. 475, was an action on a note given by one Pratt to
the trustees of a church as a subscription to enable them to procure a bell.
Pratt died before the bell was purchased. Held, that the note was an offer
and could be revoked until acted upon by purchasing the bell. The death of
the offerer revoked the offer and the note could not be collected.

**The Parties may fix a time during which the Offer will
remain Open**. — If it is not accepted within such time the offer
lapses. In the absence of any express limitation of time the
offer is construed to be open for a reasonable time. What constitutes a reasonable time depends entirely upon the circumstances of the case, the relations of the parties, and other facts
which would tend to determine what would be fair and just
under the circumstances. In some cases it might be a few
days and in others a number of months.

In *Stone* v. *Harmon*, 31 Minn. 512, there was a written offer to sell certain
real estate and no time was stated for its acceptance. The court held that
the offer remained open for a reasonable time and that acceptance after nearly
a year was not within a reasonable time.

7. CONSIDERATION

Consideration in an Executory Contract. — Another element
necessary to support an executory contract is what we term
consideration. There must be some value received to make a
contract enforceable, unless the terms thereof are fully carried
out or executed. Therefore there must be consideration in every
executory contract.

A contract under seal is in a way, under the common law, an
exception, for the seal is said to import a consideration, and the
instrument being sealed, no other evidence of consideration is
required. Now, however, in a few of the states, the seal is by
statute regarded as only a presumption of consideration in an
executory contract and is not sufficient without some actual consideration. But if the seal is used on a gratuitous promise for
the purpose of creating a consideration, the effect is the same
as at common law.

In *Aller* v. *Aller*, 40 N. J. L. 446, a father gave his daughter a written
instrument under seal by which he promised to pay her $312. This was
understood to be a part of the money which the father had owed his wife, now
deceased, and he felt it should go to the daughter, although there was no legal
obligation. The defense to this promise was want of consideration. Held,
that as the promise was intended to be a gratuitous one the seal imported
sufficient consideration.

Consideration in an Executed Contract. — A contract that has
been executed will not be set aside because of lack of consideration; it is therefore those contracts which have not yet been
carried out that we are to consider.

In *Matthews* v. *Smith*, 67 N.C. 374, plaintiff purchased of defendant a
quantity of fertilizer and gave his note for it. When it became due he said
the fertilizer was not good and had injured his land; still he paid the note, and
then brought suit to recover the money paid. Held, that as he had paid the
money with a full knowledge of the facts he could not maintain his action.

Consideration for a Gift. — A familiar illustration of lack of
consideration is the case of a gift. A mere promise to give a
present is void for want of consideration, but when the promise

is executed by the delivery of the gift the defect is remedie
and the gift can not be reclaimed.

In the case of *Brewer* v. *Harvey*, 72 N.C. 176, plaintiff's father poin
out a colt to her when she was but twelve years old and said, " This is yc
property ; I give it to you." It was known by the family as her colt, but t
father kept possession of it until he died. Plaintiff brought an action
recover the horse. Held, that it being a gift, there was no valuable conside
tion. To make the agreement valid there must have been a delivery. Th
having been no delivery, the title did not pass to the daughter.

In *Camp's Appeal*, 36 Conn. 88, N handed C some money to put in the savin
bank for him, and when the books were brought back he said, " I give y
these bank books." C kept them, and in an action by N's administrator
recover the books it was held that this was a good delivery, sufficient to c
stitute a complete gift.

The Consideration must have Value. — Consideration defin
is said to be a benefit to the party promising or a loss to t
party to whom the promise is made.

It is not necessary that the consideration be adequate in val
to the thing promised, but it must be of some value in the ey
of the law. It will be seen that it would be impossible for t
courts to require an adequate or full consideration, as they wou
then have to determine the merits of every bargain.

In the case of *Hamer* v. *Sidway*, 124 N.Y. 538, one Story promised
nephew, William, that if he would refrain from drinking liquor, using tobac
swearing, and playing cards or billiards for money until he should beco
twenty-one years of age he would pay him $5000. William lived up to
part of the agreement and upon becoming of age asked his uncle for payme
His uncle answered that he had set apart the money for him in the bank. 1
court held that the promise to pay this money was founded upon a good co
sideration, as it is enough that something be done or forborne by the party
whom the promise is made. He had a right to do these things if he wish
The suspension or forbearance of these legal rights sustained the agreemen

Bainbridge v. *Firmstone*, 8 A. & E. (Eng.) 743, was a case in wh
defendant obtained plaintiff's consent to let him weigh two boilers belong
to plaintiff and promised to place them back in the shape in which
found them. Defendant took the boilers apart and weighed them and tl
refused to put them together again, claiming there was no consideration
his promise to put them back. Held, that the plaintiff gave up the right wh
he had, to refuse to let them be weighed. There was a detriment to plain
in parting with the possession of them for even so short a time. This con

ted a sufficient consideration, and defendant was obliged to replace the
oilers.

Wolford v. *Powers*, 85 Ind. 294, was an action on a note given in considera-
on of a parent naming a child after the maker of the note. The court held
at this was based upon a sufficient consideration. The parent surrendered
s right to name the child.

A Promise may be a Sufficient Consideration. — The con-
deration must come from the promisee, and it may consist of
present act or a promise in the future. It may be to give or
o something, or to refrain from doing something which the
omisee has a legal right to do. For instance, a promise to
rbear suit and extend the time of payment of a claim is held
be a good consideration for a promise.

In *Flanagan* v. *Kilcome*, 58 N.H. 443, defendant promised to pay plaintiffs
ertain sum if they would drop a lawsuit which they had commenced against
r. This was done, but she did not pay it and suit was brought for the sum
omised. It was held that there was a valuable consideration for the prom-
, even though it be shown that she would have succeeded if the suit had
me to trial. The plaintiffs surrendered their right to have it tried.

In *Pennsylvania Coal Co.* v. *Blake*, 85 N.Y. 226, the firm of C. A. Blake &
. were indebted to plaintiff. Plaintiff agreed to extend their time of pay-
nt upon receiving, as collateral security, a mortgage upon land owned by
zabeth Blake, wife of C. A. Blake, who had no interest in the firm. This
s an action brought to foreclose that mortgage. The court held that it was
de for a good consideration, the consideration being the agreement on
part of plaintiff to grant a longer time to C. A. Blake & Co. and to forbear
sue said firm.

Consideration for the Discharge of a Debt. — But the payment
a smaller sum of money in satisfaction of a larger one is not
valuable consideration for the discharge of a debt, as it is, in
t, doing no more than the party is already legally bound to do.
is is one case in which the court will look into the amount of
consideration and determine whether or not it is adequate.

In *Ayres* v. *C. R. I. & P. R. Co.*, 52 Iowa 478, one Q entered into a contract
ouild a certain section of road for defendant. After building a part Q in-
ned the defendant that he owed for supplies and could not go on at the
tract price. Defendant told him to go on and his actual expenditures
ld be met and his creditors paid. Held, that the agreement was without
sideration, as it simply bound Q to do what he was already under a legal
gation to do.

If something else than money is taken in part satisfaction
the debt, the rule will be different.

This is seen in the case of *Jaffray* v. *Davis*, 124 N.Y. 164, in which (
fendant, who was owing plaintiff a certain amount on open account, gave
plaintiff his promissory note for one half the amount secured by a chat
mortgage under an agreement that it would be accepted as payment in fu
Held, that this was a valid agreement upon sufficient consideration and th
action could not be brought for the balance. Here defendant gave ext
security and deprived himself of the legal title to the goods so mortgaged.

In *Wharton* v. *Anderson*, 28 Minn. 301, defendant leased premises
plaintiff for five years at $250 per month. Thereafter plaintiff agreed to
certain reduction in consideration of defendant's paying promptly. Held, th
the promise to take less was without consideration and could not be enforce

But if the amount due is in dispute, the promise to pay a
sum in settlement of the disputed claim is valid, even thoug
such sum be less than that actually due. The liquidation of th
claim constitutes a good consideration.

Riley v. *Kershaw*, 52 Mo. 224, was an action to recover rent and tax
alleged to be due. The defense was that a new agreement had been enter
into between the parties, by which, in consideration of the defendant's payi
the rent monthly instead of quarterly, a smaller sum was stipulated to be pa
and that this smaller sum was actually paid in full satisfaction of all clain
Held, that the payment of a part of a debt is no satisfaction of the whole de
even although agreed to be taken as such. But in case of a dispute a co
promise fairly made and faithfully carried out will be upheld.

Accord and Satisfaction. — This is the settlement of a claim l
compromising the amount which is in dispute, or by giving som
thing else than that which was originally agreed upon.

Lee v. *Timken*, 23 App. Div. (N.Y.) 349, was a case where plaintiff's h
band before his death transferred to plaintiff certain real estate which w
subject to a mortgage of $10,000, and gave other property to the defendant,
daughter, upon her agreement to pay off and discharge the mortgage. T
widow sued for $6000, which she claimed to be due under the agreement, a
alleged that $4000 had been paid. The defense was accord and satisfaction
that this $4000 had been paid and accepted in full satisfaction of the daught
obligations. The court held that the defense, if true, was a good answer
the complaint, as the payment direct to the mother instead of applying it
the mortgage was a sufficient consideration to support the agreement to acc
it in full payment. So accord and satisfaction, if proved, was a good defen

Settlement to avoid Litigation. — A settlement to avoid litigation, where the party forbears to sue or consents to drop a pending suit, is a good consideration, and the promise made for this consideration can be enforced.

In *Parker* v. *Enslow*, 102 Ill. 272, plaintiff had been in the habit of going to defendant's store and filling his pipe from tobacco left on the counter for the use of the public. Defendant, for a joke, mixed powder with the tobacco, and when the plaintiff lit it an explosion followed and injured his eyesight. Plaintiff threatened, and was intending to sue defendant. As a compromise and settlement of this cause of action, defendant gave plaintiff the promissory note here sued upon. The court held that as the note was given in settlement of a threatened suit, if the payee supposed or believed that he had a cause of action and the note was given and accepted in good faith as a compromise, it is supported by a sufficient consideration and could be enforced.

Compromise with Creditors. — If several creditors of a party agree with each other and with the debtor to accept a part of what he owes each of them in discharge of the whole debt, the forbearance of each one is the consideration to the others, who might otherwise lose the whole. A compromise with creditors is therefore held to be for a good consideration, and such an agreement can be enforced.

In *Pierce* v. *Jones*, 8 S.C. 273, Jones & Co., an insolvent firm, entered into a written agreement with their creditors whereby the creditors were to accept twenty-five cents on the dollar in payment of their several claims and give receipts in full, provided that all of the creditors assented to the agreement. Held, that this was a valid agreement, and that the firm by complying therewith was discharged from the balance of the indebtedness.

Consideration for Extension of Time. — But a promise to extend the time of payment of a debt already due is void for want of consideration unless the debtor makes some concession; as, giving some security, paying interest in advance, or doing something that will form a consideration for the promise to extend the time.

Warner v. *Campbell*, 26 Ill. 282, held, that an agreement to extend the time of payment of a promissory note upon the payment of the interest in advance is valid, as it is founded upon a valuable consideration.

Moral Obligations. — A distinction is sometimes made between "good" consideration and "valuable" consideration. In defining these terms, Blackstone says, "A good consideration is such

COM. LAW. — 3

as that of blood, or of natural love and affection, when a ma
grants an estate to a near relative; being founded on motives
generosity, prudence, and natural duty; a valuable consideratio
is such as money, marriage, or the like, which the law esteer
an equivalent given for the grant: and is therefore founded o
motives of justice."

Accordingly it was held by some old authority that a mor
obligation was a sufficient consideration to make a promise vali

But the courts are now practically united on the point th
neither a moral obligation nor a "good" consideration is suf
cient to make a promise valid and enforceable at law.

In the case of *McElven* v. *Sloan*, 56 Ga. 208, Sloan & Co. sued McElv
Bros. on a promissory note given by them, the consideration for which was t
payment of a note against their father, who was dead. Before his death t
father had become insolvent and had gone through bankruptcy. Held, th
this claim against their father did not impose such an obligation upon the
as to constitute a valid consideration to support the new note given.

The Consideration must be Legal. — The doing or promisin
to do an illegal act is not sufficient consideration to support a
agreement.

In *McBratney* v. *Chandler*, 22 Kan. 692, plaintiff sued for services in p
senting the claim of the Miami Indians at Washington. It was contended th
the services were those of a lobbyist and illegal. The court held it was
the jury to decide whether the services were those of an attorney in drawi
papers and making agreements, or of a lobbyist in influencing the legislato
If the former, he could recover; if the latter, the consideration was illegal a
void, and he could not recover. If for both, the illegal part of the conside
tion vitiated and avoided the whole contract.

A Consideration must be Possible. — A promise to do an i
possible act is never a sufficient consideration to support
promise. This does not mean a mere pecuniary impossibili
but an obvious physical impossibility. The non-existence of t
thing given as consideration would render the consideration vo
and a promise made thereon invalid.

Gibson v. *Pelkie*, 37 Mich. 380, was an action on an agreement concerni
a judgment which plaintiff was to collect, retaining one half for his servic
It appeared that no such judgment existed. Held, that as the subject-matt
of the contract was not in existence there was no valid contract.

In *Rogers* v. *Walsh*, 12 Neb. 28, plaintiff bought of defendant what she pposed were, and what appeared to be, tax warrants of York County, but ng issued by the county commissioner without authority, they were void. ere was an action to recover the price paid. Held, she might recover, for ile the articles she bought resembled county bonds, they were really worth- s paper and the tax warrants did not exist. The agreement was therefore d for want of consideration.

The Consideration must be Present or Future. — A past con- leration is no consideration at all, for it confers no value. It simply some act or forbearance in time past, which has been nferred without incurring any legal liability. If afterwards, om a feeling of thankfulness or good will, a promise is made the person by whose acts or forbearance the promisee has been nefited, such promise is gratuitous and can not be enforced.

In *Summers* v. *Vaughan*, 35 Ind. 323, plaintiff sold defendant an engine and chinery and took a note for same. This action was to recover on the note. fendant claimed that after the sale the plaintiff had warranted the machinery, ereas in fact it was defective. The court refused to consider such a war- nty, as, being made after completion of the contract of sale, which was in iting, it was without consideration and void.

In *Dearborn* v. *Bowman*, 3 Met. (Mass.) 155, Bowman was nominated for nator. Plaintiff rendered services and furnished literature to advance de- dant's cause, but without any solicitation on defendant's part. After the ction defendant gave plaintiff his note for $60 for such services. The court d that the note was void for want of consideration. Past performance of vices constitutes no consideration for an express promise, unless the services re performed at the express or implied request of the defendant.

But if there has been, either expressly or impliedly, a request r the act or forbearance beforehand, the consideration for a omise to pay afterwards will be valid, because it is then evi- nt that the act was not intended to be a gratuity, and the ole is but one transaction.

8. REALITY OF CONSENT — MISTAKE

Mistake. — After the parties have entered into the apparent reement, the questions arise as to whether the minds of the rties have met on the same thing in the same sense, and

whether the consent of both parties was given under such c:
cumstances as to make it a real expression of intention.

The parties may not have meant the same thing. It may n
have been the intent of one or both of two parties to make
contract into which they have been brought by the misrepr
sentations of a third party. Should such a condition be occ
sioned by the carelessness of either party, he is not excusec
as when a man, able to read, signs a contract thinking it
something different from what it really is.

Walker v. *Ebert*, 29 Wis. 194, was an action on a promissory note. I
fendant proved that at the time he signed the note he was unable to re
or write the English language, and that it was represented to him, and
believed it to be, an agreement in reference to a patented machine, about whi
the party to whom he gave the note had been talking to him. Held that t
note, having been procured by false representations as to the character of t
instrument itself, and the maker being ignorant of its character and having
intention to sign such a paper, the note was void.

The mistake as to the nature of the transaction must be mutu
and must arise from some deceit which ordinary diligence cou
not foresee or from some accident which ordinary diligen
could not avert.

Nevius v. *Dunlap*, 33 N.Y. 676, was an action brought to reform a bor
The court held that to entitle plaintiff to a decree reforming a written instrume
he must show that the part omitted or inserted in the instrument was omitt
or inserted contrary to the intent of both parties and under a mutual mistak

Again, the mistake may be in the identity of the one wi
whom the party deals. X may enter into a contract, thinkir
and intending to contract with Y, when in fact he has bee
dealing with Z. There is no meeting of their minds, for X nev
contemplated dealing with Z.

Boston Ice Co. v. *Potter*, 123 Mass. 28, was an action for the price of i
furnished to defendant from April 1, 1874, to April 1, 1875. The defenda
was supplied with ice by plaintiff in 1873 and, becoming dissatisfied, terminat
his contract and made a new one with the Citizens Ice Company. Just befc
April, 1874, this company sold out to plaintiff. The court found that t
defendant had no notice of the change. Held, the plaintiff could not recov
as there was no meeting of the minds of these parties to this action. A m
has a right to select and determine the persons with whom he will **deal, a**
can not have others thrust upon him without his consent.

There may be a mistake as to the subject-matter of the thing contracted for, as where one party contracts expecting to receive one article and the other party thinks the agreement refers to another. The parties clearly have not agreed upon the same thing and the agreement is void.

Kyle v. *Kavanagh*, 103 Mass. 356, was an action to recover for the purchase price of land. It transpired that the defendant was negotiating for one piece of land and the plaintiff was selling another. It was held by the court that, as their minds did not meet on the subject-matter, they could not be said to have entered into a contract, and although there was no fraud on the part of the plaintiff, the mistake alone was a good defense.

The mistake may be as to the existence of the thing contracted for.

In *Thwing* v. *Hall*, 40 Minn. 184, plaintiff made a contract to sell certain timber lands to defendant, thinking they contained seven million feet of fine timber, defendant also believing there was good lumber there. The facts were that, unknown to either party, the land had been practically stripped of good lumber. Defendant sent a man who mistook the location and reported good timber. Held, a mutual mistake, which was a sufficient cause for the court to cancel the contract. There was a mistake as to the existence of the thing contracted for.

There may be a mistake by one party as to the intention of the other. In such a case it appears that if the second party knows that the first party is mistaken in his intention the contract is void.

In *Parrish* v. *Thurston*, 87 Ind. 437, plaintiff sold to defendant a buggy and harness and received a promissory note signed "E. K. Parrish." There was a man by that name living near Shelbyville, the place where the sale was made, who was wealthy and was known to both parties. The note was really made by E. K. Parrish of Hamilton County, a man entirely unknown to plaintiff. Plaintiff supposed he was getting a note signed by the man from Shelbyville, and the defendant knew that plaintiff believed this. As soon as plaintiff learned the truth he tendered back the note and sought to rescind the contract. Held, that the contract could be rescinded, as the silence of defendant, when honesty required him to correct the mistake of plaintiff, amounted to fraud.

The cases make the following distinction: If the second party knows that the first party is under a misapprehension as to what

the first party is *getting*, the contract is not voided, but if t
first party is under a misapprehension as to what is *promised*
the second party, and the second party *knows* of the misappr
hension, the contract is void.

In *Smith* v. *Hughes*, L. R. 6 Q. B. (Eng.) 597, plaintiff offered to sell
fendant some oats, and showed a sample. Defendant wrote the next day t
he would take them at the price named. He afterwards refused to take t
oats on the ground that they were new oats and he thought he was buyi
old oats. Nothing had been said at the time of the sale about their being c
oats, but the price was high for new oats. Held, that in order to relieve t
defendant from liability it was necessary to show not only that the plaint
believed the defendant thought that he was buying old oats, but that t
plaintiff believed the defendant thought the plaintiff was contracting to s
old oats.

Misrepresentation. — Misrepresentation is defined as an inn
cent misstatement of fact as distinguished from fraud or a willf
misstatement, and as thus defined it is almost, if not entirel
identical with mistake.

A party in making a misstatement, either does it willfull
which is fraud, or does it innocently, which is a mistake ; st
many writers and judges make a distinction between misrepr
sentation and mistake.

9. REALITY OF CONSENT — FRAUD

Fraud Defined. — Fraud is a false representation of fact, mac
either with a knowledge of its falsity or recklessly, wit
out belief in its truth, with the intention of having it act
upon by the complaining party, and actually inducing him to a
upon it. Aside from vitiating the contract, fraud is an actio
able wrong, and the party guilty of fraud is liable for deceit.

Fraud may be actual.

In *Holmes's Appeal*, 77 Pa. St. 50, a party about to purchase a farm ask
the owner whether the neighborhood was sickly or not, and declined to pu
chase if it was. The owner assured him that it was free from sicknes
whereas fever and ague were prevalent in the locality. The court held th
the agreement to purchase could not be enforced, it having been induced
the vendor's misrepresentations.

Fraud may also arise where there is active or artful concealment.

Jones v. *Edwards*, 1 Neb. 170, was an action brought for damages because alleged fraud in the sale of a horse. Jones bought the horse when he had a eeney, stiffness in the neck, and other ailments. He cut the cords of his ck and doctored him up. Later Edwards came and wanted to buy a farm am. Jones said he had what he wanted, and showed him this one and other horse, saying they were sound, as far as he knew, but that he never rranted a horse. He did not say a word as to the former ailments. Held, at it was fraud on the part of Jones in not acquainting the defendant, lwards, with conditions affecting the value of the horse, which, if known, uld have prevented defendant from buying.

One who conceals a fact which he ought, as a legal duty, to sclose is guilty of fraud.

Smith v. *Ætna Life Insurance Company*, 49 N.Y. 211, was an action upon life insurance policy. The defense was fraud in obtaining it. In the phyian's examination it was asked whether insurer had cough, occasional or bitual expectoration, or difficulty in breathing. The answer was, " No ugh; walking fast upstairs or up hill produced difficulty in breathing." ie facts were that he had raised blood for two and one-half years and that died three months after the policy was issued. Held, that there was a udulent concealment and misrepresentation which would avoid the policy.

The false representation may arise from the suppression of e truth, amounting to the suggestion of a falsehood.

In *Grigsby* v. *Stapleton*, 94 Mo. 423, plaintiff sold defendant a herd of cattle the ordinary market price, knowing that they had Texas fever, a disease not sily detected by one having had no experience with it. He did not disclose is to defendant. Held, that plaintiff was guilty of a fraudulent concealment, r which he was liable.

Caveat Emptor. — In a sale of goods in which the buyer can spect them the rule of *caveat emptor* is said to apply. The rm means, " let the buyer beware," and its application de ates that a vendor is under no obligation to communicate the cistence of even latent defects in his wares unless, by act or aplication, he represents that such defects do not exist.

In *Lucas* v. *Coulter*, 104 Ind. 81, defendant leased certain premises for one ar and defended an action for rent on the ground that they became unfit for s business. It appeared that the woodwork shrank and cracked the plaster,

causing dust to fall on the musical instruments which defendant kept in sto
Plaintiff made no representations or warranties. Held, there was no impli
warranty and the tenant must determine for himself, before engaging t
premises, as to their safety and fitness for his business.

Effect of Non-disclosure. — Mere non-disclosure does not vitia
a contract unless the parties stand in a relation of confidence
each other, and one party has the means of knowing facts th
are inaccessible to the other. He is then bound to tell ever
thing that is likely to affect the other party's judgment. Su
contracts are said to be *uberrima fides* contracts, that is, the
require the " utmost good faith," such as contracts of fire ar
life insurance and for the sale of land.

In *King* v. *Knapp*, 59 N.Y. 462, plaintiff purchased of defendant at an aucti
sale a lot in New York City, paying ten per cent down. Printed handbi
were circulated containing a diagram of the lot, which represented it to
25 x 100 feet, the handbill also stating this to be the size. Relying on t
description, the plaintiff purchased the premises without inspection. As
matter of fact a building upon the adjoining lot, which had stood there for ov
twenty-five years, encroached upon the premises. This was known to t
defendant, but there was no mention of it in the handbills or at the sa
Plaintiff refused to complete the sale and brought this action to recover t
amount paid. Held, the plaintiff had bought under the suppression of
material fact, and the contract could not be upheld.

It is held also in contracts for the sale of shares of stock in
company that the utmost candor and fullness of statement a
required of the promoter and of those who make statemen
upon the strength of which purchasers subscribe.

In *Brewster* v. *Hatch*, 122 N.Y. 349, defendants acquired options on certa
mining land. A prospectus was then issued describing the property and se
ting forth the terms and conditions upon which a company was to be organize
The proposed capital stock was $1,500,000, divided into shares of $10 eac
Plaintiff and others subscribed for about 61,000 shares, and the company w
organized and completed the purchase of the land. After paying the cost
purchase and other expenses, there remained on hand 58,235 shares of stoc
which were divided among the defendants, as previously agreed, and for whi
they paid nothing. When plaintiffs subscribed they did not know that d
fendants were to receive any stock without paying for it. This was an acti
to recover for the benefit of the corporation the value of the shares so di
tributed. Held, that the plaintiffs were led to believe that the defendan

re acting in the interest of all the investors and that defendants knew the
aintiffs so believed; that the relations of the parties were those of trust and
nfidence, binding the defendants to the exercise of good faith and requiring
em to disclose the information they possessed affecting the value of the
operty.

The statement must be a misrepresentation of fact. A mere
pression of opinion which turns out to be without foundation
a statement of intention which is not carried out will not
validate the contract.

In *Gordon* v. *Butler*, 105 U.S. 553, defendant borrowed money of plaintiff
d gave as security a mortgage upon real estate containing some sandstone
arries which had not been sufficiently worked to show their value. Defend-
t furnished the certificates of two persons, saying they had lived near the
ce for twenty years and giving the value of the property in their best judg-
nt to be an amount one hundred and fifty per cent more than the loan.
on a sale under foreclosure the land brought one-sixth of the amount of the
n. Plaintiff sued, charging fraud. Held, he could not recover; that an
tion will not lie for an expression of opinion, however inaccurate, in regard
the value of property which depends upon contingencies that may never
ppen.

The representation must be a statement of something that
ists or has happened; for instance, that a wagon cost $50 and
t that the wagon is worth $50, which would be a statement of
inion; or that if you buy this wagon you can sell it again in
e spring for $50, as this is merely a prediction for the future.
The law tolerates considerable prevaricating by the tradesman,
the matter of puffing his goods or wares, provided the thing
rgained for is open to the inspection of the buyer.

Poland v. *Brownell*, 131 Mass. 138, was a case in which plaintiff bought
t a half interest in defendant's stock of goods and business. He looked
er the stock and books and had ample opportunity to investigate. Held
it he had no right to hold the seller upon his representations of the value
the goods or the amount of business he had previously done. The Judge
d, "It is everywhere understood that such statements and commendations
e to be received with great allowance and distrust." (This case is another
istration of the rule of *caveat emptor*.)

The representation in order to render the contract void because
fraud, must be made with a knowledge of its falsity or with-
t belief in its truth.

Cowley v. *Dobbins*, 136 Mass. 401, was an action for fraud in that defenda represented to plaintiff that William Dobbins left an estate of $40,000 abo all liabilities, whereas in truth he was insolvent. The evidence showed th defendant believed her representations to be true. Held, no action would I against her.

If a man makes a false statement, honestly believing it to I true, he is not liable for fraud. He can be held only when I knows it to be false or has no knowledge either of its truth c falsity. The false statement must be made with the intentic of its being acted upon. It need not be intended that the part to whom it is made shall act upon it but that he shall lead som one to act.

In *Eaton* v. *Avery*, 83 N.Y. 31, defendant made false representations to mercantile agency as to the financial responsibility of the firm of Avery Reggins, of which he was a member. This firm asked credit of plainti Plaintiff went to the mercantile agency and obtained the information given I defendant, and relying on this he extended the firm credit. In an action f fraud it was held that the purpose for which such information is given t mercantile agencies is to enable them to furnish it to their subscribers fc guidance in extending credit ; and that the defendant would therefore I liable, as the case justified the finding that the false statements were mac with the intent to defraud any person who might inquire of the agency.

Sheldon v. *Davidson*, 85 Wis. 138, was an action for deceit in which it wa claimed that the defendant, in order to induce plaintiff to lease certain prem ises, concealed the fact that a barn thereon did not belong to him. But was not shown that this concealment induced plaintiff to lease the premis* and for this reason it was held that an action would not lie.

The false representation therefore must actually deceive, a in the case of *Eaton* v. *Avery*. If Eaton had not bee deceived by the information, he could not have succeede in his suit.

The effect of fraud on a contract is to give the injured part grounds for an action for damages for deceit. And the perso who has been led into a contract by means of the fraudulen misrepresentations may either affirm the contract and compe the fulfillment of the agreement or he may avoid it, provide that he signifies his intention to do so as soon as he become aware of the fraud. If he accepts any benefits under the cor tract after he learns of the fraud, the contract is affirmed.

Crooks v. *Nippolt*, 44 Minn. 239, was an action brought to recover the ount paid by plaintiff on a contract to buy a certain piece of real estate, on e ground that defendant's agent in making the sale showed plaintiff another d more valuable lot instead of the one sold. It appeared that after plaintiff rned of this he applied to defendant twice for an extension of time within ich to carry out his contract as to another payment. He also endeavored have the contract acknowledged so that it might be recorded. Held that should have rescinded upon the discovery of the fraud, and that his acts, er knowledge of the fraud, amounted to an affirmance and terminated the ht to rescind.

Duress. — Duress is defined to be some unlawful constraint ercised upon a man whereby he is forced to do some act ainst his will. It is actual or threatened violence or imprison- ent.

A contract entered into by a party under duress is voidable his option. The duress must be inflicted or threatened by a rty to the contract or one acting for him and with his knowl- ge, and the subject of the duress must be the contracting rty himself or his wife, parent, or child.

In *Morrill* v. *Nightingale*, 93 Cal. 452, plaintiff procured several promissory tes to be executed by defendant under coercion and intimidation, caused by eats of arrest, and he also had a warrant of arrest issued by a Justice of the ace not for the purpose of punishing defendant for a crime but to compel n to pay the money or execute the notes. Held that this constituted duress d was a good defense to the action to recover on the notes.

Wrongful detention of goods or damage to them does not con- itute duress, nor does threatened arrest in lawful prosecution.

Undue Influence. — In the creation of a contract undue influ- ce arises where the parties are not on an equality as to knowl- ge or capacity.

A promise made by a child to its parent, a client to his attorney, patient to his physician, a ward to his guardian, or a person his spiritual adviser, will not necessarily be set aside by the urt, but such relations call for clear evidence that the party nefited did not take advantage of his position.

Hall v. *Perkins*, 3 Wend. (N.Y.) 626, was a case in which a simple-minded, norant young man was induced by his uncle, a justice court lawyer, to accept conveyance of land worth $240 in satisfaction of a claim of $500. The

uncle was one of the executors of the estate which owed plaintiff. Held, t█
from the nature of the transaction, the inadequacy of the consideration, █
relative character, capacity, and connection of the parties, fraud and imp█
tion might well be presumed.

Bainbrigge v. *Browne*, 18 Ch. Div. (Eng.) 188, was an action to set as█
a deed given by children, who were of age, to their father. The court he█
that the father must show that the deed was executed with a full knowle█
of its contents and with a free intention of giving the benefit conferred.

Undue influence, like duress, renders the contract voidable █
the instance of the injured party.

10. SUBJECT–MATTER

The Object of a Contract must not be Illegal. — Another con█
tion is necessary to the formation of a binding contract and th█
is that the object of the contract must not be contrary to la█
Certain things are forbidden by law, and if these things are █
the contemplation of the parties at the time the contract █
entered into, it is not enforceable, otherwise the law would █
aiding in an indirect way what it expressly forbids.

Wells v. *The People*, 71 Ill. 532, was a case in which the school law provi█
that a teacher should have certain certificates of qualification. The sch█
directors employed plaintiff to teach school for six months at $45 █
month. He had no certificate, but obtained one after he had taught th█
months. He then learned that he could not collect his pay as he had █
qualified, so he canceled his contract with the consent of the directors a█
they hired him under a new contract for the remaining three months █
$90 per month. It seemed clear that the intent was to recompense him █
the time already taught. Held, that the first contract was void and by t█
second there was an attempt to do indirectly what the directors could not █
directly, which rendered the second contract void. But the plaintiff co█
recover reasonable pay for his services for the last three months.

This principle applies only to executory contracts, for if t█
contract has been voluntarily executed by the parties it is bin█
ing, as the law will not compel the return of anything acquir█
under such a contract any more than it will compel its perfor█
ance. The rule is that if parties have voluntarily completed █
contract, illegal as to the subject-matter, the law will leave the█
where they are.

Illegal Objects. — The object of the contract may be illegal express statutory enactment or because of rules of the com-on law. The statutes declare some contracts illegal and void d impose a penalty for the making of some others without dering the contracts void. A statute requiring a lawyer or a ysician to be licensed renders a contract made without com-ance with it void.

In *Gardner* v. *Tatum*, 81 Cal. 370, plaintiff, a physician, was called by de-dant on March 8, 1883, and continued to visit the patient until October 2, 3. Plaintiff's application for a certificate to practice medicine was granted rch 12 of the same year. Held, he could not recover any compensation the services rendered before the procuring of the certificate upon any tract express or implied, the contract being illegal and against public icy.

In *Buckley* v. *Humason*, 50 Minn. 195, the plaintiff, acting as a real estate ker in Chicago, purchased certain property for defendant. The ordinance Chicago requires all real estate brokers to be licensed and fixes the license at $25, providing a penalty for its violation. Plaintiff at this time had no nse. In an action for his commissions it was held that he could recover hing for his services. Business transacted in violation of law can not be foundation of a valid contract.

A law requiring weights and measures to be sealed as a con-ion precedent to a sale of goods by a merchant, renders a tract made in violation thereof void.

In *Eaton* v. *Kegan*, 114 Mass. 433, a statute provided that all oats and meal uld be bargained for and sold by the bushel. Held, plaintiff could not over the price of the meal and oats sold by the bag.

Sometimes a statute simply imposes a penalty and does not validate the contract, as seen in the following case: —

Pangborn v. *Westlake*, 36 Iowa 546, was an action to compel the payment of ote given in purchase of a city lot. A statute existed that provided a pen-y of $50 for selling any lot in a town before the plat thereof was recorded. e court held that as a general rule a penalty prescribed by statute for the ng of an act implies a prohibition which will render the act void. This is always so, however, as the court will look to the language and subject-tter of the statute and the purpose sought to be accomplished, and if from s it is manifest that it was not the intent to render the prohibited act void, vill be so construed. It was therefore held that the note was valid.

In this country statutes against wagers or bets have bee
passed in most of the states, and all wagers are now practical
declared contrary to public policy and void.

In *Love* v. *Harvey*, 114 Mass. 80, plaintiff made a wager of $20 with defen
ant that the body of one Dr. Cahill was buried on a certain side of the ma
avenue in Holywood cemetery. The stakeholder, although forbidden so to c
paid the $40 left with him to defendant. Held, that all wagers are unlawf
The party receiving the money from the stakeholder after being forbidd
to receive it is liable to the other for a return of the money even though he
the winner of the wager.

Statutes in many states also prohibit the desecration of tl
Sabbath day, and any contracting done on that day contrary
the statutes is void.

Handy v. *St. Paul Globe Publishing Co.*, 41 Minn. 188, was an action broug
for breach of contract. Plaintiff was employed by defendant to take char
of the real estate advertising in the daily, Sunday, and weekly editions of e
fendant's paper. A statute of the state forbade any work on Sunday exce
that "of necessity and charity." The court held that issuing and publishi
a paper on Sunday was unlawful. The contract was for illegal work in p
and was therefore void.

Clough v. *Goggins*, 40 Iowa 325, was an action on a promissory note ma
on Sunday. The court held that contracts made on Sunday are void, ane
promissory note made upon that day will not support an action.

In some states it is illegal for one to follow his "ordina
calling" or work, in others to make any contracts, etc. T
different statutes differ so materially that no general rule can
laid down as to what acts are prohibited.

Aside from the contracts declared unlawful and void by statu
there are contracts which are illegal at common law. The cour
will not enforce an agreement to commit a crime or to do a ci
wrong.

White v. *Kuntz*, 107 N.Y. 518, held, that in a composition of a debtor w
his creditors, any contract with one of them whereby he is to receive m
than his *pro rata* share is void and any security given upon such a promise
void.

Contracts against Public Policy. — All contracts, which if e
forced would be contrary to the good of the public or oppos
to the welfare of the community, are said to be against pub

icy and therefore void. Those contracts which tend to injure
government in its relations with other countries, those with
en enemies which involve any communication over the border
e, and those in restraint of trade, are illustrations of this class
contracts.

n *United States* v. *Grossmayer*, 9 Wall. (U.S.) 72, Ernstein, a resident
Macon, Ga., was indebted to Grossmayer of New York when the Civil War
ke out. Through an agent Grossmayer took cotton in payment and had
tored in Savannah. The government confiscated it and Grossmayer made
m against the government. Held, that all intercourse with an enemy is
iwful, and notwithstanding that the parties sustain the relation of debtor
creditor, the plaintiff above does not present a valid claim.

All agreements looking to the aid of hostile actions against a
ndly state are unlawful as being contrary to public policy.
contract to raise funds to aid an insurrection in a friendly
te would be such an agreement.

n *Kennett* v. *Chambers*, 14 How. (U.S.) 38, a contract was made in Cin-
ati, after Texas declared itself independent of Mexico, but before being
gnized as independent by the United States, whereby plaintiff agreed to,
did, furnish money to a Texas general to enable him to raise and equip
ps to fight against Mexico. Held, such a contract was void.

A contract to break a law of a sister state is also against
lic policy.

Graves v. *Johnson*, 156 Mass. 211, was an action for the price of intoxi-
ng liquors, sold and delivered by plaintiff in Massachusetts to a Maine
l keeper with a view of their being resold by defendant in Maine, contrary
he laws of that state. Held, that the contract had in view the breaking
he laws of Maine and could not be maintained.

Agreements to prevent or hinder the course of justice are
gal; as, to agree to conceal a crime of which one has knowl-
e, to refrain for a certain consideration from prosecuting a
ninal, to agree not to testify as a witness, to influence a wit-
s's testimony, or to bribe a juror.

Partridge v. *Hood*, 120 Mass. 403, held that a contract to deed a certain
e of property, where the real consideration was an agreement to drop a
inal prosecution against the grantor's son, was void as against public
cy.

A contract tending to injure the public service is contrary
public policy and therefore void. Such a contract is an agreeme
by a public officer to assign his salary to a creditor or an und
taking to influence the action of a legislature by lobbying or
agreement to hinder or prevent competition for public contrac

Agreements which tend to promote and encourage litigati
are also void; that is, it is not legal to speculate in lawsu
A may have a cause of action against B but it is not lawful
C to buy the action for the purpose of instituting suit. T
rule was formerly more strict than now. The holding in m
states at the present time is that an attorney can institute a s
on a "contingent fee," which means that he is to receive for
services a percentage of what he recovers. In the earlier da
this was forbidden.

Agreements contrary to good morals are illegal. So also
contracts which affect the freedom or security of marriage,
an agreement not to marry, and contracts made in considerat
of the procuring or bringing about of a marriage, or mut
agreements to obtain a divorce.

Sterling v. *Sinnickson*, 5 N.J.L. 756, was an action upon a written ins
ment promising to pay plaintiff $1000 provided he was not married within
months. Held, that the contract was void as against public policy.

In *Cross* v. *Cross*, 58 N.H. 373, plaintiff, who was the wife of defend
received from him certain notes secured by mortgage and in return she dee
to him the land covered by the mortgage. This transaction was part of
agreement between the parties to separate. It was further agreed that plai
was to obtain a divorce on certain grounds and defendant was to allow
papers in the action to be served upon him and make no defense, also that
children were to be divided between them, etc. Held, that the whole tra
action was illegal and void, and the law would not aid either party in enfor
their unlawful contract.

Restraint of Trade. — There is another class of agreeme
known as contracts in restraint of trade which are prohibi
by law as against public policy. It is for the good of the c
munity and the welfare of the individual that competition
trade should exist and that every man should be free to eng
in the occupation or vocation he may prefer. Still it is but
that a man in selling out his business shall include with it

good will, and refrain from opening up a like business at the next door or on the same street. The rule is, therefore, that if the restraint imposed upon the one party is not greater than the protection the other party requires, the contract is valid.

In *Herreshoff* v. *Boutineau*, 17 R.I. 3, plaintiff hired defendant as a teacher of languages for six months, and defendant covenanted not to teach the French and German languages anywhere within the state of Rhode Island for one year thereafter. Held, that this covenant was unreasonable and void ; the restriction extended beyond what was apparently necessary for the protection of plaintiff.

In *National Benefit Company* v. *Union Hospital Company*, 45 Minn. 272, the parties thereto consisted of two companies engaged in issuing benefit certificates entitling the holders to care and medical treatment in case of sickness or injury. Plaintiff had acquired a good business in Minnesota, Wisconsin, and northern Michigan, and entered into a contract with defendant agreeing for a certain consideration to refrain for three years from doing business in this territory except with railway employees. Held, that the contract was valid and not void as being in restraint of trade. The question of the reasonableness of the restraint depends upon whether it is such as to afford a fair protection to the party in whose favor it is made.

From the nature of the case it will be seen that a covenant to refrain from engaging in the same business within the same city might be reasonable in a grocery business, while in another business, the limitation of the whole state would be only just, as in the case of a manufacturer of heavy machinery requiring a wider territory for his sales.

In *Perkins* v. *Clay*, 54 N.H. 518, defendant sold his cart and butcher business for $90 and agreed that he would not carry on the same business on the same route for two years. Held, that this agreement was reasonable and valid.

In *Guerand* v. *Dandelet*, 32 Md. 561, defendant sold his dyeing and scouring establishment, and leased the premises to plaintiff, entering into a covenant that he would not at any time thereafter engage in a like business in the city of Baltimore. Held, that this covenant was valid, as it was not too comprehensive in its restriction.

In *Diamond Match Co.* v. *Roeber*, 106 N.Y. 473, defendant, who was engaged in the manufacture and sale of matches throughout the United States, sold his stock of machinery and good will to plaintiff. He covenanted that he would not, at any time within ninety-nine years, engage in such business in any of the states or territories except Nevada and Montana. Held, that the covenant was valid, as the restraint was coextensive only with the interests to be protected.

11. OPERATION OF CONTRACT

Parties acquiring Rights under Contracts. — We have now considered every element necessary for a valid and binding contract, and the question arises as to the extent and limitation of the rights conferred and of the obligations incurred.

As a general principle we learn that only the parties to a contract acquire any rights under it. It is clear that it can not impose liabilities upon any one not a party to it. A man can not voluntarily and without being asked to do so pay another man's debts and then seek to establish himself as a creditor. There is an apparent exception to this rule in the case of any one interfering with the contract of master and servant and inducing the servant to break his contract of employment. Some authorities hold that a party so interfering is liable for damages, and some hold that unjustifiably to induce one to break any contract is actionable.

In *Walker* v. *Cronin*, 107 Mass. 555, plaintiff conducted a shoe factory and employed a large number of people. The defendant with the intent to injure plaintiff's business induced a number of the employees to leave. The court held that plaintiff could recover damages.

It is held by some of the courts that a man can not acquire rights under a contract to which he is not a party, such as for A and B to enter into a contract, the consideration being that A shall confer some benefit upon X, a third party. Does X acquire the right under such an agreement to institute an action against A if the contract is not executed? The English courts say no. The Massachusetts and Michigan courts hold with the English courts that no action can be maintained by one not a party to the agreement for whose benefit a promise is made.

In *Linneman* v. *Moross*, 98 Mich. 178, a father agreed with his son that he would revoke a provision in his will in favor of his daughter and devise the same property to the son in consideration of the son's paying the daughter $10 a month as long as she might live. The daughter was not a party to the agreement. Held, that she could not enforce it.

The New York courts in the celebrated case of *Lawrence* v. *Fox*, 20 N.Y. 268, held that X, the third person, for whose benefit a promise was made by A, upon a consideration from B, the promisee, might maintain an action upon the promise, provided that he was the person directly intended to be benefited, and provided that B, the promisee, was at the time under an existing obligation to X, which he sought to discharge by giving X the benefit of A's promise. The facts in this case were that one Holly, at the request of defendant, loaned to defendant $300. Holly stated at the time that he owed that sum to the plaintiff and had agreed to pay it to him the next day. The defendant, in consideration of the loan, promised Holly that he would pay the sum to plaintiff on the next day. The plaintiff sued the defendant on this promise and the court held that he could recover on the promise, although he was not a party to it.

This rule as applied in New York State has been very largely adopted throughout the United States.

In *Dean* v. *Walker*, 107 Ill. 540, X sold certain real property to defendant, the property being mortgaged to plaintiff. As a part of the purchase price defendant agreed with X to assume the mortgage and pay the amount named therein to plaintiff. Held, that plaintiff, who was not a party to this agreement, could claim the benefits thereof and maintain an action to recover the amount of the mortgage from defendant.

Assignment of Rights. — Having now determined upon whom the rights and liabilities fall, we must ascertain how and when other persons may take their places and succeed to their rights, if at all. It is well established that the promisor can not assign his liabilities under the contract; that is, the promisee can not be compelled to accept performance from any but the promisor. This is only just, for if A contracts with B to have him do a certain thing for him, A is entitled to know with whom he is dealing, as he may have taken into consideration B's particular adaptability to the work.

This rule is qualified in the case of B undertaking to do certain work for A in which no particular knowledge or skill is required. He can then have the work done by another, but still B is responsible for the work being well done.

In *LaRue* v. *Groezinger*, 84 Cal. 281, one H agreed to sell to defendant all the grapes he might raise in a certain vineyard during a period of ten years, and defendant agreed to pay therefor $25 per ton. At the end of five years H sold the vineyard and assigned the contract to plaintiff. Defendant refused to accept grapes from plaintiff, saying he had no contract with him. Held, that the contract could be assigned, as it was not for services of a personal nature.

The ice case on page 36 seems almost in conflict with this decision, and in most cases the holding seems to be that the promisor can not assign his liability unless the agreement contemplates that some one else is to do the work or aid in it. This is true in the case of a contractor agreeing to build a house, as it is plainly within the contemplation of the parties that he will employ men to do part or all of the work.

As to the rights of parties under the contract, we find that at common law the only way such rights can be transferred to a third party is by a new agreement between all of the parties. The equity courts, however, permit an assignment in many cases, under which the assignee can enforce the contract, but the party liable must be given notice of the assignment. In such cases the assignee takes no better title than his assignor has; the assignment carries with it all of its defenses. Rights under contracts are assignable by statute in most of the states, and the assignee can enforce them in his own name. The above rule does not apply to negotiable instruments, which will be treated in another chapter.

Aside from the assignment of the rights under a contract by the voluntary acts of the parties, they may also be transferred by operation of law. In the assignment of a lease of land, certain covenants in the lease, which are said to concern the demised premises, pass to the assignee, such as covenants to repair, to pay rent, etc.

In *Salisbury* v. *Shirley*, 66 Cal. 223, it was held that the person who takes an assignment of a lease is liable on the covenants to pay rent and taxes the same as the original lessee.

By the death of the person all of his rights under his contracts pass to his executor if he leaves a will, or to his administrator if he dies without one. This is not the rule if the contract depends upon his performing some acts of personal service or skill. In such cases the contract dies with the party.

In *Lacy* v. *Getman*, 119 N.Y. 109, plaintiff contracted with M to work upon his farm as an ordinary farm laborer for one year from March 1. In July M died. Held, that his death terminated the contract.

By the bankruptcy of a party all of his property as well as his rights under his contracts pass to the trustee.

12. STATUTE OF FRAUDS

Outline. — In the year 1676, a law was passed in England, entitled " An act for the prevention of frauds and perjuries." This statute required that written evidence should be supplied in proving certain contracts.

The statute commonly called "the fourth section of the statute of frauds " provides as follows : " No action shall be brought whereby to charge

1. Any executor or administrator upon any special promise to answer damages out of his own estate ;
2. Or whereby to charge the **defendant** upon any special promise to answer for the debt, default, or miscarriage of another person ;
3. Or to charge any person upon any agreement made in consideration of marriage ;
4. Or upon any contract for sale of lands, tenements, or hereditaments or any interest in or concerning them ;
5. Or upon any agreement that is not to be performed within the space of one year from the making thereof ; unless the agreement upon which such action shall be brought or some memorandum or note thereof, shall be in writing and signed by the party to be charged therewith or some person thereunto by him lawfully authorized."

Object. — The object of this statute was to lessen the perjury in the testimony of witnesses, especially in the important cases included therein, and it therefore required that these contracts be evidenced in writing. In nearly all of the states of the Union this statute has been reënacted in somewhat the same form, although the language of the different statutes varies. This statute does not render oral contracts void, but says that no action shall be brought on them. It takes away the remedy. When action is brought in court upon such contracts, it is necessary to show the written agreement. The oral agreement is valid, and after it is made, a sufficient writing may be given.

Bird v. *Munroe*, 66 Me. 337, was a case in which a verbal contract was made. The contract belonged to the class required by the statute of frauds to be in writing. It was broken, and the parties afterwards entered into a written agreement containing the terms of the oral contract. After the writing was signed an action was brought for a breach of the contract which occurred before the written agreement was executed. Held, that the contract was sufficient to satisfy the statute. The writing was not the contract itself, but the evidence necessary to prove it.

The statute of frauds is a defense, solely, and the party availing himself of it must set it up, otherwise it is waived.

When Memorandum is Sufficient. — The writing need not be a formal contract. A memorandum or note containing the terms of the agreement, if signed by the party to be charged or his authorized agent, is sufficient.

Hurley v. *Brown*, 98 Mass. 545, was an action to compel defendants to perform their part of the following contract and to convey the land to plaintiff.
$50   "LYNN, April 14, 1866.

"Received of John and Michael Hurley the sum of fifty dollars in part payment of a house and lot of land situated on Amity Street, Lynn, Mass. The full amount is $1700. This bargain is to be closed within ten days of the date hereof." This was signed by the parties. The defense claimed that the writing was not sufficient, as there were several houses and lots on the street. It was shown that defendant owned no other house and lot on the same street. The court held that the writing was sufficient, and that evidence could be given as to the particular house meant.

The memorandum or note required to be in writing need merely contain the agreement and may consist of several writings or a number of letters and memorandums.

Promise of an Executor or Administrator. — The promise of an executor or administrator to answer damages out of his own estate, that is, to render him personally liable for the debts of the deceased, must be in writing. But the writing does not import any consideration, and there must be a consideration to this as to any contract.

In *Smithwick* v. *Shepherd*, 4 Jones (N.C.) 196, Shepherd, who owed plaintiff for board, died. Defendant, his administrator, in a conversation with plaintiff stated that " he would see it paid " or, " it should be paid." Held, that the promise was not enforceable because it was not in writing.

Promise to answer for the Debts of Another. — In the case of a promise to answer for the debt, default, or miscarriage of another, there must be three parties; the debtor, the creditor, and the person who guarantees the debtor's account. To bring the case under the rule requiring a writing there must not be an absolute promise to pay, but a promise to pay if the other defaults.

To illustrate, A goes to a grocery with B and says, " Give B a bill of groceries, and if he fails to pay for them, I will." Such a promise is under the statute and must be in writing, but if A says, " Give B the bill of goods and I will pay for them," or, " I will see that you are paid," this is an independent promise, making A the principal debtor, and is not within the statute.

In *Boston* v. *Farr*, 148 Pa. St. 220, plaintiff, a physician, brought suit to recover for services rendered defendant's stepson. Defendant said to plaintiff, " Go and get a surgeon and do all you can for the boy ; I will see that you get your pay." Held, the jury were justified in finding that it was an original promise on the part of defendant by which he charged himself with the bill, and did not come within the statute.

The test seems to be whether the party for whose debt the promise is made continues to be liable; if so, the promise is within the statutes.

Agreements in Consideration of Marriage. — The agreement here meant is not the promise to marry, but the promise to settle property or to make a payment of money in consideration of, or conditioned upon, a marriage.

In *McAnnulty* v. *McAnnulty*, 120 Ill. 26, it was held that a verbal agreement made by the woman before marriage, whereby she released and renounced all interest in her proposed husband's estate after his death, was void under the statute of frauds.

Contracts for the Sale of Lands or Hereditaments, or any Interest in or Concerning Them. — This section does not apply to the deed of conveyance of land, as that must be written and sealed without statutory requirement. But the statute here refers to any agreement to buy or sell land or to any interest in or concerning lands, as a grant of a right of way over one's land which is an interest concerning the realty and within the statute. Here a nice question often arises as to whether or not trees, crops, grass, and ore are real or personal property. If the former, all contracts concerning them are within the statute. The distinction seems to be that before they are severed from the land the natural products, such as trees, grass, etc., which grow without cultivation and the labor of man are parts of the realty, and if sold standing, the buyer to cut them, the contract is within the statute.

Powers v. *Clarkson*, 17 Kan. 218, held that wild grass growing on uncultivated land is a part of the realty, and an attempted transfer of such grass by parol is void.

Harrell v. *Miller*, 35 Miss. 700, held that the term "land" embraces not only the soil, but its natural products growing upon and affixed to it. Therefore a sale of growing timber is within the statute of frauds, and void unless in writing.

But if the owner of the land is to cut them, the sale is not completed until they are severed, therefore it is not a sale of a part of the realty and so not within the statute.

In *Killmore* v. *Howlett*, 48 N.Y. 569, defendant, an owner of some woodland, entered into a parol agreement with plaintiff by which defendant agreed to cut cordwood and deliver the same to plaintiff at Syracuse for $5 per cord. Defendant performed part of the agreement, and then as the price of wood went up refused to deliver more, claiming the contract was void under the statute of frauds, as being for the sale of an interest in real estate. Held, that as it was a sale of the trees when severed, and as the plaintiff was not to have any property in the trees until they were severed, the contract was not for a sale of an interest in real estate, and so not within the statute.

The same rule applies to coal and ore.

Riddle v. *Brown*, 20 Ala. 412, holds that a contract granting the right to dig and carry away ore from a mine is for the sale of an interest in real estate and must be in writing.

But if the products are growing crops which are harvested annually, and planted and cared for by the labor of man, the general rule is that they are personal property, even when attached to the soil.

Marshall v. *Ferguson*, 23 Cal. 65, was an action upon an oral contract for the sale of wheat and barley which was not yet cut. The defense was that since it was an interest in real estate the agreement must be in writing. Held, that as it was a sale of a growing crop, the product of periodical planting and cultivation, it did not come within the provisions of the statute, and was valid if made orally.

Agreements not to be performed within the Space of One Year. — The mere fact that the contract may or may not be completed within one year is not sufficient to bring it within the statute. It must be the plain intent and purpose of the contract that it is not to be performed within that time, to bring it within the statute. If its performance depends upon a contingency that may or may not happen within the year, no writing is necessary.

Kent v. *Kent*, 62 N.Y. 560, was an action on a contract whereby plaintiff agreed to work upon K's farm and to receive his pay after K's death. Plaintiff entered upon such employment and K died five years thereafter. Held, that the contract of employment was not within the statute, as the time was uncertain, and might have been less than one year, depending as it did upon the length of K's life.

Wahl v. *Barnum*, 116 N.Y. 87, held that a contract of partnership to continue for three years was void under the statute of frauds unless in writing.

An agreement to support a person during his lifetime is not within the statute as he may die within the year.

In *McCormick* v. *Drummett*, 9 Neb. 384, Z, a stepfather, gave D, his stepson, the use of his farm during Z's lifetime in consideration of D's supporting Z and his wife during their lives. Held, that such an agreement is not within the statute.

But a contract for a year's service to be entered upon in the future, even the next day, must be in writing under the statute.

In *Oddy* v. *James*, 48 N.Y. 685, about the middle of March the parties thereto entered into a verbal agreement by which defendant employed plaintiff to superintend his cement works for one year from April 1 next. Plaintiff worked until August 3, when defendant discharged him. Plaintiff sued, and defendant set up that the agreement was void under the statute of frauds. Held, for the defendant. The contract was not to be performed within one year, so must be in writing.

A lease of land in New York State is expressly regulated by statute and is an exception to the above rule. A lease for one year or less need not be in writing, and this is true although the lease is not to commence until a future date. In other states all leases are required by statute to be in writing. By the common law it was not required that any lease be written, but this was changed in England as well as in the different states by the statute of frauds.

13. SALE OF GOODS ACT

Conditions. — Section seventeen of the English statute of frauds provides : " No contract for the sale of goods, wares, and merchandise, for the price of ten pounds sterling or upwards (see Appendix for amounts in different states) shall be allowed to be good except

1. The buyer shall accept part of the goods so sold, and actually receive the same; or
2. Give something in earnest to bind the bargain, or in part of payment;
3. Or, that some note or memorandum in writing of the said bargain be made and signed by the parties to be charged by such contract or their agents thereunto lawfully authorized."

This section is reënacted in most of the states. The amount involved necessary to bring the contract within the statute varies in the different states. As will be seen, the statute includes most of the articles regarded as personal property under the terms, "goods, wares, and merchandise." A close question comes up when the goods are in process of manufacture. If it is held that it is a sale of labor, and of material to be made up, it is not a sale of goods, wares, and merchandise, but a contract for "work, labor, and services," and does not come within the statute. In England the test is that if at the time of delivery the subject-matter of the transaction is a sale of goods, wares, and merchandise, it is within the statute, and the rule has been followed in Minnesota, Missouri, and other states.

Brown v. *Sanborn*, 21 Minn. 402, held that an agreement to purchase at $5 per ton the flax straw to be raised from 45 bushels of flaxseed, it appearing that from 20 to 50 tons were raised, was within the statute of frauds as a contract for the sale of goods and chattels. The court said, "It is essentially a contract for straw and not for labor and skill in producing the straw."

In *Burrell* v. *Highleyman*, 33 Mo. App. 183, the agreement was for three pieces of furniture, which were to be finished up and covered according to defendant's express order. The consideration of the transaction was over $50.

Held, that when the subject-matter of a contract is a chattel to be afterwards delivered, it is a sale of goods and not a contract for work, labor, and services, although work is to be done on such chattel before delivery.

In New York. — In New York the rule is that if the article is in existence at the time of the agreement, it is within the statute, although some work is to be done upon it before delivery, but it is not within the statute if the article is not in existence at the time of the formation of the contract, as flour to be ground from the wheat or nails to be made from the iron.

Parsons v. *Loucks*, 48 N.Y. 17, was an action to recover damages for a breach of contract. It was a parol contract that the defendants should manufacture and deliver to plaintiff at New York City ten tons of book paper of a certain quality, plaintiff to pay thirteen cents a pound therefor. Held, that the contract was valid, and not within the statute. The court said the distinction was between the sale of goods in existence, at the time of making the contract, which was within the statute, and an agreement to manufacture goods, which was for work and labor, and not within the statute.

In Massachusestt. — In Massachusetts a still different rule is followed, which is, if the contract is for articles in existence or the kind the vendor makes in the ordinary course of his business, even though not at the time in existence, it is within the statute ; but if the articles are to be manufactured especially for the purchaser and not for the general market, it is not. ·

In *Goddard* v. *Binney*, 115 Mass. 450, defendant went to plaintiff's shop and gave his verbal order for a buggy to be made for him according to specific directions and marked with his monogram. The price was $675. After the buggy was finished and the bill had been presented several times, plaintiff's shop burned and the buggy was destroyed. Held, that the contract was not within the statute applying to the sale of goods and the title to the buggy was in defendant, as this article was manufactured especially for the purchaser and upon his special order and not for the general market. It was not in existence at the time of the contract, nor was it such an article as the plaintiff in the ordinary course of his business manufactured for the general market.

One of Three Conditions Necessary. — Of those contracts which are within the statutes the law requires one of the three following conditions : that there be a part payment on account (to bind the bargain, as is often said), or a receipt and acceptance by the buyer of at least part of the goods, or, if neither of the above provisions is complied with, a written note or memorandum of the contract signed by the party to be charged. This memorandum must contain all the essential terms of the sale.

Stone v. *Browning,* 68 N.Y. 598, held that a writing simply acknowledging the purchase of goods, without stating the price or terms of the contract of sale, is not a sufficient memorandum of the contract to satisfy the statute of frauds. All of the essential parts of the contract must be evidenced by the writing.

14. DISCHARGE OF CONTRACT

Discharge by Agreement. — As the contract is created by the agreement of the parties, so the parties may, if they choose, terminate and discharge it in a like manner. This may be termed a waiver or rescission of the contract. If the contract is executory, each party may waive his rights under it, and the waiver of the rights of one is the consideration for the waiver of the rights of the other. It is virtually a new contract, the subject-matter of which is the waiver of the old contract, and all of the elements of a contract are necessary to constitute a valid waiver. If one party has performed his part of the contract, there must be some consideration for his release of the other party.

In *Collyer* v. *Moulton,* 9 R.I. 90, Moulton and Bromley, copartners, entered into a contract with plaintiff who agreed to build them a wire bending machine. Moulton and Bromley dissolved and Moulton withdrew from the firm, after which plaintiff agreed to release him from the agreement and look to Bromley. Held, that this release of Moulton was not binding, as it was without consideration. If Bromley had agreed to pay plaintiff the full amount if plaintiff would release Moulton, this promise would have been a valuable consideration for the release.

A waiver may be effected by the substitution of a new contract which so changes the terms of the old one that it either expressly or impliedly waives the old agreement, but the intention to discharge the old contract must be clear. The contract may by express terms provide for its own discharge, as, for instance, a stipulation that one party may terminate it upon giving certain notice or performing certain conditions.

Moore v. *Phœnix Insurance Co.*, 62 N.H. 240, was an action on a policy of insurance. The policy provided that if the premises should become vacant and remain unoccupied for a period of more than ten days, without the assent of the company indorsed upon the policy, the policy should become void. The premises became vacant and remained so for over three months. They were then occupied and thereafter burned. Held, that by the terms of the policy it was terminated and discharged by the vacancy, and subsequent occupation did not revive it.

Discharge by Performance. — This is the termination of the contract contemplated by the parties when it is made. The terms having been carried out and the conditions performed, the contract is satisfied and discharged. This of course requires performance upon both sides. If but one party has performed, he alone is discharged and not the contract, for it remains in force until all of its provisions are carried out. If the contract is for the sale of a horse for $100, the contract is discharged when the horse is delivered and the money paid. If the horse is delivered but payment not made, it is discharged as to the seller but not as to the purchaser.

To constitute a performance the terms of the contract must be carried out as to time, place, and conditions. Although a substantial performance is held good, the party will be liable for the damages caused by his deviation from the exact terms of the contract.

Nolan v. *Whitney*, 88 N.Y. 648, was an action to recover on a contract for building defendant a house. The court found that he had endeavored to live up to the agreement and, acting in good faith, had substantially performed his part. He could therefore recover, notwithstanding some slight defects in the plastering for which compensation would be made to the defendant.

Gillespie Tool Co. v. *Wilson*, 123 Pa. St. 19, was an action to recover the contract price for drilling a gas well. The contract called for a certain depth and diameter. Plaintiff had drilled the required depth, but the diameter of part of it was less than the contract specified. The only excuse for this was the saving of time and expense. Held, that this was not a substantial compliance and he could not recover, although the well answered every purpose a larger one would.

When the contract calls for the payment of money, the party to whom it is to be paid need not accept a note or check. But if it is accepted, the question arises as to whether or not this discharges the original contract, or whether the note or check is to be regarded as a conditional payment. If it is but a conditional payment, it does not discharge the contract until it is paid. It is the intent of the parties that governs here, but in the absence of any proof of intent to the contrary the presumption is, in most of the states, that it is taken conditionally.

Stone & Gravel Co. v. *Gates Iron Works*, 124 Ill. 623, held that the taking of a note for a preëxisting debt was no payment unless the creditor expressly agreed to take the note as payment and to run the risk of its being paid. The giving of a receipt for the amount is not enough to establish such a positive agreement.

In some states, the courts hold exactly the contrary view as to the taking of notes.

Dodge v. *Emerson*, 131 Mass. 467, held, that the giving and acceptance of a promissory note for a preëxisting debt is presumptive evidence of payment.

A contract in which the performance of one party is to be satisfactory to the other gives rise to a nice question and we are confronted with the inquiry, can the whims and personal taste of the party for whom the work is done prevent the fulfillment of the agreement when the performance is to all intents and purposes well accomplished? The answer seems to be that if it is a matter of personal taste, as a contract for painting a portrait or a contract for the sale of goods where the parties can be put *in statu quo* (*i.e.* the same condition in which they originally stood), the agreement will be strictly construed and the buyer will be the sole judge.

In *Brown* v. *Foster*, 113 Mass. 136, plaintiff expressly agreed to make a suit of clothes for defendant that would be satisfactory to him. The clothes were made and delivered, but defendant declined to accept them. Plaintiff proved that they could easily be altered and made to fit. But the court held that under the agreement it was for the defendant alone to decide whether or not he would accept the clothes. It was the plaintiff's fault if he entered into a contract that made his compensation dependent upon the judgment and caprice of another.

But if it is a contract for work or labor which does not involve the question of personal taste, as for machinery or mason work, the courts hold that the party for whom the work is performed must be satisfied when in justice and reason he ought to be satisfied.

In *Hawkins* v. *Graham*, 149 Mass. 284, plaintiff agreed with defendant in writing to furnish and set up a heating system in defendant's mill according to certain specifications, and he was to be paid upon its satisfactory completion. If the system was not satisfactory, he was to remove it at his own expense. Held, that the question as to whether the system was satisfactory was to be determined, not by the particular taste and liking of the mill owner, but by the judgment of a reasonable man.

Legal Tender. — The payment of money must be made in what is termed legal tender, unless the creditor consents to accept something else. Legal tender is money which Congress has declared must be accepted if offered in payment of an undisputed debt. All gold coins and silver dollars are legal tender for any amount. Silver coins of denominations less than the dollar are legal tender in amounts not exceeding ten dollars. Minor coins such as nickel and copper pieces are legal tender in amounts not exceeding twenty-five cents. Gold and silver certificates are not legal tender. United States treasury notes are legal tender in any amount. United States notes or "greenbacks" are legal tender in any amount, except for duties on imports and interest on the public debt. National bank notes are not legal tender, but are accepted by the United States government for all debts except duties on imports. In actual practice the national bank notes and the gold and silver certificates are taken without question and pass as freely as any other kind of money, and their acceptance constitutes good payment. The receipt of counterfeit money does not constitute payment, and it can be returned within a reasonable time and good money demanded in its place.

Tender. — The creditor may refuse to accept the money which the debtor claims is due him. In such a case if the debtor makes a sufficient tender of the amount he will be relieved from paying any costs in a suit against him for the debt. To constitute a sufficient tender the exact amount of money must be produced and offered, and the offer must be made unconditionally, that is, it must be made without any reservation. Even the offer to pay upon condition that the creditor give a receipt for the money is not a good legal tender. Unless the contract provides a place of payment, the tender must be made to the creditor personally if he is within the state.

Impossibility of Performance. — We have seen on page 34 that when the act to be performed is an impossibility on the face of it, no contract exists, as such an act is not a valid consideration. But the question comes up when the impossibility arises after the formation of the contract, and the rule then is that it does not excuse performance.

In *Anderson* v. *May*, 50 Minn. 280, plaintiff contracted in March to raise and deliver to defendant 591 bushels of beans. Plaintiff delivered only 152 bushels because most of his crop was destroyed by early and unusual frost. Held, that this did not excuse his non-performance. When such causes may intervene they should be guarded against in the contract.

But if the promisor makes his promise conditional upon an event, the happening of which makes the performance impossible, this of course excuses him, as where a clause is inserted providing for the contingency of fire, or strikes, or floods. If the promise is made unconditionally, the promisor takes all risk.

There are contingencies which may arise, however, which the courts hold are sufficient excuse for not fulfilling the contract. Among these are impossibilities arising from a change in the law of one's own country.

In *Cordes* v. *Miller*, 39 Mich. 581, Miller leased from Cordes, a wooden building in Grand Rapids, Mich., for ten years. The lease contained this covenant, "If said building burns down during this lease, said Cordes agrees to rebuild the same in a suitable time, for said Miller." Miller occupied the premises for two years, when it was destroyed by fire. About the time of the fire an ordinance was passed prohibiting the erection of wooden buildings within certain limits which embraced this site. Held, that the covenant was released by the ordinance making its fulfillment unlawful.

Another contingency which will excuse the failure to fulfill is where the continued existence of a specific thing is necessary to the performance of the contract. The destruction of that thing through no fault of either party discharges the contract.

Walker v. *Tucker*, 70 Ill. 527, was a case in which the lessee of a coal mine covenanted in his lease to work the same during the continuance of his lease in a good and workmanlike manner. The court held he was excused from further performance when the coal mine became exhausted.

Cleary v. *Sohier*, 120 Mass. 210, was a case in which plaintiff entered into a contract with the defendant to lath and plaster a certain building. After he had partially completed his part of the contract the building burned. Held, that the plaintiff was excused thereby from fulfilling the remainder of his contract, and could recover a reasonable amount for the work already done.

A contract for the rendering of personal services is discharged by the death or illness of the promisor.

In *Spalding* v. *Rosa*, 71 N.Y. 40, defendants contracted with plaintiffs, who were proprietors of a theater, to furnish an opera troupe to give a certain number of performances. The leader and chief attraction of the company became ill and unable to sing, and the defendants did not appear. In an action to recover damages for the breach it was held that as the illness of the chief singer made it practically undesirable and impossible to appear without him, and as it was caused by circumstances beyond his control, it constituted a valid excuse for non-performance.

Discharge by Operation of Law. — Where security of a higher nature is substituted for inferior security a merger of the less into the higher takes place. The common illustration of this rule is the case of a judgment taken on a simple contract, the amount owing on the contract being merged in the judgment.

Another illustration is the case of a contract under seal made by the same parties and containing the same subject-matter as a simple contract then existing. The simple contract is merged in the specialty.

Clifton v. *Jackson Iron Co.*, 74 Mich. 183, was a case in which the owner of land on contracting for its sale, reserved the timber, with the right of removal for a specified time. Before the expiration of this time he conveyed the land to the purchaser by warranty deed under seal without any such reservation. Held that the contract became merged into the deed and discharged by it, and the timber passed to the purchaser.

Discharge by Alteration of a Written Instrument. — If a written instrument is altered or erased in a material part by a party to the contract, or by a stranger while the instrument is in the possession of the party to it, and with said party's consent and without the consent of the other party to the instrument, the contract will be discharged, if the alteration is made with an intent to defraud; but if innocently made there can be recovery on the original consideration.

Wood v. *Steele*, 6 Wall. (U.S.) 80, was an action on a promissory note dated October 11, 1858, and made by Steele and Newson, payable to their own order one year from date. It was indorsed by them to Wood, the plaintiff. "September" had been stricken out and "October" put in as the date. The change was made after Steele had signed the note as surety and without his knowledge or consent. Held, that it was a material alteration and extinguished Steele's liability.

But if the alteration be made without intention to defraud, there can be a recovery on the original contract.

In *Owen* v. *Hall*, 70 Md. 97, at the maturity of a joint promissory note a renewal note was given which was invalidated as to one of the makers on account of a material alteration made after he signed. The alteration was the insertion of the words "with interest" without his knowledge or consent. Held, that a recovery could be had against him on the original cause of action, as there was no fraudulent intent in the alteration.

Discharge by Bankruptcy. — In 1867 there was enacted by Congress a United States bankruptcy law. This enactment was repealed in 1878, and from that time down to 1898 there was no national bankruptcy law, although in several of the states bankruptcy laws were enacted. They proved inefficient, however, and in 1898 a new national bankruptcy law went into effect.

Voluntary and Involuntary Bankruptcy. — This act provides that "Any person owing debts, except a corporation, shall be entitled to file a voluntary petition in bankruptcy."

"Any natural person, except a wage earner, or a person engaged chiefly in farming or the tillage of the soil, any unincorporated company, and any corporation engaged principally in manufacturing, trading, printing, publishing, mining, or mercantile pursuits, owing debts to the amount of one thousand dollars or over, may be adjudged an involuntary bankrupt upon default or an impartial trial, and shall be subject to the provisions and entitled to the benefits of this act. Private bankers, but not national banks or banks incorporated under state or territorial laws, may be adjudged involuntary bankrupts."

Duties of Bankrupt. — As soon as the voluntary **petition is** filed, or after the hearing upon the involuntary petition, if allowed, the party is a bankrupt, and it is then his duty to attend the first meeting of his creditors, if directed by the court or a judge of the court, and also the hearing upon the application for his discharge. He must also comply with the lawful orders of the court; examine the proofs of claims filed against his estate; execute such papers as shall be ordered by the court; execute to his trustee a transfer of all his property in foreign countries; inform his trustee of any attempts of his creditors to evade the provisions of the bankruptcy law, coming to his knowledge, or of any attempt on the part of creditors to prove false claims; prepare, make oath to, and file in court within ten days, unless further time is granted, after the adjudication, if an involuntary bankrupt, and with the petition if a voluntary bankrupt, a schedule of his property, showing the amount and kind of property, the location thereof, its money value in detail, and a list of his creditors, showing their residences, if known (if unknown, that fact to be stated), the amounts due each of them, the consideration thereof, the security held by them, if any, and a claim for such exemptions as he may be entitled to, all in triplicate, one copy of each for the clerk, one for the referee, and one for the trustee; and when present at the first meeting of his creditors and at such other times as the court shall order, submit to an examination concerning the conduct of his business, the cause of his bankruptcy, his dealings with his creditors and other persons, the amount, kind, and whereabouts of his property, and, in addition, all matters which may affect the administration and settlement of his estate; but no testimony given by him shall be offered in evidence against him in any criminal proceeding.

The bankrupt is entitled to the same exemptions as are allowed any debtor by the laws of the state in which he resides.

Acts of Bankruptcy. — Certain acts of a person are called acts of bankruptcy and render him liable to be adjudged an involuntary bankrupt upon the petition of his creditors. The law provides that these acts of bankruptcy by a person "shall consist of his having conveyed, transferred, concealed, or removed, or per-

mitted to be concealed or removed, part of his property with intent to hinder, delay, or defraud his creditors, or any of them; or
transferred, while insolvent, any portion of his property to one or
more of his creditors with intent to prefer such creditors over his
other creditors; or suffered or permitted, while insolvent, any
creditor to obtain a preference through legal proceedings, and not
having at least five days before a sale or final disposition of any
property affected by such preference vacated or discharged such
preference; or made a general assignment for the benefit of his
creditors, or, being insolvent, applied for a receiver or trustee for
his property, or because of insolvency a receiver or trustee has
been put in charge of his property under the laws of a state, or
a territory, or of the United States; or admitted in writing his
inability to pay his debts and his willingness to be adjudged a
bankrupt on that ground."

The petition can be filed any time within four months after
the act of bankruptcy has been committed.

Trustee and Creditors. — As soon as a person is adjudged a
bankrupt a meeting of his creditors is called, at which time they
can examine the bankrupt, elect a trustee, and do any other business proper at the time.   As soon as the trustee is elected and
has filed his bond, he becomes vested by operation of law with the
title of the bankrupt to all of his property except that exempt by
law, to all property transferred in fraud of creditors and to all
rights arising upon his contracts and agreements.   It is then
the duty of the trustee to collect the assets, which he divides
among the creditors whose claims have been accepted.

Discharge in Bankruptcy. — The bankrupt, after one month
and within twelve months after being so declared, may file an application for a discharge in the court of bankruptcy, and the judge
shall grant the discharge unless at the hearing held thereon it
shall appear that the bankrupt has "committed an offense punishable by imprisonment as herein provided; or with intent to conceal his financial condition, destroyed, concealed, or failed to keep
books of account or records from which such condition might
be ascertained ; or obtained property on credit from any person
upon a materially false statement in writing made to such person

for the purpose of obtaining such property on credit; or at any time subsequent to the first day of the four months immediately preceding the filing of the petition, transferred, removed, destroyed, or concealed, or permitted to be removed, destroyed, or concealed, any of his property with intent to hinder, delay, or defraud his creditors ; or in voluntary proceedings been granted a discharge in bankruptcy within six years; or in the course of the proceedings in bankruptcy refused to obey any lawful order of, or to answer any material question approved by, the court."

The discharge of the bankrupt acts as a discharge of all of the debts and contracts of the bankrupt at the time of the filing of the petition except a certain class of debts which are tinged with wrong or fraud, or debts due the government, or debts due creditors who were not duly notified of the proceedings.

Discharge by Breach. — We have already considered how a contract may be terminated and discharged by fulfilling the terms thereof. We have now to consider how it may be discharged by failure or refusal of one or both of the parties to fulfill the agreement. When the terms of the agreement have been broken, there arises in the place of the contract a new obligation under which the party in default is placed. That obligation is to pay to the other party the damage arising therefrom. The injured party acquires a new right through the breach called a right of action.

The contract may be broken in any one of three ways. A party may renounce his liability thereunder or he may, by his own acts, make it impossible for him to fulfill, or he may wholly or partially fail to perform, what he promised.

Breach by Renouncing Liability. — When one party to the contract renounces his liability thereunder before performance is due and declares that he will not perform, a breach of contract arises and the injured party may at once institute an action for damages.

Windmuller v. *Pope*, 107 N.Y. 674, was an action to recover damages for breach of contract. The parties entered into a contract whereby plaintiff sold to defendant 1200 tons of old iron to be delivered at a certain time. Before the time expired defendant notified plaintiff that he would not receive nor pay for any of the iron. Plaintiff thereupon sold the iron elsewhere. Held that the plaintiff was justified in treating the contract as broken at that time, and was entitled to bring action immediately without tendering delivery or waiting the expiration of the time fixed for the performance.

If during the course of the performance one of the parties clearly refuses to continue with his part, the contract is broken, and the other party is excused from further performance, — in fact, he must not go on if his continuing would increase the damage.

In *Clark* v. *Marsiglia*, 1 Denio (N.Y.) 317, defendant delivered to plaintiff a number of pictures to be cleaned and repaired. After he had commenced defendant gave him orders to stop, as he had decided not to have the work done. Plaintiff, however, finished the work and claimed the whole amount of the contract. Held that he had no right to increase the amount of damages by going on with the work. When the contract was broken he was entitled to just compensation for the injury he had sustained by the breach of the agreement.

Breach by Making Performance Impossible. — If one of the parties puts it out of his power to perform before the performance is due, the other party need not wait, but may consider the contract broken.

In *Wolf* v. *Marsh*, 54 Cal. 228, Marsh promised in writing to pay Wolf a certain sum of money. The note contained the following condition : " This note is made with the express understanding that if the coal mines in the Marsh Ranch yield no profit to me this note is not to be paid and the obligation herein expressed shall be null and void." Thereafter and before the mines had yielded anything defendant sold them. Held, that the yielding of profit by the mines was a condition precedent to the payment of the note, but Marsh had rendered the happening of that condition impossible by selling the mines, and the obligation therefore became absolute.

And this is true if the impossibility is created after the contract is performed in part.

In *Woodberry* v. *Warner*, 53 Ark. 488, Woodberry, the owner of a steamboat, employed Warner, a pilot, at a salary of $720 per year with the further agreement that as soon as the net earnings of the boat should amount to $8000 he should become the owner of a one-fourth interest. In about two years Woodberry sold the boat. Held, that as he had put it out of his power to fulfill the contract, he was liable to Warner for the value of his services over and above his regular wages.

In order that one party may recover damages for a breach of contract on the part of the other the first party must show that the second party's promise was not dependent upon the acts of the first party; that is, if A is to draw a ton of coal for B for $7, A can not sue B for payment until he has performed his own part.

In *Weber* v. *Clark*, 24 Minn. 354, defendant owned a farm of 200 acres and agreed to pay plaintiff $100 if he would find a purchaser for it. Plaintiff found a man who bought part of it, and then sued for the $100. Held, that he could not recover, as he was not entitled to the money until he had performed his part of the contract and found a purchaser for the whole farm.

This rule does not apply to contracts in which the promises are independent of each other. Here a breach by one does not discharge the other.

Tracy v. *Albany Exchange Co.*, 7 N.Y. 472, was an action for breach of covenant in a lease which provided that plaintiff might have the refusal of the premises at the expiration of the lease for three years longer. When the lease expired defendant refused to renew it at the same rate, but asked $200 per year more. Plaintiff was somewhat in arrears of rent at the expiration of the first lease. Held, that the payment of the rent was not a condition precedent to the right of the plaintiff to a renewal of the lease, the covenant to renew and the covenant to pay rent being independent promises. Plaintiff could bring his action for breach of the contract to renew, although he was guilty of default in the payment of his rent.

Breach by Failure to Perform — Entire and Divisible Contracts.

— It is clear that when one party wholly fails in the act that was the entire consideration for the second party's promise, and that must be done before the second party can be required to perform his part, the second party will be excused. But certain cases come up in which one party has done part of what he promised or a part of the contract has been carried out, and we have to consider whether or not the whole contract has therefore failed. In other words, is it an entire or a divisible contract? A common illustration of the cases under which this question arises is an agreement to deliver and pay for goods in installments at different times.

The English rule, which holds all contracts of this class as divisible, is followed in *Myer* v. *Wheeler*, 65 Iowa 390, in which plaintiff sold to defendant ten car loads of barley, like sample, to be delivered from time to time on the railroad tracks at Calmar, Iowa, and defendant was to pay seventy cents per bushel for each car load when delivered.   After the first car was delivered defendant refused to allow more than sixty-five cents, saying that the barley was not equal to sample, but urged plaintiff to ship balance.   Plaintiff refused. Held, that the contract was severable, and that the refusal to pay for the first car load did not entitle plaintiff to rescind and refuse to deliver the other car loads; that plaintiff could recover the actual value of the car delivered, and defendant could recover damages for the failure to deliver the other nine cars.

But the courts in this country generally seem to hold the contrary view, and make the test the real intent of the parties.   If it was intended to be all one contract, the courts do not make it divisible because it is to be executed or carried out at stated periods.

In *Norrington* v. *Wright*, 115 U.S. 188, plaintiff made a contract of sale to defendant of 5000 tons of iron rails for shipment from a European port at the rate of about 1000 tons per month, beginning in February, the whole contract to be shipped before August.   Plaintiff shipped only 400 tons in February and 885 tons in March.   As soon as defendant learned of the failure of plaintiff to ship as agreed, he refused to accept and pay for what was shipped, and sought to rescind the whole contract for the failure to ship 1000 tons per month.   In this case the contract was held to be entire and not divisible, and the defendant had the right to rescind the whole contract.

Representation and Condition. — Certain failures to perform are not considered of sufficient importance to invalidate the contract, but merely give rise to a right of action for the damages caused. If one of the terms of the contract is but subsidiary and does not defeat the main object of the contract, a breach of such term does not discharge the contract.   Such a term is styled a representation and not a condition.   A statement descriptive of the subject-matter or of some material incident, such as, the time or place of shipment, is generally regarded as a condition.

In *Filley* v. *Pope*, 115 U.S. 213, a contract provided for the sale of iron to be shipped from Glasgow as soon as possible.   It was shipped from Leith. Held, that the buyer might refuse to accept.   The place of shipment was a material incident and a warranty or condition precedent, upon the failure of which the other party might repudiate the whole contract.

A representation is a separate stipulation and neither suspends nor defeats the agreement.

In *Davis* v. *Meeker*, 5 Johns. (N.Y.) 354, defendant sold plaintiff a wagon for $50 and represented at the time of the sale that he had been offered $50 for it by different persons. The wagon was not really worth over $25. Held, that this was not a warranty and constituted no grounds for an action.

15. DAMAGES

Nature and Extent. — As we have already learned, the party who is guilty of a breach in the performance of his part of the contract may be compelled by the courts to make good the loss incurred by the other party. If the contract be discharged by the breach, the party not in default is released from further performance. He may also recover a *pro rata* amount upon the part performed if he has done anything under the contract. In certain cases there is also provided the extraordinary relief of an injunction or a specific performance.

If the action brought by the party not in default is for money damages, the amount allowed will be the loss or injury caused as the natural result of the breach or that would ordinarily be within the contemplation of the parties. The object is to compensate the party injured and not to punish the party in default.

In *Beeman* v. *Banta*, 118 N.Y. 538, defendant contracted to construct a refrigerator for plaintiff who was engaged in preparing poultry for market, and with a knowledge that plaintiff intended to make use of it at once for freezing and keeping chickens for the May market, expressly warranted that the freezer would keep them in perfect condition. This it failed to do, and as a consequence a large number of chickens spoiled. It was held that the plaintiff, in an action on the warranty, could recover as damages the difference in the value of the refrigerator as constructed and its value as it would have been if made according to contract, and that he could also recover the market value of the chickens lost, less the cost of getting them to market and selling them.

Specific Performance and Injunction. — The special relief of specific performance and injunction is granted only when money damages do not constitute an adequate remedy, as in a contract calling for the conveyance of land. The particular place could not be duplicated elsewhere, and it might have a special value to the purchaser for which money would but poorly compensate him. Specific performance would therefore be decreed at the instance of the purchaser compelling the vendor to convey, but it would not be decreed against the purchaser to compel him to accept the property because there would be an adequate remedy at law in the way of damages, as the owner could sell to some one else, and the difference between what the purchaser had agreed to pay and what he could get for the land after the breach would be the amount of his damages.

So also the remedy by injunction is exercised only in special cases in which damages would not afford adequate relief to the injured party.

In *Cort* v. *Lassard*, 18 Ore. 221, plaintiff, a theatrical manager, sought to restrain defendants, who were acrobats, from performing at a rival theater in the same place. Defendants had agreed to perform for plaintiff exclusively for six weeks, and plaintiff alleged that he had prepared for them and advertised them and that he would lose large profit, as they were unique attractions. Held, that when a contract stipulates for special, unique, or extraordinary personal services, involving special merit, skill, or knowledge, so that in case of default the same services could not be easily obtained elsewhere nor be compensated for by an action at law, a court of equity will be warranted in applying its preventive remedy of injunction.

16. DISCHARGE OF RIGHT OF ACTION

By Mutual Agreement.—As the breach of a contract gives rise to a right of action for the damages suffered, we have to determine how this right may be discharged, and we find there are three means by which it may be effected. The parties may discharge the right by mutual agreement if a valuable consideration be given, as a payment in satisfaction of the damages or an instrument under seal.

In *Hale* v. *Spaulding*, 145 Mass. 482, defendant agreed in writing to pay plaintiff six sevenths of any loss he might be subjected to as the indorser of a certain note. Thereafter plaintiff executed under seal, a receipt " in full satisfaction of defendant's liability on the document." This discharged the right of action on the original agreement.

By Judgment.—The party may prosecute the right of action in the courts and obtain a judgment, the right of action being then merged in the judgment.

By Statute of Limitations.—If the right of action is not merged in a judgment or discharged by consent within a given time, the law will refuse to enforce it by reason of the lapse of time under what is termed the statute of limitations.

This statute, which was first enacted in England, provided that all actions upon account, and some others, shall be commenced and sued within six years. Like the statute of frauds it has for its object the discouraging of litigation and the suppression of perjury, as the lapse of time makes the proof less certain and the resurrection of old and stale claims would be a fruitful field for fraud and perjury. A provision analogous to the English statute has been enacted in all of the states. In New York and most of the other states the period is six years on contracts not under seal and twenty years on sealed instruments or judgments of the court duly recorded. Certain other actions are barred in three, two, and one years. (See Appendix, p. 351.)

The statutes in the different states vary, and in a number of them negotiable instruments are not barred for a longer time than simple contracts. In the most of the states real property actions are given a longer period to run.

When the Time under the Statute Begins.—The time begins to run from the day the injured party would be entitled to bring a suit for the claim.

Sturgis v. *Preston*, 134 Mass. 372, was an action to recover money paid under mistake. Held, that it was barred unless the action was brought within six years from the date of the payment of the money, because the right of action accrued upon that day.

Most of the statutes provide that the absence of the defendant from the state at the time the cause of action arises will postpone the running of the statute until his return.

In *Engel* v. *Fischer*, 15 Abb. N.C. (N.Y.) 72, it was held that a person who comes within the state with the purpose of continuing therein, concealed under a fictitious name to avoid pursuit by his creditors, is not to be regarded as having come within the state within the meaning of the statute until the day he is discovered.

If the plaintiff is under disability, such as infancy, insanity, or imprisonment at the time the right of action arises, the time will be extended. But the disability must exist at the time the statute begins to run or it will have no effect.

New Promise.—The promise or right of action may be renewed, either by a new agreement, which by some of the statutes must be in writing, or by a payment on account. The statute then begins to run under the new promise or after the new payment.

In *Blaskower* v. *Steel*, 23 Ore. 106, plaintiff, between the years 1878 and 1885, sold to H a quantity of cigars. On May 18, 1885, there was a credit on the account. The court held, that this credit revived the whole account for a further statutory period, and the claim would not outlaw until six years after the payment.

QUESTIONS ON CONTRACTS

1. Define contracts.
2. Mention the elements necessary to constitute a binding contract.
3. Distinguish between executed and executory contracts.
4. A agrees to give B $10 for delivering to him one ton of hay. B delivers the hay, but A has not yet paid him for it. Is the contract executed or executory on A's part? On B's part?
5. What are formal contracts? Simple contracts?
6. What is necessary to constitute a seal?
7. Distinguish between oral and written contracts.
8. Distinguish between express and implied contracts.
9. Brown gives Whitmore a power of attorney to sell his house and lot. Whitmore, without Brown's knowledge, purchases it himself and makes the deed to himself. Is the contract binding? Give reason.
10. Who is an infant? In general, is a contract made by an infant valid? Is it void? What are the rights of the infant after becoming of age in reference to the contracts made during his infancy?
11. Carpenter, an infant, traded with Smith a flock of sheep for a horse; later, becoming tired of his bargain, he tendered back the horse and demanded his sheep. At the time of the trade Carpenter stated that he was over twenty-one years of age, when, in fact, he was but eighteen. Could he recover back his sheep?
12. Smith, becoming tired of the trade, tendered back the sheep and demanded the horse, claiming his right to disaffirm the contract because Carpenter was not of age. Could he recover his horse?
13. Carpenter, after he becomes of age, is in debt and his creditors seek to recover the sheep on the ground that the contract was made during Carpenter's infancy. Can they succeed?

14. Edwards, an infant, agrees with Larkin to purchase his automobile. After Edwards becomes of age and before he has disaffirmed the contract, Larkin sues him for damages because of his failure to take the machine. Was the contract binding, or was Edwards bound to disaffirm the contract upon becoming of age?

15. In question 11, could Carpenter tender back the horse and demand his sheep before he became of age?

16. In question 11, though the horse dies after Carpenter received it, could he still disaffirm the contract and demand his sheep back?

17. In question 11 Carpenter demands back his sheep, but does not offer to return the horse. Can he get his sheep and keep the horse, in case the horse is living and he still has him?

18. What class of infants' contracts are void instead of voidable?

19. What class of infants' contracts are valid and binding?

20. One Stewart sold to Haines, an infant, a suit of clothes, which were necessaries and with which he was not properly provided. The suit was reasonably worth $25. Stewart charged him $50 for it. In an action to recover the $50, could Haines succeed? If not, what could he recover, if anything?

21. Are doctor's services necessaries? Are articles of jewelry necessaries?

22. Strong, an infant and a son of a laboring man, bought of plaintiff a gold watch worth $50. Plaintiff sought to hold Strong for the price of the watch, claiming that it was for necessaries. Could he recover?

23. In the above case, if Strong was the son of a bank president and a wealthy man, would the contract be for necessaries?

24. In the last case, if Strong's father had already provided him with a good gold watch before he purchased the watch of plaintiff, could plaintiff recover as for necessaries?

25. Can an insane person make a valid contract?

26. A contracted with B, an insane person, not knowing of B's insanity. B's condition was such that it was not noticeable at times that he was of unsound mind. Under their contract A purchased a horse and wagon of B and paid him a fair price for it, and afterwards disposed of the wagon. Could B repudiate the contract?

27. In the above case B had been judicially declared insane by the courts. Could B repudiate the contract?

28. A knew of B's insanity. Could the contract be set aside?

29. In question 20, if Haines had been a lunatic instead of an infant, could Stewart have recovered?

30. Rogers, while intoxicated to such a degree that he did not know what he was doing, sold his gold watch, worth $50, to Bush for $5. After becoming sober, he tendered back the $5 and demanded the watch. Could he recover?

31. Can a married woman now make a contract in her own name? Could she under the common law?

32. What is offer and acceptance?

33. Baker offers to sell Holt his automobile for $600. Holt replies, "I will accept your offer and take the machine at $600, provided you will accept $300 in cash and my note at two months for the balance." Is this a valid contract? Give reason.

34. Fitch has two typewriters, a Remington and a Smith Premier. He offers to sell Carey the Remington for $75. Carey writes back, telling him that he will pay him $75 for the Smith Premier. Is this a valid acceptance of the offer?

35. A murder having been committed in the city of Rochester, the mayor offers a reward of $1000 for information that will lead to the apprehension and conviction of the murderer. O'Laughlin of Elmira gives such information, through which the murderer is convicted. At the time he gives the information he has no knowledge that any reward has been offered, but after learning of it claims the reward. Give holdings in different states.

36. Smith's horse became frightened while being driven along the canal and went in. Jackson, who was driving near, saw him and went to the rescue and spent time and labor in helping to get the horse and wagon out. After they had succeeded in their efforts Jackson claimed $10 for his services. Could he recover?

37. When does an offer become effectual? When does an acceptance become binding?

38. In what mode or way must the acceptance be made?

39. Defendant wrote plaintiff on the 21st of June that he would sell him his piano for $250. On the 25th of June plaintiff deposited in the post office an acceptance of the offer. This letter in the regular course of the mails reached defendant at noon on the day of the 26th, but about nine o'clock on the morning of the 26th defendant sold the piano to another party and sent plaintiff word. Could plaintiff recover damages for breach of contract against defendant, or was the contract not yet completed?

40. In the above case suppose defendant sent the offer to plaintiff by a messenger. Plaintiff instead of replying by the messenger sent the letter through the mail, but before the letter reached defendant he had sold the piano. Could plaintiff recover for breach of contract?

41. Suppose in question 39 defendant about six o'clock in the afternoon of the 25th telegraphed plaintiff withdrawing his offer. This message was sent a few hours after plaintiff had mailed his acceptance of the offer. Was the acceptance binding or was the withdrawal of the offer sent in time?

42. In question 40 if defendant in his offer had told plaintiff to reply by mail, could plaintiff recover?

43. If in question 39 defendant had died on June 23, would plaintiff's acceptance on the 25th without notice of his death have been good?

44. Define consideration. When is consideration necessary in a contract?

45. What effect has a seal in regard to consideration?

46. Stone promises to give his grandson $100 when the grandson becomes of age. Stone does not fulfill his promise. Can the grandson compel him to pay?

47. If in the above case Stone had paid the $100, could he recover it back?

48. One Powers promised Evans $100 provided he would name his child after Powers. The child was so named and Powers refused to pay. Could Evans recover?

49. Blake owed Ayers $500 which was due July 1. July 2 Blake paid $400, and Ayers in consideration of getting the money then, agreed to accept it in full payment. Thereafter Ayers sued for the balance of $100. Could he recover?

50. In the above case if Blake had given $400 and two sheep worth $5 each, could Ayers have recovered the remaining $90?

51. In question 49 if the sum owed by Blake to Ayers had been in dispute, Ayers claiming it to be $500 and Blake claiming it to be $350, and they had agreed upon a settlement of $400, which was paid and accepted in full payment, could Ayers then sue for the balance of $100 which he claims to be due? Why?

52. Ayers owes Blake $100 which is due. Blake makes a promise to extend the time of payment one year. Thirty days after Blake makes this promise to extend the time of payment, he sues Ayers for the amount. Ayers claims the account is not yet due. Can Blake recover?

53. In the above case Ayers gives Blake a chattel mortgage on his household furniture in consideration of the extension of one year. In that case can Blake sue before the year has elapsed?

54. Gibson rescues Rogers from being run over by a railroad train. Out of a spirit of thankfulness Rogers promises to give Gibson $100. Failing to keep his promise, Gibson sues him. Can he recover?

55. Gilbert who is unable to read or write the English language signs a paper which is represented to him to be an agreement for a particular kind of paint. It turns out to be a promissory note for $50. Is the note valid?

56. A contracted with B to purchase a horse which stood in B's stable. A thought he was buying the bay horse, while B thought he was selling a brown. Could A recover damages for B's refusal to deliver the bay horse?

57. Define fraud.

58. A sells B his grocery store and stock of goods. B has an opportunity of inspecting the store, and does look through it. The most of the stock had previously been injured by a flood which filled A's cellar. B purchases, and later upon discovering this, sues A for damages. Can he recover?

59. In the sale of goods where the buyer can inspect them, what rule is said to apply?

60. What are *uberrima fides* contracts?

61. Gordon sells Brownell a horse, tells him that he is the best horse in the neighborhood, and that if he keeps him until fall he can sell him for $50

more than he pays for him. As a matter of fact the horse is an inferior animal and Brownell loses on his purchase. Can he recover damages from Gordon?

62. If Gordon had represented that the horse was but eight years old, when in fact it was twelve, but Gordon believed it was only eight, could Brownell have recovered damages?

63. If in the above case when Gordon stated the horse was but eight years old he knew that he was twelve, but made the statement falsely, still Brownell knew all the time that the horse was twelve years old and was not deceived by the statement, could Brownell recover damages of Gordon?

64. Define duress.

65. A is threatened with imprisonment and physical injury, unless he signs a note that is presented to him. He signs it. Is the note valid?

66. If the physical injury and imprisonment had been threatened to A's wife unless A signed the note, would the note have been valid?

67. If the threat had been to break a valuable piece of statuary belonging to A, unless A signed the note, would the note have been valid?

68. Is a promise made by a child to his parent or a patient to his physician void? Does it come under a different rule from an ordinary promise?

69. A was employed by B to do an unlawful act. After A has performed his part of the agreement he sues B for his pay. Can he recover?

70. If B had paid A, could he recover the money?

71. A statute in New York State requires a physician to have a certain license before practicing. A physician practicing without such a license sues for his services. Can he recover?

72. A makes a wager with B that C will be elected governor of New York State at the coming election. C is defeated and the money is paid to B. A brings an action to recover the money wagered. Can he succeed?

73. A, who is an important witness against B, a criminal on trial, is promised $100 by B if he will refrain from testifying. He refuses to testify against B, and later sues B for the $100. Can he recover?

74. A promises B $500 provided he does not marry in two years. At the end of two years, B, having kept his promise, demands the $500. Can he recover?

75. Cross sold his meat market to Sterling and agreed that he would not engage in the same line of business in the same city, which had 10,000 inhabitants, for the period of ten years. Was this agreement valid?

76. If in the above case Cross had agreed not to engage in the same business within the state for a period of ten years, would the agreement have been valid?

77. If in question 75 Cross had been engaged in manufacturing automobiles, would the restrictions in that case have been valid? Would the restrictions in question 76 have been valid?

78. A and B go into a grocery store together. B is asked by the grocer to pay an account which he owes. Being unable to pay it he refuses. A

thereupon without B's knowledge or request pays the bill to save his friend's credit. He then seeks to recover the amount from B. Can he recover it?

79. Liman owes Davis $500. Liman agrees to sell one Noble a team of horses, provided he will pay him $50 in cash and will pay Davis $500 within ten days. Noble takes the team and pays the $50 in cash. Liman in the meantime departs from the country. Davis brings action against Noble for the $500. Can he recover?

80. A undertakes to do certain work for B in the nature of some fine decorating and interior finishing in B's house. A assigns the contract to C, who seeks to go on with the work. Can he complete the work and recover of B?

81. What is the statute of frauds and what is its object?

82. A, who was administrator of the estate of one Shepherd, stated orally to B, a creditor of Shepherd's, that he would see that B was paid the sum due him; if it did not come out of the estate he would pay it himself. The estate did not pay. Could the promise be enforced?

83. If in the above case Shepherd was still living and A was a friend of his, could B collect on A's promise?

84. Clarkson agrees to sell Miller all of the grass growing on his farm for the coming season. The contract is not in writing. Can it be enforced?

85. If the contract had been to sell all of the pine lumber to be cut on his farm by the purchaser, could the contract have been enforced?

86. If the contract had been to sell the wheat growing on his farm, could an oral contract have been enforced?

87. If Clarkson was to have cut the grass and timber himself and to have delivered it to Miller, could the contract have been enforced?

88. A employs B to work for him for the period of one year from the coming March. Must this contract be in writing to be valid?

89. If the agreement had been to work for B during the life of A, would the oral contract have been valid?

90. In February, A leases his farm to B for one year from the following March. Must this lease be in writing to be valid in New York State?

91. Under the sale of goods act, if the sale amounts to the sum specified therein or over, in what three ways may the contract be rendered valid?

92. Burrow goes to Sanburn's wagon factory and orders a wagon made according to his special design, with his coat-of-arms on the sides and finished up in some particular way. The price for the wagon is to be $200. When it is nearly completed, but before it is delivered, the factory burns. Under the New York rule, who loses?

93. Under the Massachusetts rule, who loses?

94. Under the English rule, who loses?

95. If in the above case the order had been for a wagon of the style and kind regularly manufactured by this party, who would lose under the New York rule? Under the Massachusetts rule? Under the English rule?

96. What is necessary to discharge a contract by performance?

97. A owes B $100. He tenders him a check for $100 in payment of the debt. Must B accept it ?

98. In the above case, if B does accept, does it discharge the original contract ?

99. Emerson enters into a contract with Foster who agrees to build him an engine and boiler for his flour mill. The contract is that the engine and boiler shall be constructed and installed in complete running order to the entire satisfaction of Emerson. Foster does the work, and the plant seems to run satisfactorily; but Emerson is not satisfied, says he does not want it, and orders Foster to take it out. Expert machinists claim that the work is done in a satisfactory manner. Must Emerson accept it, or has he the right to reject it under the agreement ?

100. A orders a suit of clothes of B, his tailor, and specifies that he will not take them unless they are satisfactory to him, he being the sole judge. The suit, as far as any third party could determine, is a good fit; but A says he does not want it, it is not satisfactory to him. Can he refuse to accept the suit ?

101. A agrees with B to manufacture and deliver 1000 pairs of shoes in 90 days, but because of a strike in A's factory he is unable to fulfill his agreement. Is the strike which renders the performance of the contract practically impossible an excuse for his non-performance ?

102. If in the above case A's agreement to furnish the shoes to B had stipulated that the contract was subject to strikes, etc., would he have been liable for non-performance ?

103. A employs B to paint his house. When the work is partially done the house burns. Does this excuse B's non-performance of his contract, and can B recover a portion of his pay ?

104. What do we mean when we speak of the merger of one contract into another ?

105. Hall gives Wood his promissory note, payable one month after date. Wood changes the note, making it payable twenty days after date. What effect has this upon the instrument ?

106. If the alteration was made without any intention to defraud, could Wood recover on the original contract ?

107. Who may file a voluntary petition in bankruptcy ?

108. Who may be adjudged an involuntary bankrupt ?

109. What are the duties of a bankrupt after he has been adjudged such ?

110. When may a bankrupt file a petition for his discharge from his debts ?

111. Edwards sues Adams on a note given for $100. Adams sets up the defense that one year after giving the note, and before the commencement of the action, he filed a petition in bankruptcy and received his discharge. Is the defense good ?

112. A employs B to deliver 100 loads of stone for him within 30 days, for $100. After he has delivered 10 loads, B, within 3 days after the agree-

ment is made, throws up the contract and says that he will not perform any further. What remedy has A ? May he proceed at once with his remedy, or must he wait until the 30 days have expired ?

113. In the above case, B, after delivering 5 loads, refused to perform further until he received his pay for the whole contract. Had he the right ?

114. For breach of the contract to deliver the stone, what would be the damages that would be allowed for the injury ? That is, by what rule would they be measured ?

115. When is the special remedy of a specific performance granted ?

116. When a right of action for damages is sued in the courts and placed in judgment, what do we say becomes of this right ?

117. Define the statute of limitations. What is its object ?

118. When does the period under the statute of limitations begin to run ?

119. Does the fact that the plaintiff is an infant or an insane person at the time the right of action arises affect the running of the statute of limitations ?

SALES OF PERSONAL PROPERTY

1. IN GENERAL

Sale and Barter. — A sale is a contract between parties to give, and to pass, rights of property for money which the buyer pays or promises to pay to the seller for the thing bought. As stated in this definition a sale is a contract and subject to all of the requirements of a valid contract. The parties must be competent to enter into a binding contract. There must be mutual assent and there must be a consideration. If there is an absence of consideration, the transfer is a gift. The price or consideration must be paid or promised in money. This distinguishes sale from barter, which is the exchange of one article of personal property for another.

In *Commonwealth* v. *Packard*, 5 Gray (Mass.) 101, defendant was tried for the unlawful sale of intoxicating liquor. It was proved by a witness that he called for intoxicating liquor at defendant's hotel, that a waiter by defendant's order gave it to him and that he offered to pay, but the defendant would not take anything. Held, that it was not a sale but a mere gratuity or gift, and the defendant was discharged.

As a general thing the same rules apply to a barter as to a sale, and we can consider that the law applicable to a case of barter is practically the same as that explained in this chapter on sales. It seems, however, that the power or authority vested in an agent to sell does not give authority to barter.

In *Edwards* v. *Cottrell*, 43 Iowa 194, it was held that the mortgage of a chattel, with power of sale by the mortgagee upon default in payment, confers upon him no right to barter the mortgaged property or to dispose of it otherwise than for cash.

Transfer of the Right of Property. — There must be a transfer of the right of property, that is, a transfer of the absolute property in the thing sold, in order to constitute a sale. This "absolute property" is a term used to distinguish it from a special property, or right in personal property. For instance, when property is pledged, the special property passes to the pledgee and the general title remains in the owner. The transfer of a special property in a chattel constitutes bailment and will be considered in another chapter.

Sale and Bailment. — The rule is that if the identical thing is to be returned, even though in a different form, as wheat ground into flour, it is a bailment; but if the identical thing is not to be returned, the general rule is that it is a barter or a sale.

In *Hyde* v. *Cookson*, 21 Barb. (N.Y.) 92, plaintiff and one Osborn entered into an agreement whereby plaintiff furnished certain hides to Osborn who took them to his tannery and manufactured them into sole leather, and was to return them to plaintiff in New York. Plaintiff was then to sell them at his discretion, and when sold the net proceeds less costs, commissions of plaintiff, expenses, etc., were to go to Osborn for tanning. If there was any loss, Osborn was to stand it. Osborn failed before the contract was completed and assigned to defendant. Defendant refused to deliver the hides to plaintiff, claiming it was a sale and the title was in Osborn. Held, that it was not a contract of sale but a bailment, the right of property remaining unchanged, and plaintiff was entitled to the hides.

It is held that the delivery of logs to be sawed into boards is not a sale but a bailment. The importance of the distinction is realized when we perceive that if it is a bailment the title does not pass from the original owner by the delivery, but if the transaction constitutes a sale, the title passes. The question often arises when the stock or material delivered is destroyed by fire, or otherwise, and it is required to be determined upon whom the loss shall fall. An exception to the rule is the case of a warehouseman who receives grain and mixes it with like grain in the same storage. Here there is evidently no intention to return the identical grain, but some of the same kind; still some cases hold that this transaction is one of bailment in which title does not pass, but others follow the general rule and hold it a sale under which the title passes to the warehouseman.

2. FIXTURES

Personal and Real Property. — In treating of the law applicable to the sale of personal property it is necessary for us to distinguish between personal and real property. We understand in a general way that real property is land and rights issuing out of and concerning it. As distinguished from this, we learn that personal property is property of a personal or removable nature, and includes all property rights not included in the classification of real property. Personal property is also called chattels. We often find much difficulty in distinguishing between the two classes of property. It is plain that a house and lot or a farm is real property, and it is equally apparent that a horse and wagon or a suit of clothes is personal property.

But the standing of certain articles known as fixtures is less clearly defined. By the early English law any interest in land less than the absolute title or freehold was called personal property, but in the United States this is not the rule. The only interest in land that can be classed as personal property at the present time is the lease.

In *Taylor* v. *Taylor*, 47 Md. 295, A at the time of his death left a will giving his real estate to a certain party and his personal estate to his son absolutely. A owned a number of leases of property, some of which were to run for ninety-nine years. Held that these leases passed as personal property to the son.

Fixtures are Chattels. — In regard to fixtures, we learn that they are chattels, either actually or constructively affixed to the land. In some cases they can not be removed and are considered part of and pass with the land, while under other conditions they may be separated from the realty and do not pass with it. The early common law was most favorable to the landowner, regarding anything attached to the realty as his property, but the rule was relaxed, at first in favor of the tenant who erected fixtures for use in his trade or business, which were held to be removable. Now, however, the question arises not only between landlord and tenant, but also between mortgagor and mortgagee, and vendor and vendee. A person selling his farm must know what he can remove and what he has sold with the land. The tenant must determine what he can take with him and what passes to the landlord because of its attachment to the realty. Different rules have been laid down by different courts.

One of the tests often applied is the intention of the party annexing the chattel to the land. This intention is inferred from the nature of the article affixed, the relation of the party making the annexation with the owner of the land, the structure and mode of the annexation and the purpose for which it is to be used.

In *Hinkley* v. *Black*, 70 Me. 473, plaintiffs entered into possession of a tract of land under a contract for its purchase, and erected large and substantial buildings with engines and machinery for manufacturing an extract of bark for tanning purposes. Plaintiffs failed to pay for the land, so never acquired title. In an action to recover the machinery and engines it was held that they were a part of the realty, and could not be sold as personal property as against the owners of the land.

In *Ottumwa Woolen Mill Co.* v. *Hawley*, 44 Iowa 57, it was held that the machinery of a woolen mill, consisting of looms, carders, breakers, condensers, etc., were part of the realty. The looms were fastened to the floor by screws, and the carders were kept in position by their own weight, one weighing 3000 pounds. The spinning jacks were fastened by cleats nailed to the floor. The question in this case arose between the purchaser under a mortgage and the owner. The court said that of the three requisites generally considered necessary to constitute a chattel a part of the realty, the first, that of physical attachment, is very uncertain, and the only value to be attached to it is in determining the intention of the owner in making the annexation. The second, being application to the use or purpose to which that part of the realty with which it is connected is appropriated, is met in this case by the use of the machinery in the mill. The third requisite, being the intention of the party making the annexation, was held by the court to be the controlling consideration in determining the whole question.

It seems that there are other tests that have to be applied in connection with the intent, to determine whether or not the chattel is a part of the realty. One is the mode and degree of the annexation. That is, if the chattel is so firmly and securely affixed to, and incorporated into, the building that it can not be removed without injury to itself and the building it is generally not removable. Under the common law the mode and degree of annexation was practically the controlling question.

Murdock v. *Gifford*, 18 N.Y. 28, holds a rule contrary to that in the case of the *Ottumwa Woolen Mill Co.* v. *Hawley*, as in this case it was held that looms in a woolen factory, connected with the motive power by leather bands and so attached to the building by screws holding them to the floor that they could be removed without injury to themselves or the building are chattels. The question arose between the mortgagor and mortgagee.

In *Despatch* v. *Bellamy*, 12 N.H. 205, it was held that an engine used in a building and so placed that it can not be removed without taking down part of the building is a fixture ; while loose, removable machinery not attached to the building is not regarded as part of the real estate. The engine in this case could not be removed without taking the boards off the side of the building, and the boilers were set in brick, requiring the wall to be torn down to remove them. In this case the question arose between the grantor and the purchaser.

A person may not intend to make a permanent improvement, but the chattel may be so firmly annexed that the law will not permit him to carry out his intention of removing it. In such a case the damage to the realty must be very pronounced to constitute the chattel a part of the real property if it is the expressed intent of the party that the chattel shall remain personalty.

Hendy v. *Dinkerhoff*, 57 Cal. 3, was an action to recover possession of a steam engine and boiler. One Lampson was in possession of land under a contract to purchase from defendant, the contract providing that in case of failure to purchase, all tools should belong to defendant. Plaintiff later leased an engine and boiler to Lampson and the agreement was that if Lampson failed to pay, plaintiff might retake them. The engine was built into the masonry so that it could not be removed without destroying the masonry and the wall to which it was affixed, but it was held that even as against the defendant, the owner of the land, the chattel remained the property of the plaintiff.

But, on the other hand, the fact that it may be removed without such injury does not necessarily make it personalty.

Goodrich v. *Jones*, 2 Hill (N.Y.) 142, held that fencing material that has been used as part of the fences on a farm, but is temporarily detached without any intent to divert it from such use, is a part of the realty and passes by a conveyance of the farm to a purchaser.

Gas and water pipes running under the floors and between the walls are not removable fixtures, but gas fixtures, chandeliers and water faucets screwed in through holes in the walls or floors are removable when erected by a tenant. Stoves and furnaces put up in the usual way by a tenant are treated as furniture and are removable, but if built into brickwork they are non-removable fixtures.

In *McKeage* v. *Hanover Ins. Co.*, 81 N.Y. 38, it was held that gas fixtures simply screwed on to the gas pipes, and mirrors which are not set into the wall but put up afterwards and supported by hooks so driven into the wall that they can be removed without injuring the walls, form no part of the realty and do not pass by deed or mortgage of the premises.

In *Towne* v. *Fiske*, 127 Mass. 125, it was held that a portable hot-air furnace resting by its own weight upon the ground, put into a house by a person in possession under an agreement for a deed to the premises to be given him, does not become a part of the realty, although connected with the house by a cold air box and pipes and registers in the usual way. So gas fixtures in a house, although attached by screws to pipes are not a part of the realty.

Another test is the appropriation of the chattel to the use or purpose of that part of the realty to which it is connected. It seems that an article which is essential to the use for which the building or land is designed, or which is especially adapted to the place where it is erected, is regarded as a non-removable fixture, although it is but slightly connected with the realty. This rule is illustrated in the case of the *Ottumwa Woolen Mill Co.* v. *Hawley* on page 87.

In *Dudley* v. *Hurst*, 67 Md. 44, it was held that machinery used in the canning business, part of which is attached to the soil and other parts of which are necessary to the use of the part so attached, is a fixture that will pass to the mortgagee. When the principal part of the machinery is a fixture by actual annexation, such part of it as may not be so physically annexed, but which if removed would leave the principal part unfit for use and would not of itself, standing alone, be well adapted for general use elsewhere, is considered constructively annexed.

Bishop v. *Bishop*, 11 N.Y. 123, held that poles used necessarily in cultivating hops, but which are taken down for the purpose of gathering the crop and piled in the yard with the intention of being replaced in season next year, are a part of the realty.

In *McRea* v. *Central Bank*, 66 N.Y. 489, plaintiff as mortgagee claimed the machinery in a building erected expressly for use as a twine factory. The machinery was heavy and was fastened to the floor by bolts, nails, and cleats and was attached to the gearing. Most of the machinery could have been removed without material injury to the building and used elsewhere. It was proved that the machinery was put in the building for permanent use. Held, that the evidence was sufficient to find an intent to make the machinery part of the realty. The court said the criterion of a fixture is the union of three requisites: 1, Actual annexation to the realty or something appurtenant thereto; 2, Application to the use or purpose to which that part of the realty to which it is connected is appropriated; 3, The intention of the party making the annexation to make a permanent accession to the freehold. In such cases the court said the purpose of the annexation and the intent with which it is made are the most important considerations.

This last rule in the case of *McRea* v. *Central Bank* does not apply between landlord and tenant, as it is held that the tenant can not intend articles for permanent use on land that does not belong to him. This rule inaugurates the theory of constructive annexation and is contrary to the common law, which requires actual annexation to the realty.

Snedeker v. *Warring*, 12 N.Y. 170, was a case in which the owner of realty, after giving a mortgage, placed on his ground in front of his house a statue of Washington, made by himself, and weighing about three tons. It was on a base three feet high. This base rested upon a foundation built of mortar and stone. The statue was not fastened to the base, nor the base to the foundation. Held, that the statue was a part of the realty and that it was as firmly attached to the soil by its own weight as it could have been by clamps and screws. In the same case a sun dial, similarly placed, was also held to be realty.

Rogers v. *Crow*, 40 Mo. 91, was a case where the builders of a church left a recess in which an organ was to be placed. The organ was required to complete the design and finish of the building and was attached to the floor and intended to be permanent. Held, that the organ was a part of the realty and passed to the purchaser of the land.

Force pumps, pipes, and shafting, and machinery attached by spikes, nails, and butts, are part of the realty.

Symonds v. *Harris*, 51 Me. 14, held, that machinery used in a sash and blind factory and attached to the mill by spikes, bolts, and screws, and which was operated by belts running from the permanent shafting driven by a water wheel under the mill, was part of the realty.

Under the rule of constructive annexation some cases hold that machinery, permanent in its character and essential for the purposes of the building becomes realty, although not actually attached thereto.

Illustrations of this class of fixtures are ponderous machinery kept in place by its own weight, cotton gins, and duplicate rollers for a rolling mill, all of which are held to pass with the realty.

Deal v. *Palmer*, 72 N.C. 582, held that a carding machine not fastened to the house and requiring several men to move it, is a fixture, and passes with the land to a purchaser.

Other cases hold that machinery is personal property unless actually annexed. Such cases hold that heavy machinery in a factory screwed to the floor but removable without injury is not realty.

In *Hubbell* v. *Savings Bank*, 132 Mass. 447, it was held that a mortgage of land does not cover machinery upon the floor of a building on the land, supported by iron legs fastened to the floor by screws only for the purpose of steadying it, and which, although of great weight and adapted for use in the business carried on in the building, can be removed without injury to the building and used elsewhere. The machinery in dispute consisted of a large engine lathe, a small engine lathe, an iron planer, and an upright drill.

Relation of the Parties. — The relation of the parties has some weight in determining the character of the fixtures. As between landlord and tenant the presumption is that tenants do not intend the improvements to be additions to the realty, and they are therefore allowed greater rights in removing the chattels than any other class of persons. For the encouragement of trade and the promotion of industry the rule has been established that trade fixtures erected by a tenant are removable. A carpenter shop, a ballroom, and a bowling alley erected on blocks or posts have all been held to be removable.

Holmes v. *Tremper*, 20 Johns. (N.Y.) 29, held, that a cider mill and press erected by a tenant, holding from year to year, at his own expense and for his own use in making the cider on the farm, are not fixtures that pass with the realty.

In *Conrad* v. *Saginaw Mining Co.*, 54 Mich. 249, it was held that as between landlord and tenant under a mining lease, engines and boilers erected by the tenant on brick and stone foundations, bolted down solidly to the ground and walled in with brick arches; also dwelling houses erected by the tenant for miners to live in, standing on posts or dry stone walls, where the intent was not to make them a part of the realty but merely to use them in the mining operations, will be regarded as " trade fixtures " and may be removed by the tenant at or before the termination of the lease.

Carlin v. *Ritter*, 68 Md. 478, held, that as between landlord and tenant wooden structures or buildings resting by their own weight on flat stones laid upon the surface of the ground without other foundation are not part of the realty. But if the building is a permanent structure on a foundation it becomes part of the real estate.

The tenant must exercise his right to remove fixtures before the expiration of his term. If he does not remove them before he surrenders the premises, he can not reënter and claim them.

In *Dostal* v. *McCaddon*, 35 Iowa 318, defendant after his lease had expired entered upon plaintiff's premises to remove a vault and safe he had constructed, and this action was brought to restrain him from removing them. Held, that the tenant could not exercise his right of removing trade fixtures after he had surrendered possession of the premises.

When the question arises between vendor and vendee or mortgagor and mortgagee the presumption is stronger against the vendor and mortgagor, as being the owners of the realty they are supposed to have intended the improvements to be permanent. The parties may agree that the chattels annexed are to remain as personalty, and effect will be given to the agreement.

In *Smith* v. *Whitney*, 147 Mass. 479, the tenant's lease provided that he might erect buildings for manufacturing purposes and remove them within the limit of his lease. He erected a brick engine house complete in itself. The engine and boiler were on a solid foundation of masonry. Held, that the tenant had a right to remove the house, and the engine and boiler as well.

The nice question as to whether or not trees, grass, and growing crops are realty or personal property often comes up and has been discussed on page 55.

3. PARTIES TO A SALE

Seller and Purchaser. —The parties to a sale are the seller or vendor and the purchaser or vendee. The general rule is that no man can sell goods and convey a valid title unless he is the owner or his duly authorized agent. Possession is not an essential to the right to sell, ownership being enough, and the rightful owner can sell what is wrongfully held by another.

Webber v. *Davis*, 44 Me. 147, was an action to recover the value of a horse once owned by defendant and which was stolen from him. After the horse was stolen plaintiff paid defendant $20 for him and agreed to run his own risk of finding him. The horse was worth $60, but if he was not found, plaintiff was to lose his $20. A few weeks afterwards plaintiff located the horse but defendant first got possession. Held, that plaintiff could recover on the ground that title will pass by a sale without delivery from the true owner, although at the time of the sale the goods were in the wrongful possession of a third person.

Seller must have Good Title. — The principle of a holder in good faith which is discussed under the negotiable instrument law does not apply in the sale of personal property, the general rule being that one can not give a better title than he himself has.

In *Williams* v. *Merle*, 11 Wend. (N.Y.) 80, a master of a boat took four barrels of potash from plaintiff's warehouse and turned them over to the clerk of his principal, the boat owner, who sold them to defendant, a broker, who paid a reasonable price for them. In an action to recover them it was held that a purchaser of personal property is not protected against the claim of the true owner, although he purchase in good faith and for a valuable consideration, if the vendor has no title or authority to sell.

In *Moody* v. *Blake*, 117 Mass. 23, A, falsely representing himself to be a member of a firm, bought goods in their name from plaintiff who sent them to the firm. On the refusal of the firm to receive them A got possession of the goods from the carrier and sold them to defendant who bought them for value and in good faith. Held, that plaintiff could recover the goods of defendant. The defendant had no better title than his vendor.

However innocent therefore the person may be who buys property from one not the owner, he obtains no title whatever, except in a few special cases, as, for instance, negotiable instruments. It follows then that a person buying goods that were either lost or stolen has no claims on them as against the true owner.

Hoffman v. *Carow*, 20 Wend. (N.Y.) 21, held, that an auctioneer who sells stolen goods is liable to the owner, notwithstanding that the goods were sold and the proceeds turned over to the thief without knowledge that they were stolen.

A thief acquires no title and can convey none, and no matter how many sales or transfers of the property there may have been after the thief disposed of it before it came into the possession of the holder, the true owner can recover. It makes no difference that the purchase was made in good faith and for full value.

In *Breckenridge* v. *McAfee*, 54 Ind. 141, plaintiff brought an action for the value of wheat which his hired man had stolen and sold to defendant. Held, that a thief acquires no title to property stolen and can confer none on a person to whom he sells the same. And such person is liable to the owner for the value of such goods without regard to his innocence or good faith in making the purchase.

Pledgee may Sell. — An exception to the rule that a person not the owner can not sell personal property is the case of a pledgee, or one with whom the chattels are left as security for money loaned, as he can sell after default in payment by the owner. So also the master of a vessel can sell the cargo in cases of absolute necessity, but actual necessity must exist or the purchaser gets no title.

Factor may Sell. — A factor or commission merchant is a person to whom goods are shipped or consigned for the purpose of sale. A sale made by him conveys a good title and binds the original owner under statutes passed in most of the states, even though he goes beyond his authority and sells when he is not authorized to do so by the owner; but the factor or commission merchant must have actual possession or he will not give a good title if he exceeds his authority. This statute is limited to mercantile transactions and applies only to factors or commission merchants.

If the owner of goods trusts the possession of them to another, thereby enabling the other party to hold himself out to the world as having not only the possession but also the ownership of the goods, a sale by such party to a person without notice who acted upon the strength of such apparent ownership will bind the true owner, if the person having possession is one who from the nature of his employment might ordinarily be taken to have the right to sell.

In *Nixon* v. *Brown*, 57 N.H. 34, plaintiff employed one M to purchase a horse for him. M bought the horse, paid for it with plaintiff's money, and took the bill of sale in his own name. He afterwards informed the plaintiff of what he had done and showed him the bill of sale, but plaintiff allowed him to go away with the horse and the bill of sale. M went to the defendant, who had no knowledge of the agency, showed him the bill of sale and sold him the horse. The court held that the plaintiff could not recover the horse from the defendant.

As we have learned in contracts the purchaser must be a party competent to contract except in the case of necessaries.

4. THE CONTRACT OF SALE

Contract may be Executory or Executed. — The contract of sale, like other contracts, may be executory or executed. In the executory contract of sale the title has not passed to the purchaser. It is simply an agreement to make a transfer at some future time. In the executed contract the title has passed and the sale is complete. At the time of the sale the subject-matter or thing sold must be in existence. If it has ceased to exist, the sale is void.

Dexter v. *Norton*, 47 N.Y. 62, was an action to recover damages for breach of a contract by defendant to sell and deliver to plaintiff 621 bales of cotton bearing certain marks and numbers specified in the contract at a certain price. After defendant had delivered 460 bales the remaining 161 bales were destroyed by fire without fault or negligence of the defendant. The court held that where a contract is made for the sale of certain specified articles of personal property under such conditions that the title does not vest in the vendee, if the property is destroyed by accident without the fault of the vendor so that delivery becomes impossible, the vendor is excused from delivery.

Potential Existence. — Regarding the sale of things not yet in existence, if they are such as the natural products or expected increase of what is already owned, they are said to have a "potential existence" and may be sold. Therefore a man may sell a crop of hay to be grown on his fields, the wool to be clipped from his sheep, or wine to be produced from his vineyard.

Rochester Distilling Co. v. *Rasey*, 142 N.Y. 570, was an action based upon the following facts: In February, 1890, Rochester Distilling Co. recovered a judgment against one Lovell. In April, 1890, Lovell, being a tenant on a certain farm, gave one Page whom he owed, a chattel mortgage on all the crops which were already sown, and those which were yet to be sown. Very little seed was in the ground at that time. On July 5, the Rochester Distilling Co. levied upon the growing crops and later at public sale purchased them. July 15, Page foreclosed his mortgage and sold the growing crops to Rasey, the defendant in the case. The Rochester Distilling Co. brought suit against Rasey for the recovery of the title to the crops. It was held by the Court of Appeals that an unplanted crop is not in potential existence, and therefore cannot be the subject of either mortgage or sale.

But when the subject of the contract is to be acquired afterwards, as the land from which one expects to raise the hay or grain, or the sheep from which one expects to clip the wool, the article can not be sold. A valid agreement however may be made to sell it, that is, an executory contract to sell it can be entered into. The question as to whether the contract of sale is executed or executory is important when the property is lost or destroyed, for if it is an executed contract, the vendee loses, if it is executory, the vendor.

When Title Passes. — We may here ask, when does the title pass from vendor to vendee? Is it when the goods are delivered or when the contract is completed? The answer seems to be that the title vests in the vendee immediately upon the completion of the contract of sale without regard to the fact of whether or not the goods are delivered.

In *Terry* v. *Wheeler*, 25 N.Y. 520, there was a sale of lumber in the vendor's yard. The pieces sold were designated and the price paid, but the vendor agreed to deliver the lumber at the railroad station. The lumber was destroyed before such delivery. Held, that it was an executed contract of sale. The title had passed and the loss fell on the purchaser.

In an executory contract, it being but a promise to sell, the title does not pass until the sale is completed.

In *Fitch* v. *Beach*, 15 Wend. (N.Y.) 221, there was an agreement for the sale of a boat load of lumber, part of which was landed and the unloading of the remainder suspended until an inspector could be procured to measure it. After waiting a day the vendor reloaded the lumber landed and went away. In an action for wrongfully taking the lumber it was held that the title had not passed, as something remained to be done between the vendor and vendee, namely, the measuring and sorting of the lumber. The only remedy would be damages for breach of contract.

It is often difficult to determine whether the parties have entered into a contract of sale or simply into an agreement to sell. The intention of the parties in this respect is controlling.

In *Callaghan* v. *Myers*, 89 Ill. 566, it was held that in an agreement to purchase a lot of books, if a part of the price is paid, possession given, and the amount to be paid if the books should prove to be as represented is fixed, the title will pass as against the creditor of the vendor. Whether the sale is complete and the title passes depends upon the intention of the parties.

Intention. — When the intention of the parties is not clear, certain rules are observed in determining it. If the chattels in contention are not agreed upon, or are not separated from a larger number or quantity, it is clear that the parties intended only an executory contract. For instance, if A buys 10 horses out of a drove of 50, there is no complete contract until the particular 10 have been designated or separated from the rest. If the articles are not ready for delivery, or there is still something to be done on them, it is but an executory agreement.

McConihe v. *New York & Erie Railroad*, 20 N.Y. 495, was an action to recover damages upon a contract under which plaintiff was to furnish material and build 15 lumber cars for the defendant at $475 per car, to be paid six months from the date of delivery. The defendants were to furnish iron boxes for the cars of a model made by them. When the cars were completed, excepting the part prevented by the default of the defendants in not furnishing the boxes, they were destroyed by fire while in the possession of plaintiff and without his fault. Held, that the title to the cars was still in plaintiff, and he could not recover for labor and material.

But if it is the sale of an article in bulk the title passes, although it has not been measured, if it is the apparent intent that it shall pass; and in the cases in which it is the sale of part of a bulk or mass, all of the same quality, it is not necessary to have the part sold separated in order to have the title pass.

In the case of *Chapman* v. *Shepard*, 39 Conn. 413, A sold B a quantity of bags of meal on board ship at a certain price per bag. B, without paying A, and before the bags were counted, sold 500 bags to C, who gave his promissory note. Thereafter C informed A of his purchase and was told he could remove the bags when he pleased, but after he had removed part A refused to let him remove the remainder. Held, that the title had passed to

Know all Men by these Presents, That

I, Edwin P. Nichols, of Rochester, Monroe County, New York, party of the first part, for and in consideration of the sum of three hundred dollars ($300.00)——————— lawful money of the United States, to me in hand paid, at or before the ensealing and delivery of these presents by Albert Connolly of the same place, party——————— of the second part, the receipt whereof is hereby acknowledged, have bargained and sold, and by these presents do grant and convey unto the said part y of the second part, his executors, administrators and assigns, one team of gray horses, one heavy wagon, one set of harness, one top buggy, and one set of sleighs

To have and to hold the same unto the said part y of the second part, his executors, administrators and assigns for ever. And I do for myself, my heirs, executors and administrators, covenant and agree, to and with the said part y — of the second part, to warrant and defend the sale of the said property,——————— hereby sold unto the said part y — of the second part, his executors, administrators and assigns against all and every person and persons whomsoever.

In Witness whereof, I have hereunto set my hand and seal the second day of September, in the year one thousand nine hundred and five.

Sealed and delivered in the presence of

Henry R Brown   *Edwin P. Nichols*

State of New York
City of Rochester } S.S.
County of Monroe

On the Second day of September in the year one thousand nine hundred and five before me personally came

——————— Edwin P. Nichols, ———————

to me known, and known to me to be the individual described in, and who executed the foregoing instrument, and he acknowledged that he executed the same.

G. H. Dillingham

Com. of Deeds.

B, as it was the evident intent of the parties that it should, and it had also passed from B to C. Upon the sale of a number of articles from a mass of the same quality and value, a separation of the part sold is not necessary to pass title; but the ruling is other,wise when the articles composing the mass are of different qualities and values, making not only separation, but selection, necessary.

Contracts in Writing. — By the statute of frauds, certain contracts of sale should be in writing. This was fully treated on page 58 in the chapter on contracts. To satisfy the statute, the writing need not be in any particular form, but must contain a description of the property purchased and other elements of the agreement, signed by the purchaser or party to be charged. In sales of any importance it is customary to execute a formal bill of sale and deliver it with the property sold as illustrated in the form on the preceding page.

It is a safe plan to require a bill of sale, as the buyer then has the warranty of title from the vendor as well as a formal certificate that he is the owner and purchaser of the property mentioned.

5. CONDITIONAL SALE

Installment Sales. — We have discussed sales only from the standpoint of the absolute conveyance or transfer of the property. We now take up those cases in which the passing of the title is conditioned upon certain acts which may or may not be performed. It is common in business for certain articles such as pianos, sewing machines, or wagons to be sold conditionally, the title to remain in the vendor until the purchase price shall be fully paid. This mode of making sales is employed by all installment dealers who sell goods on weekly or monthly payments. The payment of the last installment is a condition precedent to the passing of the title to the purchaser. As between the original parties, a conditional sale is valid and the title does not pass until the condition is fulfilled, even though the property is given into the possession of the vendee at the time the parties enter into the contract.

McRea v. *Merrifield*, 48 Ark. 160, was an action to recover an engine, sawmill, and lot of tools sold by plaintiff under a contract of sale which expressly agreed that the title should remain in the vendor until the purchase price was fully paid. Payment was never fully made. Held, that the title did not pass to the purchaser until the payment was made. The contract constituted a conditional sale and the vendor could recover the property.

But the doors are opened for the entrance of fraud if the party in possession, that is, the vendee, is enabled to present every appearance of ownership when the title does not rest in him. A third party who purchases of him without notice of the title in the vendor may easily be imposed upon and defrauded. Still the general rule is that in the absence of any fraud in the conditional sale it is valid against third persons. The seller can give no better title than he possesses.

McIntosh v. *Beam*, 47 Ark. 363, was an action to recover a mule sold conditionally by plaintiff to a third party, the title to remain in the vendor until the animal was paid for. The mule was sold by this third party to defendant, who bought it in good faith for a valuable consideration and without notice of the conditional sale. Held, that the plaintiff could recover. The purchaser acquired no better title than his vendor.

Filing Conditional Contracts. — Statutes have been passed in many of the states requiring every such contract of sale to be filed, and if it is not, the condition is void as to persons who buy of the party in possession without notice of the conditional contract. In New York, in a few special cases, the delivery to the vendee of a copy of the contract takes the place of filing.

In *Moyer* v. *McIntyre*, 43 Hun (N.Y.) 58, plaintiff on August 5, 1885, sold a wagon to one Smith for $72.50. Five dollars was paid in cash and a note for the balance was given by Smith to plaintiff. This note provided that the title to the wagon was to remain in plaintiff until the note was paid, and that plaintiff might take possession of the wagon whenever he felt insecure. After Smith had been in possession of the wagon about eight weeks he sold it to defendant, who took it without notice of plaintiff's claim, paying therefor $10 in cash and applying $55 on an old debt owing to him by Smith. Plaintiff tendered defendant $10 and demanded the wagon. Upon being refused he brought this action to recover it. Held, that by the laws of 1884 this contract must have been filed, and as that was not done the conditions in the note were void as to defendant who purchased in good faith and without notice.

Sale on Trial. — Sale on trial or on approval is another form of conditional sale, the goods being delivered subject to the approval of the intended purchaser, and if not found satisfactory or as represented, they are to be returned. If they are returnable within a given time and they are retained beyond that time, it will be presumed that the purchaser has approved and the sale is absolute. If no time for the trial or examination is agreed upon, it must be made within a reasonable time, and if the purchaser does not accept or return the goods within a reasonable time, he will be deemed to have approved and the sale is consummated.

When anything is yet to be done to the goods to put them in a deliverable shape, in the absence of a contrary intention, the performance of these things is a condition precedent to the passing of the title.

In *Cornell* v. *Clark*, 104 N.Y. 451, a railroad company entered into a contract to purchase 20,000 ties at 55 cents each for first-class ties and 35 cents for what should be adjudged second class. They were to be delivered by the vendor and counted and inspected by a person named. The company advanced 15 cents each as they were delivered. The ties were never inspected nor classified. The company failed, and it was held that the title in the ties had not passed to the company, the ties requiring yet to be counted and classified.

Butler v. *Lawshe*, 74 Ga. 352, held, that if there was an agreement by which an iron press was to be sold by the pound and was to be weighed, the contract of sale was executory until it was weighed, but if the price was fixed, the contract was executed on delivery. The press was sent by the vendor to the vendee by a drayman and the vendee gave instructions as to where it was to be delivered. The jury found that it was not to be weighed, therefore the title had passed.

Chattel Mortgage. — The chattel mortgage is another form of conditional sale. It consists of the sale of certain chattels or goods, subject to defeat upon the payment by the vendor or mortgagor of a certain debt or the performance of a certain obligation. It differs from a conditional sale in that the title passes to the purchaser at once, but it is liable to be defeated upon the fulfilling of certain conditions, while in a conditional sale the title does not pass until the conditions are fulfilled.

McCoy v. *Lassiter*, 95 N.C. 88, held, that the difference between a pledge and a chattel mortgage is that in the former the title is retained by the pledgor, while in the latter it passes to the mortgagee.

Delivery to the pledgee is essential, but in a chattel mortgage it is not necessary as between the parties, and by statute filing or registration is substituted for delivery so as to make it effective as against third parties, such as purchasers or creditors.

Tannahill v. *Tuttle*, 3 Mich. 104, held, that by a mortgage of chattels the whole legal title to the property passed to the mortgagee conditionally.

The chattel mortgage is a means frequently employed by a borrower of money to secure the loan. The goods may remain in the possession of either party, but if they are allowed to remain in the mortgagor's possession, the statutes of nearly all of the states require that the mortgage shall be filed with some public officer, where it may be open to the inspection of the public. It is usually required to be filed with the town clerk, county clerk, or registrar of deeds, if it is to be binding as to third parties who may buy the mortgaged property in good faith and without notice of the mortgage. As between the parties themselves the mortgage is valid without being filed, or in fact without being executed in any formal way.

The subject of chattel mortgages is regulated by the statutes of the several states, and now it is the almost universal rule that the mortgagor keeps possession of the goods mortgaged, the filing of the mortgage taking the place of the change of possession.

Requirements of Mortgage. — The mortgage is required by statute to be in writing, and to contain the names of the parties and a description of the property covered. The filing of the mortgage is notice to all the world, and any one buying the property thereafter is supposed to have notice of it. In New York and some other states it is necessary to file a renewal of the mortgage each year, and a failure to file such renewal at the expiration of the year renders the mortgage of no more effect than if it had never been filed.

An ordinary form of chattel mortgage used in New York state is shown on the following page : —

To all to whom these Presents shall come, KNOW YE THAT

I, Charles Pollock, of Rochester, Monroe County, New York, party of the first part, for securing the payment of the money hereinafter mentioned, and in consideration of the sum of one dollar to __me__ duly paid by _____ _____ Edward Frank, of the same place, party _____

of the second part, at or before the ensealing and delivery of these presents, the receipt whereof is hereby acknowledged, have bargained and sold, and by these presents do grant, bargain and sell unto the said part__y__ of the second part, __one typewriter, one typewriter desk,__ one fireproof safe, and six office chairs. _____

To have and to hold, all and singular the goods and chattels above bargained and sold, or intended so to be, unto the said part__y__ of the second part, __his heirs,__ executors, administrators and assigns for ever. **And __I__** the said party__ of the first part, for __myself,__ __my__ heirs, executors and administrators, all and singular the said goods and chattels above bargained and sold unto the said part__y__ of the second part, __his__ heirs, executors, administrators and assigns, against __myself__ the said party__ of the first part and against all and every person or persons whomsoever, shall and will warrant, and for ever defend. **Upon Condition,** that if__I__ the said party__ of the first part, shall and do well and truly pay unto the said part__y__ of the second part, __his__ executors, administrators or assigns, the sum of Two Hundred Dollars ($200.00) according to the terms of a note this day executed and delivered to said Edward Frank, which note with interest thereon will fall due on the tenth day of March in the year one thousand nine hundred and six,

then these presents shall be void. **And __I__** the said party__ of the first part, for _____ __myself, my__ executors, administrators and assigns, do covenant and agree to and with the said part__y__ of the second part, __his__ executors, administrators and assigns, that in case default shall be made in the payment of the said sum above mentioned, __or the interest thereon__

then it shall and may be lawful for, and __I__ the said party__ of the first part, do hereby authorize and empower the said part__y__ of the second part __his heirs,__ executors, administrators and assigns, with the aid and assistance of any person or persons, to enter __the__ dwelling-house, store, and other premises and such other place or places as the said goods or chattels are or may be placed, and take and carry away the said goods or chattels, and to sell and dispose of the same for the best price they can obtain; and out of the money arising therefrom, to retain and pay the said sum above mentioned, __with the interest thereon__

and all charges touching the same; rendering the overplus (if any) unto __me__ _____ or to __my heirs__ executors, administrators or assigns. **And** until default be made in the payment of the said sum of money __the party of the first part is__ to remain and continue in the quiet and peaceable possession of the said goods and chattels, and the full and free enjoyment of the same. If from any cause said property shall fail to satisfy said debt, interest, costs and charges, the said __party of the first part doth__ _____ covenant and agree to pay the deficiency.

In Witness whereof, I, the said party__ of the first part, have hereunto set __my__ hand and seal the __tenth__ day of __September,__ one thousand nine hundred and __five.__

Sealed and delivered in the presence of

W. H. Hunter   *Charles Pollock*

Foreclosure. — After default in the payment of the mortgage, the mortgagee must foreclose the mortgage in order to cut off all of the rights of the mortgagor. The procedure differs under the statutes of the different states. It consists in giving notice to the mortgagor and selling the property at public sale. The mortgage itself may contain provisions for the foreclosure. The mortgagor is usually allowed the time until the date of the sale in which to pay the amount due and redeem the property mortgaged.

6. WARRANTIES

Classification. — We have seen that a condition in a contract of sale which is required to be performed before the contract is completed will defeat the sale if it is not carried out. A condition is one of the essential elements of such a contract. Aside from this there are certain warranties which are collateral undertakings on the part of the seller to be responsible in damages if certain conditions as to quality, amount, or title of the article are not as represented. The warranty is a separate contract, and, if made at a different time from the contract of sale, it must be supported by a separate consideration. If made at the same time, the consideration of the sale will also operate as a consideration for the warranty. There are two classes of warranty, express and implied.

Express Warranty. — The express warranty, as its title would indicate, is an express undertaking or agreement made by the seller. No special form of words is necessary to create a warranty. Any statement framed with the intention of making a warranty will be so construed. It must be distinguished from a mere expression of opinion on points regarding the chattel, of which the seller had no special knowledge and on which the buyer may be expected to exercise his own judgment. A warranty is an assertion of a fact of which the buyer is ignorant.

In *Hunter* v. *McLaughlin*, 43 Ind. 38, the vendor in selling a patent right in a ditching machine, exhibited the letters patent and the model and stated that if properly constructed it would work well. It was claimed that it was properly constructed and did not work well. It was not shown that the vendor had ever made and used a machine constructed after this model or that he represented that he had made and used one. The court held that the statements were nothing more than mere expressions of opinion, which for aught that appeared the vendor might have honestly believed.

Stroud v. *Pierce*, 6 Allen (Mass.) 413, held, that a statement by a piano agent that the instrument is " well made and will stand up to concert pitch " is a warranty, it being a representation of fact.

If the representation is a warranty, the contract will not be broken by a breach, but an action for damages will arise. If it is a mere expression of opinion, there is no remedy if it turns out to be unfounded.

In *Anthony* v. *Halstead*, 37 L. T. N. S. (Eng.) 433, the following memorandum was given: " Received from C. Anthony, Esq., £60 for a black horse, rising five years, quiet to ride and drive, and warranted sound up to this date, or subject to the examination of a veterinary surgeon." Held, to be a warranty of soundness and not a warranty that the horse was quiet to ride and drive.

Burge v. *Stroberg*, 42 Ga. 88, held, that a statement that a horse is fourteen years old is a warranty that he is no older.

Pritchard v. *Fox*, 4 Jones (N.C.) 140, held, that a warranty that a soda fountain was in good condition is broken if, from inherent defects in construction existing at the time of the sale, it was liable to get out of order from time to time.

A general warranty is held not to include defects apparent on simple inspection and requiring no skill to discover them, nor defects known to the buyer.

In *Dean* v. *Morey*, 33 Iowa 120, defendant sold to plaintiff a horse that was a cribber. Held, that he was not bound to disclose this fact to plaintiff, as the horse was subject to the inspection of the buyer, and a simple examination of the horse's mouth would have shown the defect.

An express warranty must be distinguished from the mere praising or puffing of his goods by an owner; as, the statement by an agent that he has the best plow on the market or by a driver that his team is the best in the city.

Implied Warranty. — Implied warranty differs from express warranty in that although it exists in the contract of sale, it is not mentioned or stated in express words. In every contract of sale there is an implied warranty of title when the goods sold are in the possession of the vendor at the time of the sale, unless, of course, there is an express agreement to the contrary; but in cases in which the goods are in the possession of a third party, there is no such implied warranty and the purchaser buys at his peril.

In *Huntingdon* v. *Hall*, 36 Me. 501, defendant sold plaintiff a small house which was on another man's land and not occupied by defendant. There was no express warranty of title. This action was brought to recover damages on an implied warranty of title, as defendant did not own the house. Held, that there was no implied warranty of title in this case. The implied warranty arises when the vendor is in possession of the chattel himself, but when the chattel is in the possession of another the purchaser buys at his peril.

Long v. *Hickingbottom*, 28 Miss. 772, held, that in the sale of a chattel, if possession at the time is in another and there is no covenant of warranty, the rule of *caveat emptor* applies, and the party buys at his peril. But if the seller has possession of the article sold, and he sells it as his own and for a fair price, he warrants the title.

As to the implied warranty of quality, we find the maxim, *caveat emptor*, meaning "let the buyer beware," to be the general rule of our law. When there has been a sale of specific goods which the buyer has an opportunity to inspect, he buys at his own risk as to quality, unless there is an express warranty. There is no implied warranty of the quality.

In *Frazier* v. *Harvey*, 34 Conn. 469, defendant sold to plaintiff some hogs which, unknown to both parties, had a disease of which they died later. This was an action on the implied warranty of soundness of the hogs. Held, that when there is no express warranty and no fraud in the sale of personal property, the purchaser takes the risk of its quality and condition.

But when the chattel is to be made or supplied to the order of the purchaser, there is an implied warranty that it is reasonably fit for the purpose intended, if that purpose is communicated to the seller.

Tabor v. *Peters*, 74 Ala. 90, held, that the vendor of a patent churn, being himself the manufacturer, and contracting to furnish the purchaser with a quantity of churns, must be held to have warranted that they were useful and reasonably suitable for the intended purpose; and if they proved to be worthless, there would be a breach of the implied warranty which would be a good defense against an action for the purchase price.

If the sale is by sample, there is an implied warranty that the quality of the bulk is equal to that of the sample.

In *Myer* v. *Wheeler*, 65 Iowa 390, plaintiff sold defendant 10 car loads of barley like sample, to be delivered from time to time. Defendants had never seen the barley. Held, that there was a warranty that the barley would be equal to the sample.

In *Graff* v. *Foster*, 67 Mo. 512, defendant bought some oranges of plaintiff, to be like samples exhibited by plaintiff. In an action for the purchase price, defendant claimed that the oranges were greatly inferior in quality to sample, and set up breach of the implied warranty. Held, that it is not necessary that the word "warranty" shall be used. It is sufficient if the seller undertakes that the goods shall be as represented. So, if the seller exhibits samples as fair specimens of the stock and agrees to deliver goods equal in quality to the samples, and the purchaser buys, relying on this promise, it is a warranty.

To constitute a sale by sample it must appear that the contract of the parties was made solely with reference to the sample exhibited.

In *Day* v. *Raguet*, 14 Minn. 273, plaintiff sold to defendant whisky which was to be five per cent better than a sample shown. Held, that it was not a case of sale by sample.

In a sale by description there is an implied warranty that the goods shall be salable or merchantable, aside from the fact that a condition precedent to the sale is that the goods shall answer the description. In such a case, the buyer having no opportunity to inspect the goods, the rule of *caveat emptor* does not apply, and the buyer has a right to expect that he is getting a salable article answering the description in the contract, and not an article that is worthless.

In *Weiger* v. *Gould*, 86 Ill. 180, plaintiff sold defendant oats and represented them to be a good grade of white oats, such as defendant was purchasing at forty cents. Held, that he must deliver merchantable oats and can not deliver wet, dirty oats.

When a person buys of a manufacturer an article made for a particular purpose, there is an implied warranty that it is fit for the desired purpose, also that it is free from latent defects arising from the process of manufacture and unknown to the purchaser which render the article unfit for the purpose intended.

In *Rodgers* v. *Niles*, 11 Ohio St. 48, defendant agreed with plaintiff that he would deliver to him at a future time three steam boilers with which to run the engines in his roller mill. Held, that there was an implied warranty that the boilers should be free from all such defects in material or workmanship, either latent or otherwise, as would render them unfit for the usual purposes of such boilers.

Delivery and Payment. — To complete the sale it is necessary for the seller to deliver the goods and for the purchaser to pay for them, and unless there is an express agreement to the contrary these acts are concurrent. Delivery in this sense does not necessarily mean the passing of the article itself, but rather the passing of the ownership or title. That is to say, the delivery need not be actual; it may be constructive. It is actual when the article itself is handed over. It is constructive when a bill of sale or a receipt is handed over instead.

7. REMEDIES FOR BREACH

Rights of Vendor. — The parties may not fulfill their contract of sale and the question then arises as to what are their respective rights. The vendee may refuse to complete the contract of sale by declining to accept the goods, or after accepting and retaining the goods, he may refuse to pay the purchase price. In case the goods have not been delivered and the title has not passed to the purchaser, the vendor may elect to avail himself of any one of three remedies. First, he may resell the goods, after having tendered them and been refused, and recover damages for the loss, if any. Second, he may hold the goods for the vendee and sue for the entire purchase price, or, as his third remedy, he may keep the goods and sue for the damages, which will be the difference between the contract price and the market price at the time and place of delivery.

Dustan v. *McAndrew*, 44 N.Y. 72, was an action brought on a contract for the sale of certain hops, which defendant had refused to take. Plaintiff placed them in the hands of a broker who sold them for a fair price and then brought this action for the difference between the contract price and the price for which the hops were sold. The court held for plaintiff, and said that on the failure of the purchaser to perform, the vendor as a general rule has his choice of three remedies: (1) To hold the property for the purchaser and recover of him the entire purchase money. (2) To sell it, after notice to the purchaser, as his agent for that purpose, and to recover the difference between the contract price and that realized at the sale. (3) To retain it as his own and recover the difference between the contract price and the market price at the time and place of delivery.

Bagley v. *Findlay*, 82 Ill. 524, was a case in which the purchaser refused to take the goods for which he had contracted and the court said, " When the vendee of specific goods refuses to take and pay for them, the vendor may store them for the vendee, giving him notice that he has done so, and then recover the full contract price; or he may keep the goods and recover the excess of the contract price over and above the market price of the goods at the time and place of delivery; or he may, upon notice to the vendee, proceed to sell the goods to the best advantage and recover of the vendee the loss if they fail to bring the contract price."

Some cases do not allow the first remedy mentioned in *Dustan* v. *McAndrew*, and hold, that the vendor can either retain the goods and sue for the difference between the contract price and the market value, or resell the goods and sue for the loss. But in the case of a resale the vendor must be fair and obtain the reasonable value of the article, as otherwise the price received will be disregarded and the difference between the market price and the contract price will rule.

If the title and possession have passed to the purchaser, the only remedy is an action against the purchaser for the contract price, or if not for the contract price, for the reasonable value of the goods.

Stoppage *in Transitu*. — There is another class of remedy by which the seller may obtain the purchase price if the title has passed to the buyer but the physical possession is in the vendor, and that arises from his lien upon the goods. As soon as the goods are in the actual possession of the vendee the lien is lost. After the title may have passed to the purchaser, still the actual possession or custody, as we have learned, may yet be in the vendor, or the goods may be in transit; that is, on the road to delivery, in the possession of the railroad or express company. When the goods are in the custody of the seller, he may hold them under his lien for the purchase price, and when in transit the law gives the unpaid vendor the right to intercept them,

if he can, and thereby prevent them from reaching the purchaser. This right, called "stoppage *in transitu*," exists when
the purchaser becomes insolvent after the sale or was insolvent
when the sale was made, though the fact was unknown to the
vendor. The right of stoppage *in transitu* extends not only to
the vendor himself but to an agent who, upon the order of his
principal, has purchased goods and paid for them with his own
money. So also a third person who advances the money for the
purchase and takes an assignment of the bill of lading can exercise the right of stoppage *in transitu*.

In *Gossler* v. *Schepeler*, 5 Daly (N.Y.) 476, plaintiff advanced the money
on a cargo of iron for defendant and received the bill of lading as security for
the advance. Plaintiff sent the bill of lading to defendant, who became insolvent before he received the goods. Held, that plaintiff could stop the goods
in transit and could retake them and compel the defendant to deliver to him
the bill of lading.

This right can be exercised only against an insolvent or bankrupt person. By an insolvent is meant one unable to pay his
debts in the usual course of his business.

In *O'Brien* v. *Norris*, 16 Md. 122, it was held that the right of stoppage *in
transitu* was not defeated by showing that the vendee was actually insolvent
at the time of the purchase, unless it was shown that such insolvency was
known to the vendee, when, of course, he would be held to have contracted
with that in mind. Technical insolvency, as being declared a bankrupt, is not
necessary, and suspending of payment is sufficient to justify a vendor in exercising the right of stoppage *in transitu*.

In *Durgy Cement Co.* v. *O'Brien*, 123 Mass. 12, it was held that the fact
that the vendee's notes went to protest because of his inability to pay them in
the regular course of business was sufficient to justify plaintiff in exercising
the right of stoppage *in transitu*.

If the vendor stops the goods when the purchaser is solvent,
he does so at his peril, and will be obliged to deliver the goods
in addition to becoming liable for damages to the vendee. In
order to exercise the right the goods must be in transit. It is
held that the transit begins when the seller has delivered the
custody of the goods to the carrier and extends to the time
when the actual possession and custody of the goods are acquired by the purchaser. In other words, the goods are liable

to stoppage *in transitu* as long as they are in the possession of the carrier, and as soon as delivered to the buyer or his agent the right ceases. No particular form is necessary in order to exercise this right. It is simply required that notice be given the carrier not to deliver the goods, and that it be given in time for the carrier or transportation company, by using reasonable diligence, to notify its agents to hold them. The usual mode is a notice to the carrier stating the vendor's claim and forbidding delivery to the vendee or requiring that the goods be held subject to the vendor's orders.

In *Jones* v. *Earl*, 37 Cal. 630, the vendor delivered to the agent of the carrier in possession of the goods, a letter to the effect that the vendee had been served with an attachment and that he desired to save the goods. He gave the agent a bill of particulars of the goods and directed him to deliver them to no one but the vendor's agent, who would be there to look after them. Held, to be a sufficient notice to stop the delivery of the goods.

In *Mottram* v. *Heyer*, 5 Denio (N.Y.) 629, plaintiff made demand of the defendants when the goods were in the customhouse and after the bills of lading and freight receipts had been given to defendants. Defendants were insolvent. Held, that this demand was not sufficient. It must be made of the carrier, in whose custody the goods are, under such circumstances that the carrier may prevent their delivery to the vendee. The vendor's right of stoppage *in transitu* does not cease on the arrival of the goods at the point of delivery, but when they come into the vendee's actual or constructive possession.

The right of stoppage *in transitu* is defeated in case the bill of lading is in the hands of the vendee and he transfers it to a third person who in good faith pays value for it. The third party can hold the goods.

Rights of Vendee. — We have treated thus far only of the rights and remedies of the vendor. There are also certain rights that the buyer has which it is necessary for us to consider. The vendor may fail to deliver the goods or there may be some defect in the goods delivered. When the vendor refuses to deliver the goods and the title to them has not passed to the buyer, the buyer's remedy is to sue for damages for breach of the contract. If the purchase price is unpaid, the damages will be the difference between the contract price and the market price of the goods at the time and place of delivery, but if the purchase price has been paid, this sum should be added to the amount that may be recovered.

In *Harralson* v. *Stein*, 50 Ala. 347, it was held that a purchaser can recover as damages from a vendor who refuses or fails to deliver the goods bought, the difference between the agreed price and the market price at the time they ought to have been delivered, that is, the loss which the vendee would suffer if he had to go out and buy the articles in the market.

Specific Performance. — Another remedy is offered the buyer in certain few cases, and that is specific performance.   Generally damages for the breach is an adequate remedy, but when, because of the peculiar nature of the property and the difficulty of obtaining it elsewhere, specific performance alone can compensate the vendee, it will be granted by a court of equity.

Treasurer v. *Commercial Mining Co.*, 23 Cal. 390, was an action to compel the defendant to issue to plaintiff 46 shares of capital stock of the company. It was shown that the stock had no fixed market value, that it was fluctuating and uncertain in value, and therefore the damages arising from a breach of the contract to deliver such stock could not be ascertained.   Held, that specific performance would be allowed, because damages would not afford a full and adequate remedy.

When the goods delivered do not correspond to the articles sold, the buyer may rescind the contract and sue for damages. Also, if some warranty has been violated, he can recover damages, although he will not be allowed to return the goods if the title has passed to him, but the contrary is the rule when the title has not passed to the buyer.

QUESTIONS ON SALES OF PERSONAL PROPERTY

1. Define a sale.   Distinguish between a sale and a gift.
2. Distinguish between sale and barter.   Between sale and bailment.
3. A delivers to B 100 yards of cloth to be made into coats.   When the coats are nearly completed B's shop burns and the coats are destroyed.   Upon whom will the loss fall?
4. Brown delivered two black walnut logs at Smith's sawmill.   Smith in return was to give him 500 feet of planed pine lumber.   What was the transaction, a sale, a barter, or a bailment?
5. Distinguish between real and personal property.
6. Define fixtures.
7. Mention the three requisites which are necessarily combined to make a fixture a part of the realty as laid down in McCrea against Central Bank.

8. Under the common law which of these three is the most important?

9. In a majority of the cases at the present time which of these requisites seems to be controlling?

10. Higgins owned some land which was mortgaged to Green. He erected on this land a sawmill and placed therein an engine which was built in masonry, and put in other machinery which was fastened to the floor, all of which he intended at the time to be permanent. Green foreclosed the mortgage and obtained the property. Who was entitled to the engine and machinery?

11. In the above case, if the machinery had been set on the floor and held there by its own weight, who would have been entitled to it?

12. Edwards, who is the owner of a house and lot, is repairing and painting his house. While the painters are at work the blinds are removed for the purpose of painting. Before they are replaced Edwards sells the house and lot to Gray. Are the blinds a part of the realty which passes to Gray, or are they personal property, and can Edwards remove them?

13. In the above case do the chandeliers and gas fixtures which are screwed into the gas pipes pass to Gray or remain the property of Edwards?

14. Do the gas and water pipes, themselves, pass with the realty to Gray or remain the property of Edwards?

15. Wells, who rents a house of Myles, places a furnace in the cellar and connects it with the house by pipes and registers in the usual way. It is not attached to the floor. When Wells moves, Myles refuses to allow him to take the furnace, claiming it belongs to the realty. Who gets the furnace?

16. A large stamping machine weighing ten tons is used in a building on B's land which passes to C, the purchaser, under a mortgage foreclosure. The machine is not fastened to the building, but kept in place by its own weight. To which does it belong, B or C?

17. In the above case if B had been merely a tenant and had placed the stamping machine in the building for his own use and C had been the owner of the land, could B have removed the machine at the end of his tenancy, or would it have become the property of C? If B had left the machine in the building and ten days after his tenancy expired had gone back to claim it, would he have been entitled to it?

18. Name the parties to a sale. Who can sell?

19. B sold to Smith a horse which had broken out of the pasture lot and wandered away, its whereabouts at the time being unknown to its owner. Later it came back to B's farm and Smith claimed it. Could he recover?

20. Gordon loses his watch and it is afterwards picked up on the street by Hogan, a jeweler. Hogan puts it in his shop and sells it to Lane. Gordon discovers it in the possession of Lane and sues for its recovery. Lane bought the watch in good faith, believing it to belong to Hogan, and paid what it was reasonably worth. Who gets the watch?

21. In the above case, if Hogan had stolen the watch, would the result have been any different?

22. C, a commission merchant, receives a car load of watermelons from Logan & Co., with instructions to hold them until Logan & Co.'s agent arrives. C sells them to Weaver as soon as they are received. Logan & Co. brings an action against Weaver to recover them. Who is entitled to the melons?

23. A, a horse dealer, employed B to purchase a horse for him to match one he then owned. B bought a horse, taking bill of sale to himself. A knew of this and allowed B to keep the horse and bill of sale. B sold the horse without authority to X. Could A recover the horse from X?

24. Clark, a farmer, sells to Spence in the spring, the hay and corn that he shall raise on his farm during the coming season. The corn has not yet been planted. Is the sale good?

25. Clark also sells to Spence the wool from 100 sheep which he agrees to buy within 30 days, but which he does not yet own. Is the sale good?

26. B goes to A, a cattle dealer, and out of a herd of 50 cattle in the field buys 10, pays for them, and promises to take them the next day. Without picking out the particular 10, he leaves. Has the title in these 10 passed to B or is it still in A?

27. In the above case suppose B, before leaving, picked out and branded the 10 cattle, paid the purchase price, and agreed to call and drive them away the next day. Did the title pass to B or was it still in A?

28. A also goes to C, a grain merchant, and buys 50 bushels of wheat out of a bin containing several thousand bushels. He pays for the wheat, but it is not measured. That night the warehouse burns. Upon whom does the loss of the 50 bushels of wheat fall, A or C?

29. Define a conditional sale.

30. Mahoney buys a stove from Fisher, paying $5 down and signing a contract which provides that the stove has been merely leased to Mahoney, the title remaining in Fisher until the whole purchase price of $40 is paid. Mahoney at once sells the stove to Burns, who gives him $20 for it, believing the stove belongs to Mahoney. Can Fisher take the stove from Burns?

31. If the above transaction takes place in a state requiring conditional contracts to be filed, and the above contract is not filed, who is entitled to the stove?

32. The above stove is sent to Mahoney by Fisher for trial, to be returned if not found satisfactory, no specified time within which it must be returned being given. Mahoney keeps the stove a year without offering to return it and then, when a bill is presented for the stove, he says that it is not satisfactory and offers to bring it back. Has the sale been completed, and can Mahoney be compelled to pay?

33. Define chattel mortgage.

34. In the case of a chattel mortgage, who is entitled to the possession of the property, the mortgagor or the mortgagee?

35. If the mortgagor makes default in payment, what must the mortgagee do to obtain absolute title to the chattel?

36. What is a warranty? Does it differ from a condition? If so, how?

37. What different classes of warranty are there?

38. Coon, a sewing-machine agent, sells a machine to Mrs. Randall, telling her that it is the best machine on the market, and that it runs so easily that it will nearly run alone. She finds out that the machine is of inferior quality, runs hard, and does not work well, so seeks to recover damages for breach of warranty. Does the representation constitute a warranty?

39. Is a representation that a horse is sound and fourteen years old a warranty?

40. A sold a team of horses to B. He was driving the horses when the sale took place and immediately delivered them over. It was found afterwards that the horses did not belong to him, and an action was brought against him for breach of warranty. Was there any warranty? If so, what?

41. Suppose at the time A sold the horses he did not have them in his possession, but stated that they were in C's livery stable. B brought an action against him for breach of warranty. Was there any warranty? If so, what?

42. Frank sold a car load of apples to Jeffreys, nothing being said as to their quality. They were in the possession of Frank at the time they were sold, and each party had an opportunity to inspect them. It was found that they were of an inferior grade, and Jeffreys sued for damages for breach of an implied warranty of quality. Could he recover? What rule would apply?

43. X contracted to make for Y a new improved hayrack. When Y received it he found that it was not suitable for the purpose for which it was purchased and would not remain in position on the wagon. Was there any implied warranty on the part of X?

44. Meyer purchased a quantity of cloth from Scott. The order was taken from a sample which Scott carried with him. When the cloth was received it was an entirely different quality, being much lighter in weight. Meyer sued for damages on an implied warranty that the cloth was to be like the sample. Was there such an implied warranty and could he recover?

45. A sold B 100 barrels of sugar to be delivered in 30 days. When the time for delivery arrived, B refused to accept the sugar or pay the purchase price. What three remedies had A?

46. If the sugar had been delivered and accepted by B, but B had refused to pay for it, what remedies had A?

47. If A resides in New York and B in Rochester, and B becomes bankrupt after the sugar has been shipped by A but before it reaches Rochester, what special remedy has A?

48. If the goods had reached Rochester and had been delivered to B, but had not yet been disposed of and had been still in his possession, would A have had the same special remedy?

49. If, in question 45, B had been ready to receive the sugar but A had refused to deliver it, what damages could B have recovered?

50. What is specific performance, and when is it granted by the court?

NEGOTIABLE INSTRUMENTS

1. IN GENERAL

Definition. — A negotiable instrument may be defined as a written instrument or evidence of debt which may be transferred from one person to another by indorsement and delivery, or by delivery only, so that the legal title becomes vested in the transferee. The principal forms of negotiable instruments are promissory notes, bills of exchange, and checks.

Negotiable instruments are an important factor in business transactions of the present day, passing from hand to hand, in a sense, as a substitute for money. As a means of transferring funds and paying debts the check is as common among business houses as the money itself, while the promissory note is an equally important factor of our business system. The note is taken to the bank when the borrower desires money advanced to him by that institution. It is given to close a business transaction when so agreed if the date of payment is a day in the future; and as a large part of the business of to-day is transacted on credit, we can see the great usefulness of the promissory note as a transferable evidence of debt.

The term "negotiable" is applied to these instruments because they pass freely from hand to hand, they by their terms providing for such transfer.

Basis of Negotiable Instrument Law. — It is a common statement that the negotiable instrument law is based upon, and derived from, the customs of merchants. In the early law there is but little mention of commercial questions, any dispute arising between merchants and customers having been decided on the spot by a special court or committee that sat to administer speedy justice to the merchants at the markets or great fairs. These markets or fairs were held from time to time in the different cities in which the mercantile pursuits were largely carried on by merchants of different nations. These disputes were not determined by any fixed law but by the customs of the merchants. In the old English law books it was said that justice was administered "while the dust fell from the feet," so quickly was the court supposed to act. This practice finally developed into certain rules which were taken up and enforced by the courts and became the basis of our mercantile laws.

As the merchants dealt between different countries, it is easy to understand that the customs of the different nations came to be much the same, and the laws founded upon these customs had much similarity. The result is therefore that the negotiable instrument law, which is based more directly upon these customs than is any other branch of the law, does not materially vary in the different jurisdictions.

Statute Law. — It is very important that contracts which are to pass from hand to hand and from state to state with almost the freedom of money should be subject to practically the same laws and rules, and to this end a statute law covering the principal questions concerning negotiable instruments has been adopted in many of the states, giving a uniformity that renders these instruments more freely negotiable than they would otherwise be. We speak of negotiable instruments as contracts, and in reality they are written contracts, possessing special characteristics which give them privileges and qualities different from those in ordinary contracts.

Principal Characteristic. — The principal characteristic of a negotiable instrument, and that which makes it pass freely as a substitute for money, is that in the hands of a third party who purchases it in good faith and for value before it is due, it is enforceable, while the original holder, perhaps, could not enforce it for the reason that the party who made the instrument has a good defense or counterclaim. As soon, however, as an innocent purchaser comes into possession of it for value he can not be prevented from collecting because of any defenses existing between the original parties. In other contracts the purchaser acquires only the right of the party from whom he buys, but in the case of negotiable paper he may acquire a better title than the original holder.

Essential Conditions. — The question arises as to what conditions are essential to constitute a contract a negotiable instrument.   In general we find that no exact form need be followed, although custom has prescribed forms that are very generally used, but it is required that a negotiable instrument must be: —

1. In writing.
2. Properly signed.
3. Negotiable in form.
4. Payable in money only.
5. The amount must be certain.
6. It must be payable absolutely.
7. To the order of a designated payee or bearer.
8. At a certain time.

The Instrument must be in Writing. — The first requirement is that the instrument be in writing.   No oral contract could be negotiable.   By a written contract we mean one in either writing or printing, and the writing may be executed with any substance, as ink or pencil.

The whole instrument must be written.   No essential part, as the names of the parties, or the amount, can be omitted from the writing.

In *Currier* v. *Lockwood,* 40 Conn. 349, it was held that the following instrument was not a promissory note,

" $17.14.   BRIDGEPORT, CONN., Jan. 22, 1863.

"Due Currier & Barker seventeen dollars and fourteen cents, value received.

"FREDERICK LOCKWOOD."

This is merely a due bill.   It does not contain a promise to pay. A bare acknowledgment of a debt does not in legal construction import an express promise to pay.

The Instrument must be signed by the Party executing It. — It is usual that the signature be made by writing the name of the signer, but it is not necessary, as he may affix his mark or any other character intended to be a signature.

In *Brown* v. *Butchers' & Drovers' Bank*, 6 Hill (N.Y.) 443, the bank sued Brown as the indorser of a bill of exchange. The indorsement was made with a lead pencil and in figures, thus, " 1. 2. 8.," no name being written. It was known that they were in Brown's handwriting and that he meant them as his indorsement. It also appeared that he could write. The court charged the jury that if they believed the figures were made by Brown as a substitute for his proper name with the intention of binding himself as indorser, he was liable. The judgment was for the plaintiff. This was held to be correct. A person may be bound by any mark or designation he thinks proper to adopt, provided he uses it as a substitute for his name, and intends to bind himself.

It is usual to place the signature at the close of the instrument, but if it is shown that it is meant for a signature, it may be placed on any other part except where the statute requires that the name be subscribed.

Taylor v. *Dobbins*, 1 Strange (Eng.) 399, is an English case decided in 1720 which holds that it is sufficient if the maker writes the note with his own hand, and there need be no subscription in that case, for it is sufficient if his name is in any part of it.

The Instrument must be Negotiable in Form. — The instrument must be payable to " Order " or " Bearer." If made payable to a particular person or persons only, it is not a negotiable instrument, and falls under the rules governing a simple contract. In other words, the intent of the party making the instrument to execute a negotiable paper must appear by some express words showing such a purpose.

Chamberlain v. *Young*, 1893, 2 Q. B. (Eng.) 206, was an action on the following instrument : —

" Five months after date pay to _____ order, the sum of one hundred and fifty pounds, for value received.

(Signed)   " E. MALCOLM TOWER.
" To Mr. A. J. YOUNG."

The defense claimed it was not a bill of exchange. The court held that it was a bill of exchange payable to order, and was valid. It virtually said pay to the order of the drawer.

The Instrument must be Payable in Money, and the Amount must be Definite and Certain. — The very reason it must be payable in money is that if it were payable in any other commodity the value could not be definite and certain. If payable in a given number of bushels of wheat, the person taking it would be obliged to determine the value of wheat at that place; the value at another place might be materially different.   By the term " money " is meant the legal tender of the country; that is, a note payable in Spanish money is not a negotiable instrument in the United States.   (See " Legal Tender," page 63.)

Thompson v. *Sloan*, 23 Wend. (N.Y.) 71, was a suit on a note made and dated at Buffalo, N.Y., for $2500, payable twelve months after date at the Commercial Bank of Buffalo, N.Y., in *Canadian money*.   Held, that it was not a negotiable note.   A promissory note, in order to be negotiable within the meaning of the law merchant, must be payable in current money and not in the money of some other country.

The sum payable is considered fixed and certain if it is a given amount with interest, or payable by stated installments or with exchange (the bank's charges), or with the costs of collection in case payment is not made at maturity.

Dodge v. *Emerson*, 34 Me. 96, was an action on a note " payable to the Protection Insurance Co., or order, for $271.25, with such additional premium as may arise on policy No. 50, issued at the Calais Agency."   Held, that the instrument was not a negotiable instrument, the amount payable being indefinite and uncertain.

Lent v. *Hodgman*, 15 Barb. (N.Y.) 274, held, an instrument not negotiable as uncertain which provided as follows : " Pay A. B. for 68 bushels of wheat in store, at 3 cents below first quality wheat."

In *Fralick* v. *Norton*, 2 Mich. 130, a note for $60, but $50 if paid by January 1, was held not negotiable, as uncertain.

In *Parsons* v. *Jackson*, 99 U.S. 434, certain bonds certified " that the Vicksburg, Shreveport & Texas Railroad Co. are indebted to John Ray, or bearer, for value received, in the sum of either £225 sterling or $1000 lawful money of the United States of America; to wit, £225 sterling if the principal and interest are payable in London, and $1000 lawful money of the United States of America if the principal and interest are payable in New York or New Orleans."   Held, that in the absence of an express designation as to the place where the bonds were to be paid, the instruments were not negotiable, as the amount to be paid was uncertain.   The judge said, " One of the first rules in regard to negotiable paper is that the amount to be paid must be certain, and not be made to depend on a contingency."

In a Negotiable Instrument there must be a Designated Payee. — There must be no uncertainty as to the person to whom the money is to be paid. The instrument must be made payable to a certain person, or his order, or to the bearer. It need not name the payee, but it must be payable to a person or persons who can be definitely ascertained at the time of payment. If payable to A *or* B, it is not a negotiable instrument under the law merchant, but it has been so rendered by statute in some states.

Smith v. *Wilding* (Wisconsin case) was an action on a written instrument drawn as follows:—

"$2500. La Crosse, Wisconsin, Sept. 2, 1897.

"Four months after date I promise to pay to the order of twenty-five hundred dollars. Value received. "John Wilding."

Held, that is was not a negotiable instrument, as it neither designated the payee nor left a blank space for the payee's name.

Shaw v. *Smith*, 150 Mass. 166, was an action by the administrator of the estate of F. B. Bridgman on the following instrument:—

"$126. Belchertown, July 19, 1873.

"For value received I promise to pay F. B. Bridgman's estate, or order, one hundred twenty-six dollars on demand, with interest annually.
"Eugene Bridgman."

It was contended that this was not a promissory note because there was no definite payee, but the court held that, as the promise was to pay F. B. Bridgman's estate and he was dead and administrators had been appointed, the payees were in existence and ascertainable. They were therefore designated with sufficient definiteness, and the instrument was negotiable.

Musselman v. *Oakes*, 19 Ill. 81, was an action upon an instrument purporting to be a promissory note, payable to "Olive Fletcher or R. H. Oakes." Held, the instrument was not negotiable, as it was not payable to a certain person. This was payable to Fletcher or Oakes, but to which it was not certain.

Noxon v. *Smith*, 127 Mass. 485, was an action on a note payable to "the Trustees of the Methodist Episcopal Church or their Collector." Held, to be a negotiable instrument, as it was not payable to different persons in the alternative but to a certain designated payee, the trustees of the church, their collector being but their agent and payment to him would be payment to them.

The Instrument must be Payable absolutely and Unconditionally. — If the instrument is so drawn that any condition may arise which would render it of no effect, it is not a negotiable paper.   Consequently, a promise to pay a certain sum out of a designated fund is not negotiable, and this is the case even though the fund exists at the time or the condition that would nullify the contract never arises.

In *Richardson* v. *Carpenter*, 46 N.Y. 660, an instrument in the following form was held not to be a negotiable instrument, as the money was payable out of a particular fund.   " Please pay A, or order, $500 for value received out of the proceeds of the claim against the Peabody Estate, now in your hands for collection, when the same shall have been collected by you."

Blake v. *Coleman*, 22 Wis. 415, was an action on a promissory note in the usual form, on the back of which was indorsed, " The conditions of the within note are as follows : L. S. Blake or bearer is not to ask or expect payment of said note until his, Coleman's, old mill is sold for a fair price."   It was shown that this indorsement was made at the time the note was given.   The note was given for a new fanning mill, and the defendant still had his old one on hand.   Held, that this indorsement qualified the note and made it a mere agreement, and not being a negotiable instrument it could not be collected upon until the agreement was fulfilled.

Worden v. *Dodge*, 4 Denio (N.Y.) 159, was an action on an agreement in which defendants promised to pay to plaintiff or order $250 with interest, payable one half in two years and the other half in three years " out of the net proceeds, after paying the cost and expenses, of ore to be raised and sold from the bed on the lot this day conveyed by Edward Madden and Edwin Dodge, which bed is to be opened and the ore disposed of as soon as conveniently may be."   Held, that the payment of the amount depended on a contingency, so the agreement was not a promissory note.   A promissory note must be payable absolutely and not dependent upon some contingency or event.   Here the fund might not be adequate.

But the promise is not made conditional by designating a place of payment in the instrument.

The Time must be Certain. — The time of payment must be definite and fixed.   That is, the date of payment must be definitely stated, or it must be on or before a certain definite date, or at a certain time after the happening of an event that is sure to occur or on demand.   A note payable a certain number of days after the death of a person is negotiable, the date being certain because the time is sure to arrive.

Shaw v. *Camp*, 160 Ill. 425, held, that the following was a negotiable instrument, as the meaning was that it should be payable after the death of the maker. "After my death date I promise to pay Hanson Camp or order the sum of $750 without interest."

But the contingent event must be certain to occur or the promise will not be absolute.

Kelley v. *Hemmingway*, 13 Ill. 604, was an action on an instrument in the following form : —

"CASTLETON, April 27, 1844.

"Due Henry D. Kelley fifty-three dollars, when he is twenty-one years old, with interest."   "DAVID KELLEY."

Plaintiff proved that Henry D. Kelley became of age before the action was commenced. The court held that the instrument was not negotiable, as payment was contingent on an event that might or might not happen. The money was therefore not payable "absolutely and at all events," and the paper lacked one of the necessary elements of a negotiable instrument.

Duffield v. *Johnston*, 96 N.Y. 369, was an action brought to recover the last two payments on the following instrument : —

"THOMAS JOHNSTON, ESQ.:

"*Dear Sir :* (1) Please pay to J. J. Duffield, or order, the sum of six hundred and sixty-six dollars when the brown stone work of your eight houses situated on the south side of East One Hundred and Fifth Street, between Second and Third Avenues, City, is topped out.

"(2) The sum of four hundred dollars when the stoops of said eight houses are set.

"(3) The sum of three hundred and seventy-five dollars when the brown stone work of the said eight houses is completed ; and charge the same to me, and oblige, yours, etc.,

"WM. CHAVE."

Held, that it was not a bill of exchange because not payable absolutely. It was payable only upon condition that the work should be done as specified, and might never become payable.

The law simply requires that the time of payment shall be sure to arrive.

2. PROMISSORY NOTES

Definition. — A promissory note is an unconditional written promise made by one or more persons to pay to another or his order or bearer a certain sum of money at a specified time.

The party who makes the note and whose promise is contained therein is called the *maker*, and the party to whom the promise is made is called the *payee*.

Form. — There is no exact form of note required by law; in ordinary business practice it is printed in blank and filled in. It may or may not draw interest, but will not unless provided for in the note. The following form is a common one : —

If the note is without interest the words "with interest" are omitted. In this note Dickson is the maker and Strouss is the payee. If Strouss, the payee, wishes to obtain the money before the note matures, he indorses it by writing his name upon the back, and he is then also called the *indorser*, the person to whom he transfers it being called the *holder* or *indorsee*.

The above note is an illustration of a several note, as there is but one maker. There may be also a joint note and a joint and several note.

In a joint note there are two or more makers and the obligation to pay rests upon the makers jointly, and they must be sued together; if one is released the other or others can not be held.

In *King* v. *Hoare*, 13 M. & W. (Eng.) 494, it was held that a judgment against one of two joint debtors is a bar to an action against the other on the same debt.

When two or more persons make a note and agree to pay jointly and severally the form is substantially as follows : —

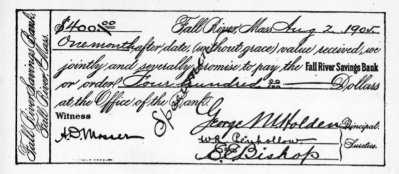

Upon this note the makers may be sued together or either one can be held severally for the full amount.

If the last note should be drawn in the form of the several note, but be signed by Holden and also by one or more sureties, it would be construed by law to be a joint and several note.

Dart v. *Sherwood*, 7 Wis. 523, was an action against the signers of the following promissory note as joint makers.

"$400. RIPON, WIS., Nov. 4, 1856.

"Thirty days after date, for value received, I promise to pay Putnam C. Dart, or order, four hundred dollars with interest, at the rate of twelve per cent per annum.
"J. C. SHERWOOD,
"WM. C. SHERWOOD, Surety."

Held, by the court to be a joint and several note; joint because signed by both parties and several because each defendant promised severally.

In *Ely* v. *Clute*, 19 Hun (N.Y.) 35, the following note was held to be joint and several, and separate judgments might be rendered against the two makers.

"$270. STOCKTON, March 14, 1875.

"One day after date I promise to pay Lorenzo Ely, or bearer, two hundred and seventy dollars at the post office in Stockton. Value received with use.
"THOMAS W. CLUTE.
"J. B. CLUTE."

In a few of the states the distinction between joint, and joint and several notes has been abolished, and all notes signed by two or more parties have been declared to be joint and several.

Signatures. — The construction of a signature may be to a certain extent ambiguous, and it may be well to note the effect of a signature which is apparently intended to be made by an agent or attorney to bind his principal.

It is plain that if the maker or any other party signing executes the signature in any of the following forms, the principal alone is bound, provided of course the agent acts within his authority: James Lane by George Chapman, Agent; James Lane by his agent, George Chapman; James Lane by George Chapman; George Chapman, agent for James Lane; or George Chapman for James Lane.

Long v. *Colburn*, 11 Mass. 97, was a case which held that the signature "Pro William Gill — J. S. Colburn," on a promissory note, was the signature of the principal, William Gill, and that he was bound by it.

On the other hand we find the courts holding that the agent alone is bound by such signatures as the following: George Chapman, Agent; George Chapman, agent of James Lane; George Chapman, president, or treasurer, etc., or George Chapman, president of the Genesee Gas Co.

Davis v. *England*, 141 Mass. 587, was an action on a promissory note in the form, "I promise to pay," and signed, "W. H. England, President and Treasurer Chelsea Iron Foundry Co." Held, that the signature made it the note of England and not of the company.

McClellan v. *Robe*, 93 Ind. 298, held, a note in the usual form in which several persons signed and after their names added, "trustees of the G. Lodge, etc.," rendered the signers individually liable, the words added being but descriptive of the parties.

When the signature to the instrument is made by the agent writing the name of the principal followed by the agent's name, the courts differ as to the effect given. Such a signature as James Lane, George Chapman, Agent, or Genesee Gas Co., George Chapman, President, is held by some courts to be the principal's signature, and he alone is bound.

Liebscher v. *Kraus*, 74 Wis. 387, was an action brought on the following promissory note: —

"$637.40.   MILWAUKEE, Jan. 1, 1887.

"Ninety days after date we promise to pay to Leo Liebscher, or order, the sum of six hundred and thirty-seven dollars and forty cents, value received.

"SAN PEDRO MINING & MILLING CO.,
"F. KRAUS, President."

Plaintiff demanded judgment against the corporation and Kraus as joint makers. The court held that it was the note of the company alone and that Kraus signed for the company as its president. The signature alone showed plainly enough that Kraus was acting as officer or agent of the company.

Other courts hold that it is the signature of both the principal and the agent, and that both are liable.

Mathews & Co. v. *Mattress Co.*, 87 Iowa 246, was an action on a promissory note against The Dubuque Mattress Co. and John Kapp. The note read "we promise to pay" and was signed "Dubuque Mattress Co., John Kapp, Pt." Held, that Kapp was personally liable. Where a person signs a note and adds thereto his name of office, and there is nothing on the face of the instrument to show he does not intend to be bound, he is personally liable, because the name of the office is merely descriptive of the person.

And still other courts hold the signature to be ambiguous and allow evidence to explain it.

Bean v. *Pioneer Mining Co.*, 66 Cal. 451, was an action on a promissory note reading "we promise to pay" and signed "Pioneer Mining Company, John E. Mason, Supt." Held, that the signature was ambiguous and parol evidence was admissible to show that it was understood by the payee to be the note of the company, and that the consideration for which it was given passed to the company.

The body of the instrument may contain statements that will explain the instrument, but the printed heading of the paper does not necessarily prove agency.

Casco National Bank v. *Clark*, 139 N.Y. 307, was an action against Clark and Close on the following promissory note: —

> "$7500.   BROOKLYN, N.Y., Aug. 2, 1890.
>
> "Three months after date, we promise to pay to the order of Clark and Chaplin Ice Company, seventy-five hundred dollars at Mechanics Bank, value received.   JOHN CLARK, Pres.
>
> "E. H. CLOSE, Treas."

(margin: Ridgewood Ice Co.)

Defendants claimed that they had signed as officers of the Ridgewood Ice Company and had not become personally liable on the note. But the court held that the name of the company printed on the margin of the paper did not create any presumption that the note was made by the company, and that the officers of the company had a right to obligate themselves.

Discharge. — The agreement of the maker of a note or of the acceptor of a bill of exchange is that upon the date of maturity of the note or bill he will pay absolutely the amount named therein to the payee designated therein or to his order.

His promise is absolute, and it can be discharged only in some one of the ways in which a contract can be discharged, as by payment, lapse of time, etc.

The only condition he can require is that the holder surrender the note or bill, and the maker is not obliged to pay without receiving the instrument, as otherwise, if it were lost, it might be presented by a person purchasing of the finder, and so payment might be compelled the second time. Relief in such a case is generally given the payee, however, by compelling the maker to pay upon being furnished a bond to indemnify him against any loss because of the reappearance of the note.

3. BILLS OF EXCHANGE

Definition. — A bill of exchange, or draft, is a written order from one person to another to pay to a third party or his order a certain amount of money at a specified time.

A common form of a bill of exchange is : —

In this bill of exchange the American Book Company is the drawer, the National Park Bank is the payee, and Davis is the drawee. After Davis has accepted the bill he is called the acceptor.

Bank Draft. — When the drawer and drawee are banks the bill of exchange is known as a bank draft and constitutes a common method of paying the debts of parties residing in different localities. The form is as follows: —

Merchants Bank of Rochester,

Rochester, N.Y. *Dec. 22. 1905* No. **225273**

Pay to the order of *Charles M. Allen* payee $ *100.*00

One hundred no/100 ——————— Dollars

To The
Chemical National Bank. *William G. Gancourt*
New York City.
drawee *drawer* Cashier.

Allen owes Brown of Albany $100 and wishes to pay him, therefore he goes to his bank in Rochester and purchases a draft on a New York bank and sends it to Brown. This draft he has made payable to himself and on the back indorses "pay to the order of William Brown" and signs "Charles M. Allen." The draft might have been made payable to Brown on its face, but the advantage of the other form is that when the draft is returned to the Merchants Bank, having been indorsed by Brown, it contains a complete record of the transaction, and in case of a dispute is a receipt which Allen could procure for use in evidence. The banks have an arrangement among themselves through the clearing house and their correspondents in the large financial centers like New York and Chicago, by reason of which they can issue these drafts. The New York or Chicago draft is as readily accepted as the money itself, and is unhesitatingly cashed by banks anywhere. Here it may be seen how the bill of exchange or bank draft acts as a convenient transfer of obligation without the necessity of conveying money between distant points.

The bill of exchange and promissory note like the bank draft may be transferred by the payee, and so may pass from hand to hand, and thus take the place of money.

Bills of Exchange may be either Foreign or Inland. — A foreign bill of exchange is a bill drawn in one state or country and payable in another state or country. An inland bill of exchange is one made payable in the same state in which it is drawn.

The last illustration is an inland bill. A foreign bill is sometimes drawn in duplicate or triplicate, and upon the payment of one the other or others become void. The several copies are termed a set, the object in having them so drawn being that if one is lost, the other, or others, will reach their destination. In the earlier times the custom was to send each copy by a different route, thus assuring safety and dispatch. The first copy presented was the one paid. A common form for a foreign bill is : —

But the custom of issuing bills in a set is fast becoming obsolete, and the practice between the states is to draw foreign bills in the same form as inland bills.

Time and Sight Drafts. — Drafts are also drawn as either time or sight drafts. The following is a sight draft, that is, it is payable on presentation. A time draft is one payable at a given time after demand or sight or date.

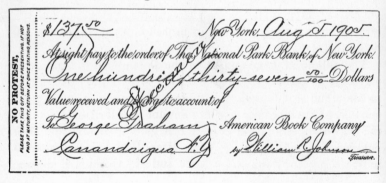

The draft is a common means employed by business houses to collect debts due them from parties residing in other places. The creditor draws upon the debtor, naming a bank as the payee, for the purpose of making the collection.

Acceptance. — A bill of exchange being an order on the drawee to pay a certain amount of money to a third party, it is not binding upon the drawee until he has accepted it. The acceptance is signified, if a sight draft, by payment; if a time draft, by the drawee writing the word "accepted" across the face of the draft and signing his name. After he has accepted the bill, he becomes the acceptor and his obligation is then fixed and absolute and can be enforced against him, his position becoming much the same as that of the maker of a note. According to the law merchant, the acceptance could be either oral or written, but by statute in most of the states it must be in writing. Barring the case of an acceptance for honor, which will be discussed later, the only person who can accept a bill is the drawee.

In *Cook* v. *Baldwin*, 120 Mass. 317, it was held that the words "I take notice of the above, Henry Baldwin" written on a bill of exchange do not necessarily import an acceptance, and parol evidence of a refusal can be shown. The court said a bill of exchange may be accepted by an oral promise to pay as well as by a written one, or by such language and conduct on the part of the drawee, when the bill is presented to him, as justifies the payee in believing that he consents to pay it.

National Park Bank v. *Ninth National Bank*, 46 N.Y. 77, was an action to recover the money paid on a forged draft, which the plaintiff had accepted and paid. The court held that the plaintiff could not recover. It is a well-settled rule that it is incumbent upon the drawee of a bill to be satisfied that the signature of the drawer is genuine, and he is presumed to know the handwriting of such drawer, and if he accepts or pays a bill to which the drawer's name has been forged, he is bound by the act and can neither repudiate the acceptance nor recover the money paid.

The Bill must be presented to the Drawee for Acceptance or Payment. — Until accepted the drawer is the party liable to the payee. He agrees that the drawee will accept it or he himself will pay it if proper presentment and demand be made upon the drawee, and notice of dishonor be given him. If the bill is payable a certain length of time after sight or on demand it must be presented for acceptance and the acceptance secured before the time will begin to run. The acceptor should always include the date in his acceptance on this kind of draft. If the bill is payable at sight or on demand, it must be presented to the drawee for payment within a reasonable time. If the drawee refuses to accept, the drawer must be duly notified and he thereupon becomes liable for the bill. But if the bill is payable a certain number of days after date or upon demand or upon a day specified, it need not be presented for acceptance, presentment for payment being sufficient. Still it should be presented for the purpose of securing the drawee's acceptance and thus making him liable upon the instrument and at the same time giving him an opportunity to prepare to pay the bill.

In *Chambers* v. *Hill*, 26 Tex. 472, a bill of exchange dated December 18, 1851, was not presented for payment until two years and nine months thereafter. The draft contained no specific date for payment. Held, that the draft was payable on demand and must be presented for payment within a reasonable time to hold the drawer and indorser; and that an unexplained delay of two years and nine months is unreasonable and the drawer and indorser are released.

In *Wallace* v. *Agry*, 4 Mason (U.S.) 336, a bill drawn June 18 at Havana, Cuba, on Williams in London, payable sixty days after sight and presented in London on October 31, having been kept by the holder in Boston from July 6 to September 29, was found to have been presented within a reasonable time.

Aymar v. *Beers*, 7 Cowen (N.Y.) 705, held, that a bill drawn on December 12 in New York, "three days after sight," and presented January 10 in Richmond, Va., having been in the payee's hands during that time, was presented within a reasonable time under the circumstances of the case.

When the drawee refuses to accept, the bill is said to be dishonored.

Acceptance for Honor. — Mention has been made of acceptance for honor. This is also known as acceptance *supra protest*. When the bill has been dishonored and protested, a third party who may or may not be the drawer accepts it to protect the drawer or any of the other parties to the instrument. The obligation of such an acceptor is to pay the bill if upon a further presentation of it to the drawee for payment, at maturity, it is again dishonored and duly protested, and due notice is given to such acceptor.

Virtual Acceptance. — There is another mode of acceptance known as "virtual" acceptance, which is practically a promise to accept. If the virtual acceptance consist of a written unconditional promise to accept a bill already drawn or one to be drawn in the future, it is binding in favor of one who has taken it with a knowledge of the acceptance and in reliance thereon. The promise must clearly describe the bill and must be absolute in its terms.

4. CHECKS

Definition. — A check is a draft, or order, drawn on a bank or banker, directing payment on demand by the bank to a third person or his order or to bearer, of a certain sum of money. A common form of check follows : —

New Haven, Conn. *Aug 15* 190 *5*   No. **849**

THE MERCHANTS NATIONAL BANK,

Pay to the order of

James Farley $200 00

Two hundred 00/100 ———— Dollars.

H. E. Eldridge

A check is drawn by a party having money on deposit in the bank and, as shown in the definition, is a special form of bill of exchange with the bank as drawee. In the above check Eldridge is the maker or drawer, the Merchants Bank of New Haven, Conn., is the drawee, and Farley is the payee. A check is intended for immediate payment upon presentation, and the implied contract of the drawer is that the bank will pay the check. In case it does not, the drawer is liable absolutely, and no notice of dishonor is necessary.

Harrison v. *Nicollet National Bank*, 41 Minn. 488, was an action for damages for protesting the following instrument before it was due.

"45 WASHINGTON AVENUE SOUTH,
  "HARRISON THE TAILOR,

"$199.92.   "MINNEAPOLIS, MINN., March 27, 1888.

  "On April 14 pay to the order of E. Harrison one hundred and ninety-nine $\frac{92}{100}$ dollars.   "J. T. HARRISON.

"To CITIZENS' BANK,
  "Minneapolis, Minn."

Payment was demanded and the instrument protested on April 14. The plaintiff contended that it was a bill of exchange and entitled to days of grace, while the defendant claimed that it was a check and not entitled to grace. Held, that one of the essentials of a check is that it shall be payable on demand and, as this was payable in the future, it was not a check but a bill of exchange and entitled to grace.

Check must be Presented without Delay. — But the payee of a check must present it for payment within a reasonable time, or the drawer will be discharged from loss occasioned by his delay. What would be a reasonable time would depend upon circumstances, but it is generally considered that the check should be presented within a day after its receipt.

Grange v. *Reigh*, 93 Wis. 552, was an action against the drawer of a check. After banking hours on July 20 defendant drew and delivered to plaintiff in Milwaukee, where plaintiff resided, a check for $1211 upon the South Side Savings Bank of that city. The check was not presented on July 21, although the bank was open and would have paid it at any time during the banking hours of that day. The bank failed, and did not open after that date. The court held that the party receiving a check must present it for payment within a reasonable time in order to preserve his right of recourse on the drawer in case of non-payment; and when such party resides and receives the check at the place in which the bank is located, a reasonable time for such presentation reaches, at the latest, only to the close of banking hours on the succeeding day. The defendant in this case is therefore discharged from liability.

In *Mohawk Bank* v. *Broderick*, 13 Wend. (N.Y.) 133, a check drawn on the Mechanics & Farmers Bank of Albany was transferred by defendant to Meyers and by him deposited in the Mohawk Bank of Schenectady. This bank retained the check 23 days before presentment, although a daily mail passed between Schenectady and Albany, a distance of 16 miles. When presented payment was refused. Held, that the holders had not used due diligence in making presentment, and were not entitled to maintain an action against the payee who had negotiated the check.

Certified Checks. — A check purports to be drawn upon a deposit made by the drawer in the bank upon which it is drawn, and although in fact there may be no such deposit, it is still a check.

Checks pass freely between parties as money, yet, unless the drawer is known to have on deposit in the bank funds sufficient to meet the check, or unless his solvency is known, a person is not safe in accepting the check. It is therefore customary in such cases to have the bank certify the check, that is, the cashier or teller stamps the word "certified." and the date with his signature on the face of the check. The bank then takes the amount from the drawer's deposit and puts it in a separate account. The result is that the check is thereafter the check of the bank rather than of the drawer, and it is good as long as the bank is solvent. When the holder has the check certified, the bank by so certifying becomes the principal and only debtor, and the holder by accepting the certified check discharges the drawer. But if the drawer procures the certification before delivering the check, he is not released from further liability.

Minot v. *Russ* and *Head* v. *Hornblower*, 156 Mass. 458, were two cases arising from the failure of the Maverick National Bank and decided together by the court. In the first case the defendant on October 29, 1891, drew a check on the Maverick National Bank payable to plaintiff, who informed him that the check must be certified by the bank before it would be received. On the same day the defendant presented it to the bank for certification. The bank complied by writing on the face of it " Maverick National Bank. Pay only through clearing house. J. W. Work, Cashier. A. C. J., Paying Teller." After the check was certified the defendant, on October 31, 1891, delivered it to plaintiff for a valuable consideration. The bank stopped payment Monday morning, November 2, 1891.

In the second case on Saturday, October 31, 1891, defendants drew their check on the Maverick National Bank payable to plaintiffs and delivered it to them. As the check was received too late to be deposited by the plaintiffs for collection in time to go through the clearing house that day, plaintiffs procured the certification of the check by the bank during banking hours in the following form : " Maverick National Bank. Certified. Pay only through clearing house. C. C. Domett. A., Cashier." At that time the defendants in both cases had on deposit sufficient funds to pay the checks, and the bank on certification charged to the defendants accounts the amounts of the checks which they credited to a ledger account called certified checks. It was held that in the first case the defendant was not released by the certificate, as he had procured it himself, and in the second case he was released as the payee obtained a certification in his own behalf instead of getting the check paid.

In *Boyd* v. *Nasmith*, 17 Ont. (Can.) 40, the payees of a check took it to the bank on which it was drawn on the afternoon of the day they received it from the drawer and had it marked "good." The amount was charged to the drawer's account. Payment was not demanded of the bank, and it suspended payment that evening. Held, that the drawer of the check was discharged from all liability thereon.

5. NEGOTIATION

Definition. — By negotiation we mean the transfer of a negotiable instrument from one person to another in such a way that the transferee is the legal holder thereof. Almost all other claims and contracts can be assigned, although that was not the rule of the common law. A negotiable instrument, however, is particularly intended to be readily transferred. To aid the freedom with which it may pass from one to another, it has the distinctive feature of being collectible in the hands of a third party, even though it is subject to certain defenses in the hands of the original payee.

Indorsement. — Negotiable paper is transferred by indorsement and delivery, that is, by the payee signing his name on the back with directions as to the party to whom payment shall be made and handing it over to the transferee. When an instrument is made payable to a certain person or bearer, an indorsement is not necessary to give a good title to the transferee, delivery being sufficient, but if it is payable to a certain person or order, the indorsement is necessary to give title.

Blank and Full Indorsement. — For the purpose of transfer, the indorsement must be made by the party to whom the instrument is payable. In the note on page 124, Strouss may owe James McConnell, and if he hands him Dickson's note in payment, he may write on the back, "Pay to the order of James McConnell," and sign "Eugene M. Strouss." This would be called an indorsement in full, or special indorsement, and if McConnell wishes to transfer, he must again indorse to his transferee.

In *Lawrance* v. *Fussell,* 77 Pa. St. 460, defendant made a note payable to plaintiff. Plaintiff indorsed it to another party by special indorsement. It was not shown that plaintiff had taken up the note as indorser upon the maker's failure to pay. Held, that no title was shown in plaintiff. If the note had been indorsed in blank, the possession would have been sufficient evidence of ownership, but when a note is specially indorsed, it can not be negotiated except by indorsement, and can be sued upon only by the special indorsee.

In the case of the Dickson note, Strouss, in transferring, might have indorsed by simply signing his name, " Eugene M. Strouss." Such a form is called an indorsement in blank and makes the instrument payable to bearer.

Restrictive Indorsement. — By this form of indorsement the indorsee is made the agent of the indorser, and the form might be as follows : —

Pay Henry Fox, or order,
for collection and credit,
to my account. JAS. WILSON.

Obligation of Indorser and Drawer. — The obligation of an indorser to a transferee, like that of the drawer of a bill, is that the indorser will pay the instrument provided the maker does not, and also provided it is duly presented for payment and upon refusal is duly protested and notice of protest given the indorser. In domestic bills and notes the protest may be omitted and instead notice of non-payment may be given the indorser. It will be seen that the contract of the maker of a note or the acceptor of a bill is absolute. Each is liable in any event, but the contract of the indorser and of the drawer of a bill is conditional upon the failure of the maker or acceptor to pay upon proper protest and notice to him.

Indorsement without Recourse. — If the indorser of the Dickson note wished to avoid any personal liability, he would indorse " without recourse " and sign " Eugene M. Strouss." By the indorsement " without recourse," the indorser expressly stipulates that he will not be liable if the maker does not pay, but he is held to impliedly warrant that the signatures of the maker and all prior indorsers are genuine, that is, that they are not forgeries. The intent and purpose of such indorsement is to pass title to the instrument.

In *Lomax* v. *Picot*, 2 Rudolph (Va.) 247, the court said : " An indorsement without recourse is not out of the due course of trade. The security continues negotiable, notwithstanding such an indorsement. Nor does such an indorsement indicate that the parties to it are conscious of any defect in the security, or that the indorser does not take it on the credit of the other party or parties to the note. On the contrary, he takes it solely on their credit, and the indorser only shows thereby that he is unwilling to make himself responsible for the payment."

Indorsement ; How made. — The indorsement must be on the instrument itself or on a paper attached to it. The indorsement must relate to the entire instrument ; a part can not be transferred by indorsement, or a part to one party and the remainder to another.

Hughes v. *Kiddell*, 2 Bay (S.C.) 324, was an action against the indorser of a note. The note was given by one David Bush to the defendant Kiddell for £473 sterling. Kiddell afterwards made the following indorsement : " I assign over to Hudson Hughes the sum of $1930.50 as part of this note of hand.
"BENJAMIN KIDDELL."
Afterwards he made another indorsement and assigned the residue to Hughes. The court held that each indorsement was bad, as it affected only part of the note, and that being so, two bad indorsements would not constitute one good one.

Any writing intended to transfer the title to the instrument will be construed as an indorsement.

Adams v. *Blethen*, 66 Me. 19, was an action against the indorser of the following note : —
"LINNEUS, May 30, 1873.
"I promise to pay James H. Blethen, or order, $137.50 at ten per cent interest, on demand. "EBENEZER TOZIER."
On the back of this note was written, " I this day sold and delivered to Catherine M. Adams the within note. JAMES H. BLETHEN."
Held, that the defendant assumed all of the liability of an ordinary indorser. This indorsement but expressly stated what every indorsement impliedly states, a sale or transfer of the note. The liability of an indorser can be limited or qualified only by express terms.

Where the name of the payee or indorsee is wrongfully designed or misspelled, he may on the instrument as therein described add his proper signature.

Presentment and Demand. — As has been said, to fix the liability of the drawer or indorser, the first step is presentment to the drawee or maker and demand. Bills of exchange payable a certain time after sight are presented for acceptance; notes, checks, and bills payable on demand or sight are presented for payment. Presentment consists in exhibiting the instrument to the payor or handing it to him, while demand is a request to either accept or pay it as the case may be. If the paper is payable at a bank the mere fact that at the time of maturity the paper is at the bank at which it is payable is sufficient presentment and demand, provided the bank has knowledge of the fact.

Presentment and demand must always be made at the place designated in the instrument. Promissory notes are often drawn in the following form, designating the place of payment : —

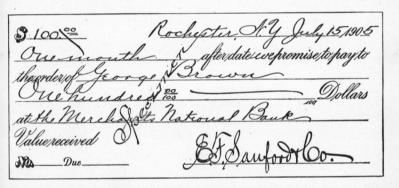

This is called a bank note, but the place of payment designated may be some other place than a bank.

In *Brooks* v. *Higby,* 11 Hun (N.Y.) 235, a bill was drawn on N. F. Mills, 114 South Main St., St. Louis, and by him accepted. The notary's certificate stated that the bill was presented for payment "at the place of business of N. F. Mills, St. Louis." It appeared that Mills had two places of business in St. Louis. The court held that the certificate was insufficient, as it did not show at which place presentment was made. The bill was addressed to Mills at a particular place and by him accepted at that place, making it the place of payment, and a due presentment and demand of payment at that place was necessary in order to charge the indorser.

In case there is no designated place of payment, it is said that the paper is payable generally. This means that it is payable at the place of business or residence of the maker of the note or acceptor of the draft, and when he has a known place of business, that should have preference over his residence.

Barnes v. *Vaughan*, 6 R.I. 259, was an action against the indorser of a note which was not made payable at any particular place, but was left by the plaintiff at the Mount Vernon Bank in Foster for collection. The only demand made upon the maker, Northrup, was that the usual printed bank notice was mailed to him by the cashier and directed to Providence, where he lived in the early part of the month in which the notes became due. The court held that there was no legal and proper demand made upon the maker and therefore the indorser was discharged. The rule is that in order to charge the indorser payment must be demanded of the maker on the day the note becomes due, unless the note is made payable at a designated place, as at a bank named, when it is only necessary to make demand at such place; but if no place of payment is named in the note, it is necessary to present it to the maker personally or at his place of business or abode, otherwise the indorser can not be charged.

In *Taylor* v. *Snyder*, 3 Denio (N.Y.) 145, the note was dated at Troy, N.Y. The maker then and afterwards resided in Florida to the knowledge of the holder and indorsers, but presentment was made in Troy though not personally on the maker or at his residence. It was held to be insufficient. The court said, "When no change has taken place in the residence of the maker between the making of the note and the time of its payment, the intervention of a state does not dispense with the necessity of making due demand of payment."

If the maker or acceptor has neither a known residence nor a place of business, the holder need only be present with the paper and ready to receive payment at the place where the contract was made.

Malden Bank v. *Baldwin*, 13 Gray (Mass.) 154, held, that a presentment for payment at any bank in Boston, of a note payable "at bank in Boston" or "at either bank in Boston," was a sufficient demand upon the maker to charge the indorser.

Time. — Presentment for payment must be made on the day on which the instrument falls due, unless some "inevitable accident" or other legal obstacle prevents such presentment. The fact that both the holder and indorser know that the note will not be paid when due and that the maker is dead and the estate insolvent, does not relieve the holder from his obligation to make presentment and give notice of dishonor.

Days of Grace. — Drafts, bills of exchange, and promissory notes formerly had days of grace, that is, three days were added to the time stated in which the instrument should become due. The purpose of this was to give the payor in the early days of slow transportation an opportunity to arrange for payment. A note at thirty days drawn June 10 would not be payable until July 13; but days of grace have been abolished by statute in most of the states and an instrument matures on the date fixed. If given a number of days after date, the day on which the instrument is drawn is excluded; thus, a note dated January 10 payable thirty days after date is due February 9. If the date of maturity is Sunday or a legal holiday, the instrument is payable on the next succeeding business day.

Salter v. *Burt*, 20 Wend. (N.Y.) 205, was an action on a check drawn on August 9 but postdated August 21, and as checks are payable without grace, the day on which it became due fell on Sunday. It was presented for payment, and notice of non-payment was given on Saturday, August 20. The court held that it was presented before it came due. If a negotiable instrument which does not have grace falls due on Sunday, it becomes due and payable on Monday, but when grace is allowed the rule is different, and Saturday is the day it becomes due.

In the states in which days of grace are yet allowed, if the last day of grace is a holiday or Sunday, the instrument is payable on the preceding day.

Johnson v. *Haight*, 13 Johns. (N.Y.) 470, was a case in which the third day of grace fell on Sunday, November 29, and payment was not demanded of the maker until November 30. It was held that the law is well settled that demand must be made on the third day of grace unless that falls on Sunday, and then payment must be demanded on the second day of grace. Therefore in this case the indorser was discharged.

But when the time is reckoned by the month, as it is when the instrument is made payable one or more months after date, the note falls due on the corresponding date of the month in which it is due. Thus a note dated January 31, 1903, due one month after date, would mature February 28, 1903, where no grace is allowed, and if dated February 28, it would be due March 28.

Roehner v. *Knickerbocker Insurance Co.*, 63 N.Y. 160, held, that a note without grace dated December 11, payable four months after date, is due and payable April 11.

Not only must the presentment for payment be made on the right day, but it must be made at a reasonable time on that day. If presented at a bank, it must be during banking hours. In other cases the time must be at a reasonable hour.

Dana v. *Sawyer*, 22 Me. 244, was a case in which presentment for payment was made at the maker's house between eleven and twelve o'clock at night, the maker being called up from bed for that purpose. Held, that the presentment was made at an unreasonable hour, and the demand was not sufficient.

Farnsworth v. *Allen*, 4 Gray (Mass.) 453, was an action against the indorser of a note, and the defense was insufficient presentment and demand for payment. The holder did not know the maker's place of residence. He gave it to a notary who arrived at the maker's house at nine in the evening. The maker and his family had retired for the night, but he answered the bell, and upon the note being presented refused payment. Held, to be sufficient presentment; the rule is that it must be presented at such a time, regard being had to the habits and usages of the community where the maker resides, that he may reasonably be expected to be in condition to attend to ordinary business.

Newark India Rubber Mfg. Co. v. *Bishop*, 3 E. D. Smith (N.Y.) 48, was a case in which a note payable at a bank was presented after banking hours and the clerk still there refused payment, although funds had been left with the regular teller to pay it. Held, that the presentment and demand were not sufficient.

The presentment must be made by the holder or his duly authorized agent, upon the proper person, who is the maker or acceptor, or, if he is dead, his personal representative.

Stinson v. *Lee*, 68 Miss. 113, was an action against an indorser. The note was signed " A. G. Cunningham, Agent." Nothing appeared on the face of the note showing for whom he professed to act. Presentment and demand of payment was made upon S. A. Cunningham, the wife of A. G. Cunningham. Held, that the demand was insufficient. By the signature the note was made by A. G. Cunningham, and the demand to bind the indorser must be made on him.

Toby v. *Maurian*, 7 La. 493, was an action against the indorser of a note. The defense was want of due presentation. The maker died on the last day of grace. The notary called with the note and found no one but a mulatto woman who informed him of the death of the maker. The note was then protested without any inquiry or demand being made of any heirs or representatives of the deceased. Held, that demand must be made of the heirs or legal representatives of deceased unless the impossibility of such demand is shown.

Notice of Dishonor. — After payment has been refused and the instrument dishonored, notice of such dishonor must be given to the drawer of a bill of exchange and to each indorser if a bill or note, and any drawer or indorser to whom such notice is not given is discharged.

This notice under the law merchant must be given within a reasonable time, but by the negotiable instrument law adopted in many of the states it is expressly stipulated when the notice is to be given. If the parties reside in the same place, it must be given the following day. If they reside in different places, and notice is sent by mail, it must be deposited in the post office so as to go the day following the dishonor; if given otherwise than through the mail, it must be done in time to be received as soon as the mailed notice would have been.

In *Simpson* v. *Turney*, 5 Humph. (Tenn.) 419, the bank was the holder of a promissory note, payable at said bank, made by James H. Jenkins, to Anthony Dibrell, and indorsed as follows, "A. Dibrell, S. Turney, and John W. Simpson." Turney's residence was within one mile of the bank. The note was due on February 1, and was protested on that day. On February 3 notice was sent Turney from the bank. Simpson, the next indorser, gave him no notice. The court held that the notice was not given in time. If it had been given by Simpson on the 3d, it would have been good, as each indorser is given a day to notify his prior indorser, but this was not done. The notice given was not valid as to the bank, so could not be to any one to whose benefit it would inure.

Smith v. *Poillon*, 87 N.Y. 590, was a case in which the holder notified the third indorser by mail and inclosed notices for the second and first indorsers. The third indorser notified the second and inclosed notice for the first. The second indorser received the notice on the 6th, and mailed notice to the first indorser on the 7th, in time to go on the second mail closing at 1.30 P.M. The first mail closed at 9.30 A.M., and defendant contended that notice should have been sent by that mail. The court held that the notice was sufficient and that plaintiff had used due diligence in giving notice.

The notice may be given by the holder or his agent or by any party who may have to pay the debt and who is entitled to be reimbursed.

In *Stafford* v. *Yates*, 18 Johns. (N.Y.) 327, a note with two indorsers was dishonored and notice given by the holder to both indorsers. The second indorser sued the first, and it was held, that the notice was sufficient; that it was not necessary for the second indorser to give notice to the first. It was sufficient that notice was given him, and the notice of the holder inures to the benefit of any indorser.

Notice to Indorsers. — When there are several indorsers the last indorser can look to the previous one, or in fact to any one who has indorsed before him, as well as to the maker or acceptor. Therefore it often happens that the holder upon dishonor of the instrument gives notice to the last indorser, and he in turn gives notice to the prior indorser, to whom he will look to be reimbursed in case he is obliged to pay the instrument.

The notice of dishonor may be either oral or written, and can be either delivered personally or sent through the mail. Some cases hold that the postal service can not be used when the parties reside in the same town, but by statute in New York State the post office can be used even in that case.

In *Hobbs* v. *Straine*, 149 Mass. 212, plaintiff took a written notice of dishonor to defendant's office, and finding no one there, left it. The court instructed the jury that if they determined that it was left in a conspicuous place, it was sufficient. Held, that this was correct. It is sufficient to charge the indorser if the notice is delivered personally, left at the indorser's place of residence or business, or deposited in the post office addressed to him at his residence or place of business with the postage prepaid.

Waiver. — Notice may be waived, and frequently the indorser adds " protest waived," the effect of this being to waive presentment and notice of dishonor as well as formal protest.

Protest. — Protest is a formal declaration in writing and under seal, of an officer called a notary public, certifying to the demand and dishonor. When it is impossible to command the services of a notary, protest may be made by any two respectable citizens who sign as witnesses of the act of presenting. Protest of foreign bills of exchange is necessary, but it is not required in the case of notes, checks, and inland bills, although it is often employed in giving notice of their dishonor. The notary makes the presentment and demand, and upon refusal issues a certificate like the following : —

State of New York.
County of ___Monroe___ } ss.

J, ___Charles M. Allen___, one of the Notaries Public in and for the County aforesaid, **Do Hereby Certify**, that on the ___27th___ day of ___August___ in the year One thousand nine hundred and ___five___ at the request of ___Flower City National Bank___ I did present the original ___bill___, which is hereunto annexed, to ___Edgar Wood___ at ___Rochester___, N. Y., and demanded ___payment thereof ___, which was refused.

Whereupon J, the said Notary, did **Protest,** and by these presents do publicly and solemnly Protest, as well against the maker and *endorser* of the said ___bill___ as against all others whom it doth or may concern, for exchange, re-exchange, and all costs, damages and interest, already incurred or to be hereafter incurred by reason of the non-payment ___ of the said ___bill.___

And J do further Certify, That on the same day and year above written, due notice* of the foregoing demand, non-payment ___and Protest (by notice partly printed and partly written, signed by me) was given to the ___drawer and the___ several endorsers thereon by depositing notices at the post-office at ___Rochester,___, N. Y., postage fully paid, directed as follows:

To ___Eugene M. Strouss___ at ___Rochester, New York.___
To ___Joseph A. Dey___ at ___Rochester, New York.___
To ___Fred. M. Rood,___ at ___Rochester, New York.___
To ___Thomas M. Pearce___ at ___Penn Yan, New York.___

each of the above named places being the reputed place of residence of the person to whom the notice was directed, and the post-office nearest thereto.

Thus done and Protested, in the City ___ of ___Rochester___, N. Y., the day and year first above written.

In Testimony Whereof, I have hereunto set my hand and affixed my official seal.

[L. S.]

Charles M. Allen
Notary Public.

COM. LAW — 10

After attaching the instrument to this certificate the notary mails a notice after the following form to all indorsers: —

Rochester N.Y. Aug. 27, 1905

Please to take Notice, That a *certain bill of exchange drawn on and accepted* by *Edgar Wood* for *One hundred 00/100* — — Dollars dated *August 1st, 1905* payable *Rochester, N.Y.*

endorsed by you, is PROTESTED for non-payment, and that the holders look to you for the payment thereof.

Your obedient servant,

Charles M. Allen

Notary Public.

To *Eugene M. Strouss, Rochester, N.Y.*

Irregular Indorser. — Frequently there appears on the back of a bill or note the name of a person who is not a party to it and to whom it was never indorsed. Such a person is known as an irregular or anomalous indorser. The object of such an indorsement is to give additional security to the payee. Under the law merchant different states held differently as to the liability of such a party, some holding him to be a joint maker, others an indorser, and still others whatever he could prove that he intended to be. Under the negotiable instrument statute he is held to be an ordinary indorser.

Coulter v. *Richmond*, 59 N.Y. 478, was an action on a promissory note made by Anson and indorsed by defendant, payable to the order of plaintiff. The note was indorsed at the request of the maker before delivery to the payee, to enable the maker to purchase bonds of the payee. The court said: "In some states such an indorser is regarded as a guarantor, in others an indorser, and in others a joint maker; but it is well settled in this state that a person making such an indorsement is presumed to have intended to become liable as second indorser, and on the face of the paper without explanation he is to be regarded as second indorser, and, of course, not liable upon the note to the payee, who is supposed to be the first indorser ; but it is competent by proof to show that the indorsement was made to give the maker credit with the payee and others, to hold him as first indorser." In this case the latter was found to be the intention and the indorser was held as first indorser.

Such indorsements are frequently used when the payee of a note wishes to get it discounted at a bank, that is, to get the money on it. The bank requires an indorser, and the payee gets a friend to indorse the note. The irregular indorser is liable to the bank the same as any other indorser.

Accommodation Paper. — The question of accommodation paper must be discussed here, as it is an instance of the drawer or indorser of a bill and the indorser of a note becoming liable without notice of dishonor. Accommodation paper is the term used to denote negotiable instruments that have been executed without consideration and for the purpose of lending the name of the maker, indorser, or acceptor. To illustrate, A may desire a loan, so he goes to B and asks the favor. B gives him a note which A indorses and discounts at the bank. If B refuses payment at maturity because it is really A's debt, the bank can, of course, proceed against B, as his name is on the paper, but it can also proceed against A without the formality of demand and notice. The reason is apparent as, A being the real debtor, it can not be supposed that he expects B to pay, but considers himself the principal debtor.

American National Bank v. *Junk Bros.*, 94 Tenn. 624, was an action against the indorser of some notes. The defense was that notice of dishonor had not been given. It was shown that the notes were given for the defendant's accommodation and then indorsed by him to plaintiff. Such being the case, it was the indorser's duty to provide funds to meet them at maturity, and he was bound, therefore, without presentment, protest, and notice.

The Holder or Payee. — We have yet to consider the position and rights of the holder or payee of the instrument. Whether he be the original payee or an indorsee, he is the party in whose hands the instrument rests and who has the right to the money which it represents. We have already learned that negotiable instruments have a distinguishing characteristic not possessed by any other contract, which is that when they have passed into certain parties' hands under particular conditions they are valid and enforceable, although not valid between the original parties to them. The rule is generally said to be that a negotiable instrument in the hands of an innocent purchaser for value and before maturity is not subject to any of the defenses that might be interposed to it between the original parties, but this is not true of certain absolute defenses which affect the very existence of the contract, and which we will consider later.

To bring the instrument under the rule, the holder must be an innocent purchaser for value, or as it is often expressed, a " *bona fide* holder for value " or a " holder in due course." The term " *bona fide* holder " means a holder who has acquired the instrument in good faith, without knowledge or notice of any defenses or defects that could be set up against any prior holder. To constitute notice, the holder must have had actual knowledge of the defect, or his carelessness must have been so great as to amount to " bad faith."

In *Hotchkiss* v. *National Bank*, 21 Wallace (U.S.) 354, the court said : " A party who takes negotiable paper before it is due for a valuable consideration, without knowledge of any defect of title, in good faith, can hold it against all the world. A suspicion that there is a defect of title in the holder, or a knowledge of circumstances that might excite such suspicion in the mind of a cautious person, or even gross negligence at the time, will not defeat the title of the purchaser. That result can be produced only by bad faith, which implies guilty knowledge or willful ignorance."

The instrument must be complete and regular on its face.

Davis Sewing Machine Co. v. *Best*, 105 N.Y. 59, was an action to recover the value of certain notes diverted by plaintiff's president. When defendant purchased the notes they were complete and regular and signed by plaintiff's treasurer, but they were not signed by the president, although a blank ruled space with the title of his office printed thereunder was left at the foot of the instrument. It was conceded that the plaintiff was entitled to the notes unless the defendant was a *bona fide* holder thereof. The court held that any one buying commercial paper which remains incomplete and imperfect in some essential particular does not acquire the character of a *bona fide* holder.

He must be a holder " for value." This means that he must have given a valuable consideration for it, and it is not enough that it be a gift.

In *DeWitt* v. *Perkins*, 22 Wis. 473, the plaintiff, being acquainted with the defendant and knowing that he was responsible, purchased shortly before maturity a promissory note against defendant for $300, paying therefor $5. As between the original parties the note was invalid for want of consideration. Held, that the plaintiff was not a *bona fide* holder for value. The consideration paid by him was nominal. It was on the face of it merely either a gift or a subterfuge to get the note into other hands to cut off the defense of want of consideration.

We have discussed in the subject of contracts what is necessary to constitute a valuable consideration.

The purchaser of a negotiable instrument must take it before maturity, and if it is a bill of exchange that has been dishonored, without notice of previous dishonor. The mere fact that a note or bill is past due is considered sufficient notice of defect to put the purchaser on his guard, and a party buying past due paper can not be said to be a *bona fide* holder. If, therefore, in the case of a bill of exchange that has been presented for acceptance and dishonored, this fact is brought to the notice of the purchaser, he is not a *bona fide* holder.

Continental National Bank v. *Townsend*, 87 N.Y. 8, was an action of indorser against maker. The defense was a set-off against the original payee. On the last day of grace the note was indorsed to plaintiff. The question was whether or not the transfer was made before maturity. The court held that it was and that the plaintiff was a *bona fide* holder. The maker has the whole of the last day to pay, so it is not past due until the close of that day.

O'Callaghan v. *Sawyer*, 5 Johns. (N.Y.) 118, was an action by indorser against maker. Defendant offered to prove a set-off. At the time of the transfer of the note to the plaintiff it was overdue. The court held that the set-off should be allowed. The note had been long overdue and dishonored when it was indorsed, and the point is well settled that the indorser took the note subject to all the equities and to every defense which existed against it in the hands of the original payee.

6. DEFENSES

General Statement. — It can be stated as a general proposition that a *bona fide* purchaser before maturity and for value takes title free from all defects and defenses, or, as is often stated, "free from all equities" except such as affect the very existence of the instrument and which are said to constitute absolute defenses.

The absolute defenses are either cases in which no valid contract ever existed, or where the contract is declared illegal and void by statute.

No Delivery. — The instrument may never have been delivered. It is considered by the law merchant to be a sufficient delivery to hold the maker or acceptor, if it is handed over by the party himself or his agent either with or without authority, or if it gets into circulation through the negligence of the maker. The question is, did the maker deliver the instrument or was his act or representation responsible for its coming into the hands of *bona fide* holders? If this be true, he must suffer, although it was not his intention to deliver the instrument. On the other hand, if he has been deprived of the possession of the paper by fraud or theft, he can not be compelled to pay the amount named to any one, as in this case the instrument was never delivered and no contract existed.

In *Chapman* v. *Rose*, 56 N.Y. 137, defendant entered into a contract with one Miller to act as agent for the sale of a patent hay fork, and a contract was signed by both, also an order for one hay fork. Another paper was then presented to defendant which Miller said was a duplicate of the order. Defendant signed it without reading or examining it. It was the note in suit and plaintiff purchased it in good faith for value and before maturity. Held, that when one has the opportunity and the power to ascertain the exact character of the obligation he assumes, and he takes the word of another instead, he can not claim that he intended to sign a different instrument to defeat a *bona fide* holder. To avoid liability he must show he was guilty of no negligence or carelessness in signing.

If in the making of the instrument there was such fraud as would vitiate a contract, then no contract exists, and the maker or acceptor can not be held.

Walker v. *Ebert*, 29 Wis. 194, was an action against the maker of a promissory note by the holder, who claimed to have purchased for value before maturity. The defense was that defendant was a German, unable to read and write the English language, and that the payee fraudulently induced him to sign an instrument represented to him to be a contract of agency, which was in fact a promissory note. Held, that it was a good defense. The instrument never, in the contemplation of the law, existed as a negotiable instrument. The party not having been guilty of any negligence in signing, and his signature having been obtained by fraud, he was no more bound than if his signature was a forgery.

Alteration or Forgery. — Another failure of contract arises when there has been a material alteration or forgery, for in these instances the minds of the parties have not met in the contract. When the instrument has been materially altered and is in the hands of a holder in due course, not a party to the alteration, he may enforce payment thereof according to its original tenor.

Horn & Long v. *Newton City Bank*, 32 Kans. 518, was an action against Horn & Long, the makers of a promissory note. The note was given for a threshing machine, and was originally drawn payable to " H. C. Pitts' Sons Manufacturing Company," and after delivery to the company it was altered by substituting the name of " O. B. Hildreth " as payee. The alteration was made without the knowledge or consent of Long, and he never ratified the change. Horn and the payee made the change. Held, that this was a material alteration and released Long, although the bank was a *bona fide* holder for value.

Draper v. *Wood*, 112 Mass. 315, was an action against Wood & Higgins as makers of the following promissory note : —

" $1000. " NORTH HADLEY, Mar. 31, 1868.

" For value received, we promise to pay L. L. Draper, or order, one thousand dollars on demand, with interest at 12 per cent.

" GEO. A. WOOD.
" H. S. HIGGINS."

Higgins defended on the ground that the note he signed had been changed by substituting " we " for " I " and adding the words, " at 12 per cent." It was shown that Wood made the changes in good faith, but without consulting Higgins. Held, that the note was void as against Higgins.

Any alteration of a negotiable instrument which changes its legal effect is a material alteration.

Sullivan v. *Rudisill*, 63 Iowa 158, was an action upon a note. After the note was given by defendant, with Fuller as surety, the plaintiff innocently procured R to sign as surety. The court held the note void, but allowed a recovery upon the original consideration. When a promissory note has been innocently altered without any fraudulent purpose, the payee may recover in an action on the original consideration. It was also held that the signing by a party as a joint maker, after the execution by the original maker and without his knowledge and consent, is a material alteration.

There must be an intent to make the alteration, and it must be made, of course, without the consent of the maker or acceptor of the instrument. The alteration must also be made by a party to the instrument or one in lawful possession of it. The holder can not be prejudiced or injured by the act of a stranger without his consent.

In *Langenberger* v. *Kroeger*, 48 Cal. 147, a person not a party to the instrument, without authority wrote across the face of a draft the words, "payable in United States gold coin." Held, that the alteration was not such as to vitiate the draft, although, if the alteration had been made by the payee or by his instruction, it would have invalidated the bill, as the change was evidently material.

It will be seen from the foregoing paragraphs that when a signature to a negotiable instrument is forged, the party whose name is so used can not be held.

Want of Capacity to Contract. — The contract represented by the instrument may not be binding, for the reason that the party or parties did not have the capacity to contract; as, the note or bill of an infant or lunatic. Still, if a valid negotiable instrument comes into the hands of an infant, he may, if of full mental capacity, transfer it to another.

The mere fact that a contract is illegal is not an absolute defense to a negotiable instrument in the hands of a *bona fide* holder; but if the contract is expressly made illegal and void by statute, an absolute defense is created.

Equities. — Other defenses than those described as absolute are termed "equities," and are valid defenses between the original parties to the instruments, but, as we have learned, can not be set up against *bona fide* holders. Lack of consideration is a good defense as between the original parties, but not as against a *bona fide* holder for value. It is an equity, and not an absolute defense.

The fact that there is an absolute defense to an instrument does not discharge all of the parties to it, or through whose hands it has passed. As we have seen, such defense exonerates the maker or acceptor of a negotiable instrument, but it does not relieve the liability of the indorser, because every person who negotiates such an instrument warrants that it is genuine, that he has a good title to it, and that all prior parties have capacity to contract.

In *Williams* v. *Tishomingo Saving Inst.*, 57 Miss. 633, defendants indorsed a bill of exchange to which they claimed title through a forged indorsement. The court held that the indorser warranted the genuineness of the prior indorsements on the bill and also his title to the paper. Should it be ascertained even after the payment of the bill that any of the indorsements were forged, the drawee can recover the amount of the bill from the party to whom he paid it, and each preceding indorser may recover from the party who indorsed the bill to him.

7. DISCHARGE

Payment. — Negotiable instruments, like other contracts, are discharged by payment. A payment by the maker or acceptor to the holder, and the surrender of the instrument to him, ends the transaction and releases all the parties to the paper.

Slade v. *Mutrie*, 156 Mass. 19, was an action to recover the balance of a promissory note. The defendant paid plaintiff $125 and received the note and a receipt in full settlement of all accounts to date. The jury found that the plaintiff intended to receive the amount in full payment. The court said the delivery of a promissory note by the holder to the maker, with the intention of transferring to him the title of the note, was an extinguishment of the note and a discharge of the obligation to pay it.

Payment before Maturity. — But if payment is made before maturity, and the paper should again get into circulation, it would be valid in the hands of a *bona fide* holder who acquired it before maturity.

Stoddard v. *Burton*, 41 Iowa 582, was an action against the maker of a lost or stolen promissory note made January 5, 1866, payable to A or bearer, on or before January 6, 1868. The defense was that it had been paid to Thompson, a holder, on October 11, 1866. The court held that the note by its terms was payable at any time within two years after its date at the option of the maker. So it could not be said to be out of the ordinary course of business for him to pay it at any time, as that express provision was incorporated in the instrument, and the note not having been paid before maturity the plaintiff was not a *bona fide* holder.

Payment by Indorser. — Payment by one of the indorsers after the instrument has been dishonored does not discharge it, as the prior indorsers and the maker or acceptor are still liable. The payment to extinguish the instrument must be made by or for the party primarily liable.

The instrument may also be discharged by the intentional cancellation thereof by the holder or by any other act that would discharge a simple contract.

In *Larkin* v. *Hardenbrook*, 90 N.Y. 333, Loper executed a deed of certain premises to defendant, and in consideration thereof the note in suit was executed and delivered to the grantor, who thereafter intentionally canceled, destroyed, and surrendered the same to the defendant. The court said: "The rule is well settled that where the payee delivers up the obligation which he holds against another, with the intent and for the purpose of discharging the debt, in the absence of fraud, such surrender operates as a release and discharge of the obligation."

Discharge of Indorser. — An indorser or drawer is discharged by any act that discharges the instrument or that discharges a prior party. Thus, the third indorser on a promissory note would be discharged by any act that would discharge either the maker (which would cancel the instrument) or the first or second indorser. Any agreement on the part of the holder of a negotiable instrument to extend the time of payment, unless with the assent of the indorsers, discharges the indorsers' liability.

8. INTEREST AND USURY

Definition. — As the question of interest is one that very frequently arises in connection with negotiable instruments, it is well to consider it here. A common definition of interest is, "The compensation paid for the use of money." The amount upon which the interest is reckoned is called the principal. The interest is usually a certain annual per cent of the principal.

In most of the states the rate of interest is prescribed by statute and known as legal interest, and when no rate is designated by the parties this rate will prevail. In some states the legal rate is fixed at 6 per cent, in others 7 per cent. (See table, page 353.) The statutes of the different states also determine whether or not a higher rate may be agreed upon between the parties and, in most cases, say how high a rate may be charged by agreement.

The taking of a higher rate than that allowed by the statute of a particular state is called usury and is punished in some of the states by the forfeiture of all of the interest; in others, as in New York State, by the forfeiture of both principal and interest. Where such statutes exist, a person agreeing to accept usurious interest can not collect either the money due or the interest.

Originally the word "usury" was identical in meaning with interest, and meant any compensation taken for the loan or use of money, but the modern sense, as will be seen, is entirely different.

Claims on which Interest can be Collected. — Interest can be collected on all claims or amounts where it is mutually agreed by the parties that it is to be paid, as on a promissory note, which contains the words "with interest" or "with use," or some words to the same effect. It can also, without stipulation in the agreement, be collected upon debts from the time they become due until they are paid; in other words, all overdue debts draw interest. An illustration is the case of a promissory note containing no provision for interest, as such a note draws interest from the date it becomes due until it is paid, but does not draw interest before maturity.

In the matter of *Trustees*, etc., 137 N.Y. 95, the court held that interest may not be allowed in any case unless by virtue of some contract, express or implied, or of some statute or on account of default of the party, when it is allowed as damages for the default.

But when the amount of the debt is not determined and is uncertain, or where the debt consists of a running account with payments at different periods, it is held that interest does not attach.

In *Wood* v. *Hickok*, 2 Wend. (N.Y.) 501, plaintiffs were wholesale grocers and defendants country merchants. Defendants purchased different bills of goods of plaintiffs between February, 1824, and November, 1825, amounting in all to $1190.62, and made various payments, amounting in June, 1827, to $1191.25. In the suit the plaintiffs charged interest amounting to $64.87. No mention had been made of interest until in 1827, when an account was transmitted in which there was a barrel of brandy in dispute. Plaintiffs claimed it was the custom among grocers to charge interest after 90 days. Held, that the account was not liquidated, and an unliquidated running account does not carry interest unless there is an agreement between the parties that interest shall be allowed.

Compound Interest. — Interest upon interest can not be collected in the absence of a special agreement, and some jurisdictions do not allow it then.

QUESTIONS ON NEGOTIABLE INSTRUMENTS

1. Define negotiable instruments. What are the principal classes?

2. Name and explain the principal source of the negotiable instrument law.

3. Name the principal characteristics of a negotiable instrument.

4. Is the following a negotiable instrument? "Rochester, N.Y., Aug. 3, 1903. Due John Brown, one hundred dollars. Value received. George Smith."

5. An instrument is written in lead pencil in the following form: "Buffalo, N.Y. I, George Smith, promise to pay to Thomas McCarty, or order, fifty dollars. Value received." Mention three particulars in which this paper is not in the usual form.

6. "Philadelphia, Pa., Sept. 1, 1903. Five months after date I promise to pay George Williams the sum of twenty-five dollars. Value received. E. D. Parsons." Is this a negotiable instrument?

7. Is a promissory note payable in Mexican money a negotiable instrument?

8. Is there any reason why the following is not a negotiable instrument? Explain. "Three months after date, for value received, I promise to pay Charles Benham, or order, one hundred dollars, or ninety-five dollars if payable two months after date. Signed Elmer Clark."

9. Is an instrument payable to one of three different persons named negotiable?

10. State whether or not the following is a negotiable instrument. "For value received, I promise to pay to Thomas Rice, or order, one hundred dollars when he shall be married. Charles Ellis."

11. Draw a promissory note, and name each party to it.

12. Name three forms of promissory notes and illustrate each.

13. "One month after date, for value received, I promise to pay E. F. Sherwood, or order, two hundred dollars. James Grant, Edward F. Grant." What kind of promissory note is the above?

14. A note is signed James Willis by John Rogers, Agent. Which of the two parties does the signature hold?

15. A note is signed Frank Getman, agent of William Carr. Which is liable on the note, Getman or Carr?

16. A note is signed Erie Gas Co., Edward Booth, President. What is the effect of this signature in different states?

17. What is the agreement of a maker of a note as to paying the same?

18. Draw a bill of exchange. Designate the different parties to the same.

19. How does a bank draft differ from a bill of exchange?

20. Distinguish between foreign and inland bills of exchange.

21. Distinguish between time and sight drafts.

22. What is meant by accepting a draft, and what is the party called who accepts it?

23. What is the obligation of the party accepting the draft before and after the acceptance?

24. When must a presentment for acceptance be made?

25. When acceptance is refused what is said of the bill?

26. Define acceptance *supra protest*. Define virtual acceptance.

27. Draw a check. Designate the parties.

28. "The Merchants Bank of Rochester, Rochester, N.Y., Aug. 25, 1903. Thirty days after date pay to the order of George Harris one hundred and fifty dollars. William Copeland." Is this a check, or is it a draft?

29. When must a check be presented to the bank for payment? Upon whom will the loss fall in case of delay?

30. A check on a Rochester bank is given to A by B in Rochester on July 25. It is not presented for payment on the 26th, and on the 27th the bank fails. Is it A's or is it B's loss?

31. What is a certified check? If the check is certified by the drawer before its delivery and the bank fails before the check is paid, who loses? If the payee secures the certification after the check has been delivered to him and the bank fails before payment, who loses?

32. What is meant by negotiation of a negotiable instrument, and how is it accomplished?

33. Illustrate a full or special indorsement. A blank indorsement.

34. What is the contract or the undertaking of the indorser? Upon what is it conditioned?

35. When the indorser wishes to avoid personal liability, how may he indorse?

36. The indorsement on a one hundred dollar note is as follows: "Pay to X or order fifty dollars of the within note. Signed, Y." Is this a good indorsement?

37. Define presentment and demand.

38. If a note is payable at the Alliance Bank of Rochester, N.Y., where must presentment and demand be made?

39. When must presentment for payment be made?

40. Define days of grace.

41. When a negotiable instrument with days of grace falls due on Sunday, which is the last day of payment? If the instrument has no days of grace, which is the last day of payment?

42. A note without days of grace falls due on July 3, which is Sunday. What is the last day of payment?

43. If a note has days of grace, the last day of grace being Monday, July 4, what is the last day of payment?

44. A note was presented the day it matured at the maker's residence between eleven and twelve o'clock at night. Payment was refused. Was the presentment good?

45. A note was presented to the wife of the maker. No effort was made to present it to him personally. Was the presentment good?

46. After the instrument has been dishonored, what notice, if any, is required, and to which of the parties must it be sent? When must it be sent?

47. If no notice is sent to any of the indorsers, what is the effect?

48. What is protest, and upon what negotiable instruments is it necessary?

49. Define an irregular indorser. Define accommodation paper.

50. What is necessary to constitute the holder a *bona fide* holder for value?

51. Plaintiff purchased a negotiable note before maturity. The note on its face was for $500. The purchaser was acquainted with the maker and knew that he was solvent. He paid $25 for the note. Was he a *bona fide* holder?

52. If the purchaser had taken the above note after maturity and paid the face value, $500, for it, would he have been a *bona fide* holder?

53. A becomes the *bona fide* holder for value, of a note upon which the maker's name was forged. Can he collect of the maker? Can he collect of the indorser?

54. A made and delivered a promissory note payable three months after date to the order of B. B after receiving the note changed the time of payment to four months without the knowledge or consent of A. Did this affect A's liability on the instrument?

55. C becomes a *bona fide* holder for value, of a promissory note which was given from A to B without consideration. C sues A on the note and A sets up the defense of no consideration. Can C recover?

56. B executed a promissory note to C for $100 payable three months after date. One month after date he paid the note. The note instead of being destroyed was lost and came into the hands of X, a *bona fide* holder for value. Can X recover on the note?

57. Define interest. Define usury.

58. Brown makes a note for three months, but says nothing in reference to interest. He pays the note nine months after having made it. Can interest be collected upon it, and, if so, for how long?

AGENCY

1. IN GENERAL

Definition. — An agent is a person employed by another to do some act or acts for the employer's benefit or on his account. The person for whom the agent acts is called the principal. Agency is the legal relation existing between the principal and the agent. A person dealing with the agent is known as the third party.

The principal must be a person competent to make contracts, for no one can make a contract through an agent which he has not the power to make himself. The agent, since his acts are the acts of his principal, is not necessarily required to be competent to make a contract; therefore we find it to be the general rule, that any person with sufficient understanding to transact the business committed to his charge may be an agent. Infants or married women may be so employed, and may bind their principals by a contract which they could not make themselves.

It can readily be seen how impossible it may be for any one person to transact all his business without assistance; consequently we can easily realize the vast scope and great importance of the law of agency.

Classes of Agents. — Agents are usually divided into two classes, general and special.

General Agent. — A general agent is one who is authorized to transact all of his principal's business of a particular kind, or in a certain place. Having received from his principal a general authority to do certain acts, he is not limited to the performance of a specific act, but is permitted a certain amount of discretion in carrying on the particular line of business for which he is employed. The acts of a general agent, while acting within the scope of his authority, will bind his principal, whether or not they are in accordance with his private instructions. If he is apparently clothed with authority, the principal is bound.

Munn v. *Commission Co.*, 15 Johns. (N.Y.) 44, was a case concerning a general agent, and the court said: " The distinction is well settled between a general and a special agent. As to the former, the principal is responsible for the acts of the agent, when acting within the general scope of his authority, and the public can not be supposed to be cognizant of any private instructions from the principal to the agent; but where the agency is a special and temporary one, there the principal is not bound, if the agent exceeds his employment."

Special Agent. — A special agent is one who is appointed for a special purpose, or to transact a particular piece of business. He is given but limited authority. His acts do not bind his principal beyond the scope of the particular authority given him.

It is readily seen that the distinction is a difference in degree rather than in kind. In the case of a general agent there has been general power delegated, the authority is necessarily broad, and a person dealing with such agent may reasonably infer that he has the authority usually conferred upon such agents under like circumstances; while in the appointment of a special agent, the object is to accomplish a special purpose or to carry out a particular piece of business, and one would naturally infer the authority was limited.

2. RELATION OF PRINCIPAL AND AGENT

Agreement. — The relation of principal and agent may be created in several different ways. The ordinary way is by agreement, as where one man employs or appoints another to represent him in a certain transaction or in a general way. This is really an agency by contract, except in case of a gratuitous agent, and all the rules governing contracts govern also the relations of the principal and agent as between themselves.

The reason why a gratuitous agent is not an agent by contract is that, there being no consideration, the agreement can not be enforced as a contract, as we have learned in the chapter on contracts.

An agent by agreement may be appointed orally except in the following cases : —

First. Where by the terms of the agency the service is not to be performed within one year ; then, by the statute of frauds, the agreement must be in writing.

In *Hinckley* v. *Southgate*, 11 Vt. 428, defendant made a parol agreement in February with plaintiff that plaintiff would carry on defendant's gristmill for one year from April 1, next. Plaintiff offered to perform, but defendant would not allow him. It was held by the court that the case was clearly within the statute of frauds, since the work was not to be performed within one year ; consequently the parol agreement could not be enforced.

Tuttle v. *Swett*, 31 Me. 555, was an action upon a parol agreement to employ plaintiff for three years to labor for defendant in making powder casks, for which he was to be paid a certain price per day. Defendant refused to permit him to work, and it was held that the agreement could not be enforced, since the labor was not to be performed within one year and the contract was not in writing.

Second. When the contract between the principal and the third party is required to be under seal, the authority of the agent to execute the instrument must itself be under seal.

Hanford v. *McNair*, 9 Wend. (N.Y.) 54. Here A by writing, not under seal, authorized an agent to enter into a contract for the purchase of a quantity of lumber. The agent entered into a sealed contract for such purchase. Held, an agent can not bind his principal by sealed instrument unless he has authority under seal to do it.

In *Johnson* v. *Dodge*, 17 Ill. 433, the question was as to the proper authority of the agent to sell land. The court said the power to convey land must be in writing and under seal, as the land can be conveyed only by deed, and the power to convey must be of equal dignity with the act to be executed.

Power of Attorney. — The formal method of appointing an agent is by a written instrument under seal known as a power of attorney.

A form similar to that shown on the following page is used when the power conferred is the authority to sell and convey certain real estate. When the power conferred is to execute a deed, mortgage, or any other instrument that is to be recorded,

Know all Men by these Presents. That

I, John E. Martin, of Albany, Albany County, New York
have made, constituted and appointed, and by these presents do make, constitute and appoint
Joseph A. Dey, of Rochester, New York, my *true and lawful attorney*
for me *and in* my *name, place and stead* to grant, bargain, and
sell all my real estate situated in the said Rochester, New York,
or any part thereof, for such price, and on such terms, as to him
shall seem best, and for me and in my name, to make, execute,
acknowledge, and deliver good and sufficient deeds and conveyance for the same, either with or without the covenants of warranty: ————————————————————————
giving and granting unto my said attorney full power and authority to do and perform
all and every act and thing whatsoever requisite and necessary to be done in and about the
premises, as fully to all intents and purposes, as I *might or could do if personally*
present, with full power of substitution and revocation, hereby ratifying and confirming all
that my *said attorney or* his *substitute shall lawfully do or cause to be done by*
virtue hereof.

In Witness Whereof, I *have hereunto set* my *hand and seal the* 18th
day of October *in the year one thousand nine hundred and* five

Sealed and delivered in the presence of

H. D. Hopkins

John E. Martin

State of New York
City *of* Albany   } *SS.*
County of Albany

On the eighteenth ——— *day of* —— October ——— *in the year nineteen*
hundred and five ———————————— *before me personally came* ———
———————— John E. Martin , ————————————
——————————————————————————

to me known and known to me to be the individual described in, and who executed the foregoing
instrument and he duly ——— *acknowledged that* he *executed the same.*

W. H. Parsons   Notary Public

the power of attorney must be so executed as to entitle it to be recorded in the same place. This requires that it shall be acknowledged in substantially the form shown on page 162 before a notary public, or some other officer empowered by law to take such acknowledgment.

This form may be used to confer other authority by inserting, in place of the authority to sell real estate, the exact authority intended.

Ratification. — The second way in which the relation of principal and agent may be created is by ratification.

The assent of the principal to the act of the agent may be given either before or after the agent's act. If given before, then it is an agency by agreement and has already been explained. If given after the act has been performed by the agent, it is a ratification of this act and gives the same effect to it as though there had been a previous appointment. This may be true in a case where the agent had no previous authority whatever, or where the agent had some prior authority but exceeded this authority in the particular act. The ratification operates as an extension of the authority to this act.

In *Merritt* v. *Bissell*, 84 Hun (N.Y.) 194, it was held that where a person was clothed with some authority as agent, the ratification by his principal of his unauthorized acts relates back and makes such acts of the agent the acts of the principal from the beginning, the same as though they had been duly authorized at the start.

The ratification to bind the principal must be made with a knowledge of all the material facts ; if made under a misunderstanding, or through a misrepresentation, the principal will not be bound. The principal must repudiate the agent's unauthorized act within a reasonable time after he learns of it, or he will be presumed to have ratified it. The ratification may be by express words or by accepting the benefits of the act.

In *Pike* v. *Douglass*, 28 Ark. 59, A without authority purchased a bill of goods for persons about to form a copartnership, in their name and on their credit as partners. They received the goods and sold them. One of the partners afterwards repudiated the purchase, claiming that the other partner was to buy the goods and that the agent had no authority to buy for him, and he so advised the sellers.   Held, this was not sufficient.   He should have restored the goods, but as they kept the goods they were liable as partners ; they had ratified the act by retaining the benefit.

But if the principal ratifies the act it must be as a whole, for he can not accept the benefits of a part and reject the remainder.

An axiom of the law is, " A man can not take the benefits of a contract without bearing its burdens."

In *Eberts* v. *Selover*, 44 Mich. 519, a subscription agent canvassing for a history to cost $10, had a book for signatures, and on this it was printed that no terms except those printed thereon should be binding.   A justice of the peace consented to sign on condition that his office fees from that time to the time of delivery of the book should be taken in payment.   This was agreed, and he was given a written memorandum by the agent to that effect.   Held, if the company ratified the contract it must be upon the terms agreed upon.   As the agent went beyond his authority they could repudiate the contract and refuse to deliver the book, but they could not repudiate part and still hold the subscriber.

Necessity. — The third way in which the relation between principal and agent may be created is by necessity.

This is where the relations or positions of the parties are such that the authority of the principal is presumed.   The leading illustration of this is the case of husband and wife.   The wife can contract for the necessities of the household and bind the husband for their payment.

Benjamin v. *Dockham*, 134 Mass. 418, was an action for the price of milk delivered to defendant's wife, who because of his cruelty was living apart from him.   Held, that as the wife is authorized by law to pledge her husband's credit, it is a case of compulsory agency and her request is his request.

Another illustration is that of a shipmaster, who has authority in case of necessity to purchase supplies for the vessel and pledge the credit of the owner.

In *McCready* v. *Thorn*, 51 N.Y. 454, an action was brought against the owners to recover for services and advances rendered to the master of the ship.   The master was running the vessel under an arrangement with the owners whereby the master was to furnish everything and divide the profits, but the plaintiff had no notice of this.   The owners of the vessel were found liable for moneys and labor so advanced.

3. OBLIGATION OF PRINCIPAL TO AGENT

Compensation. — The principal is under obligation to the agent to compensate him for his services.

When the agreement fixes the compensation the agent is to receive, this, of course, will control.

Wallace v. *Floyd*, 29 Pa. St. 184. Here the plaintiff agreed to work for a given time at a certain salary. He stayed beyond the time, and nothing was said about the salary for the additional period. It was held that he could recover the salary only at the rate agreed upon. It was said that the best valuation of services was that mutually agreed upon by the parties themselves.

In the absence of an express contract, the law will imply an agreement to pay what the services are reasonably worth, unless it can be fairly inferred that the services were intended to be gratuitous.

Even if the service was unauthorized but is subsequently ratified, and the benefit is accepted by the principal, the agent, ordinarily, can recover for the service to the same extent as though the service had been originally authorized.

In *Gelatt* v. *Ridge*, 117 Mo. 553, plaintiff was employed to sell real estate on the owner's terms. He sold on other terms, but the principal ratified the sale. Held, that the agent was entitled to his commissions as originally agreed.

The principal is also under obligation to reimburse the agent for any sums which he may have paid out, or for which he may have become individually liable in the due course of his agency and for the principal's benefit.

Maitland v. *Martin*, 86 Pa. St. 120, was a case in which a broker purchased for B certain bonds which B left in his hands several years, when he directed that they be sold. It was then learned that three of the bonds had been repudiated by the state where issued. Held, that the broker might be reimbursed. That the loss fell on B if the broker acted within the lines of his duty and in good faith.

The agent is further entitled to indemnity from his principal for the consequences of any act performed within his authority and in the execution of his employment. But to be entitled to indemnity the act must be lawful, or the agent must have been ignorant of the fact that the act was illegal.

In *Moore* v. *Appleton*, 26 Ala. 633, plaintiff brought an action to be reimbursed for damages which he had been obliged to pay because of certain acts performed by him as agent for defendant in dispossessing a third party of lands claimed by the defendant and which plaintiff had reason to believe belonged to defendant. Held, that the act was not manifestly illegal, and that the law implies a promise of indemnity by the principal for losses which flow directly and immediately from the execution of the agency.

4. OBLIGATION OF AGENT TO PRINCIPAL

Agent must obey Instructions. — The agent is under obligation to his principal to obey the principal's instructions. So long as the agent carries out his instructions he is protected, but if he goes contrary to them and loss ensues, he is liable for the damage; as, where an agent is instructed by his principal to send a certain claim for collection to A, and instead he sends it to B and loss ensues, the agent is liable.

In *Whitney* v. *Merchants Union Express Co.*, 104 Mass. 152, the Express Company received for collection a draft with instructions to return at once if not paid. They instead held the draft until the drawee wrote for some explanation. They then failed to present it for two days after the drawee had received a reply from the drawer, and at this time the drawee became insolvent. Held, that the Express Company was liable to the drawer.

Agent must use Judgment. — The agent owes the duty to his principal to exercise judgment and skill necessary to the prudent and careful discharge of his agency. This prudence and skill can generally be said to be the same as is ordinarily observed by prudent and careful men, under similar circumstances and engaged in similar business.

Whitney v. *Martine*, 88 N.Y. 535, was a case where an attorney was employed as agent to loan moneys on bond and mortgage. He made loans when the parties giving the bonds were insolvent and took mortgages on realty already mortgaged. The principal lost, and it was held that the attorney was liable to his principal for the loss.

Thus, an agent to purchase a car load of wheat must exercise and possess only such knowledge and skill as is common to careful dealers in grain; while an agent to purchase an expensive and intricate engine is bound to exercise the caution and skill of an engineer.

Fiduciary Relation. — There exists between the principal and his agent what is said to be a fiduciary relation, which means that their relations are such that the utmost good faith is required in their dealings. An agent can not, therefore, acquire any rights that are contrary to the interests of the principal. He must not act for both the principal and the third party in a transaction without their consent.

Walker v. *Osgood*, 98 Mass. 348, was an action by a real estate agent for commissions. Defendant had employed him to sell or trade his farm and the agent effected an exchange and made an agreement with the third party that he was to receive from him a commission. It was held by the court that the broker was the agent of the owner and could not act for the third party, and if he exacted from the third party a promise of compensation, he could not recover of the owner for his services, even though an exchange or sale was effected. The interests of the parties are adverse, and an agent for one can not act for the other without his knowledge and consent.

Neither must the agent use his position or authority for his own benefit.

In *Bunker* v. *Miles*, 30 Me. 431, defendant was employed by plaintiff to buy a certain horse for him for $80 or as much less as he could, and was to have $1 for his trouble. Defendant bought the horse for $72.50, and returned to plaintiff no part of the $80. The court allowed plaintiff to recover the balance of $7.50, holding that the agent could not make a profit for himself out of the transaction.

An agent authorized to sell or rent will not be permitted to buy or lease the property himself without the principal's consent.

Kerfoot v. *Hyman*, 52 Ill. 512. Here plaintiff owned certain land and employed defendant to sell it for a certain amount. The defendant bought it himself and took the title in the name of a third party, but for his own benefit without the owner's consent, and at the same time had a part of it sold for as much as he obtained for the whole of it for the plaintiff. Held, that the agent must account to the plaintiff for the excess received, and the remainder not sold will revert to the principal.

Also an agent commissioned to compromise a claim can not purchase it at a discount and then enforce it in full against the principal. The agent is under obligation to his principal to render a true account of all of the proceeds and profits of the agency.

In the absence of an express agreement to the contrary the agent must render an account to his principal upon demand or within a reasonable time.

Subagents. — Another obligation of the agent to his principal is to act in person, except when authorized either by his principal or by established custom, to appoint subagents. The reason for this is obvious; the principal employs the agent because of his confidence and trust in his ability and honesty to act in his stead, and the agent appointed can not delegate to another the duty or trust which has been confided to him.

Still, an agent can in some cases appoint subagents to perform duties which do not involve an exercise of his discretion, but are merely mechanical or ministerial acts.

In *Renwick* v. *Bancroft*, 56 Iowa 527, A was employed to sell a piece of realty and to fix the price, etc. After looking over the property he employed B to find a purchaser and B did find such a purchaser and sold the property. It was held that the agent might properly appoint such a subagent, as there was no discretion placed in the subagent, and A could employ such party as he wished to help him in carrying out the agency.

Sometimes, from the nature of the case, it is implied that the agent is to appoint another agent for his principal. In that case the first agent is relieved from liability for the acts of the third party if he himself uses care and discretion in his appointment; whereas if he but employs a subagent, he is personally liable to the principal for the acts of the subagent to the same extent precisely that he would be in case they were his own acts.

A very interesting illustration of this point is the case of a man depositing at his home bank commercial paper payable at some other city. The question then is, does the owner of the paper authorize the home bank to appoint subagents, or does he authorize it to employ additional agents in his behalf?

It is evident that, whichever view is maintained, it is within the contemplation of the parties that the home bank can not execute the agency alone but must have aid at the point where the note or paper becomes due. If the correspondent bank is a subagent, then the home bank is liable for its acts the same as for its own; but if the home bank had the authority to appoint the correspondent bank an agent for the principal, the correspondent bank is liable directly to the principal, and the home bank, if it used care in appointing the agent, is exonerated.

In New York, Michigan, and some other states the first theory is held.

Allen v. *Merchants Bank*, 22 Wend. (N.Y.) 215, is a case where a draft was drawn by plaintiff in New York on a Philadelphia merchant and deposited by plaintiff in the Merchants Bank of New York. Defendant bank sent the draft to the Philadelphia bank. It was presented by the Philadelphia bank notary, but he did not properly protest it, and because of the lack of the proper protest plaintiff lost. Held, that the bank receiving a draft is liable for any neglect of duty in the collection, whether arising from the default of its officers, its correspondents abroad, or the agents of its said correspondents.

The second theory is held in Iowa, Massachusetts, Pennsylvania, and other states.

In *Guelich* v. *National State Bank*, 56 Iowa 434, a bill of exchange was deposited with defendant bank of Burlington, Iowa, against a New York party. Defendant sent it to the Metropolitan Bank of New York for collection. This bank failed to present it for payment and protest in proper time. Held, when the holder of a bill of exchange, payable at a distance, deposits it in a local bank for collection, he thereby assents to the course of business of banks to collect through correspondents, and the correspondent bank becomes his agent and is responsible to him direct for its negligence in failing to present the bill within the proper time.

Gratuitous Agent. — It may be well to note also the legal relation of the agent who undertakes to perform some service for the principal without compensation.

In such a case the promise being without consideration is not enforceable, and the agent can not be held liable for neglecting or refusing to perform.

Thorne v. *Deas*, 4 Johns. (N.Y.) 84. Here A and B were joint owners of a vessel and A voluntarily undertook to get the vessel insured, but neglected to do so, and the vessel was lost. Held, that no action would lie against A for his non-performance, though damage resulted to B, as there was no consideration for A's promise.

But if the agent enters upon the performance of the undertaking, he is bound to exercise skill and care in what he does.

In *Williams* v. *Higgins*, 30 Md. 404, a party undertook voluntarily and gratuitously to invest money for another. It was held that in such a case the gratuitous agent must use due diligence and exercise proper caution or he will be liable, and if he is given positive instructions, he will be liable if he disregards them.

The question of gratuitous agent often comes up in the case of bank directors, who fill their offices without compensation.

Delano v. *Case*, 121 Ill. 247, held, if bank directors are guilty of negligence in permitting their bank to be held out to the public as solvent, when in fact it is insolvent, and thereby induce parties to deposit their money there and it is lost, such depositors may recover from the directors, as they are bound to exercise care and dilligence in their offices.

5. OBLIGATION OF PRINCIPAL TO THIRD PARTY

Scope of Authority. — The main object of agency is to effect a contractual relation between the principal and the third party. The identity of the principal may be disclosed or it may be withheld. In the case of either a disclosed or an undisclosed principal, he is bound by such acts of the agent as are within the actual or apparent scope of his authority.

The difficult question then is to determine what is the scope of his authority. If the principal clothes the agent with apparent authority to do an act, the principal is bound, although the agent had private instruction to the contrary, or had a limit put upon this authority.

A doctor might employ an agent to buy him a particular horse. He has no apparent authority to buy a team or any other horse. But when a stock dealer employs an agent to buy horses for him, the agent has apparent authority to buy a team, although he may have had private instructions to the contrary. The one is clearly a special and the other a general agent.

It seems settled that when the agent has apparent authority the principal is bound. It is only required in such a case that the person dealing with the agent, acting with average prudence and in good faith, is justified in believing that the agent possesses the necessary authority.

Notice to Agent. — It is the rule that notice to the agent of anything within the scope of the agency is notice also to the principal. And the principal is chargeable with knowledge of all the facts that have been brought to his agent's attention in the transaction in which the agent is acting for the principal.

If this were otherwise, the principal would be in a position to claim ignorance whenever he might wish to do so, and therefore would be in a better position than if he dealt with the third party direct.

6. LIABILITY OF PRINCIPAL FOR TORTS OR WRONGS OF AGENT

General Rule. — The principal is liable for the contractual obligations of his agent in his behalf, and there are various ways in which he can be rendered liable by the agent for the agent's torts or wrongful acts.

The rule is that the principal is liable for the wrongs committed by the agent in the course of his employment and for the principal's benefit.

This is obviously true where the principal commands or ratifies the act, and we find that it is also true where the principal neither ratifies nor commands it. The law considers that when a person chooses to conduct his affairs through another, he must see that they are managed with due regard for the rights and safety of others.

Dempsey v. *Chambers*, 154 Mass. 330, was an action for damages in breaking a plate-glass window. It was proved that the party who delivered coal for the defendants, and in so doing broke the window, was not authorized to deliver coal for them, and they did not know of his doing it. Later, after they knew of the broken window, they presented a bill for the coal. Held, that by ratifying the acts of this man they become liable for his negligent acts.

Fraud and Negligence. — Fraud is one of the wrongs of frequent occurrence in the relation of agency, the agent having made false and fraudulent representations in carrying out his principal's business. It is the general holding that the principal is liable for the agent's fraud in the course of the principal's business and for his benefit.

The negligence of the agent is among the wrongs for which the principal is liable, if such negligence was committed in the ordinary discharge of the agency.

In *Brady* v. *Railroad Co.*, 34 Barb. (N.Y.) 249, an agent failed for four days to present a draft and the party drawn on failed. Held, that the principal was liable for the negligence of his agent in not presenting the draft in proper time.

When the wrong is committed by the agent in the course of his employment, and even to benefit himself personally and not his principal, some authorities hold that the principal is nevertheless liable.

In *Cobb* v. *Railway Co.*, 37 S.C. 194, an engineer willfully and unnecessarily blew the whistle and frightened a horse. Held, that the railway company was liable for acts done by its engineer maliciously, wantonly, and willfully while in the exercise of his duties, whether in the course of his employment or not.

Others hold the principal is not liable.

In *Stephenson* v. *Southern Pacific Co.*, 93 Cal. 558, a railway engineer intentionally and wantonly backed his engine toward a street car that was crossing the track, with the simple intent of frightening the passengers, without colliding with the car. As a result the plaintiff, a passenger, was frightened and jumped from the car and was injured. Held, that the act of the engineer was without any reference to the service for which he was employed and not for the purpose of performing his employer's work, and that the principal was not responsible.

Liability for Malicious Wrongs. — But it is held that the principal is not liable for the malicious wrongs or crimes of the agent, unless he expressly authorized the same. There is an exception to this in the case of laws or statutes which are said to be in the nature of police regulations designed to promote the safety and health of the community. In cases of this kind the principal is liable, even though the agent act directly contrary to instructions and without his knowledge and consent. The laws regulating the speed of automobiles on the public roads, and those prohibiting the selling of liquor on Sunday or to children, may be mentioned as examples under this head.

Commonwealth v. *Kelley*, 140 Mass. 441, has relation to a statute which prohibited the closing on Sunday of curtains or blinds, so as to obscure the interior of premises where liquor was sold. The owner had given instructions that they be kept open, but the bartender, without his knowledge, closed them. Held, that the owner was liable. The statute forbids him to do the prohibited act, or permit it to be done, and it includes the acts of his servants as well as his own.

7. OBLIGATION OF THIRD PARTY TO PRINCIPAL

It is clear that the third party is liable to the principal for contracts entered into with the agent, within his authority, or which are subsequently ratified by the principal.

The third party is also liable to the principal for moneys or property obtained from the agent by duress or fraud; hence, if an agent is compelled to pay illegal charges to protect his principal's interest, the principal may recover of the third party.

The third party may also be liable to the principal for fraud or wrong, or for collusion with the agent to injure the principal.

Mayor v. *Lever*, 1891, 1 Q. B. 168, is an English case in which the plaintiff was proprietor of gas works. It was the duty of the company's manager to obtain and recommend bids for coal and supplies. Defendant bribed him to recommend his bid, and added the price of the bribe to the bid. In an action against them, it was held that plaintiff could recover the damages from the agent who had accepted the bribe, or from the defendant who had given it. They were joint wrongdoers, and could be held jointly or severally.

He is also liable for unlawfully interfering with the agent in the performance of his duties as agent.

In *Railroad Co.* v. *Hunt*, 55 Vt. 570, it was held, that maliciously to cause the arrest of plaintiff's engineer while running a train, and then to delay the train and thereby damage the company, is actionable, and the railroad company can recover for such damages from the person so causing the arrest.

8. OBLIGATION OF AGENT TO THIRD PARTY

When an agent makes a contract on behalf of his principal, he may in certain cases bind himself. If he holds himself out as having authority to act for a principal in a transaction in which he has no such authority, he is liable to the third party for the damages suffered.

In *Kroeger* v. *Pitcairn*, 101 Pa. St. 311, A, the agent for an insurance company, obtained and delivered to B a policy of insurance on B's store, containing a clause that no petroleum should be kept on the premises. B told A it was necessary to keep a little, and A assured him if he kept only a barrel it need not be noted in the policy, and was all right. The store burned, and B could not recover because he had a barrel of petroleum. Held, A, the agent, was liable, as he gave positive assurance in excess of his authority.

The agent is also presumed to represent not only that he has authority, but that his principal was competent to give such authority.

In the case in which there is no real principal, but the one so represented is fictitious, the agent himself becomes the principal, and is liable as such.

Lewis v. *Tilton*, 64 Iowa 220, held, an unincorporated organization can not be a party to a contract, and persons contracting in the name of such an organization are themselves personally liable either as being themselves in fact principals, or as holding themselves out as agents for a principal which never in law existed.

In some instances, the agent expressly pledges his credit, and of course in such cases he is liable.

9. TERMINATION OF THE RELATION OF PRINCIPAL AND AGENT

The agency may be terminated by limitation, by acts of the parties, or by a change in the condition of the parties.

Termination by Limitation. — If the contract of agency is by its terms to continue for but a limited time, the agency terminates when the time expires; or if the particular business for which the agency was created has been completed, the agency is terminated.

Moore v. *Stone*, 40 Iowa 259. An agent was employed to negotiate for the purchase of certain land. He obtained the contract for the conveyance, the first payment was made, and the agent was paid for his services. Held, the agency was then terminated as the object for which the agency was created had been accomplished. Here the agent, after he was paid for his services, bought in the property at tax sale, and plaintiff sought to set it aside on the ground that he was still his agent, but as the agency was held to be terminated, the court refused to interfere.

Termination by Act of the Parties. — Under certain conditions either party may terminate the relation. This may be done by mutual agreement, by the principal revoking the agent's authority, or by the agent renouncing the agency.

Since the principal appoints the agent, and the relation is one of confidence for his own protection, he has the power to terminate it at will. It is therefore the general rule that the principal may terminate the agent's authority at any time and with or without good cause. This of course gives the agent a claim for damages if the agency is revoked contrary to agreement.

It may be well to note here the distinction between the power to terminate the agency and the right to terminate it. The principal generally has the power, but if it violates an agreement with the agent, he does not have the right to so terminate the agency, and he is therefore liable to the agent for damages.

In *Standard Oil Co.* v. *Gilbert*, 84 Ga. 714, there was a written contract for one year, fixing the agent's compensation. This was renewed the next year, and from then on was lived up to, but nothing was said about the agreement. Held, that there was a tacit renewal from year to year, and that the principal could not, during the year, deprive the agent of his salary before the expiration of the year. Though the power of revocation existed, the right to revoke did not exist.

The revocation of the agency by the principal need not be made in any formal way, but may be by oral instructions or by written notice. In some cases it may be implied by the conditions; as, when a principal gives an agent authority to sell his house, and before the agency is executed it is destroyed by fire, in which case a revocation must be implied.

A revocation is binding only upon those who have notice of it. The principal must therefore not only give notice to the agent but to those who upon the strength of the previous authority are likely to deal with him; otherwise he may be held for the acts of the agent after the revocation.

There is a class of cases in which the principal has no authority to revoke the agency. This is where, as it is said, the agency is coupled with an interest; as when the agent has an interest in the subject-matter of the agency by way of security.

For example, when a person has possession of personal property with power to sell and apply the proceeds to the payment of a debt due the agent, such a case constitutes a power coupled with an interest.

In *Knapp* v. *Alvord*, 10 Paige Ch. (N.Y.) 205, a cabinet maker on going abroad, employed an agent to carry on his business, and gave him the full and entire control of his property, with a written power to sell any or all of the furniture or stock, and apply the proceeds to the security or payment of a certain note, indorsed by said agent and a third party, or for any renewals upon which the agent might become liable. Held, the agent had a power coupled with an interest which survived the principal's death, and the agent could sell after such death.

As to the rights of the agent to renounce the agency, it seems that he also has the power but not the right to renounce at will. And it may be either express or implied; as, if the agent abandons his work, the principal may consider the agency as renounced.

10. CHANGE IN CONDITION OF THE PARTIES

The agency may also terminate by a change in the condition of the parties.

Death. — The death of either the principal or the agent terminates the agency and it is no longer binding on the estate of the deceased or the survivor. And in this case no notice of the termination need be given to third parties. The agency terminates upon the principal's death, and any contract made thereafter by the agent is a nullity.

Farmers Loan and Trust Co. v. *Wilson*, 139 N.Y. 284, held that the power of an agent to collect rent due his principal ceased upon the principal's death, unless the agency was coupled with an interest. And payments made thereafter do not bind the principal's estate, although made in ignorance of his death.

Insanity. — If either the principal or the agent become insane, the effect is to terminate the agency, as the principal is no longer competent to enter into a contract, and the agent, if insane, is not competent to carry out the intentions of the principal. But if the principal has not been legally declared insane, persons dealing with the agent in ignorance of his insanity are protected.

Any other cause that may render the agent incompetent to carry out the agency will also terminate the agency, as the illness of the agent or his imprisonment.

Bankruptcy. — The mere insolvency of either party does not affect the agency, but it will be terminated when either party becomes technically bankrupt, because when a party becomes a bankrupt his property passes out of his hands and he is unable to carry out any contract in reference to it. The above rule does not apply, however, when the agency is coupled with an interest. In the case of the bankruptcy of the agent his authority ceases except to perform some formal act not involving the transfer of any property.

Marriage. — Under the common law many restrictions were placed about a married woman, the control of her property passing to her husband. Consequently, upon her marriage, any contract of agency in which she was principal was dissolved, as she no longer had the power to deal with her own property. But every state has passed laws enlarging the rights of married women, and in most instances giving them full power to own and manage their property and to carry on their own separate business. The result is that a married woman may appoint agents, and the act of marrying does not affect her status in a business way and therefore has no effect on the relation of principal and agent, nor does it dissolve an agency then existing.

War. — It is the general law in the different states in this country that the existence of a state of war between the country of the principal and that of the agent terminates the agency. This is because of the rule prohibiting all trading or commercial intercourse between two countries at war.

QUESTIONS ON AGENCY

1. Define agent. Define principal.
2. Brown & Co. appointed one Cary, who was but 19 years old, as their agent to buy certain goods for them. Later they refused to take the goods, setting up that the agent was an infant and the contract could not be enforced. Was this a good defense to the contract?
3. Into what two classes are agents divided?

4. X, a farmer, is on his way to town and Y, his neighbor, asks him to bring back for him a wheel for his mowing machine, which has been broken. X agrees to do this without any compensation. X forgets to obtain the wheel and returns without it. Y is unable to proceed with his work and sues X for damages. Can he recover?

5. The Brown Medicine Co., by oral agreement, employ Hartman, who is an experienced agent, to travel for them, advertising and selling their medicines. By their agreement he is to travel in every state in the Union and is to spend not less than two weeks in each state. Hartman before commencing his work obtains a better offer elsewhere, and the company sue him for breaking the contract. Can they recover?

6. An agent was authorized to sell a car of coal for his principal at $6 a ton. Contrary to his authority he sold it for $5 per ton, and received $120 down. The principal accepted the $120 and delivered 20 tons of coal, then refused to deliver more until the full price of $6 a ton was paid. Could the principal refuse to deliver the balance under the contract?

7. A man running an automobile through the country meets with an accident and is unable to proceed farther. Another party, who is a stranger to him, comes along with a horse and wagon and the first party asks to be driven to the nearest railroad station, 4 miles away. When he reaches there he refuses to pay anything for the services. Can the man with the horse and wagon recover anything? If so, how much?

8. A party employs an agent to sell certain shares of railroad stock for him at par value. The agent sells them for $10 a share above par and then remits his principal the par value of the stock. Can the agent retain the balance, or can the principal recover it from him?

9. Brown & Co., through the Merchants Bank of Rochester, draw on S. P. Kendall, merchant, of New York City. The Merchants Bank forward the draft to their correspondent, the Chemical National Bank of New York City. This bank negligently fails to present the draft for one week, and in the meantime S. P. Kendall becomes insolvent. Brown & Co. sue the Merchants Bank of Rochester. Can they recover?

10. The American Bicycle Co. opened a store in Buffalo and placed X there in charge of the business. He employed Y as head clerk at $20 per week. X was expressly instructed by the company not to pay any employee over $10 per week. Y worked several weeks and sued for his wages. Could he recover?

11. A is driving on the city streets, and through the negligence and carelessness of the street car motorman he is run into and injured. Can A recover of the street car company?

12. An agent, without any authority so to do, accepts a bill of exchange in the name of his principal, believing that the principal will ratify his act. The principal refuses to ratify. Is the agent liable?

13. An agent was employed by A to sell his team of horses. In a railroad accident the horses were killed. Did this terminate the agency?

14. A appointed B, his agent, to represent him for one year at a salary of $100 a month. At the end of 3 months he discharged him without cause. Could A so discharge his agent, and if so, was he liable to B for damages?

15. In the above case B deals with parties as the agent of A after he has been discharged. The parties with whom he deals have no knowledge of his discharge. Can they hold A on the agreement made by B?

16. An agent employed to sell goods for his principal, sells to B the day after his principal's death, neither B nor the agent knowing that the principal is dead. Can B hold the principal's estate on the contract?

17. If in the above case the principal had become insane, but had not been legally so declared, could the principal have been held?

BAILMENT

1. IN GENERAL

Definition. — Bailment is defined as a delivery of some chattel by one party to another, to be held according to the special purpose of delivery, and to be returned or redelivered when that special purpose is accomplished. As we have already seen, a bailment differs from a sale, in that the title to the property does not pass in a bailment. Practically every case in which one receives and holds or handles the property of another, without buying it or receiving it as a gift, is a case of bailment. When one borrows or lends a book, hires a horse, or sends a package by express, he is within the rules of bailment. Where the possession but not the title has passed to the vendee, which case we have considered in the chapter on sales, we find that the vendee holds as bailee; as, for instance, when property is taken on trial.

Hunt v. *Wyman*, 100 Mass. 198, was an action for the price of a horse. Plaintiff had the horse for sale and agreed to let defendant take it and try it; if he did not like it he was to return it on the night of the day he took it in as good condition as he got it. Almost as soon as the horse was delivered to defendant's servant it escaped from him without the servant's fault and was injured so that the defendant could not try it. The horse was not returned in the time stated. Held, to be a bailment and not a sale, therefore the plaintiff could not recover.

In *Nelson* v. *Brown*, 44 Iowa 455, it was held that a contract acknowledging the receipt of grain for storage, "loss by fire and the elements at the owner's risk," with the option to the party receipting for it to return grain of equal test and value, constitutes a bailment which is converted into a sale whenever the bailee disposes of the grain.

The parties to a bailment are the bailor, or the owner of the chattel who delivers it over, and the bailee, who is the party vested with the temporary custody of the chattel.

Classification. — Bailments are generally classified according to the Roman law under five heads.

1. Deposit; a bailment of goods to be kept by the bailee gratuitously for the benefit of the bailor.

2. Mandate; a delivery of goods to the bailee who is to do something to them gratis.

3. Loan for use; a loan of personal property for the benefit of the bailee without recompense.

4. Pledge or pawn; a bailment as security for a debt.

5. Hiring, which is the loaning of a chattel for a consideration or reward.

Another and more practical division of the subject of bailment is made according to the benefit or recompense as follows: —

1. Bailment for the benefit of the bailor; deposit and mandate.

2. Bailment for the benefit of the bailee; loan for use.

3. Bailment for the benefit of both the bailor and bailee; pledge and hiring.

The last Bailment, for the mutual benefit of both parties, is again classified as ordinary and exceptional, the exceptional bailments being those of postmaster, innkeeper, and common carrier. All other cases of bailment for mutual benefit of bailor and bailee are ordinary bailments.

Degrees of Diligence and Care. — In all cases of bailment a certain degree of diligence or care is required of the bailee. A lack of the required diligence or care is termed negligence and renders the bailee liable.

By the early authorities the diligence or care required of the bailee was classified into degrees, and to a certain extent this division is still adhered to. The absence of the required diligence renders one liable for negligence. Where the bailment is for the benefit of the bailor alone, no benefit nor remuneration accruing to the bailee, it is not expected nor required of the bailee that he shall exercise the degree of care or diligence necessary in a case in which he is paid for his services. So it is said he is bound to exercise slight diligence toward the property in his care and is liable for gross negligence.

In the case of a bailment for the benefit of both parties, a benefit accrues to the bailee and a greater degree of diligence is demanded of him than in the former case, therefore it is required that he exercise ordinary diligence and he is liable for ordinary negligence. The bailment for the sole benefit of the bailee, being without any benefit to the bailor, imposes upon the bailee a greater degree of diligence than in either of the other cases, and it is said that great diligence is exacted of him while he is answerable for even slight negligence.

Ordinary care is defined to be the care which persons of ordinary prudence under like circumstances are wont to bestow upon their own property of the like description. Slight care or diligence is something less than ordinary care, yet not amounting to an utter disregard of the property. It may be said to be the care that might be exercised by a very careless person. Great care or diligence, on the other hand, is that which would be exercised under similar circumstances by a more than ordinarily prudent and careful person.

In *First National Bank* v. *Ocean National Bank*, 60 N.Y. 278, plaintiff deposited bonds in defendant's vaults for safe keeping and defendant charged nothing therefor. The vault was burglarized and the bonds stolen. The court held that a gratuitous bailee is liable only for gross negligence and is not bound to take any special or extraordinary measures for the security of the property intrusted to him.

In *Mariner* v. *Smith*, 5 Heisk. (Tenn.), 203, Smith left $900 in gold at the counting house of Mariner & Curtis to be sold if 50 per cent premium could be had. The gold was placed, in the presence of Smith, in the safe of Mariner & Curtis where the firm kept their own money. The safe was afterwards broken open and the gold, as well as the money belonging to Mariner & Curtis, was taken. The court held that the question as to whether the bailment was for reward or not depended upon the intention and contract of the parties. The liability of a bailee without reward is to be determined by his *bona fide* performance of the fairly understood terms of the contract, which will be ascertained by the express contract explained by the surrounding circumstances, or by the failure to perform the terms of the contract as it was understood by the parties at the time.

Besides the degree of care or diligence that is demanded of the bailee, the law requires that he act honestly and in good faith. He must not abuse his trust nor sell, pledge, or otherwise deal with the property in his hands as though he were the owner.

Tortious Bailee. — In the case of a tortious bailee, that is, one who holds the possession of the property through an unlawful or wrongful act, as theft, trespass, and fraud, or having received it in a rightful way misappropriates it or applies it to a use other than that intended, he is liable to account absolutely for the property, and although it may be injured or lost while in his possession, but without his fault, he must nevertheless account for it.

A thief who steals a horse, and while driving it is run into by a runaway team which kills the horse, is liable for the value of the horse, although he was guilty of no negligence. Or, if a man hires a horse to drive to Albany and instead goes to Troy, and on the way the horse is injured without the fault of the bailee, still he is absolutely liable.

In *Fisher* v. *Kyle*, 27 Mich. 454, defendant hired a horse of plaintiff to drive to a certain place. He drove beyond the place stated, and the horse fell dead while being driven. The defendant was held liable for the value of the horse. A person who hires a horse for a specific journey and drives him beyond that journey takes upon himself all the consequences of such additional drive, and if the horse dies while being so driven, the hirer is liable.

Liability Varied by Contract. — As a general rule the parties to a bailment may by contract vary the rights or liabilities of the parties, making the liability of the bailee either greater or less than it would otherwise be, except that the law will not allow the bailee to be exempt, even by contract, for the consequences of his own willful misconduct.

In *Archer* v. *Walker*, 38 Ind. 472, A and B were partners in the banking business. To enable the firm to draw sight drafts on New York they borrowed from B a number of U. S. bonds and deposited them in New York as collateral security against overdrafts. The firm expressly agreed in writing that the bonds were "to be returned or accounted for to B." The bonds were stolen from the bailee in New York. Held, that the firm was liable to B for the loss.

2. BAILMENT FOR THE BAILOR'S SOLE BENEFIT

Deposit and Mandate. — This class of bailment arises frequently in everyday life. Every undertaking of a friend or neighbor to hold or convey an article of personal property gratuitously and as a favor comes under this class. A man may gratuitously take the chattel belonging to another to keep it in his custody. To illustrate, A stores B's wagon in his barn gratuitously ; or he takes it to perform some work upon it, as to paint it without charge ; or it may be he carries it from one place to another, as to take B's wagon home for him. A bailment for the bailor's benefit may come under any one of these three classes, or it may combine two or all of them.

Two of the divisions of the Roman law are included under this head. They are deposit, which is the placing of a chattel with the bailee to be kept by him without pay, and mandate, which is the bailment of a chattel upon which the bailee is to do something gratuitously.

Liability of Bailee. — An agreement by the bailee to carry out the gratuitous bailment, as we have seen, can not be enforced because of the lack of consideration, but when the bailee receives the property and carries out the bailment, he is bound to do it with care, and he will be liable for gross negligence or for wrongful acts in relation thereto. The act of the bailor, in surrendering the possession of the chattel upon the faith of the bailee's undertaking, furnishes sufficient consideration. A person who finds property and takes it into his possession is a gratuitous bailee, and is bound to care for it as such.

It is often a difficult question to determine whether it is a gratuitous bailment or a bailment for the mutual benefit of the parties, that is, whether or not the bailee is entitled to compensation. The original intent of the parties is the test. If the bailee receives the chattel in the usual course of his business, and business usage and his ordinary method of dealing give him the right to demand compensation, the bailment is not considered gratuitous, even though nothing was said as to compensation.

Pattison v. *Syracuse National Bank*, 4 T. & C. (N.Y.) 96, was an action to recover the value of bonds stolen from the defendant's bank, where they had been deposited by plaintiff for safe keeping. Nothing was said about compensation at the time of the deposit. Held, that if the defendant had the right to demand compensation by its course of dealing with depositors, the bailment was not gratuitous. The degree of diligence required of defendant depended upon whether or not the bailment was gratuitous.

But if the bailee undertakes the service for a near relative or personal friend, or out of mere charity or favor, and if the trust puts him to but little trouble and the bailment is out of his usual course of business, it is presumed to be without compensation.

In *Dart* v. *Lowe,* 5 Ind. 131, plaintiff, a merchant in Peru, Ind., being about to go to Cincinnati, had placed in his hands by Thayer, another merchant, $81 with which to buy goods for Thayer. When Thayer handed plaintiff the money he remarked that he would rather pay him for his trouble than go himself. To this plaintiff made no reply. This, with other money, was stolen from plaintiff on his way and through no gross negligence on his part. Plaintiff bought goods on credit for Thayer and charged him nothing for his services as buyer. The question arose as to whether it was a bailment for hire or a gratuitous bailment. The court held that to render the bailee liable for negligence as a bailee for reward when he is acting without the scope of his ordinary occupation, it must be expressly proved that he was to receive a compensation. The court further held that when the bailment is for the sole benefit of the bailor, the law requires only slight diligence and makes him liable only for gross negligence.

Bailment through an Agent. — Either party to a contract of bailment may act through an agent, and delivery to the agent of the bailee is delivery to the bailee.

Degree of Care Necessary. — In this class of bailment, as we have seen, only the lowest degree of care and diligence is required of the bailee; that is, slight care, and he is not held liable for loss or injury unless guilty of gross negligence, as was held in *Dart* v. *Lowe.*

Griffith v. *Lipperwick,* 28 Ohio St. 388, was an action to recover the value of certain government bonds, deposited by plaintiff with defendants as gratuitous bailees and stolen from defendant's banking house. The bonds, when deposited, were in a tin box, the key of which was retained by plaintiff. Defendants had a small burglar proof safe in which they kept similar bonds of their own and other depositors, but plaintiff's and similar bonds of another depositor were kept outside, the other depositor consenting that his should be so kept. Held, to be a question for the jury as to whether or not this was gross negligence. Good faith generally requires that such bailee should keep the goods intrusted to him with as much care as he ordinarily keeps his own of the same kind, and he should also keep them with such degree of care as would be reasonable, considering the nature of the goods and the circumstances of the bailment.

McKay v. *Hamblin,* 40 Miss. 472, held, that when there is no contract for the safe keeping of property and no compensation agreed to be paid for the custody of the same, the party in possession is a mere depositary, and, in the event of loss, is liable only for gross neglect.

Ordinary care may be defined as the care which a prudent man takes of his own property; less care might be expected when the bailor knows the bailee's habits and the place in which he is to keep, or the manner in which he is to handle the goods, for when he knows these conditions, the law presumes that he agrees that the goods should be so treated.

Coggs v. *Bernard*, 2 Ld. Raymond 909, was an early English case that was decided about the year 1700. The defendant, it seemed, undertook without compensation to move some casks of brandy from one place to another, but by his carelessness a quantity was spilt. It was held that if a man undertakes to carry goods safely and securely he is responsible for any damages they may sustain in the carriage through his negligence, although he is not a common carrier and is to have nothing for his services.

In *Spooner* v. *Mattoon*, 40 Vt. 300, plaintiff and defendant were soldiers in camp, occupying tents 10 rods apart. Plaintiff had considerable money, and fearing it might not be safe, left it with his friend, the defendant, without expectation of reward, for safe-keeping. For two nights he so left it, and came for it in the morning. On the third morning he did not call for it, and defendant started for plaintiff's tent with the money. He put it under his arm inside of his vest, so that the pocketbook would not be seen. It slipped out and was lost. Held, that the defendant was not guilty of gross negligence, so was not liable.

No absolute rule can be laid down as to just how a gratuitous bailee must care for the chattel in his charge. The circumstances of the case control; that is, different care would be required of the person who receives a watch or a valuable vase, from that expected of the person who receives a wagon or a load of stone. It is said that a gratuitous bailment seldom demands skilled labor or care, and the gratuitous bailee is excused from the results of inevitable accident, accidental fire, etc.

Use of Property. — In bailments of this class the question arises as to whether or not the gratuitous bailee may use the thing bailed to him. Clearly, he can not make any use of it except for the bailor's benefit, otherwise the bailment would not be included in this class. When the bailee accepts the custody of an animal, he undertakes to feed and care for it. Proper care would require him to drive a horse for exercise, to milk a cow, etc., but the profits derived from the use of the animal in this class of bailment go to the bailor. The bailee has a right to incur such expenses in caring for the thing bailed as are necessary.

In *Devalcourt* v. *Dillon*, 12 La. An. 672, A deposited in the hands of B merchandise to be sold, the proceeds to be applied on a debt which he owed to B. Held, that whatever useful and necessary expenses B incurred in fulfilling the bailment were chargeable to A.

Termination. — This class of bailment is terminated either by the accomplishment of the purpose of the bailment or by the express act of either party. The bailee may surrender the article bailed, and so terminate the relation, or the bailor may make a demand and recover the chattel. When the bailment is for the purpose of accomplishing some act, as the delivery of a chattel from one place to another, the bailee, after undertaking the bailment, must accomplish it with at least slight care, or be responsible for breach of contract. But by mutual assent, the bailment may be terminated at any time. The delivery of the identical chattel is necessary. If it is in a bettered condition, the bailee derives no benefit; and if in worse, it is not his loss unless due to his gross negligence. If it is lost, he is liable in so far as the loss is due to his lack of slight diligence or care.

3. BAILMENT FOR BAILEE'S SOLE BENEFIT

Definition. — This class of bailment consists of the gratuitous loan for use. The bailee is what we call in ordinary language, the "borrower." When a man lends his lawn mower or his bicycle to a friend to use and afterwards to be returned, the loan is a bailment for the bailee's sole benefit.

The bailor must voluntarily give the possession of the article to the bailee without exacting any recompense for its use. This bailment must be distinguished from the loan of something that is to be consumed and afterwards to be paid back in kind, as flour or grain, which was under the Roman law, *mutuum*, or a "loan for consumption," but which is in fact no bailment at all, but a barter; that is, the exchange of the particular property for another of a like kind.

The loan may be for a definite period or at the will of the bailor, who may terminate it whenever he pleases.

In *Clapp* v. *Nelson*, 12 Texas 370, plaintiff sued to recover the possession of a wagon and two mules which he had loaned to the defendant for "a day or two," but which defendant had neglected to return. Held, that when property is loaned for a definite period or for a day or two or a week or two, if it is not returned at the end of the longer period, the lender can bring an action for it without first making a demand for the property.

Responsibility of Bailee. — The bailee being the only one benefited, the duty devolves upon him to exercise the highest degree of care or diligence in the use of the chattel, or, as it is expressed, he is bound to use great diligence, and is responsible for every loss which is occasioned by even slight negligence.

In *Hagebush* v. *Ragland*, 78 Ill. 40, defendant borrowed a horse of plaintiff to drive on a visit to his brother, and when the horse was returned it was so injured that it died. The court held the defendant liable, and said that when an animal is borrowed without hire, the borrower is bound to take extraordinary care of it, and if a failure of such duty results in injury to the lender, the borrower will be liable.

Bennett v. *O'Brien*, 37 Ill. 250, held, that the loan of domestic animals necessarily involves their keeping, and the expense thus incurred by the borrower is not a compensation to the lender which changes the gratuitous character of the bailment. In a suit brought by the lender against the borrower of a horse which dies in the possession of the latter, it devolves upon the borrower to show that he exercised extraordinary care toward the property borrowed.

Wood v. *McClure*, 7 Ind. 155, held, that the borrower is to use extraordinary diligence in regard to property loaned to him, and is responsible for the slightest neglect; but if the property perish, or is lost or damaged, without any blame or neglect on his part, the owner must sustain the loss.

Great diligence, then, is such as one more than ordinarily careful would bestow upon his property under like circumstances. Such a high degree of care being required of the gratuitous bailee, he is held strictly to the terms of the bailment, and when he deviates from these terms he is liable for the loss or damage ensuing.

In *Martin* v. *Cuthbertson*, 64 N.C. 328, plaintiff borrowed a horse to ride to the residence of one Cline and return next day, but instead he rode a mile and a half farther and in a different direction. The horse died during its absence on the third day after leaving home. It was admitted that there was no negligence. Held, that without regard to the question of negligence the bailee is liable for any injury which results from his departure from the contract.

But where the borrower, while using the chattel within the terms of the bailment, encounters some accident whereby the thing loaned is injured or lost without even slight negligence on his part, he is not liable.

Watkins v. *Roberts*, 28 Ind. 167, was an action for the value of a horse loaned by plaintiff to defendant. The defense was that while defendant, who had borrowed the horse to go to a certain place and return, was on his way, and without any fault or negligence on his part, he was met by some cavalry soldiers of the United States, who forcibly took the horse from him. It was held to be a good defense, and rendered the defendant free from liability.

If the chattel is injured or destroyed by inevitable accident or by fire, or if it is an animal and dies a natural death, the loss will not fall upon the bailee unless he is in fault.

In *Beller* v. *Schultz*, 44 Mich. 529, plaintiff loaned a flag to defendant. After it was hoisted a hailstorm came up and damaged it. Held, that in the absence of proof that defendant had failed to take due care of the flag he was not liable. A borrower of property is not an insurer, even though it be gratuitously loaned.

Use of Property. — As we have seen, this class of bailment carries with it the right to use the chattel, subject to such conditions and limitations as the bailor may be reasonably supposed to have made. Such expense as may be necessary to preserve the chattel while in use is to be paid by the borrower, as feeding and sheltering a horse or other domestic animals. But any extraordinary expense which wholly preserves the property for the owner may properly be chargeable to the bailor.

As soon as the bailment is ended, either by the expiration of the term, the act of the bailor, or the mutual agreement of the parties, the borrower must immediately deliver the property to the bailor or his order.

4. BAILMENT FOR MUTUAL BENEFIT

Definition. — This class of contract differs from those just considered in that the benefits to be derived are mutual instead of being confined to one side. It is a business transaction rather than an act of favor or friendship.

Bailments of this class may consist of (1) the hired service about a chattel, (2) the hired use of a chattel, or (3) pledge or pawn.

In mutual benefit bailments it is essential that there be a recompense for the use of the chattel or for the work to be bestowed upon it. The amount may be definitely fixed or, in the absence of an agreed price, it may be such as shall be determined to be just and reasonable.

In *Chamberlin* v. *Cobb*, 32 Iowa 161, plaintiff owned a horse for which he had no use, and, to avoid the expense of keeping it, requested defendant to take it and do his work with it in consideration of its feed and keep. Held, to be not a mere gratuitous loan, under which defendant would be required to exercise extraordinary care, but a contract for the mutual benefit of both parties, under which defendant was required to exercise ordinary care in the keeping and care of the animal.

Like all other bailments, the possession of the chattel must be intrusted to the bailee, and as in other contracts, the parties must be competent to contract and the object of the bailment must be lawful.

Hired Service about a Chattel. — In the hired service about a chattel the bailment may be for the purpose of having the chattel stored or cared for, or it may be for the purpose of having work performed upon it, or for the purpose of having it carried from place to place. Among the hired custodians who store or care for property are safe depositaries, who for a consideration keep valuables in a safe place, and warehousemen, who for a certain charge keep goods and merchandise in storage. The hired work upon a chattel includes that of the wagon-maker who takes a wagon to repair it, of the watchmaker who takes a watch to adjust it, and of other classes of mechanics who receive chattels to bestow labor of different kinds upon them. The hired carriage of a chattel may be performed by a private carrier, who for hire undertakes to transport a particular chattel, or the public or common carrier who follows as a business the conveying of chattels or persons. Private carriers are within the usual rules of a mutual benefit bailment, while public carriers, including railroads and express companies, come within a special class, having exceptional liabilities imposed upon them by law, which will be discussed later.

Pennewill v. *Cullen*, 5 Harr. (Del.) 238, was an action against the owner of a boat, for damage to a load of corn which was spoiled by water getting into it. Defendant's boat was generally employed to carry coal for a certain party from Philadelphia to New York and on returning to bring lime to defendant. Three or four times the boat had carried loads for other parties. The question was as to whether or not the defendant was liable as a common carrier. The court held the test to be whether the defendant held himself out to the public as engaged in the business of a common carrier. It was not necessary that his trips should be regular between the same places. If engaged in the business of carrying grain for others generally, to and from any point, he was a common carrier. But if he kept his vessel for his own use, he would not be liable as a common carrier, even though he chartered or hired it to another by special agreement.

In the bailment for hire the degree of care or diligence required of the bailee is said to be ordinary diligence, or such care as a prudent person exercises toward his own property under like circumstances. He is therefore liable for loss or injury to the chattel caused by ordinary negligence or, in other words, a failure to bestow ordinary care and diligence.

In *Jones* v. *Morgan*, 90 N.Y. 4, plaintiff stored certain household goods in a building owned by defendant and rented by him for that purpose. Plaintiff had a room allotted to her. Most of the goods were stolen by employees in charge of the buildings. Held, that the defendant was a bailee for hire and bound to exercise ordinary care and prudence. The plaintiff was given a judgment.

In *Maynard* v. *Buck*, 100 Mass. 40, defendant was a drover who received cattle to drive from Brighton to Worcester, for hire. He received two head of cattle from plaintiff and while driving them the herd became frightened by a train and the two wandered away. Held, that the defendant was bound to use the same care in regard to the cattle that men of ordinary prudence would exercise over their own property under the same circumstances. The plaintiff recovered.

While the chattel is in the possession of the workman employed in working upon it, if it is destroyed by inevitable accident or through some natural cause and without any fault upon his part, he will not be liable.

A greater degree of care is required of the safe depositary who stores jewelry and valuables than is required of a cattle keeper. So the exact care and precaution required of the bailee depends much upon the circumstances of the particular case.

Morehead v. *Brown*, 51 N.C. 367, was a case in which a bailee, to store and keep cotton for hire, permitted it to remain with the roping off, the bagging torn, and the under portion in the mud and water so that it became stained and much of it was destroyed. The court held that there was a want of ordinary care and the defendant was liable.

A keeper of horses who carelessly leaves doors or gates open so that the animals are lost or injured can be held liable.

In *Swann* v. *Brown*, 51 N.C. 150, defendant, a keeper of a livery stable, permitted the owner of certain horses to go into the stable at a late hour of the night and take them out, in consequence of which, a horse belonging to plaintiff made his escape and was lost either by passing out with the other horses or afterwards, as the door was left partly open. Held, that the defendant was guilty of lack of ordinary care and was liable. Ordinary care was said to be that degree of care which, under the same circumstances, a person of ordinary prudence would take of the particular thing were it his own.

When the bailee is to perform some work upon the chattel, he must exercise such skill as a prudent workman of the same class would bestow upon a similar undertaking. And for a failure to exercise ordinary skill he will be liable as for a lack of ordinary diligence.

In *Smith* v. *Meegan*, 22 Mo. 150, defendant took plaintiff's boat to make certain repairs upon it. Held, that he was bound to use ordinary diligence in the care of the boat and was liable for any damages to it occasioned by launching it into the river at a time and under circumstances of great danger which ought to have been foreseen and which resulted in the destruction of the boat.

Thus it is apparent that the skill required in different cases varies greatly according to the nature of the work required, but in all cases honesty and good faith are required of the bailee.

The bailee, for hire, has the right to the undisturbed possession of the chattel during the accomplishment of the purposes of the bailment, and when the work is completed he has the right to demand suitable compensation. This compensation may be fixed in advance or left to be computed later on a basis of what is just and reasonable.

Redelivery. — When the service required by the bailment has been completed, it is the bailee's duty to deliver the chattel to the bailor, and it is the duty of the bailor to pay the compensation. The delivery back must be to the bailor, his agent, or to his order. It is customary for warehousemen who conduct places of storage, also wharfingers who keep wharves on which goods are received and shipped for hire, to give to the bailor, or owner of the goods, at the time the goods are delivered, a receipt known as a warehouse or wharfinger's receipt. These receipts are generally considered as representing the property itself and are assignable from one person to another, and the warehouseman is held to be the bailee of the person to whom the receipt is transferred.

Dodge v. *Meyer*, 61 Cal. 405, holds, that a bill of lading represents the property for which it is given, and by its indorsement, or delivery without indorsement, the property in the goods may be transferred where such is the intent in making the indorsement or delivery.

Lien. — Although, as we have said, it is the duty of the bailee to deliver back the chattel, still he may keep possession until he is paid for his services on the chattel or payment has been tendered to him. The bailee therefore is said to have a lien upon the chattels for his services.

Harris v. *Woodruff*, 124 Mass. 205, held, that a person has a lien for the expenses incurred and skill bestowed upon a horse delivered to him to be trained to take part in running races.

Low v. *Martin*, 18 Ill. 286, held, that a warehouseman has a lien for proper charges upon grain stored in his warehouse, and he may retain possession of it to secure the payment of such charges.

This lien holds only for the service bestowed upon the particular chattel, and lasts only while the bailee retains possession.

In *Tucker* v. *Taylor*, 53 Ind. 93, defendant, a mechanic, received a wagon to repair. In payment for his labor he was to have the use of the wagon and a horse to take a journey. After the work was done the defendant permitted the owner to take the wagon with the understanding that it was to be returned at a later day and the horse sent with it so that he could make the journey. The owner having failed to furnish the horse and wagon, the defendant asserted his lien and sold the wagon. This action was brought by the original owner to recover the wagon. Held, that defendant lost his lien when he relinquished the possession of the wagon to the owner. The court also held that there was no lien if the agreement was that the labor should be paid for on a future day.

Hired Use of a Chattel. — The hiring of a chattel for use is frequently illustrated in everyday transactions. The hiring of a horse at a livery stable, or the hiring of a rowboat on the river, are each included in this class. After the contract is made it is the bailor's duty to deliver the chattel and to allow the bailee or hirer to have possession for the agreed purpose or during the stipulated time.

In *Hickok* v. *Buck*, 22 Vt. 149, defendant leased plaintiff a farm for one year, and agreed to provide a horse for plaintiff to use during the term. He furnished a horse at first, but took it away and sold it before the expiration of the term. Held, that plaintiff had an interest in the horse for the period, and could recover damages from defendant for taking it away.

It is the bailee or hirer's duty to use the chattel with care, and for no other purpose than that for which it was hired. He also has a further duty to return it at the termination of the bailment and to pay the consideration for its use. As in other instances of a mutual benefit bailment, the bailee must use ordinary care and diligence. This is the rule only when the chattel is used as agreed. And if the bailee uses the hired property in a way materially different from that mutually agreed upon, he is in most instances liable absolutely for any resulting loss or injury. This is illustrated in the case of *Fisher* v. *Kyle*, on page 183.

Pledge or Pawn. — This class of mutual benefit bailments consists of the loan or deposit of a chattel as security for some debt or agreement. This mode of securing a debt differs from a chattel mortgage in that the possession is transferred in

the pledge, while in the case of a chattel mortgage the possession is generally retained by the owner. In the mortgage the
title passes conditionally to the mortgagee, while in a pledge it
remains in the bailor.

Collateral security is another term applied to this class of
bailments, but the term has a broader meaning and includes
chattel mortgages as well. The name " pawn " is the old expression, and is still in use as applied to a class of persons called
pawnbrokers, who make a business of loaning money on articles
of personal property deposited with them. But the same object
is accomplished by the banker who loans money and accepts as
collateral security, stocks, warehouse receipts of grain, bills of
lading, etc. From this we can see that the subject of a pledge
may be any kind of personal property, including bills and notes,
certificates of stock, bonds, and bank deposits. But the thing
pledged must be in existence, for if it has ceased to exist, the
pledge is void; as, in a case where the chattel has been burned
or, if an animal, it is dead.

Boynton v. *Payrow*, 67 Me. 587, held, that the giving of a savings bank
book to a third person for delivery to a creditor as security for a debt will
create a valid pledge of the book and deposit.

The pledgee must exercise ordinary care and diligence toward the thing pledged, and when the property is delivered as
security for a particular loan, it can not be held as security for
any other.

In the case of *Baldwin* v. *Bradley*, 69 Ill. 32, a quantity of whisky was
pledged for money borrowed, and a few weeks later another lot was pledged
for another loan. Each pledge and loan was separate from the other. Held,
that each pledge was security for the loan made at the time, and not both for
the first loan.

The bailee must keep the chattel in his possession, and if he
voluntarily surrenders possession to the owner, the benefit of the
bailment or pledge as security is lost. An exception is the redelivery of the thing pledged to the bailor for some temporary
purpose and with the understanding that the pledgee is again to
have possession, in which case the security is not lost.

The pledgee has the right to use the chattel pledged if it is of such a nature that it requires use; for instance, a horse may be driven for exercise. But if the article pledged would be the worse for usage, then the pledgee is prohibited from using it. All profits derived from the article pledged belong to the pledgor and must be accounted for to him, but all necessary expenses for the keeping of the property are chargeable to the owner.

In the case of *Androscoggin Railroad Co.* v. *Auburn Bank*, 48 Me. 335, it was held that when a pledgee holds as collateral security bonds upon which interest accrues at certain periods, the pledge necessarily implies an authority in the pledgee to collect the interest and hold it on the same terms as the pledge itself.

The pledgee has a right to the undisturbed possession of the chattel pledged. After the pledgor has made default in paying the debt secured, the pledgee may sell the chattel, after giving the pledgor a reasonable notice of the time and place of sale, which notice must be preceded by demand of payment. The sale, unless the pledgee is a pawnbroker, must be by public auction, and the goods must be struck off to the highest bidder.

In *Stearns* v. *Marsh*, 4 Denio (N.Y.) 227, defendant sent plaintiff ten cases of boots and shoes as collateral security for a note of defendant's, due November 5, which plaintiff held. From November 2 to 15 plaintiff advertised an auction sale of boots and shoes and sold the goods so pledged on the latter date without any notice to defendant. They sold for a very low price, and plaintiff sued for the balance of the note. The shoes were worth the face of the note. It was held that he could not recover. The pledgee can not sell the pledged property until he has called upon the debtor to redeem the property, and he must also give him notice of the time and place of sale.

In case the pledged property consists of notes, bills, or bonds, which will soon become due, the proper procedure is to hold them until maturity and collect them if possible, applying the proceeds on the debt.

Union Trust Co. v. *Rigdon*, 93 Ill. 458, held, that a pledge of commercial paper as collateral security for a debt does not, in the absence of a special power to that effect, authorize the pledgee to sell the security so pledged either at public or private sale upon default of payment of the original debt by the pledgor. The pledgee is bound to hold and collect the same as it becomes due, and apply the net proceeds to the payment of the debt so secured. The pledgee has no right, unless in extreme cases, to compromise with the parties to the security for a less sum than its face value.

The pledgor has the further remedy of bringing an action in the equity court to foreclose his claim upon the article pledged, and when large amounts are involved, this is a frequent procedure. When the original debt has been discharged without recourse to the property pledged, the pledgor is entitled to the return of his chattels, the object of the bailment having been accomplished. But before the pledgor is entitled to the return of the chattels pledged, the principal debt and also the interest and all necessary expenses incidental to the pledge must be paid. A tender made by the pledgor to terminate the pledge must include both the interest, if any, and all such necessary expenses.

5. INNKEEPERS

Definition. — Aside from the classes of bailment already discussed there are mutual benefit bailments which, because of the extraordinary diligence and care required of the bailee, are termed exceptional bailments. Innkeepers and common carriers are the principal illustrations of this class.

An innkeeper is one who keeps a house, or inn, for the lodging and entertainment of travelers. In the modern sense he is a hotel keeper, an inn being the same as our hotel or tavern. The innkeeper or hotel keeper differs from a boarding-house keeper in that his is a public calling and he is required by law to receive and give accommodations to all persons of good behavior who apply and offer to pay for their accommodation, unless his house is full. Boarding-house keepers, or restaurant keepers, can receive or refuse such persons as they please.

In *Pinkerton* v. *Woodward*, 33 Cal. 557, it was held that an inn is a public place of entertainment for all travelers who choose to visit it. It is distinguished from a private lodging or boarding house in that the keeper of the latter is at liberty to choose his guests, while the innkeeper is obliged to entertain and furnish all travelers of good conduct and means of payment, everything which they have occasion for as travelers on their way. A traveler who enters an inn as a guest does not cease to be a guest by proposing to remain a given number of days, or by ascertaining the price that will be charged, or by paying in advance for his entertainment. This question arose in a suit to recover gold dust brought by plaintiff to defendant's hotel and, at defendant's suggestion, deposited in the safe, from which it was afterward stolen. The court held the landlord liable, and stated the rule to be that an innkeeper is liable as an insurer of the goods of the guest committed to his care unless the loss is occasioned by the act of God, or the public enemy, or by the neglect or fraud of the guest.

Neither a company owning the sleeping cars attached to a train nor a steamship company can be held to be an innkeeper.

In *Pullman Palace Car Co.* v. *Smith*, 73 Ill. 360, Smith purchased a ticket on the Palace Car Company's car and while asleep on the trip his money was taken from his vest pocket, the vest being under his pillow. In an action for the money it was held that Palace Car Companies are not liable as innkeepers.

Clark v. *Burns*, 118 Mass. 275, held, that a steamship company is not liable as an innkeeper for a watch worn by a passenger on his person during the day or kept within reach at night, although the passenger pays a round sum for transportation, board, and lodging.

Guests. — The relation of innkeeper arises only with reference to such parties as are his guests, a guest being one who as a transient traveler partakes of the entertainment of the inn or hotel. He may be a guest, although he does not stay over night.

In *Read* v. *Amidon*, 41 Vt. 15, plaintiff and his father drove to defendant's hotel with their horse and wagon. They had the horse cared for, went in and laid off their coats, had dinner and staid until evening, when they left. The court held that this created the relation of innkeeper and guest.

In *Walling* v. *Potter*, 35 Conn. 183, plaintiff resided about half a mile from defendant's hotel. Plaintiff went to the hotel one evening, staid all night and had his breakfast, for which he paid. Held, that the relation of innkeeper and guest existed, and the defendant was liable as such for money lost by plaintiff at the hotel.

A person receiving a gratuitous accommodation is not a guest. To create the relation of guest the innkeeper must receive pay for the accommodation.

Innkeeper's Liability. — The innkeeper is a bailee of the property and baggage of the guest, and this includes the horse that is placed in the innkeeper's stable as well as the wearing apparel, jewelry, and money of the guest. By the common law the responsibility of the innkeeper as bailee was exceptionally great. He was in most cases held to be an insurer of the goods and liable if they were lost, even without any fault on his part, unless the loss was occasioned by the guest's negligence or by an act of God, — flood, lightning, etc., — as illustrated in the case of *Pinkerton* v. *Woodward*, which we explained on page 197.

In *Hulett* v. *Swift*, 33 N.Y. 571, plaintiff's goods were destroyed by fire while he was a guest at defendant's hotel. The cause of the fire was unknown, but plaintiff was free from negligence. Held, that the innkeeper was liable. An innkeeper is an insurer of property committed to his custody by a guest unless the loss be due to the negligence or fraud of the guest, or to the act of God or the public enemy.

Other cases go so far as to relieve the innkeeper from liability in case of loss if he can show positively that he was in no way negligent, but this is a modification of the common law rule.

In *Howth* v. *Franklin*, 20 Tex. 798, it was held that when property committed to the custody of an innkeeper by his guest is lost the presumption is that the innkeeper is liable for it, but he can relieve himself from that liability by showing that he has used extreme diligence.

The innkeeper is responsible for the acts of his servants and employees the same as for his own acts.

Rockwell v. *Proctor*, 39 Ga. 105, was a suit against defendant, an innkeeper, for a coat which had been left by plaintiff who was a guest at defendant's hotel. The coat had been given to a negro in charge. Held, that the defendant was liable as innkeeper for the act of his servant.

Therefore the innkeeper is liable for any theft of the guest's property, and he is not excused on the plea that he selected his servants carefully and performed his own duty well.

Limitation of Liability. — The statutes in most of the states now allow the innkeeper to relieve himself from the extreme rigor of the common law, permitting him to limit his responsibility for money and valuables by requiring the guest to deliver them into his special custody. This is generally done by requiring that they be placed in the innkeeper's safe. But notice of this requirement must be given to the guest, or the common law liability will attach.

Bodwell v. *Bragg*, 29 Iowa 232, held, that the mere posting of notices in the room of a guest, limiting the liability of the landlord if certain directions are not observed, does not operate as notice to the guest unless he reads it or his attention is called to its contents.

Termination of Relation. — The liability of the innkeeper for the guest's personal property exists as long as the owner of the property maintains his relation as guest of the hotel or inn.

MacDonald v. *Edgerton*, 5 Barb. (N.Y.) 560, held, that if a person after becoming a guest at an inn goes away for a brief period, leaving his property with the intention of returning, he is to be considered as still continuing a guest, and if his property is lost during his absence, the innkeeper is liable.

Sasseen v. *Clark*, 37 Ga. 242, held, that when a hotel keeper sends his porter to the cars to receive the baggage of persons traveling, and there is delivered to the porter the baggage of a traveler who becomes the guest of the hotel, the liability of the innkeeper begins at the delivery to the porter and continues until redelivery to the actual custody of the guest. If the porter takes charge of the baggage to deliver to the car, the liability of the innkeeper continues until the baggage is so delivered.

But after the relation of guest has ceased, the innkeeper is liable for property left with him only as an ordinary bailee.

Innkeeper's Lien. — As we have seen, the innkeeper is compelled to receive any proper person who may apply for accommodations, but he need not receive those who can not pay, and he may require payment to be made in advance.

When he is not paid in advance, the law gives him a lien for all unpaid charges upon the property which the guest has brought into the house and placed in the custody of the innkeeper as bailee.

In *Threfall* v. *Borwick*, L.R. 10 Q.B. (Eng.) 210, A went to the defendant's inn and staid there with his family, taking with him to the inn as his own a piano which he had hired of the plaintiff. When A left the inn he was in debt to defendant and defendant detained the piano by virtue of his lien as innkeeper. Held, that defendant could hold the piano under such lien.

The innkeeper can detain the property until he is paid, but if he voluntarily surrenders it, the lien is lost. Statutes in most of the states now give boarding-house keepers a like lien, but by common law it extended only to innkeepers.

6. COMMON CARRIERS

Definition. — Common carriers also belong to the class of exceptional bailments. Like innkeepers they are as a general rule required to serve all alike and can not choose their customers. They are also bound to exercise a greater degree of care and diligence toward property placed in their possession than any of the ordinary bailees.

A carrier is defined to be one who undertakes to transport personal property from one place to another. He may be either a private carrier who comes under the class of ordinary bailees or a common carrier who is subject to special rules. A common carrier is one whose regular calling is to transport chattels for all who may choose to employ and remunerate him, while a private carrier is one who transports goods gratuitously or only in special cases.

Pierce v. *Milwaukee Railway Co.*, 23 Wis. 387, was an action to recover the value of eight bundles of bags which had been used in transporting grain and were then on their return empty. Defendants sought to avoid liability as common carriers by showing that it was the usage of the railroads to carry empty bags free of charge, and that they were responsible only for gross negligence. Held, that the consideration for such carriage was the patronage given the company in carrying the grain; that the carriage was therefore not gratuitous, and the defendant was liable as a common carrier.

Steele v. *McTyer*, 31 Ala. 667, was an action against defendant as a common carrier for loss of fifteen bales of cotton shipped by plaintiff on defendant's flat-boat to Mobile. The boat was wrecked by running into a log. Held, that defendant was liable, as the damage was not due to an act of God or inevitable accident.

Allen v. *Sackrider*, 37 N.Y. 341, was an action to recover damages for loss of a cargo of grain while being transported from Bay of Quinte to Ogdensburg by defendant for plaintiff. It was held that it was not enough, to charge as a common carrier, that he was the owner of a sloop and was specially employed by the plaintiffs, to make a trip for which he was to receive a stipulated compensation. Carrying for the public not being the business of defendant, he was held to be a special carrier and not liable for anything but his negligence.

A carrier may be one who operates by land or by water, the laws regulating their liability being much the same. Express, railroad, and steamboat companies are everyday examples of common carriers. In order to constitute one a common carrier two things are necessary; first, a continuous offer to the public to carry, and second, the charge of a compensation for the service.

Haynie v. *Waring*, 29 Ala. 263, held, that one who undertakes to carry goods for another gratuitously is liable only for gross negligence and not as a common carrier.

Goods and Payment for Carriage. — Common carriers are said to be carriers of "goods," and this term includes animals, money, and in fact any article of personal property that is subject to transportation. By the common law a common carrier is bound to receive without respect of persons whatever may be offered him for transportation, when the charges are paid or offered to be paid. Payment must be offered, as the carrier is under no obligation to carry free or upon credit. If he does not obtain his pay upon receipt of the goods, he may hold them until his charges are paid, the law creating a lien upon the goods for the charges and expenses in favor of the common carrier. This compensation is sometimes termed "freight" when applied to the charge for carrying goods. After the goods have been delivered to the carrier the shipper can not retake them without paying the freight, and if they are intercepted before reaching their destination, the full freight can be recovered by the carrier. The consignor or shipper is the party primarily liable for the freight and not the consignee or the person to whom the goods are shipped, unless the consignee expressly agrees to pay it.

In *Wooster* v. *Tarr*, 8 Allen (Mass.) 270, defendant shipped mackerel at Halifax upon plaintiff's vessel. In the bill of lading it was specified that they be delivered in Boston "unto Howe & Co. or to their assigns, he or they paying freight for said goods." They were delivered to parties to whom Howe & Co. had sold, and as plaintiff could not collect the freight from Howe & Co. who were insolvent, it was held that he could recover of defendant, even though the goods were purchased for and on account of Howe & Co. and shipped at their risk. The shipper is liable to the carrier for the freight, even though he does not own the goods and the carrier has waived his lien thereon.

Regulation of Charges. — The charges that may be made are in some instances regulated by statute. In the absence of any statute regulating the subject, the carrier may agree to give one party a lower rate than others, but he can not impose exorbitant or unreasonable rates or conditions upon any one.

In the case of *Johnson* v. *Pensacola Railroad Co.*, 16 Fla. 623, plaintiff sued defendant railroad company for excessive freight money claimed to have been paid. He proved that he was charged more than another shipper of lumber. Held, that as a common carrier defendant can not charge excessive or unreasonable rates of freight. The common law protects the individual from extortion and limits the carrier to a reasonable rate, but it does not require equal rates to all.

318½ *tons of Coal*, 14 Blatchf. (U.S.) 453. In this case the New Haven Railway Co., owning a dock at New Haven, refused to receive coal on its cars on said dock from a canal boat thereat, unless the master of the boat employed shovelers designated by the company, at a price fixed by the company, which was ordinarily the usual market price, to shovel the coal into tubs which were hoisted by derricks into the cars. The canal boat owners paid the company ten cents per ton for the use of the tubs and machinery. Held, that the requirements of the company were unreasonable and could not be enforced.

The carrier can retain the goods under his lien until all the freight and charges are paid.

Not only must he be a carrier for hire, but he must carry in the regular course of his business in order to be classed as a common carrier. That is, it is not sufficient that he carry goods in some particular business; he must undertake to carry for any one who asks him. The test is whether he carries for particular persons only or for every one who applies. If he holds himself out to carry for every one who asks him, he is a common carrier; but if he does not do it for every one, but carries for certain persons only, it is a matter of special contract. Or, as it is said in other words, a common carrier is one who follows the business as a public employment.

In *Satterlee* v. *Groat*, 1 Wend. (N.Y.) 272, defendant, who had been a common carrier between Schenectady and Albany, sold out all of his teams but one which he used on his farm and for a year or more entirely gave up the business. One Dows then engaged him to bring some loads for him from Albany to Schenectady. He sent his servant to bring these loads, but expressly instructed him to carry for no one else. The man brought two loads, and when he went for the third, as it was not ready, he, contrary to his instructions from defendant, took a load from plaintiff to be delivered to Frankfort. On the way one box was broken into and stolen. The servant was afterwards convicted of the theft. Held, that the defendant could not be held unless he was at the time a common carrier, and if the defendant was employed under a special contract for carrying the goods, he was not liable. The defendant having abandoned his business as a common carrier stood upon the same footing as he would if he had never been engaged in such business.

Right to refuse Goods. — As we have said, a common carrier is bound by the common law to receive whatever is offered to him to carry without respect to the persons offering. This rule is subject to three qualifications, viz. : First, the offer of the chattel must be for hire; Second, the bailment must be within the carrier's means of safe conveyance; Third, such carriage should be in the line of his vocation.

We have already discussed the first qualification. As to the second, it is but reasonable that the carrier may refuse to receive goods when he has not sufficient room or adequate facilities for carrying them safely. He is under no obligation to furnish extra equipment to satisfy an unusual demand. So, if the article carried be larger or heavier than the carrier can handle, he may refuse it on that ground. Furthermore, he may decline to receive particular property which may at the time be exposed to extraordinary danger or hazard on his route.

Phelps v. *Illinois Central Railway Co.*, 94 Ill. 548, held, that the fact that the road was under the military control of the officers of the United States Army was a sufficient excuse for defendant to refuse to receive freight while the road was in such control during the Civil War, it not being safe for the defendant to undertake the carriage of freight.

The article offered for transportation may not be in the line of the carrier's vocation. A freight carrier may not necessarily hold himself out to carry passengers. He need carry only the class of goods included in his public profession.

Johnson v. *The Midland Railway Co.*, 4 Exch. (Eng.) 367, was an action for damages against the Railway Co. for refusing to transport five tons of coal offered by plaintiff. The defendant never carried coal and did not hold itself out for any such business, and could not, unless it gave up its passenger traffic. Held, that a common carrier is not bound to carry every description of goods but only such goods, and to and from such places, as he has publicly professed to carry, and for which purposes he has conveyances.

Interstate Commerce Law. — The carrier may prescribe reasonable rules as to the time and manner of receiving goods. He can not be required to receive them at an unreasonable hour or place, and he may insist that the goods be packed in a reasonable way. But by statutes passed in most of the states the carrier is prohibited from discriminating in favor of one customer over another either in rates or privileges of any kind. The common carrier must not select his patrons arbitrarily, but must furnish equal facilities to all.

To further this object a statute was passed by the Congress of the United States in 1887 which is known as the Interstate Commerce Law. This law was designed to regulate the commerce between the states and applies to all common carriers, either by land or water, who do business in two or more states or territories. It provides that no discrimination shall be made between large or small, constant or occasional, shippers, and that no charges shall be unjust or unreasonable. It also provides that proportionate charges shall be made for long and short distances. The law further requires that the schedule of rates shall be published and filed with commissioners who are appointed to oversee the enforcement of the law and are known as the Interstate Commerce Commissioners. The act also makes it unlawful for any common carrier who comes under its provisions to enter into any combination or agreement by which the continuous carriage of freight from one point to another shall be delayed or interrupted.

All of the large railroad and express companies do business in more than one state, and therefore come within the provisions of this act.

When Liability Begins. — The common carrier becomes responsible for the goods when they are delivered to him for carriage and accepted by him in the capacity of a carrier. The delivery should be made to the agent or person whose business it is to receive freight, not to any one who may be about the place of delivery.

Trowbridge v. *Chapin*, 23 Conn. 595, was an action against the owner of a steamboat as a common carrier. It was the duty of the clerk of the boat to receive freight for transportation. Plaintiff's property was taken on board by a porter and left in a place pointed out by a person whose appearance and employment indicated that he was a common laborer. No inquiry was made by the porter as to whether the person had authority to receive the freight. Held, that it was not sufficient evidence of delivery to make defendant liable for the loss of the property.

It is not necessary, as we have seen, that the transportation shall actually begin before the common carrier's liability attaches, but rather the carrier is liable as soon as he accepts the goods. So in the case of expressmen and other carriers who go after the goods and receive them at the shipper's residence or place of business, their liability begins when they receive the goods.

Receipts. — It is always prudent for the shipper or sender of the goods to demand of the carrier a receipt for the articles delivered. This is termed a freight receipt, way bill, or bill of lading. Originally a bill of lading was given only by a carrier by water, but it is now given by all carriers. It consists of a writing showing the receipt of the goods and the terms of the contract of carriage in brief form.

7. LIABILITY OF COMMON CARRIERS

Limits of Liability. — As in the case of the innkeeper, the liability of the common carrier is exceptionally great. He is held liable as an insurer of the goods against all risks of loss or injury, except when the loss arises from the following causes: (1) by an act of God, or by a public enemy, (2) by the act of the shipper, (3) by the act of the public authority, (4) from the nature of the goods. In the early times this strict measure of responsibility was placed upon the carrier for reasons of public policy. In an age of thieving and lawlessness the carrier had many opportunities to defraud his customers, and, by collusion with thieves and robbers, to cause the shipper to be defrauded. To this absolute liability as an insurer there were only two exceptions under the common law, and these were losses occasioned either by act of God or the king's enemies. But modern methods make the reason for the rule less urgent, and modern legislation has relieved the carrier's liability in the other cases just specified.

Loss or Injury by Act of God. — This includes those causes which man neither produced nor can contend against; as, accidents caused to the goods while the carrier is within the line of duty, by lightning, tempest, earthquake, flood, sudden death, snow, rough winds, freezing, and thawing.

Denny v. *New York Central Railroad Co.*, 79 Mass. 481, held, that the rising of the Hudson River, caused by a flood, which ruined goods in defendant's warehouse, was an act of God for which defendant would not be liable.

Ballentine v. *North Missouri Railroad Co.*, 40 Mo. 491, held, that a snowstorm which blocks up a railroad to the extent that it delays and hinders the running of the cars is an act of God for which a carrier can not be held liable.

But a prudent man will foresee the less violent of these causes, such as snow and freezing, and a carrier will not be excused for loss in such cases, unless he has exercised prudence and foresight in regard to them.

In the case of *Vail* v. *Pacific Railroad*, 63 Mo. 230, fruit trees shipped on defendant's road were frozen while *en route*, and the freezing was held to be an act of God for which the company was not liable, unless caused by unnecessary delay in transporting the trees or by their careless exposure to the cold.

In *Parsons* v. *Hardy*, 14 Wend. (N.Y.) 215, plaintiff received on November 19, at Albany, a quantity of merchandise to transport by canal to Ithaca. When he arrived at Montezuma locks the winter set in, and he was prevented by ice from going farther, having had to stop on the way to repair an accident caused by being run into by a scow. Plaintiff took care of the goods at Montezuma, but the defendant took them from there. Held, that the plaintiff should have delivered them in the spring, but if the owner took them, it relieved the plaintiff and he could recover *pro rata* for the part performed. As to the time of delivery, the carrier must exercise due diligence, and is excused by accident or misfortune. It is enough if he exercises due care and diligence to guard against delay.

Loss by Fire. — Loss by fire, unless caused by lightning, is not an act of God and a common carrier is not excused from loss by this cause unless it is expressly contracted for.

Parker v. *Flagg*, 26 Me. 181, held, that unless a carrier limits his responsibility by the terms of a bill of lading or otherwise, he can not escape the obligation to deliver the goods at their destination unless prevented by the public enemy or by an act of God. A loss by accidental fire is not a sufficient excuse unless the fire be caused by lightning.

Loss or Injury by Public Enemies. — This is a loss caused by those at war with one's country.

In *McCranie* v. *Wood*, 24 La. An. 406, defendant contracted with plaintiff, a carrier by boat, to remove certain cotton belonging to plaintiff to places deemed safe from hostilities during the Civil War. It was stored where it was deemed safe, but hostilities arose in that direction and the cotton was destroyed. Held, that defendant had performed, as far as was in his power, and the goods having been destroyed by the public enemy, he was not liable.

But the violence of mobs or rioters does not bring the participants within the term "public enemies."

Loss or Injury by Act or Fault of the Consignor. — This arises when the shipper carelessly packs the goods and they are injured, or when he incorrectly addresses them so that they are delayed or lost, in which cases the carrier is not liable.

In *Klauber* v. *American Express Co.*, 21 Wis. 21, plaintiff shipped some clothing which was not entirely covered and while being transported by defendant was damaged by rain. Held, that the owner is not required to cover goods shipped so that they shall be safe from rain, mud, and fire, and the defendant here is liable. If there had been a hidden defect in the packing from which damage resulted in the ordinary course of handling, it would have been the act of the owner and the carrier would have been relieved.

In *Congar* v. *Chicago Railway Co.*, 24 Wis. 157, plaintiff shipped by defendant's road, trees and other nursery stock from Whitewater, Wis., directed to "Iuka, Ia." The consignee was a resident of Iuka, Tama Co., Ia. The defendant took them to Iuka, Keokuk Co., Ia., in consequence of which delay the stock became worthless. Defendants proved that they examined the maps and found the place in Keokuk Co. Held, that the company was not responsible. The negligence, if any, was upon the part of plaintiff in not marking the goods with the name of the county or the road by which they were to go.

Any deception or bad faith on the part of the shipper as to the article shipped, whereby it is made to appear less valuable or less liable to be injured, will relieve the carrier from responsibility for any injury.

American Express Co. v. *Perkins*, 42 Ill. 458, was an action brought against the express company to recover for the value of a package containing a wreath, made partially of glass, which was broken. The company was not informed of the fragile nature of the goods shipped. Held, that in order to charge a common carrier as insurer he must be treated in good faith, and concealment or suppression of the truth will relieve him from liability. When a package containing articles of a brittle nature is delivered to a carrier, he must be informed of the nature of its contents in order that he may use care proportionate to its fragile character, if he is to be held liable as a common carrier.

Loss or Injury arising from the Nature of the Goods. — When the loss arises, not from any act of the carrier, but because of the inherent nature of the goods, the carrier is relieved. This applies to the natural decay of vegetables and fruit and other perishable commodities, also to the loss of live stock arising from their own viciousness and habits, as when cattle gore or trample upon each other. But the carrier must take such care of live stock as prudence and foresight demand, and must feed and water them, unless the shipper undertakes this duty.

Clarke v. *Rochester and Syracuse Railroad Co.*, 14 N.Y. 570, was an action for damages for the loss of a horse shipped on defendant railway from Rochester to Auburn, which, upon arrival, was found dead. Held, that the carrier was liable, unless the damage was caused by an occurrence incident to the carriage of animals in a railroad car, and which the defendant could not by the exercise of diligence and care have prevented.

Evans v. *Fitchburg Railroad Co.*, 111 Mass. 142, was also an action for injury to a horse, and the court held that a common carrier is liable for all accidents and mismanagements incident to the transportation, but not for injuries produced by or resulting from the inherent defects or essential qualities of the article which he undertakes to transport. If the injury is produced by fright, restiveness, or viciousness of the animal, which the defendant exercised all proper care and foresight to prevent, it would be unreasonable to hold him responsible for the loss.

Loss or Injury caused by Public Authority. — An example of such a loss is a seizure of the goods by process of law, or by the direct act of one's own government.

Ohio Railway Co. v. *Yohe*, 51 Ind. 181, was an action against the railroad company for failure to deliver goods shipped by them. Their answer was that while the wheat was being shipped, one Johnson took out a writ of replevin, and by virtue of this writ the sheriff of the county seized the grain and took it out of the possession of the company. Held, that the common carrier is excused from liability when the goods are seized by virtue of a legal process and taken out of his hands.

Limitation of Liability by Contract. — The carrier in most of the states may limit his liability to a certain extent by contract with the shipper. That is, by special agreement a lighter degree of responsibility may be stipulated for. He may stipulate not to be liable for loss by fire, robbery, accidental delay, or dangers from navigation, provided he is not himself in fault;

COM. LAW — 14

but he can not contract away his liability for the fraud, misconduct, or negligence of himself, his agents, or servants. Notwithstanding his attempt by contract to limit his liability, he will still be held to the responsibility of a mutual benefit bailee, and he is required to exercise ordinary care and diligence, as well as honesty and good faith.

Camp v. *Hartford Steamboat Co.*, 43 Conn. 333, was an action against the defendant steamboat company as a common carrier for the value of goods shipped by them and lost through the boat running upon a rock and thereby springing a leak. The bill of lading given by the company when the goods were shipped provided that the company should not be responsible for damage to the goods from any perils or accidents not resulting from their own negligence or that of their servants. Held, that the exemption stipulated for was valid and lawful and the defendants were not liable.

Boorman v. *American Express Co.*, 21 Wis. 152, held, that an express company may exempt itself by special contract from its liability as an insurer; or for loss or damage of any package for over $50, unless the just and true value thereof is stated in the receipt; or upon any property not properly packed and secured for transportation; or upon any fragile fabric unless marked as such upon the package containing it, and when a receipt embodying such conditions is given to the shipper, his assent is presumed.

The carrier is also allowed to state a reasonable limit to the amount for which he shall be held liable in case of loss, unless the shipper shall state the valuation at the time of the delivery of the goods to the carrier. Express companies generally contract that in case no valuation is given, they will not be liable for a sum to exceed $50, and such a provision is generally upheld.

In *Belger* v. *Dinsmore*, 51 N.Y. 166, plaintiff expressed a trunk by defendant company and received a receipt which contained a statement that as a part of the consideration of the contract it was agreed that in case of loss the owner should not demand over $50, at which price the article was valued, unless otherwise expressed. Held, that by accepting the receipt and failing to give another valuation, the plaintiff assented to the limitation, and in case of loss could claim no more.

In *Hart* v. *Penn. Railroad Co.*, 112 U.S. 331, plaintiff shipped five horses and other property in one car, under a bill of lading signed by him, which stated that the horses were to be transported "upon the following terms and conditions which are admitted and accepted by me to be just and reasonable. First, to pay freight thereon 'at a specified rate' on the condition that the carrier is liable on the stock to the extent of the following agreed valuation : if horses or mules, not to exceed $200, etc." By the negligence of the railroad company one of the horses was killed and others injured. It appeared that they were race horses worth $25,000. Held, that the liability of the company for the horses was limited to $200 each, the limitation in the bill of lading being just and reasonable and binding on the plaintiff, even though the loss occurred through the company's negligence.

Delivery by Carrier. — The carrier is bound to transport the goods with reasonable dispatch, and by the prescribed or customary route, and at the termination of the journey to deliver them over to the consignee or his authorized agent within a reasonable time.

Berje v. *Railway Co.*, 37 La. An. 468, held, that a stipulation in the bill of lading exempting the company from liability for loss arising from delay for any cause, is unreasonable, and will not relieve the carrier from liability for losses caused by negligence.

The carrier is liable absolutely to deliver to the right party. If he delivers to the wrong party, no matter how cautiously and innocently, he is liable. Delivery on a forged order or through the fraud of a stranger will not relieve him.

In *Odell* v. *Boston Railroad*, 109 Mass. 50, plaintiff bought hay from one Swasey, to be delivered to the plaintiff at the depot of the defendants, who as common carriers were to carry the hay to plaintiff in Boston, where it was to be weighed. Swasey delivered the hay to defendants and directed them to market it in plaintiff's name and carry it to him. After the hay reached Boston Swasey directed defendants to deliver it to a third party. Held, that the title passed to plaintiff on the delivery of the hay to defendants, and they were liable to him therefor.

Powell v. *Myers*, 26 Wend. (N.Y.) 591, held, that common carriers of passengers and their baggage are liable for the latter until its safe delivery to the owner. The delivery of the baggage upon a forged order will not discharge them.

When a bill of lading has been issued by the carrier, he must deliver the goods to the holder of it. He should, therefore, demand the bill of the consignee, otherwise, if it has been negotiated, he runs the risk of being required to make good the property to a purchaser holding the bill of lading.

Forbes v. *Boston Railroad*, 133 Mass. 154, held, that the delivery of goods by a common carrier to a person unauthorized to receive them without requiring the production of the bill of lading, but relying upon such person's representation that he is the holder of it, renders the carrier liable to the person entitled to the possession of the goods without regard to the question of the carrier's negligence or care.

When the carriage is by water a delivery on the usual wharf is sufficient, but while on the wharf, goods should be handled with reasonable care. A railroad company may deliver the goods at the depot or freight house, and according to the laws of Alabama, New York, Wisconsin, Vermont, Michigan, Louisiana, and many other states, they must also notify the consignee, and they are liable as common carriers until the consignee has had a reasonable opportunity to remove the goods.

In the case of *Moses* v. *Boston Railroad*, 32 N.H. 523, ten bags of wool were delivered to defendant to be transported to Boston and then delivered to the consignee. The train arrived in Boston between one and three o'clock in the afternoon, and in the usual course of business two or three hours were required for unloading. The warehouse was closed at five o'clock, and during the night it burned. Held, that the defendant was liable as a common carrier until the consignee had had reasonable opportunity during the hours in which such goods are usually delivered, of examining them and taking them away, after being informed that they were ready for delivery. In this case he had no such opportunity to take the goods, and the defendant was still liable as a common carrier.

Massachusetts, Iowa, California, Pennsylvania, and other states hold that the delivery and safe storage of the goods in the freight depot relieve the carrier from further liability other than as a warehouseman.

In *Francis* v. *Dubuque Railroad Co.*, 25 Iowa 60, plaintiff shipped goods by defendant road to Ackley, where plaintiff resided. They arrived at 8.15 P.M. and were at once unloaded and safely placed in defendant's warehouse ready for delivery. That night the warehouse burned, and the goods were destroyed. Held, that the liability of a railroad company as a common carrier terminates and the company's responsibility as a warehouseman commences upon the arrival of the goods at the point of destination and their deposit in the warehouse of the company to await the convenience of the consignee. .

If such carriers as express companies in the cities, whose custom it is to deliver to the consignee at his residence or place of business, deliver at any other place or store the goods in the depot as is practiced by freight companies, such delivery will not be sufficient. This rule applies also to draymen and teamsters.

8. CARRIERS OF PASSENGERS

Definition. — A common carrier of passengers is one who transports persons from one place to another for hire. A public carrier may be both a carrier of goods and of passengers. The passenger may be carried by water or by land. The common carrier of passengers is bound to receive and carry alike all persons who shall apply and are ready and willing to pay for their transportation.

In *Bennett* v. *Dutton*, 10 N.H. 481, it was held that the proprietors of a stagecoach who hold themselves out as common carriers of passengers are bound to receive all who desire passage, so long as they have room and there is no legal excuse for a refusal. It is not a legal excuse that they have agreed with a connecting coach line that they will receive no passengers on certain days from a given point unless they come on a coach of said line.

Rights and Duties. — But the coach driver may refuse to carry when he has no more room or when the party applying is not a suitable person. He need not receive a drunken person, a notorious criminal, or a person infected with a contagious disease. Neither is he obliged to take persons to a place which is not on his route, or at which he is not accustomed to stop.

Atchison Railroad Co. v. *Weber*, 33 Kans. 543, held, that where an unattended passenger becomes sick or unconscious or insane after entering upon a journey, it is the duty of the company to remove him from the train and leave him until he is in a fit condition to resume his journey.

The fare required of the passenger must be reasonable, and in many states it is regulated by statute. The carrier is bound to have means and appliances suitable to the transportation, and to use all reasonable precautions for the safety of passengers. He can prescribe reasonable rules as to showing tickets, etc. The carrier is not an insurer of the lives and safety of the passengers, but he is held to a high degree of care, and will be liable for even slight negligence. While the carrier does not warrant the safety of the passengers, he is held to the highest degree of care practicable under the circumstances.

In *Ingalls* v. *Bills*, 9 Metc. (Mass.) 1, plaintiff was a passenger on defendant's coach. By reason of the breaking of one of the iron axletrees, in which there was a small flaw that could not be seen, he was injured. Held, that defendant was not answerable for the injury thus received. Proprietors of coaches who carry passengers for hire are answerable for injuries to passengers which happen by reason of any defect in the coach that might have been discovered by the most careful and thorough examination, but not for an injury which happened because of a hidden defect that could not, upon such examination, have been discovered.

In most of the states the carrier is not permitted to limit his liability for injury to the passenger. It is considered contrary to public policy to exempt the carrier from liability for even slight negligence when the lives and safety of human beings are concerned.

Baggage. — The passenger who pays his fare to the carrier is entitled to have certain baggage taken without charge, and for this baggage the carrier is liable as for the carriage of freight. Baggage in this sense includes such articles of personal necessity, convenience, and comfort as travelers under the circumstances are wont to take on their journeys. It does not include merchandise or a stock of goods used in the traveler's business.

In *Pardee* v. *Drew*, 25 Wend. (N.Y.) 459, plaintiff took passage at New York on defendant's boat and brought on board with him a trunk which was put with the other baggage. It contained silks and other merchandise he had purchased in New York for his store. The trunk was lost, and this action was brought for its value. Held, that defendant was liable as a common carrier for baggage, but it must be such articles of necessity and personal convenience as are usually carried by travelers, and in this case the carrier was not liable.

In *Dexter* v. *Syracuse Railroad Co.*, 42 N.Y. 326, plaintiff sued for the value of the contents of his trunk which was lost by defendant. It contained, aside from his wearing apparel, material for two dresses purchased for his wife, and also material for a dress intended for his landlady. Held, that the common carrier is liable for the loss of such property received as baggage as is designed for the personal use of the passenger or his family, but it does not include articles purchased for persons not members of his family. In this case the company was held liable for all but the dress intended for the landlady.

The carrier is also liable for money which the passenger includes in his baggage for his traveling expenses and personal use, not exceeding a reasonable amount.

Duffy v. *Thompson*, 4 E. D. Smith (N.Y.) 178, held, that a passenger on a voyage from a foreign country may keep money designed for small personal expenses in his trunk while on board ship, and hold the shipowner responsible for it.

If the baggage is not delivered into the actual custody and keeping of the carrier, but is retained in the possession of the passenger, the carrier is under no such liability for its safety.

Carpenter v. *New York Railroad Co.*, 124 N.Y. 53, held, that a carrier was not liable for the effects of travelers not delivered into his custody, and money retained at night and placed under the traveler's pillow was not in the custody of the carrier.

The carrier may by special contract make reasonable modifications of his liability for baggage. But the carrier can not relieve himself wholly from liability, and the limitation must be brought to the passenger's notice and must be reasonable. Conditions limiting the carrier's liability to each passenger to a given amount have been upheld.

In *Mauritz* v. *Railroad Co.*, 23 Fed. Rep. (U.S.) 765, it was held that a railroad company can not limit its liability for the safe carriage of a passenger's baggage by a notice printed upon the face of a ticket, unless the passenger's attention is called to it when purchasing the ticket, or unless the circumstances are such that it would be negligent of him not to read it. When the passenger can not read and the agent makes no explanation when he sells the ticket, the passenger is not bound. The clause in the ticket was that the company would not be liable for lost baggage excepting wearing apparel, and then only for a sum not to exceed $50.

The liability of the carrier for the baggage does not terminate until the passenger has had reasonable opportunity to take charge of it after it has reached its destination. ·If it is not claimed after a reasonable time, the carrier may store it, and his liability as a carrier ceases, he being liable thereafter only as a warehouseman.

Roth v. *Buffalo Railroad Co.*, 34 N.Y. 548, held, that when a passenger did not call for his trunk, but left it in the hands of the company over night, without any arrangement with them, and it was destroyed before morning by the burning of the depot, the company was not liable. The common carrier's liability for baggage terminates within a reasonable time after the arrival of the baggage at the place of destination, if the carrier is ready to deliver the same to the passenger.

QUESTIONS ON BAILMENT

1. Define bailment. Distinguish from sale. Who is the bailor ? Who is the bailee ?

2. What are the five classes of bailments under the Roman law ?

3. Classify bailments according to recompense.

4. What care or diligence is said to be required in the case of a bailment for the benefit of the bailor? For what degree of negligence is the bailee liable ?

5. In the case of a bailment for the benefit of both parties, what degree of care is required, and what degree of negligence renders the bailee liable ?

6. In the case of a bailment for the benefit of the bailee, what degree of care is required, and what degree of negligence renders the bailee liable ?

7. Brown steals a horse, and while riding it carefully is run into by a runaway team and the horse is killed. Brown was exercising the greatest care, and was not guilty of any negligence whatever. Is he liable for the value of the horse ?

8. A, a farmer, intending to go to town the next day, promises B that he will take two bags of wheat for him without charge. The next morning he starts away without it, and B is put to the necessity of hiring a man to take the wheat for him. Can he recover damages from A for breach of A's agreement ?

9. If in the above case A had taken B's wheat on his wagon and started to town with it, but in loading it had carelessly put a plow on the top of it, in consequence of which the bag was torn open and the wheat scattered along the road. Could B have recovered of A for the loss of the wheat ?

10. In question 8, if nothing was said by the parties as to whether or not A was to receive any compensation for taking the wheat, and he had been in the habit of doing numerous little errands for B without charge, which would the presumption be, that he was a gratuitous bailee, or a bailee for hire ?

11. Bernard, as a favor to Webster, receives a sum of money to keep for him until next day. He puts it with his own in his pocketbook which was in his coat pocket. That night Bernard's house was robbed, and the pocketbook that also contained money of his own was taken from his coat, which hung on the foot of the bed. Was Bernard liable ? What degree of care was required of Bernard ?

12. Nelson borrows a bicycle from Wood, rides it to a ball game, and leaves it in the bicycle rack unlocked. The bicycle is stolen. It was left in the same place with many other bicycles, but no one was placed in guard over it. Is Nelson liable to Wood for the bicycle ?

13. A borrows a horse of B with which to work his garden. He keeps the horse two days, and then sends it back. While A had the horse he cared for it and furnished its feed. One shoe was off, and he had the horse shod. The horse was injured during the bailment through the slight negligence of A. Was A liable ?

14. In the above case, if the horse had been injured by an accident without any negligence or fault on the part of A, would A have been liable ?

15. In question 13, if the horse had died a natural death without any fault of A, would A have been liable ?

16. Under what three divisions do we consider bailments for mutual benefit ?

17. In question 11, if Bernard was to receive $5 for caring for the money, what degree of care would be required of him, and for what negligence would he be liable ?

18. Dodge employed a keeper of a livery stable to board and care for his team. The keeper of the stable left the door open so that one of Dodge's horses got out and was kicked by another horse. Was the livery-stable keeper liable ?

19. A takes his wagon to B, who represents himself to be a wagon maker, and employs him to repair it. B is wholly incompetent and does not understand the business, and as a result the wagon is damaged. Is B liable ?

20. After the purposes of the bailment of the class in question 19 have been accomplished, what is the duty of the bailee ? Of the bailor ?

21. What security has the bailee for his services ?

22. Harris takes his desk to a cabinet maker to be repaired and revarnished. After the work is completed he sends for the desk, and the cabinet maker refuses to deliver it until he receives his pay, whereupon Harris brings an action to recover the possession of the desk. Can he succeed without paying for the work ?

23. In the above case, if the cabinet maker had let Harris have the desk, could he have compelled Harris to deliver it back to him or else pay him for his services ?

24. Define pledge or pawn. Distinguish from chattel mortgage.

25. What kind of personal property may be the subject of a pledge ?

26. What is the result when the property pledged has been destroyed by fire?

27. What degree of care and diligence must the pledgee exercise toward the property pledged ?

28. Has the pledgee the right to use the chattel pledged ? If so, when ?

29. If the pledgor makes default in paying the debts secured by the pledge, what rights has the pledgee ?

30. In case the property pledged consists of bills or notes which will soon become due, what are the rights of the pledgee ?

31. What are the two principal examples of exceptional bailments ?

32. Define an innkeeper. Distinguish an innkeeper from a boarding-house keeper.

33. Reed enters Porter's hotel, and leaving his baggage with the clerk, goes to dinner. After dinner he calls for his baggage, meaning to take the three o'clock train. The baggage is lost. Does the relation of innkeeper and guest exist between them ?

34. Swift went to Porter's hotel as a friend and guest of Porter for the purpose of visiting him and without paying anything for his accommodation. Did the relation of innkeeper and guest exist between them?

35. Hewlett becomes a guest at Porter's hotel, and while there the hotel is destroyed by fire. Porter is free from negligence. Is he liable to Hewlett for baggage lost in the fire?

36. In the above case, if Hewlett's baggage had been stolen by a servant in the employ of Porter, would he have been liable?

37. In question 35, if the hotel had been destroyed by a flood or cyclone and Hewlett's baggage lost without any negligence on Porter's part, would Porter have been liable?

38. Porter gave notice to his guests that he would be liable for money or valuables only when they were placed in the office safe, and not when they were left in their rooms. Hewlett left $1000 in bank notes locked in his trunk in his room. This was broken into and the money stolen. Was Porter liable?

39. When Hewlett applied to Porter for accommodations, Porter refused to receive him unless he paid in advance. Had Porter this right?

40. Hewlett was received as a guest by Porter, and after staying three days packed up his trunk preparatory to leaving. Porter refused to allow him to remove his trunk from the hotel until his bill was paid. Had Porter this right?

41. Define a common carrier.

42. What two requisites are necessary to constitute a person a common carrier?

43. Wooster shipped 100 barrels of flour to Allen & Co. When the goods arrived the carrier refused to deliver them until Allen & Co. had paid the charges. Had the carrier a right to so hold them?

44. In the above case suppose the carrier delivered the goods to Allen & Co. and then looked to Wooster for the freight. Wooster claimed that the agreement between the parties was that Allen & Co. should pay the freight. Could the carrier hold Wooster?

45. In the absence of a statute regulating the rates of the railroad company a common carrier charged one Johnson $1.50 a hundred for carrying freight a certain distance. The Pennsylvania Coal Company had received a special rate of $1.20 a hundred, because they were large and important shippers. Had the carrier the right to make this distinction?

46. Suppose in the above case the railroad company desired to put Johnson at a disadvantage with his competitors, as the competitors shipped all of their freight by this carrier while Johnson shipped some by another carrier. Therefore they charged Johnson $2.80 a hundred, while all other shippers had the regular rate of $1.50 a hundred. Had the railroad company the right so to charge him?

47. The Pony Railroad Company, owners of a small line of railroad being

constructed to convey passengers to a pleasure resort, were called upon to transport for plaintiff a heavy boiler. The company refused to accept it on the grounds that they had no car sufficient in size to carry it nor any facilities to transport it. Had they the right so to refuse it?

48. In the above case, if the boiler was not too large for their equipment, had they the right to refuse on the ground that they were carriers of passengers only, and did not carry freight?

49. What is the object of the interstate commerce law?

50. When does the carrier's responsibility for goods intrusted to him begin?

51. What is the liability of a common carrier for goods intrusted to him?

52. Name four exceptions to this exceptional liability.

53. Plaintiff's goods were lost by the carrier by reason of lightning striking the car in which they were contained, and the car being consumed by fire. Was the carrier liable?

54. In the above case, if the fire was caused by sparks from a fire along the course of the railway for which the company was not to blame, was the company liable?

55. If the goods in question 53 had been lost through acts of a mob of strikers, would the carrier have been liable?

56. If the goods had been lost through the act of an army while the country was at war, would the carrier have been liable?

57. Conger ships a barrel of crockery which has been but carelessly packed and with no mark placed upon it to give the carrier notice of its contents. While being handled in the usual course of transportation the crockery is broken. Is the carrier liable?

58. Clark ships a car load of cattle from Chicago to New York City. While on the way one of the cattle, being vicious, gored a number of others so that they died from their wounds. Is the company liable?

59. In question 54, if the company had expressly contracted that it would not be liable for accidental fire not caused through its negligence, would it have been liable?

60. In the same case, if the fire had been caused by the gross negligence of the company's employees, but it had expressly contracted not to be liable for fire from any cause whatever, would it have been liable?

61. The carrier receives certain goods to be delivered to one J. R. Myers of New York City. When the goods reach there, a person applies to the freight office and asks for the goods, stating that his name is Myers. The goods are delivered to him, and it later transpires that the party who applied was not the consignee of the goods, but a party who obtained them fraudulently. Can the consignee recover the value of the goods from the carrier?

62. Certain goods are carried by the New York Central Railroad consigned to one Powell at Albany. The goods reach Albany and are placed in the depot at four in the afternoon. A notice is mailed to Powell which reaches him

the next morning. Within that time a fire occurs and the goods are destroyed. Is the railroad company responsible ? State the holding in the different states.

63. Brown, a respectable person, applies to the Pennsylvania Railroad Company for transportation on one of their passenger trains, offering to pay the usual fare. Have they the right to refuse him, there being sufficient room on their cars ?

64. If Brown was drunk and disorderly, had they a right to refuse him ?

65. What is the liability of the carrier for the lives and safety of its passengers ?

66. What is baggage, and what is the carrier's liability for a passenger's baggage ?

67. Drew, a passenger on the New York Central Railroad, had his trunk checked and placed in the baggage car of the train upon which he received transportation. The trunk, which was lost, contained his wearing apparel, a dress for his wife, which he had purchased on the journey, some presents for his friends, and a sum of $20 in a purse, which money he intended to use on his journey. Was the railroad company liable for all of the contents of this trunk ? If not, for what portion of it was the company liable ?

68. If the company had expressly contracted with Drew that their liability for baggage should be limited to $50 and he had had notice of this limitation, would they have been liable for a greater amount ?

PARTNERSHIP

1. IN GENERAL

Definition. — Thus far we have treated of individuals acting alone in their business dealings, but in actual experience we find that the more important business transactions and many of the smaller ones are undertaken not by single individuals, but by several persons joining themselves together, and thus by a union of their labor, ideas, and capital they are able to accomplish better results than if each had conducted his business alone. Two merchants in the same line of business in the same neighborhood may together run a store more economically than it could be run by either separately, and at the same time they will lessen their competition. One may have business ability, an idea, or a patent, while the other may lack all of these but have the capital. Together they can accomplish results which neither alone could have attained.

When several persons thus join themselves together in business they do so either by forming a partnership, a joint stock company, or a corporation. Partnership is a legal relation based upon the expressed or implied contract of two or more competent persons to unite their property, labor, or skill in carrying on some lawful business as principals for their joint profit. The members of a partnership are called partners. The partners together are said to constitute a firm.

Executed Contract. — The partnership is formed as the result of an agreement, and this agreement or contract of partnership must be executed. An agreement to form a partnership at some future time does not constitute the parties to such an agreement partners. A partnership differs from a corporation, which will be considered later, in that it is formed simply by the contract of the parties and requires no authority from the government to create it. The contract of partnership may be entered upon by a written agreement, by an oral agreement, or in some cases by implication.

Written Contract. — It is a wise precaution to have the agreement in writing and all of the terms and conditions of the partnership expressed. The written agreement, setting forth the terms of the partnership and signed by the parties that are to compose the firm, is called articles of copartnership. A great many different clauses may be inserted, depending upon the actual agreement of the parties, but the following is a brief form containing some of the more common provisions.

ARTICLES OF COPARTNERSHIP

This agreement made and entered into this thirty-first day of October, One thousand nine hundred and three, by and between Charles Snow of Rochester, N.Y., of the first part and Edward M. Chapin of Batavia, N.Y., of the second part, witnesseth as follows: —

1. The said parties, above named, hereby agree to become partners in the business of buying and selling dry goods under the firm name of Snow & Co., said business to be carried on in the city of Rochester, or such other place or places as the parties may hereafter determine, and to continue for the term of five years from the date hereof.

2. The capital of the said partnership shall consist of the sum of ten thousand dollars, to be contributed as follows: The party of the first part shall contribute his stock of dry goods and the good will of the business heretofore conducted by him, which are together valued by the parties hereto at the sum of five thousand dollars; and the party of the second part shall contribute the sum of five thousand dollars in cash. The capital stock so formed is to be used and employed in common between the parties hereto for the support and management of said business.

3. At all times during the continuance of their copartnership they and each of them shall give their time and attention to said business, and to the utmost of their skill and power exert

themselves for their joint interest, profit, benefit, and advantage, and truly employ, buy and sell, and trade with their joint stock and the increase thereof in the business aforesaid; and they shall also at all times during the said copartnership bear, pay, and discharge equally between them all rents and expenses that may be required for the management and support of said business; and all gains, profits, and increase that shall grow or arise from or by means of their said business shall be equally divided, and all losses by bad debts or otherwise shall be borne and paid between them equally.

4. Each of said partners shall be at liberty to draw out of the funds of the firm each month for his private expenses the sum of one hundred dollars, and neither of them shall take any further sum for his own separate use without the consent in writing of the other partner. The sums so drawn shall be charged against the partners respectively, and if at the annual settlement, hereinafter provided for, the profits of any partner do not amount to the sum so drawn out in that year, he shall at once repay such deficiency to the firm.

5. All the transactions of the said copartnership shall be entered in regular books of account, and on the first day of January in each year during the continuance of this copartnership account of stock shall be taken, and an account of the expenses and profits adjusted and exhibited on said books; said profits shall then be divided, and one half carried to the separate account of each partner. Either partner shall be at liberty to withdraw at any time the whole or any part of his share of the accrued profits thus ascertained and carried to his separate account. Each partner shall have open and free access to the books and accounts of the copartnership at all times, and no material or important changes shall at any time be made in the general business of the firm, either in the buying of stock or in any other respect, by either partner without the knowledge of the other.

6. And the said parties hereby mutually covenant and agree, to and with each other, that during the continuance of the said copartnership neither of them shall indorse any note, or other-

wise become surety for any person or persons whomsoever, without the consent of the other of said copartners. And at the determination of their copartnership, the said copartners, each to the other, shall make a just and final account of all things relating to their said business, and in all things truly adjust the same; and all and every, the stock and stocks as well as the gains and increase thereof, which shall appear to be remaining, either in money, goods, wares, fixtures, debts, or otherwise, shall be divided equally between them.

IN WITNESS WHEREOF, the said parties have hereunto set their hands and seals this thirty-first day of October, 1903.

CHARLES SNOW.   [L. S.]

EDWARD M. CHAPIN.   [L. S.]

The agreement should be full and explicit, and many other provisions may be inserted, as the facts require.

Oral Contract. — As we have said, articles of copartnership are desirable, but not necessary, to the formation of a partnership. Two neighbors, each being in need of a grain drill on his farm, may purchase one, each paying half, and agreeing that each shall use it. The result is a partnership in the drill, and in case it should be disposed of each would be entitled to his half of the proceeds unless the agreement between them provided otherwise. By the statute of frauds, a contract of partnership for over one year must, in most of the states, be in writing.

In *Morris* v. *Peckham*, 51 Conn. 128, plaintiff agreed orally to assign to defendant a one half interest in an invention for making patent screw-drivers, defendant agreeing to furnish the capital to procure the patents and to purchase the machinery and stock, and they were then to engage in manufacturing the screw-drivers. After conducting the business one year, defendant refused to continue and to furnish more funds. Plaintiff brought an action to compel specific performance of the partnership agreement, claiming that the partnership was to continue for seventeen years, the life of the patent, but the court held that such a contract, not being by its terms to be performed within one year, is void under the statute of frauds unless in writing.

Virginia and some other jurisdictions hold to the contrary, and expressly declare that a contract of partnership for over one year, when made orally, is not within the statute of frauds.

Implied Partnership. — Aside from a partnership formed by an actual agreement, either oral or written, which we have just discussed, a partnership may be implied from transactions and relations, in which the word "partnership" has never been used, but from which the law will imply a partnership whether it was so intended by the parties or not. This implied partnership may be an actual partnership by implication or a partnership by implication as to third parties.

Partners. — Here the difficult question arises as to when a partnership actually exists, and who are partners. The number of persons who may unite to form a partnership is not limited, but a person, to become a partner, must be competent to contract. An infant's contract of partnership, like most of his contracts, is voidable, and may be affirmed after he becomes of age, in which case he has all of the rights, and is subject to all of the duties, of a partner.

In *Bush* v. *Linthicum*, 59 Md. 344, plaintiff and defendant entered into a written agreement of copartnership in the grocery business. After the business had been conducted for a time, plaintiff brought an action to dissolve the partnership and to have the assets applied on the debts of the firm. Defendant pleaded that he was an infant, but the court held that this did not prevent the dissolution of the partnership and the selling of its assets, and applying the same to the payment of its debts. Although an infant may become a partner, he can not be held for the contracts or debts of the firm individually unless he affirms them after becoming of age.

Kinds of Partners. — Partners are (1) ostensible or public, (2) secret or unknown, (3) nominal, (4) silent, (5) dormant, or (6) special or limited.

Public Partner. — A public or ostensible partner is one of the active and known parties. He usually participates in the business and is held out to the world as a partner.

Secret Partner. — A secret or unknown partner is one who is in reality a partner active in the management of the business, but conceals the fact both from the public and from the customers of the partnership. This course is often taken when a person risks money or credit in a business, but does not wish to assume the risks and liabilities of a partner. So long as his concealment is perfect, he is protected; but if he is at any time discovered to be an actual partner, he may be held the same as an ostensible partner.

In *Milmo National Bank* v. *Bergstrom*, 1 Tex. Civ. App. 151, defendant and one Carter were engaged as partners for one year in dealing in hides, wool, and produce, under the name of A. N. Carter. At the time Carter opened the credit account with plaintiff, he informed plaintiff that defendant was his partner. The money sued for had been loaned after defendant had withdrawn from the firm, but this was not known to plaintiff. Defendant contended that as he was a secret or dormant partner, he was not bound to give notice of the dissolution. Held, that he was liable to plaintiff for the debts contracted after the dissolution of the partnership if plaintiff was not given notice, as the credit was extended on the strength of defendant's membership in the firm.

Nominal Partner. — A nominal partner is one who is held forth as a partner, with his own consent, and is liable as a partner because he has given his credit to the firm and authorized engagements and contracts on the strength of this relation. He has no interest whatever in the business, and as between himself and the true owner there is no actual partnership, but there exists what we have spoken of as an implied partnership as to third parties, and the nominal partner will therefore be held to the same liability as to third parties to whom he has suffered himself to be held out as a real partner.

In the case of *Hicks* v. *Cram*, 17 Vt. 449, defendants were sued as partners doing business under the name of Cram & Hutchinson. Defendant Hutchinson claimed that he was not a partner and had no interest in the business, but that his son was the partner. It was shown that defendant had held himself out as a partner, and when Cram had stated that Hutchinson was a partner he had made no denial. Held, that defendant Hutchinson was liable, and that a person who suffers himself to be held out to the world as a partner in a firm will be liable for all debts which the firm contracts upon the credit of his being a member.

Silent Partner. — A silent partner is one who as between the members of the firm is an actual partner, but who takes no active part in the business of the firm except that of recovering his share of the profits. He may be known to the outside world as a partner, but in the business itself he takes no active part.

Dormant Partner. — A dormant partner does not differ materially from a silent partner, except that he is not known to the outside world. He is both a secret and a silent partner, being both unknown as a partner and inactive in the business.

Special Partner. — A special or limited partner exists only in those states in which the statutes provide for limited partnerships. By complying with the statute, such a partner may contribute a certain amount of capital and not become liable for the debts of the firm beyond the amount so contributed.

Reality of Partnership. — In the case of a partnership by implication, which has already been mentioned, a nice question often arises as to whether or not a partnership really exists. The agreement or understanding between the parties to a transaction may be such that the law will say they are partners although they did not contemplate becoming partners, but that the effect of their agreement created this relation. The early test in the English and American courts was the sharing of profits. A person who was to share in the profits was a partner, but the later holdings of the courts have departed from this rule and the test now in England and in most of the states seems to be the intention of the parties.

If the parties either expressly or impliedly enter into an association such as the law regards as a partnership, they will be held to stand in that relation. Whether such an association is intended to be formed depends upon the facts in each case.

There may be a partnership as to third parties though the parties are not partners as between themselves, as is the case where one holds himself out as a partner and by his conduct induces others to trust the firm on the strength of his being a partner. As to such outside parties, he will be so held although the intent and agreement of the parties between themselves does not create such a relation.

Powell v. *Moore*, 79 Ga. 524, was an action brought against Marbut and Powell, doing business under the firm name of S. P. Marbut. Powell denied being a partner. He contributed the use of a dwelling, storehouse, and $200, which he called a loan, and Marbut contributed his time to the business and $200. No agreement was made as to the rent of the house or the interest on the money, but Powell was to receive one half of the profits of the business as profits and not as compensation for the use of the house and money. Held, that this constituted a partnership as to third parties.

In *Hackett* v. *Stanley*, 115 N.Y. 625, defendant entered into an agreement whereby in consideration of his loaning one Gorham $750 for use in the heating and ventilating business, which sum was secured by notes of Gorham's and by a chattel mortgage, etc., and in the further consideration of defendant's services in securing sales, also in consideration of any other sums he might in his option advance, Gorham was to divide the net profits of the business equally with him. Any money advanced was to draw interest. Gorham was to have $1000 for his services in managing the business, which was to be carried on in his name. Held, that as to creditors of the business, defendant was chargeable as a partner, and that this was so although the creditors were ignorant of the agreement at the time of giving the credit.

Caldwell v. *Miller*, 127 Pa. St. 442, held, that an agreement between persons engaged in business that each is to share directly in the profits as such, constitutes them partners as to third persons, whatever their arrangements may be between themselves.

In determining whether or not the parties are partners, the fact that they are to divide the profits and to share the losses is evidence of an intent to become partners, though this does not absolutely create such a relation. That each party is to have a voice and control in the business, and that each is to invest his capital and labor in the undertaking and is not to occupy the position of clerk or manager, are generally considered facts sufficient to determine the relation one of partnership.

Meehan v. *Valentine*, 145 U.S. 611, held, that one who lends a sum of money to a partnership, under an agreement that he shall be paid interest thereon and shall also be paid one tenth of the yearly profits of the partnership business if those profits exceed the sum lent, does not thereby become liable as a partner for the debts of the firm.

Manhattan Brass Co. v. *Sears*, 45 N.Y. 797, held, that an agreement for sharing in the profits of a business is sufficient to constitute a partnership as to third parties. It is not necessary that the agreement be to share in the losses.

The authorities differ very widely as to the rules that will control in determining who are and who are not partners, and the only safe guide seems to be to discover whether the parties intended to enter into a relation which the law will consider a partnership. If so, even though they themselves did not intend to become partners and expressly stated they were not, still they will be considered to be partners.

In *Bush* v. *Beecher*, 45 Mich. 188, Beecher owned a hotel and Williams agreed in writing to hire the use of it from day to day, to keep it open as a hotel, and to pay Beecher daily a sum equal to one third of the gross receipts. Plaintiff sold Williams a bill of goods and then sought to hold Beecher as a partner. The goods were sold to Williams, and Beecher was never held out as being in partnership with him. Held, that their agreement did not constitute a partnership. The court said that there can be no such a thing as a partnership as to third persons when there is none as between the parties themselves, unless the third persons have been misled by deceptive appearances or concealment of facts.

In *Farnum* v. *Patch*, 60 N.H. 294, certain persons took a number of shares, at $25 each, in an enterprise which, according to their written agreement, was for the purpose of starting a grocery store. They thought they would not be liable for any debts except for the amounts which they subscribed, and did not consider that they were partners. Held, that their arrangement constituted their relation that of partners.

⅄2. RIGHTS OF PARTNERS BETWEEN THEMSELVES

Right to Choose Associates. — The first right of a partner is to choose those with whom he is to be associated in this relation, for as a person can not be compelled to go into a partnership against his will, so he can not be compelled to allow any one to come into the partnership without his consent. If one partner draws out or dies, his interest can not be purchased by another who can come in without the consent of the other partners; and if they give their consent, and he comes in, the result is that a new partnership is created.

The case of *Noonan* v. *Nunan*, 76 Cal. 44, held that the mere purchase of the interest in the partnership property of the estate of a deceased partner does not create a new partnership between the purchaser and the surviving partner of the old firm.

Right of Purchaser or Inheritor. — The person who buys or inherits the interest of a partner in a firm merely has the right to demand a settlement of the affairs of the company and a payment to him of his share, after the debts of the firm are paid.

Partner may Sell. — Each partner has the absolute right to sell the whole or any part of the partnership property included in the regular course of the business, but a sale of any property of the partnership not ordinarily kept for sale and not within the course of the business is not within the power of one partner. For example, one partner in a grocery business can sell the stock in the regular way, but not the fixtures and store, as such sale would not be in the regular course of the business.

In the case of *Drake* v. *Thyng*, 37 Ark. 228, Drake and Thyng were partners in the brickmaking business. While Drake was away Thyng sold the stock and plant to a third party for an insignificant and inadequate sum. Drake brought this action to set aside the sale. Held, that, while a partner may sell a part or the whole of any of the effects of a firm which are intended for sale, if the sale is within the scope of the partnership business, yet he can not, without the consent of the other partners, dispose of the partnership business itself or of all the effects, including the means of carrying it on, as this is beyond the range of a partner's implied powers.

Capital. — The capital of the partnership consists of such properties or amounts as are contributed to the common fund by the different partners at the beginning, or that may be put in thereafter. The claim of each partner to this partnership capital does not extend to any particular article, but to an interest in the whole, consisting of a right to share in the proceeds after the firm debts are paid. Aside from this, individual property of the partners may be used in the business. The store in which the business is conducted may belong to one of the partners, and he can deal with this as his own and not as a partner.

In *Nichol* v. *Stewart*, 36 Ark. 612, one partner mortgaged a certain number of bales of cotton out of the partnership crop for the payment of an individual debt. The mortgagee had notice of the partnership. Held, that the mortgagee had no right to the specific property but only a right to the ultimate interest of the mortgagor in the partnership effects, after all of the firm debts were paid, to an amount equal to the value of the cotton.

Good Will. — The good will of the firm is partnership property. The good will is defined to be the benefit arising from the connection and reputation of the firm, the fact that the business is established and going, that it has customers and is advertised throughout the section to which it looks for trade. The sale of the business as a whole, including stock, fixtures, etc., is understood to include the good will. So the trade-marks and trade name of a business are property belonging to the firm and pass with the sale of the business in the same manner as the good will, although either may be sold separately.

In *Merry* v. *Hoopes*, 111 N.Y. 415, Hoopes and Merry were copartners engaged in manufacturing galvanized iron under two trade-marks, one the "Lion brand" and the other the "Phœnix brand." Upon the dissolution of the firm defendant bought the business. Thereafter plaintiff brought this action to restrain him from the use of the above-named trade-marks, nothing having been said about them in the bill of sale. Held, that the exclusive right to use the trade-marks belonging to the firm passed to the defendant.

In the case of *Williams* v. *Farrand*, 88 Mich. 473, it was held that an assignment of all tne stock, property, and effects of a business, or the exclusive right to manufacture a given article, carries with it the exclusive right to use a fictitious name under which such business has been carried on and such trade-marks and trade names as have been used in such business.

Good Faith. — The first duty of each of the partners to the others is that of exercising the utmost good faith toward them. The reason for this is apparent when we realize how completely each partner is at the mercy of the others. Each partner really acts as agent in the transaction of the business for the firm and for the other partners.

Kimberly v. *Arms*, 129 U.S. 512, held, that if one partner is the active agent of the firm, and as such receives a salary beyond what comes to him from his interest as a partner, he is clothed with a double trust in his relations with the other partners, which imposes upon him the duty of exercising the utmost good faith in his dealings ; and if he obtains anything for his own benefit in disregard of that trust, a court of equity will compel him to account to the other partners for it.

Individual Liability. — Each partner is chargeable with any loss to the firm which arises from his own breach of duty, whether through fraud, negligence, or ignorance, but he is not liable to the company for loss arising from an honest mistake of judgment.

Charlton v. *Sloan*, 76 Iowa 288, held, that although a partner may act unwisely in incurring liabilities for the firm, the resulting loss can not properly be charged to him personally upon a dissolution, when it is not shown that his acts were wanton or fraudulent.

If one partner takes a secret advantage of the partnership, whereby he makes a profit for himself at the expense of the firm, he can be required to restore it, the courts holding that he acted for the partnership and it will be entitled to the benefits. If the lease of a building occupied by a firm expires, one member can not secretly take out a new lease in his own name and seek to sublet to the firm at an increased rate. The new lease taken in the name of one member of the firm will be declared by the courts as held by him for the benefit and use of the firm.

In the case of *Hodge* v. *Twitchell*, 33 Minn. 389, Hodge, Twitchell, and Ruby agreed to purchase real property together, each to pay one third of the cost and to divide the property equally. Twitchell called their attention to a lot and advised its purchase. While they were considering it he secretly made an agreement with the owner that if he, Twitchell, found a purchaser for the remainder of the lot at $2500, the original price, the seller would give him a certain part of the lot for his services. Twitchell then told his partners that a part was sold, but the balance could be obtained for $2500, and urged its purchase. It was taken upon his recommendation, and the portion promised Twitchell was conveyed to his wife, in pursuance of the owner's agreement. The court decided that his wife held the lot in trust for Hodge and Ruby, to the extent of their agreed interest in the venture.

Records of Transactions. — The firm must keep books of account upon which each member is bound to enter, or have entered, all of his transactions for the firm, as each partner has a right to know of all the transactions in the business.

Van Ness v. *Van Ness*, 32 N.J. Eq. 669, held, that a member of a firm whose duty it is to keep the accounts, and who claims that he has omitted to enter credits to which he is entitled, will be required to furnish satisfactory proof of the mistake he asks to have corrected.

Compensation. — One partner is not entitled to any special compensation for his services in the partnership unless it is expressly provided for. Each partner is supposed to do all that he can for the good of the partnership, and whatever he does gives him no claim for extra compensation beyond his share of the profits of the business unless he has the consent of the other partners.

Burgess v. *Badger*, 124 Ill. 288, held, that in the absence of an agreement to that effect, one partner is not entitled to charge his copartners for his services because he has done more than his just proportion of the work.

In *Gregory* v. *Menefee*, 83 Mo. 413, the claim of the surviving partner of a firm for compensation for his services in closing up the partnership business was not allowed. The court held that a surviving partner is not entitled to any compensation for such services.

Heath v. *Waters*, 40 Mich. 457, held, that the sickness of a partner is one of the risks incident to a partnership, and does not give another partner any claim for personal services in conducting the entire business unless the articles of copartnership provide for such compensation.

Partners may Sign Negotiable Paper. — It is the general rule that one member can bind the firm by signing the firm name as maker, indorser, or acceptor of negotiable paper if it is done in connection with the firm business and not for a private debt or account.

In *Wagner* v. *Simmons*, 61 Ala. 143, defendants were partners in the business of buying and selling cattle and produce. The court held that each member had the right to draw, accept, or indorse bills of exchange in the firm name, and bind the partnership as to third persons, dealing fairly and in good faith, regarding matters usually incident to the business. It is immaterial in such a case, as to persons thus dealing with one of the partners, that the other partner was not informed of the transaction and repudiated it as soon as it came to his knowledge.

The power of any partner to use the firm name on negotiable paper is presumed, and a stipulation between the partners that certain members of the firm shall not so use it will not affect third persons having no knowledge of such agreement. But this rule does not apply if it is obvious that the instrument is signed, not for the firm, but for the individual benefit of a partner.

Power of Majority. — We have discussed the power of one partner, and turning now to the question of what a majority of the partners can do, we find that they may control the ordinary conduct of the firm's business, and have power to act in all matters within the scope of the partnership affairs, but they have no power to change the nature or location of the business.

In the case of *Clarke* v. *Slate*, 136 Pa. St. 408, it was held that as a majority of the partners, while acting fairly and in good faith and keeping within the scope and purposes of the partnership, have power to direct the course of the partnership affairs, they may give a valid warrant of attorney in the name of the firm, authorizing suit upon a contract made by it, and this notwithstanding the dissent of a minority.

In the case of *Staples* v. *Sprague*, 75 Me. 458, five persons had agreed to cut and pack a quantity of ice for sale, and after deducting all expenses to divide the proceeds equally. One of the members, with the consent and approval of two others, sold a large quantity of the ice. The remaining two brought suit to charge the others for damages in selling the ice at what they claimed was too low a price. Held, that the agreement constituted a partnership, and if there be no fraud the majority of a firm can make a valid sale of property belonging to the firm without the consent of the minority.

3. LIABILITY OF PARTNERS TO THIRD PARTIES

As we have already stated, each partner is liable for all of the debts of the partnership, and this is so whether he is a secret, nominal, or ostensible partner.

In *Richardson* v. *Farmer*, 36 Mo. 35, defendants had been doing business under the name of W. H. Jopes. It was shown that Farmer was a dormant or secret partner. Held, that while the credit was given to an ostensible partner, because no other was known to the creditor, yet the creditor may also sue the secret partner when discovered, and the credit will not be presumed to have been given on the sole responsibility of the ostensible partner.

Effect of Notice. — But this is not so if fair notice is given that the company will not be liable for any particular acts of a partner, and if the notice that such acts are forbidden is given to the person with whom the partner deals, he can no longer bind the firm.

In *Yeager* v. *Wallace*, 57 Pa. St. 365, it was held that the partnership relation makes each partner the agent of the other when acting within the scope of his power, but when the agency is denied and the act forbidden by the copartner, with notice to the party assuming to deal with him as agent of the firm, the act is then his individual act, and not that of the firm.

Limit of Authority. — The authority of a partner to bind the firm by contract is limited to transactions within the scope of the partnership business, and if he seeks to charge the firm with matters outside of the scope of the firm's usual business, he must show special authority from the other partners so to do. A partnership to work a farm would not therefore give one partner any implied authority to draw bills of exchange or borrow money, while a partner in a mercantile or manufacturing company would have such authority.

In *Randall* v. *Merideth*, 76 Tex. 669, Tiernan, Randall, Sawyer, and Dyer, residing in Galveston, made a joint investment in mining property in Mexico. Tiernan was the manager in charge of the work of developing the mine. Assessments were made for the work each year for three years, and when the money for each year gave out the work was to be suspended. In 1885, although the home partners gave express orders that the work should stop when the money gave out, Tiernan kept up the work and raised money by loan from Merideth and Ailman, local bankers, who dealt alone with Tiernan, not having knowledge of his partners. Upon suit being brought by the bankers against all the partners, it was held that they could not recover of Randall, Sawyer, and Dyer without showing affirmatively that Tiernan had express authority from them to borrow money on their credit for the mining enterprise. The partners to a mining enterprise have no implied power to borrow money on the credit of the partnership.

While the presumption is that a partner has no authority to use the goods or credit of the firm to pay his personal debts nor to buy goods for his personal use with the partnership funds, still he may have express authority so to do, and in that case the transaction is valid.

In *Dob* v. *Halsey*, 16 Johns. (N.Y.) 34, one Moore and plaintiff were partners in the lumber business. Moore gave defendant some lumber belonging to the firm in payment of a personal debt. In an action by plaintiff to recover the value of the lumber the court held that when one partner delivers partnership property to a third person in payment of a private debt, and the third person knows it is partnership property, he can not hold it against the other partners, but is liable to pay the price of the goods.

In *Hartness* v. *Wallace*, 106 N.C. 427, Connelly and Deitz were copartners in the business of selling wagons until they made an assignment to Hartness. Before the assignment one Hobbs purchased a wagon of them and gave his note. Connelly assigned the note to Wallace in part payment of his individual indebtedness to him. This assignment of the note was made without the knowledge or consent of Deitz. The note was afterwards paid to Wallace. In an action by the receiver to recover this amount from Wallace it was held that the plaintiff could recover.

In *Guice* v. *Thornton*, 76 Ala. 466, it was held that when money is borrowed by one partner on his own individual credit, the subsequent execution of a note for it in the partnership name, without the consent of the other partners, is a fraud on the partnership, and does not give the creditor a right to recover from the firm on such a note.

Name. — A partnership should adopt some particular name under which to do business. This may be simply the name or names of one or more of the partners, either with or without the words "and company" added, or any other designation that the parties may adopt, but by statute in New York State the term "and company" must not be used unless it actually represents a partner.

Fraud. — The partners are held liable for the fraud and the false representations of one partner when they are made in the course of the firm business.

In the case of *Taylor* v. *Jones*, 42 N.H. 25, it was held that one partner is not liable for the wrongful acts of another partner unless they were done within the proper scope of the business of the partnership, or were authorized or adopted by him.

Notice to one Partner is Notice to All. — It is a well-established principle that notice to one partner in the course of the business is notice to all. An illustration of this is the case of partnership negotiable paper that has been dishonored, notice of which dishonor to one partner is notice to the firm.

In *Tucker* v. *Cole*, 54 Wis. 539, it was held that where timber is purchased by a firm, prior notice to one member of the firm that it was cut from land not belonging to the vendor is notice to all of the partners.

In *Frank* v. *Blake*, 58 Iowa 750, it was held that where a partnership seeks to recover as a *bona fide* purchaser of a promissory note, fraudulently procured, the burden is upon it to show that all of the members of the partnership were ignorant of the fraud at the time of the purchase.

4. REMEDIES AGAINST THE PARTNERSHIP

In the eyes of the law a partnership does not have an individuality of its own like a corporation, but it is looked upon as a collection of persons and must be sued not in the firm name but in the names of the persons composing it. In some of the states this rule has been changed, and partnerships may sue and be sued in the firm name. The members of a partnership are proceeded against for a debt of the firm in the same way that one proceeds against an individual. When the creditors of the partnership and the individual creditors of the partners come in conflict, a distinction is made and the law says they must proceed in a particular way, the object being to give the individual creditor his due out of the individual property of the partner, and the firm creditor his due out of the partnership property. If, after the partnership debts are paid, there remains a surplus, the creditors of a partner may proceed against this partner's share; but if, on the other hand, there are not sufficient partnership assets to satisfy the firm creditors, but there remain individual assets after the individual creditors are satisfied, such surplus is liable for the firm debts.

Wilder v. *Keeler*, 3 Page (N.Y.) 164, held, that upon the death of one of the partners in a firm, a joint creditor of the partnership has no claim for the payment of his debt out of the estate of the deceased partner until all the separate creditors of such partner have been paid out of his estate, and the creditors of the individual partners have no claim upon the partnership property until all of the partnership creditors are satisfied.

In case there are no partnership assets, the firm creditors are entitled to share in the individual assets of any partner equally with his individual creditors.

In *Brock* v. *Bateman*, 25 Ohio St. 609, it was held that when a partnership and several members of the firm are insolvent and there are no partnership funds for distribution among the creditors, the creditors of the firm are entitled to share equally with the creditors of each partner in the distribution of his individual assets.

5. DISSOLUTION

Duration. — When the partnership is formed, the articles of copartnership usually state how long it shall continue. Other circumstances, however, may operate to change the time, and when the relation terminates, the partnership is said to be dissolved.

Forms of Dissolution. — Dissolution may take place in any one of the following ways: (1) By provision in the articles of copartnership. (2) By the mutual consent of all the partners. (3) By the act of one or more of the partners. (4) By a change in the partnership. (5) By the death of a partner. (6) By the decree of a court of equity. (7) By bankruptcy.

1. *Contract.* — When the period for which the partnership was formed has elapsed, it is thereupon dissolved unless con-

tinued by the parties. The partnership may be formed for a temporary purpose, and in that case when the purpose is accomplished the partnership ceases.

2. *Mutual Consent.* — The partnership may be dissolved at any time by the mutual assent of all the partners, though the period for which it was formed has not elapsed.

3. *Act of a Partner.* — The firm may be dissolved by the act of one or more of the parties. This is accomplished when one partner makes an assignment for the benefit of his creditors or becomes bankrupt or, being insolvent, his interest is sold upon execution to pay his creditors. In these cases his property passes beyond his control and he can no longer perform his part as a partner. Also, where the partnership was formed for no definite period, but at the will of the parties, any partner can terminate the relation by notice to the other parties.

In the case of *Blake* v. *Sweeting*, 121 Ill. 67, Blake, Huston, and Sweeting were engaged as partners in manufacturing brick. After continuing in the business about three years Huston went away, abandoned the business, and wrote to Blake, authorizing him and Sweeting to settle the business as they pleased. Thereafter Blake and Sweeting formed a new partnership and conducted the business themselves. Held, that the acts of Huston operated as a dissolution of the old firm. A partnership, when not formed for any definite time, may be dissolved by any member of the firm at his pleasure. The withdrawal of one member is a dissolution of the firm.

4. *Change in the Partnership.* — The partnership may be dissolved by a change in the membership of the firm. A partner may withdraw from the firm, or he may transfer his interest to a stranger. In whatever way the members of a partnership may be changed, the act at once terminates and dissolves the partnership. One partner may sell his interest to another party who is satisfactory to the remaining members of the firm, and they may agree to take him in as a partner. In this case the old partnership is dissolved and a new one formed. After the partner has retired or sold out he is still liable upon all of the contracts of the firm made before dissolution, and he is entitled to his share of the assets of the firm after the debts are paid.

In *Goodspeed* v. *Wiard Plow Co.*, 45 Mich. 322, it was held that a retiring partner is bound by all previous contracts made within the lines of the business, but after the dissolution of the partnership he is not bound by any new contracts made by his former partner.

Notice. — The retiring partner, if the business is to be continued by a new firm, which may have the same or a somewhat similar name, will be liable for the debts and contracts of the firm even after he is out, if they were entered into with parties who had dealt with the firm while he was a member and had no notice of his retirement. Therefore, to render him free from liability for the debts and contracts of the new firm, he must give notice of the dissolution of the old firm. This notice must be given either orally or in writing to those who have had previous dealing with the old firm, for the retiring partner is bound unless those who have dealt with the old firm can be shown to have had actual notice.

National Shoe & Leather Bank v. *Herz*, 89 N.Y. 629, was an action brought against defendant as an alleged partner of the firm of Martin Herz & Co., to recover on four promissory notes indorsed in the name of the firm. Prior to the indorsing of the note, Herz had sold out to his partner, Rosenberg, who carried on the business in the same name. Notice of dissolution was given in the papers and sent by mail to persons who had dealt with the firm. Such a notice was sent to the bank, which never received it. Held, that the defendant was liable. To release himself he must show that the bank had actual notice of the dissolution.

But direct notice from the firm or the retiring partner is not required if the customer has actual knowledge of the withdrawal of the partner.

Aside from notice to former customers, notice to the world is necessary to enable the retiring partner to escape liability for future debts of the continuing firm or partner. The ordinary method of giving such notice by publication in a newspaper is usually held sufficient, but the paper must be one which circulates in the vicinity.

In *Meyer* v. *Krohn*, 114 Ill. 574, it was held that, as to persons who have never had any business transactions with a partnership, notice of its dissolution or the withdrawal of a member by publication in a newspaper published at the place of business of the firm is sufficient, but as to those who have had previous dealings with the firm actual notice or its equivalent must be shown to protect the retiring member from liability for debts subsequently incurred in the firm name.

A change in the name of the firm by which the name of the retiring partner is dropped and general attention is called to the fact that the firm has dissolved, is sometimes held to be sufficient notice to the general public to protect the retiring partner against future dealings of the new firm.

In *Coggswell* v. *Davis*, 65 Wis. 191, it was held that a change of a partnership name which in itself indicates who the individual partners are, may be sufficient evidence of a dissolution of such partnership ; but when the name under which the business is transacted gives no indication of the names of the persons composing the firm, a change in such name is not notice of the retirement of a person who was previously known to have been a partner in the business.

The new or incoming partner who purchases the interest of the retiring partner and becomes a member of the new partnership is of course liable for all of the debts incurred after he came into the firm, but not for any of the old debts, unless he expressly agreed for a consideration to assume them.

In *Kountz* v. *Holthouse*, 85 Pa. St. 235, it was held that an incoming partner may by agreement become liable for debts contracted by the firm previous to his entering it, but the presumption is against any such liability.

5. *Death of a Partner.* — Another change which will work a dissolution of the partnership is the death of a partner. This is really a subdivision of the preceding class, as it is a change in the partnership. The dissolution of the partnership follows necessarily immediately after a partner's death. The surviving partners have the exclusive right to the possession and management of the partnership business for the purpose of closing it out. Frequently the articles of copartnership provide how the surviving partner shall close out the business, and when such provision is made it must be followed. The surviving partner holds the partnership assets in trust for the purpose of closing up its affairs, paying the firm debts, and distributing the remaining assets among the partners or their representatives.

In *Sellers* v. *Shore*, 89 Ga. 416, it was held that upon the death of a partner the title to the personal assets of the firm is in the survivor, who is charged with the administration of the same, first for the payment of the partnership debts and second for paying over the deceased partner's share in the surplus to his legal representatives. Unless there is a surplus none of the assets constitute any part of the estate of the deceased.

6. *Decree of a Court.* — A court of equity may decree a dissolution of the firm for good cause upon the application of one or more of the partners. This relief will be granted when the partnership was entered into through fraud or for a wrongful and illegal purpose. After the partnership is formed a dissolution may be decreed because of the misconduct of one or more of the partners, but this relief will not be granted for any slight cause. Wild speculations, gross extravagance, quarrelsome and oppressive conduct, habitual intemperance, indolence and inattention to business, or any conduct which brings disgrace and discredit upon the firm, if sufficiently serious, will constitute grounds justifying such action by the court.

In the case of *Cottle* v. *Leitch*, 35 Cal. 434, it was held that when one partner having the management of the partnership affairs makes false entries in the books and defrauds his copartners of a portion of the partnership receipts, the partners thus defrauded are entitled to a dissolution of the partnership and an accounting.

In *Loomis* v. *McKenzie*, 31 Iowa 425, it was held that ill feeling and differences between partners will not justify the appointing of a receiver to wind up the affairs of the concern, when the term for which the partnership was created has not expired and it does not clearly appear that the parties would suffer loss by continuing in possession of the property.

In *Groth* v. *Payment*, 79 Mich. 290, it was held that the denial by one partner of all rights of his copartners in the partnership property and his claim of the right of exclusive possession and use of it, entitled his copartners to a dissolution of the partnership.

The rule seems to be, if it is obvious that the parties can not longer be associated together with harmony and profit the court will decree a dissolution rather than cause the partnership to be injurious to the innocent party. So also the financial inability of one partner to fulfill his part of the transactions of the firm, whether from his fault or his misfortune, will be a sufficient cause for dissolution. Insanity or permanent failure of health because of incurable disease are sufficient grounds for dissolution.

In *Raymond* v. *Vaughn*, 128 Ill. 256, it was held that the insanity of a partner does not in itself work a dissolution of the partnership, but may constitute sufficient grounds to justify a court of equity in decreeing its dissolution.

7. *Bankruptcy.* — Bankruptcy of either a partner or the firm operates as a dissolution of the partnership. This is also true when the firm or any partner makes an assignment for the benefit of creditors.

6. JOINT STOCK COMPANIES

Definition. — A joint stock company is a form of association in appearance resembling a corporation while in reality it is nothing more than a partnership.

Incorporation is expensive in England, and there the joint stock company is common, but in the United States, where the corporation is so frequently adopted, the joint stock company is in many states but seldom found.

As has been said, joint stock companies resemble corporations in form. They have officers and by-laws. Their capital is divided into shares which under their by-laws are transferable. Their by-laws generally regulate the mode of conducting their business and electing their officers. A member of a joint stock company, although he may style himself but a stockholder, is a partner, and as such is liable to the same extent and in the same manner as any ordinary partner.

In *Davison* v. *Holden*, 55 Conn. 103, the defendants and others associated themselves together without incorporation under the name of the Bridgeport Coöperative Association for the purpose of procuring meat and provisions at a lower rate for the members of the organization. Sales were made to persons not members at a higher rate, but no profit was expected beyond the expense of management. The members held meetings and elected officers. Held, that the individuals composing the association were liable personally as partners for goods purchased by the managers of the association for its benefit. It made no difference that they did not intend to become individually responsible or that they did not know or believe that they would be.

Sale of Shares. — It is generally held that under the by-laws of the company a member may sell or transfer his shares without working a dissolution of the company as would be the result in a partnership. And the death of a member does not work its dissolution. In some of the states joint stock companies are given certain privileges by statute; as, for instance, allowing them to sue or be sued in the name of their president or treasurer. The business of a joint stock company can not be changed or extended without the consent of all the members, although in its ordinary business arrangements a majority will govern.

QUESTIONS ON PARTNERSHIP

1. Define partnership. What are the objects of partnership relations?

2. How is a partnership formed?

3. A and B intending to engage in the dry goods business agree orally to invest an equal amount of cash and give their time to the business, arranging to divide the profits and losses equally. Does this oral agreement constitute a partnership? Is it advisable to form a partnership in this way?

4. If in the above case these parties in their oral agreement had expressly understood that the partnership was to continue for five years, would the agreement have been binding?

5. What is an implied partnership?

6. Name and define five principal classes of partners.

7. George Hicks and Charles Hutchinson agree to engage as partners in the business of manufacturing furniture under the name of Charles Hutchinson, Hicks's name not appearing in the firm and he taking no active part in its management. They buy lumber, and before it is paid for, the firm fails. The lumber company did not know of Hicks's partnership in the business, the lumber being bought in Hutchinson's name. Can they hold Hicks personally for the lumber?

8. Grover and Martin have been engaged for a number of years in the wholesale grocery business. They dissolve partnership, and Grover retires from the firm, though he still allows his name to remain in the firm. He is around their place of business frequently and was present when Martin stated to Edwards & Co., a firm from which they bought, that Mr. Grover was his partner. Grover did not deny this. Can Edwards & Co. hold him as a partner?

9. Stanley is doing business under the name of A. H. Stanley, he and Moore having an agreement whereby Moore, who owns the store, contributes the rent and loans Stanley $500. Stanley, on the other hand, contributes $500 and his time in conducting the business. It is agreed that the profits are to be shared equally. Are they partners as to third parties?

10. If in the above case Moore had merely furnished the store and nothing else, and the agreement had been that Stanley was to give him one fourth of the profits as rent, would they have been partners as to third parties?

11. A, B, and C are engaged in conducting business as copartners. C dies and D, C's son, who is his executor and heir, seeks to come into the firm as a partner and take his father's place. Has he that right? What right has he?

12. Leland and Scott were engaged in manufacturing and selling shoes. Leland, without the knowledge or consent of Scott, sold 100 pairs of shoes from their regular selling stock. Had he the right?

13. In the above case had Leland the right without the consent of Scott to sell all the shoes they had manufactured?

14. Suppose in question 12 Leland, without the consent of Scott, sold their machinery and lasts used in manufacturing their shoes. Had he that right?

15. A and B were copartners in conducting a carting business in which they employed six wagons and six teams of horses. A gave X a mortgage on three of the wagons to secure an individual debt. X knew that the wagons were partnership property. Had A the right to take half of the wagons as his share of the partnership assets to pay an individual debt?

16. What is the good will of a firm? Can it be sold separately from the business?

17. A firm having been engaged in manufacturing collars and cuffs under a certain brand sell out their business to X and include in the sale all of their stock and machinery. They afterwards seek to sell to Y the trade-mark or brand under which they had manufactured their collars and cuffs. X claims it. To whom does it belong?

18. Carlton and Brown are engaged as partners in buying and selling produce. Brown learns of a man who has a large quantity of wheat, and as the firm are looking for wheat and he knows that they can afford to pay $.95 a bushel for it, he goes to the owner and tells him that if he will give him one cent a bushel for his services, he will find him a purchaser for the wheat at $.95. The owner agrees, and the firm buys the wheat. Carlton learns of the transaction afterwards and sues Brown for one half of the one cent per bushel received by him. Can he recover?

19. A and B are engaged in conducting a dry goods store. A is taken sick and is obliged to go away for the benefit of his health. During the time he is gone B conducts the business alone, and later charges the firm for extra services in running the business alone. Has he a right to such compensation, there being no agreement about the same?

20. A, B, and C are partners in the hardware business. B gives the firm of Sloan & Co. a promissory note, due in 60 days, for a bill of goods bought by his firm. He signs his note in the firm name. Has he authority?

21. In the above case, suppose B gives the firm's note, payable in 60 days, in payment of his individual grocery bill. Has he the right?

22. In question 20 A and B wish to buy a quantity of stoves for sale in the course of their business. C objects. Have they the right to buy them?

23. In question 20 A and B, wishing to enlarge their stock and make a

general department store of it, decide to add a line of crockery, glassware, and groceries. C objects. Have they the right?

24. A and B were engaged as copartners in dealing in horses. A sold a horse for X, fraudulently representing it to be sound, when in fact it had the glanders, a contagious, incurable disease. X sued the partners for fraud. Was B liable as well as A?

25. Randall and Cole were engaged in the mercantile business. In the course of their business they received a note from Darrow which they indorsed. When the note became due it was not paid by Darrow but was protested, and notice of non-payment was given to Randall. In a suit against Randall & Cole, to hold them as indorsers, Cole set up the defense that he had not had notice. Could he be held, or was his defense good?

26. In the above case, when the action is brought against Randall & Cole, how should they be sued, as a firm or as individuals?

27. Keeler and Wilder, dry goods merchants, fail. The firm owns $5000. Keeler has individual assets amounting to $3000, and Wilder has individual assets amounting to $10,000. Page, a creditor of the firm, seeks to satisfy his claim out of Keeler's personal property, while Keeler has individual creditors whom he owes more than the amount of his property. Can Page so satisfy his claim? To what property must he look first?

28. Bates is a personal creditor of Keeler. Can he proceed against the partnership property to satisfy his claim? Can he proceed against the individual property of Wilder?

29. Name the different ways in which the dissolution of a partnership may be effected.

30. A and B enter into articles of copartnership, under which they agree to continue in business as partners for three years. At the expiration of three years does the partnership become dissolved? Can the parties by mutual assent dissolve the partnership before that time?

31. In the above case A sells his interest in the partnership to C. What is the result?

32. If A dies, what effect has his death upon the partnership?

33. In question 30, suppose A sells out his interest to C, who is accepted as a partner, and the firm continues under the old name of A and B. The new firm of B and C contracts with one Everetts for some merchandise. Everetts had previously sold to the old firm and had received no notice of A's withdrawal, although A has published a notice of dissolution in the paper. The firm of B and C fails, and Everetts seeks to hold A liable. Can he succeed?

34. If in the above case A had sent Everetts a notice, which he had received, could he be held?

35. If in question 33 A had mailed Everetts a notice which Everetts had never received, could A be held?

36. If in question 33 Everetts had had notice that A was no longer a partner, although it had not been sent directly to him, could A be held?

37. If in **question 33** the firm of A and B had never dealt with Everetts before, and notice of the change of partnership had been published in the local papers, could A be held?

38. In question 33 could C be held liable if the contract had been entered into by the old firm and C had not expressly agreed to pay?

39. Raymond and Loomis are engaged in partnership, but do not agree. Raymond is engaged in wild speculations, is habitually intemperate, and is bringing the business into disrepute. The term during which they agreed to conduct their partnership has not yet expired. Has Loomis the right to dissolve the partnership in an equity court?

40. If in the above case Raymond had become bankrupt, would this have had any effect upon the partnership?

41. What is a joint stock company?

42. Twenty different persons organized a yacht club, each taking one share at $25. They had certain by-laws under which they elected the officers, and stipulated that no member of the club should be personally liable for its debts. The club became bankrupt, and the creditors proceeded individually against the members for the debts of the club. Could they be held?

CORPORATIONS

1. IN GENERAL

Origin. — Such vast undertakings as the modern railroads, steamship lines, large manufacturing plants, etc., which are controlled by private parties, have made it desirable and in fact necessary for a large number of persons to join in a single enterprise that can be more successfully promoted by means of their joint capital and endeavor. There has also arisen the need of some method of organization that shall be free from certain features of the copartnership law. A necessary feature of the organization is that it shall survive the life of any one member, also that the interest of any member may be sold or transferred without affecting the organization. To interest people freely in an organization of this kind, it has also been found desirable that a member shall not be personally liable in the enterprise beyond the amount which he invests.

Under the common law there was no provision for any association of persons to meet these demands unless by a special permit or authority from the government, known as a charter — a provision too slow and costly to admit of common commercial use. The statutes in all of the states, therefore, provide now for the formation of corporations, the purpose of which is to enable a number of persons to associate themselves together under a corporate name with the privileges and protections just enumerated.

Definition. — A corporation is defined as a collection of individuals united by authority of law into one body, under a special name, with the capacity of perpetual succession and of acting in many respects as an individual.

Corporations are in the eyes of the law separate from the members who compose them. The property of the corporation is owned by it and not by the members of the corporation, and a conveyance or sale of such property must be made by the corporation, as it can not be made by the members as individuals.

In *Wheelock* v. *Moulton*, 15 Vt. 519, it was held that the stockholders, as such, can not convey the real property of the corporation, though they all join in the deed. The name and seal of the corporation must be affixed by an officer or agent having authority.

Suits in favor of or against a corporation must be brought by or against the corporation and not the individuals who compose it personally. The corporation may convey to or take from its individual members, and may sue them and be sued by them.

In *Waring* v. *Catawba Co.*, 2 Bay (S.C.) 109, it was held that a member of a corporation may maintain an action against such corporation on any just demand.

The authority of the government is always necessary for the creation of a corporation. No agreement among the members can accomplish such a result. The mere act of the members alone would result in a partnership. The corporation, therefore, being created by the government, has only such powers as are conferred upon it by its charter or act of incorporation.

Public Corporations. — There are several classifications of corporations, but the only one of sufficient importance for us to consider here is the division into public and private corporations. Public corporations are such as are created for the purposes of government and the management of public affairs. Cities, towns, and villages are illustrations of such corporations. The legislatures give them certain powers to pass laws or ordinances, to build bridges, improve streets, etc. They may take and hold property, and may sue and be sued in their corporate names.

Private Corporations. — Private corporations are such as are created for private purposes and for the management of affairs in which the members are interested as private parties. When private individuals are interested in a personal way in a corporation which is of even a public nature, as a railroad, bank, or insurance company, it is a private corporation. Private corporations are also either stock or non-stock corporations. Those formed for the pecuniary profit of their members generally have a capital stock divided into a certain number of parts called shares of stock. A member's interest is determined by the number of shares of stock which he holds in the company. This stock is represented by a written or printed certificate, which can be transferred from one person to another without the consent of the other members of the company.

Certificates. — The form of a certificate of stock is somewhat like the following : —

Incorporated under the laws of the state of New York

No. 130   10 Shares

THE MONROE COUNTY NURSERY COMPANY

Capital $100,000   Shares $100 each

This certifies that George W. Ellis is the owner of ten shares, of one hundred dollars each, of the capital stock of THE MONROE COUNTY NURSERY COMPANY of Rochester, N.Y., transferable only on the books of the Company, in accordance with the By-laws thereof, in person or by attorney, upon the surrender of this certificate.

In witness whereof, the said Corporation has caused this certificate to be signed by its duly authorized officers, and to be sealed with the seal of the corporation, this second day of September, 1903.

[SEAL]   JOHN CAREY, President.
                              WILLIAM A. WILLIS, Secretary.

Non-stock Corporation. — A non-stock corporation is one in which there is no stock to be transferred, and the membership of any individual depends upon the consent of the other members. Incorporated societies and mutual benefit societies are illustrations of this class.

Private Stock Corporations. — The class of corporations most common in this country and to which we will direct our attention, is private stock corporations.

The following are the powers and attributes of practically all private stock corporations: (1) to have continuous succession under a special name; (2) to receive and grant property, enter into contracts, and to sue and be sued in the corporate name; (3) to purchase and hold real and personal property; (4) to have a common seal; (5) to make by-laws; and (6) to limit the personal liability of its members for the corporation debts to the amount invested.

Name and Perpetual Succession. — The attribute of perpetual succession under a special name is essential to all corporations. The corporation is not subject to dissolution by the death or withdrawal of a member. A member may transfer his shares without the consent of his associates, and the transferee comes into the corporation as a member without in any way changing or affecting its existence. A necessary attribute of every corporation is a corporate name. This is essential, as the corporation, being distinct from its members, could not otherwise be known.

In the case of *Elgin Butter Co.* v. *Elgin Creamery Co.*, 155 Ill. 127, it was held that the issuance of a charter to the "Elgin Creamery Company," notwithstanding the previous licensing of the "Elgin Butter Company," does not violate the corporation act, which forbids issuing licenses to corporations having the same name.

In *State* v. *McGrath*, 92 Mo. 355, it was held that a company would not be entitled to a charter under the name of "The Kansas City Real Estate Exchange" when there is a duly incorporated company doing business under the name of "Kansas City Real Estate and Stock Exchange," as the names are substantially the same.

Real Estate. — The power to hold real estate is common to most corporations, but it is not an essential to a corporation's existence. So also the power to use a seal is ordinarily included in the privileges of a corporation, but it is not essential, as a corporation can contract without a seal.

By-laws. — The right to make by-laws is a common incident of a corporation's powers. It is unnecessary to make them when the charter is sufficiently full to provide for all contingencies, but usually the matters of detail are not included in the charter, provision being made for them in the by-laws, and every private corporation has the implied power to make them. But the by-laws to be valid must be reasonable, consistent with the charter, and within the purposes of the corporation. They are generally adopted by a majority vote of the stockholders, and having once been adopted, bind all of the stockholders whether they have assented to them or not.

Limited Liability. — One of the most important attributes of a corporation is that which exempts the stockholders from liability for the debts of the corporation. In a partnership, it will be remembered, a partner is personally liable for the debts of the firm, but this is not so in the case of a corporation except when by statute the personal liability of a stockholder is increased to a greater or less extent. For instance, the stockholder of a bank is by statute liable not only for the amount invested in his stock but also for a further sum of the same amount. It is called a double liability of the stockholder.

Incorporation. — As we have already said, a corporation can be created only by act of the government. This act may be the enactment of a special law which creates and gives power to one particular company. The constitutions of most of the states prohibit the legislature from creating a corporation by a special law except in some particular cases. The great majority of corporations are formed under the general law, which does not of itself create the corporation but authorizes persons to form a corporation by taking certain prescribed steps. It generally requires that articles of incorporation be executed by the incorporators and filed in some public office. These articles must usually set forth the names and residences of the incorporators, the name by which the proposed corporation shall be known, its principal place of business, the objects and purposes of the association (which must be lawful), the period of time for which it is to exist, the amount of capital stock and the number of shares into which it is divided, the number of directors and the names of those who are to act as directors until an election is held.

Any person who has the capacity to enter into a contract may be an incorporator. The statutes generally prescribe the number of incorporators necessary to organize.

In the matter of the *Globe Mutual Benefit Association*, 63 Hun (N.Y.) 263, it was held that a coöperative insurance company, incorporated and having by-laws under which losses are payable from weekly dues collected from policy holders, can not insure infants. The relation existing between the company and its members is one of contract, and the legal disability of an infant is inconsistent with such relation.

In *State* v. *Critchett*, 37 Minn. 13, a statute provided that the articles of incorporation shall be signed by any number not less than nine. So articles of incorporation signed by but two were invalid.

In most of the states a certain number of the incorporators are required to be residents of the state in which the company is incorporated.

2. POWERS AND LIABILITIES OF CORPORATIONS

Powers Limited. — A corporation has only such powers as are conferred upon it by its charter or articles of incorporation. These powers may be expressly conferred, or they may be implied, either because they are incidental to a corporate existence, as the right of successor and the right to have a corporate name, or because they are necessary in order to exercise the powers expressly conferred.

In *Downing* v. *Mt. Washington Road Co.*, 40 N.H. 230, a charter which gave defendant the authority to make and keep in repair a road to the top of Mt. Washington, to take toll of passengers and carriages, to build and own toll houses, and to take land for a road, was held not to authorize the corporation to establish a stage and transportation line, nor to buy carriages and horses for that purpose. Corporations have no powers except such as are given them by their charter, or such as are incidental and necessary to carry into effect the purposes for which they were established.

Implied Powers. — The powers that are incidental to a corporate existence and that will always be implied, are these : to have perpetual succession during the life of the corporation, to have a corporate name by which to contract and to sue and be sued, to purchase and hold real and personal property, to have a common seal, and to make by-laws.

A corporation has also the implied power that is reasonably necessary for the execution of the powers expressly granted and not expressly or impliedly excluded. A corporation generally has the implied power to borrow money whenever the nature of its business renders it necessary or expedient to do so.

In *Nelson* v. *Eaton*, 26 N.Y. 410, it was held that an insurance corporation, in the absence of any statutory restriction, has the power to borrow money and, as incident thereto, the power to transfer its assets in trust as security for the loan.

In *Bradbury* v. *Boston Canoe Club*, 153 Mass. 77, it was held that a corporation formed for the purpose of encouraging athletic exercises has the power to borrow money for building a club house upon lands leased by it, under the provisions of the statute that such a corporation may hold real and personal estate and may purchase or erect suitable buildings for its accommodation.

It also has the implied power to make, indorse, or accept bills of exchange and promissory notes, if such is the usual or proper means of accomplishing the results for which it was created.

In *Moss* v. *Averell*, 10 N.Y. 449, a corporation organized for the purpose of raising and smelting lead ore, was held to be a corporation having power to purchase property necessary for carrying on the business and, unless expressly prohibited by statute, can give promissory notes in payment for such purchases.

To sell or mortgage real property owned by it is another implied power of a corporation, except in the case of railroads and other companies of a public nature.

In *Dupee* v. *Boston Water Power Co.*, 114 Mass. 37, it was held that a corporation chartered with power to purchase and hold water power, created by the erection of dams, and to hold real estate may, when its water privileges can no longer be profitably used, sell its land.

But a corporation has no implied power to enter into a contract of partnership or suretyship.

In *Mallory* v. *Hanaur Oil Works*, 86 Tenn. 598, an agreement between corporations engaged in manufacturing cotton-seed oil, to select a committee composed of representatives of each corporation and to turn over to this committee the properties and machinery of each company, so that the business of each might be operated and managed for a specified time by this committee for the common benefit, the losses or profits to be shared in certain proportions, was held to be a contract of partnership. A partnership contract is not within the express or implied power of a corporation and is void even though authorized by both stockholders and directors.

In *Central Railroad Co.* v. *Smith*, 76 Ala. 572, it was held that the Central Railroad & Banking Co. of Georgia, which was authorized by its charter to construct and operate a railroad between the cities of Savannah and Macon and to organize and carry on a banking business, has no power, express, implied, or incidental, to purchase and run a steamboat on the Chattahoochee River, which is no part of its route, nor to form a partnership with a natural person for carrying on that business.

As a general rule it may be said that when a corporation is given general authority to engage in business, it takes the powers of a natural person to make all the necessary and proper contracts to enable it to attain its legitimate objects.

In *Wright* v. *Hughes*, 119 Ind. 324, it was held that a corporation organized as a life insurance company has power to borrow money and secure its payment by mortgaging its real estate. When general authority is given a corporation to engage in business, it takes the power, in the absence of charter restraint, just as a natural person enjoys it with all of its incidents, and may borrow money to attain its legitimate objects the same as an individual.

Acts *Ultra Vires*. — When a corporation performs acts not within its power to perform, the acts are said to be *ultra vires*. An *ultra vires* contract, if executory, can not be enforced; but most courts hold that if the defense of *ultra vires* will work an injustice, it will not be allowed, and this is also true if the party seeking to enforce the contract has performed his part.

In *Nassau Bank* v. *Jones*, 95 N.Y. 115, plaintiff, the bank, subscribed for stock in a railroad corporation and in this action sued for its share of the profits. Held, that the plaintiff was not authorized to make such a contract, and the courts would not enforce it.

Liability for Acts of Agents. — A corporation is liable to the same extent as a natural person for the frauds and wrongs of its agents and servants, committed in the course of their employment.

In *Goodspeed* v. *Bank*, 22 Conn. 530, plaintiff brought an action against the defendant, a banking corporation, for damages for maliciously bringing vexatious and unjust lawsuits against plaintiff. The defense was that a corporation was not liable for such a wrong, but the court held that a suit of this nature may be maintained against a corporation.

3. DISSOLUTION OF A CORPORATION

A private corporation may be dissolved in any one of four ways : —

1. By the expiration of its charter.

2. By the surrender of its charter with the consent of the state.

3. By an act of the legislature repealing its charter, under the power reserved by the state when granting the charter.

4. By the forfeiture of its franchise or charter, upon the judgment of a proper court, for misuse or non-use of its powers.

1. *Expiration of Charter.* — The charter usually stipulates that the corporation shall be formed for a certain time, as for twenty or fifty years. When this period expires, the association no longer has an existence, and is therefore dissolved.

Sturges v. *Vanderbilt*, 73 N.Y. 384, held, that upon the expiration of the term of existence of a corporation as limited by its charter it becomes extinct and no formal decree of dissolution is necessary.

A charter when granted to the corporation and accepted by it constitutes a contract between the state and the corporation. This contract exists under the clause in our federal constitution prohibiting any state legislature from passing a law impairing the obligation of the contract. The state can not, therefore, repeal the charter of a company unless it has expressly reserved that right or unless the corporation assents thereto.

In *Ruggles* v. *People*, 91 Ill. 256, a railroad company was in its charter expressly granted the right to fix the rates of toll to be charged. This was held not to confer unlimited power, but only the right to charge a reasonable rate, and a statute fixing what is a reasonable maximum rate does not impair the contract contained in the charter. The charter of a railway corporation is a contract between it and the state by which it may exercise the rights and privileges conferred until the expiration of its charter, unless by some act it shall forfeit its privileges and franchise, and, under the federal constitution, the obligation of such contract can not be impaired by subsequent legislation.

2. *Surrender of Charter.* — The dissolution may be effected by the association surrendering its charter, but the charter being a contract between the state and the association this can be done only with the consent of the state. The statutes generally provide certain formalities which must be complied with before the dissolution will be granted.

3. *Repeal of Charter.* — The state may institute a suit in the proper court to cause a corporate charter to be forfeited. The ground for such a suit is the abuse or misuse of the corporate powers, or the neglect or non-use of the same. But the mere abuse or misuse alone does not work a forfeiture of the charter. This results only from the judgment of the court after a hearing

in which the corporation has a chance to appear and present its side of the case. A forfeiture will be decreed by the courts when the corporation is guilty of acts or has omitted to do certain things which by statute are expressly made a cause of forfeiture of its franchise.

People v. *North River Sugar Refining Co.*, 121 N.Y. 582, is one of the famous trust cases. The defendant had entered into an agreement with other sugar refineries which constituted a partnership between them, whereby the control of their several businesses was to be under one board of managers, and the profits were to be divided according to a certain proportion. Held, that such action was in excess of its corporate powers, illegal and contrary to public policy, and so authorized a dissolution of the corporation. The court in the course of its opinion said: " To justify forfeiture of the corporate existence the transgression on the part of the corporation must be not merely formal or incidental, but material and serious, and such as to harm or menace the public welfare; for the state does not concern itself with the quarrels of private litigants. It furnishes for them sufficient courts and remedies, but intervenes as a party only where some public interest requires its action."

4. *Forfeiture.* — Continued neglect to exercise rights under corporate franchises and a failure to perform the implied conditions upon which the charter was granted amount to a non-user, for which the charter may be forfeited.

State v. *Atchison Railroad Co.*, 24 Neb. 143, held, that when a railway company without authority of law leases its road to another railway company with all of its rights, property, and franchises, for a long period of time, it thereby abandons the operation of its road and is subject to forfeiture.

Combinations with other corporations to form an unlawful trust or monopoly is sufficient ground for a dissolution. This is illustrated in the case of the *People* v. *North River Sugar Refining Co.*, just quoted.

Distilling Co. v. *People*, 156 Ill. 448, was an action brought to dissolve the Distilling and Cattle Feeding Co., which had been formed for the purpose of taking over the plants of five or six other distillers and running them under one head, the profits to be divided among the several stockholders. Held, that a charter authorizing a corporation to engage in a general distilling business, and to own the property necessary for that purpose, gives it no power to enter into a scheme of getting into its hands all the distilleries of the country and establishing a virtual monopoly of the business.

Method of Dissolution. — The effect of the dissolution is that thereafter the corporation no longer exists for any purpose, but the statutes in practically all of the states now make provisions under which the business of dissolved corporations may be liquidated and settled and the rights of stockholders and creditors may be adjusted. The usual method of doing this is the appointment of a receiver to wind up the corporate affairs, collect bills due to the corporation, and pay its creditors, after which the remainder is divided among the stockholders, according to the amount of stock they hold.

Mason v. *Pewabic Mining Co.*, 133 U. S. 50, held, that on the dissolution of a corporation at the expiration of the term of its corporate existence, each stockholder has the right, as a general rule, to have the corporate property converted into money, whether it be necessary for the payment of debts or not.

4. MEMBERSHIP IN A CORPORATION

Stockholders. — Membership in a corporation is acquired by the ownership of one or more shares of the capital stock in a private stock corporation. This may be acquired by subscription to the capital stock either before or after incorporation, by purchase from the corporation, or by a transfer from the owner. The certificate of stock, the form of which is given on page 249, is a written acknowledgment of the interest of the holder in the corporation. When the stock is subscribed for after the incorporation of the company, it is simply a contract between the corporation and the subscriber.

In *Greer* v. *Railway Co.*, 96 Pa. St. 391, Greer was soliciting subscriptions for the building of a railway, and took a subscription book, signed therein himself, and persuaded others to subscribe. He kept the book about six months, and then, because of a disagreement with the company, he cut out his own name from the book and returned it to the company. Held, that by placing his name in the book he had perfected a contract with the company, and was just as much bound as though he had left his name in the book.

Stock Subscriptions. — The subscriptions of several persons to an agreement to take stock in a corporation thereafter to be formed, is a continuing offer to the corporation to be formed, which may be accepted by the corporation, and is binding. The delivery of the certificate is merely evidence of the ownership of the shares, and is not necessary to make a subscriber a stockholder. A stockholder has the right to inspect the books and papers of the corporation if he has a reason so to examine them.

In *Phœnix Iron Co.* v. *Commonwealth*, 113 Pa. St. 563, a stockholder wishing to prepare a bill setting forth certain grievances against the corporation, asked to see the papers and books of the company. Held, that the books and papers of a corporation are the common property of the stockholders, and, unless the charter provides otherwise, a stockholder has the right, at proper times, to inspect them personally, and with the aid of a disinterested expert to make extracts from them for a definite and proper purpose.

Dividends. — Out of the surplus or net profits of the corporate business the directors may vote a dividend. This is a certain per cent upon the capital stock, and when the dividend is declared the stockholders are entitled to their respective shares. Until such dividend is declared, a stockholder has no legal right to a share of the profits, although upon its being wrongfully withheld a suit in equity may be brought to compel the corporation to declare a dividend.

In *Hyatt* v. *Allen*, 56 N.Y. 553, plaintiff transferred to defendant twenty shares of stock of a corporation under an agreement by which all profits and dividends upon said stock up to January 1, 1872, were to be paid to plaintiff. No dividends were declared until April 9, 1872. In an action to recover a part of this dividend as having been earned before January 1, it was held that plaintiff was not entitled to any part of it. A stockholder has no legal title to the profits until a dividend is declared.

Preferred Stock. — The dividend declared must be equal on all the stock except where a part of the stock is preferred. This means that a certain part of the capital stock is declared on the certificate to be preferred and the balance common stock. The preferred stock gives the holder rights and privileges not enjoyed by the holders of the common stock. These rights usually include a prior claim for dividends. Six per cent preferred stock would entitle the holder to an annual dividend of 6 per cent before any dividend could be declared on the common stock. Upon dissolution the preferred stock is generally paid before the common.

Transfer of Stock. — Shares of stock are transferred from one holder to another by an assignment which is usually upon the back of the certificate of stock and in a form somewhat like the following : —

For value received I hereby sell, assign, and transfer unto James D. Scott twenty shares of the capital stock represented by the within certificate, and do hereby irrevocably constitute and appoint William A. Willis my attorney to transfer the said stock on the books of the within named corporation, with full power of substitution in the premises.

Dated November 10, 1903.   GEORGE W. ELLIS.

     In the presence of

        E. A. WAGNER.

The attorney named to transfer the stock is generally the secretary of the company.

Stock in a corporation is subject to sale and transfer like any other kind of personal property. The transferee of the stock acquires all of the rights and assumes all of the liabilities arising after the date of the transfer. He is entitled to the dividends declared after the transfer and has a right to vote at the stockholder's meeting and exercise all other rights arising from his ownership.

In *March* v. *Eastern Railroad Co.*, 43 N.H. 515, it was held that the purchaser of a share of stock in a corporation takes the share with all its incidents, one of which is the receiving of all future dividends declared on such shares, and it does not make any difference at what time or from what sources the profits thus divided may have accrued.

When the statute imposes a personal liability upon the stockholders, the transferee is liable under such statute if the liability arises after the transfer. The transfer of stock must be recorded in the books of the company and a new certificate issued before the transferee appears as a stockholder on the books and has the right to vote at the corporate meetings.

5. MANAGEMENT OF CORPORATIONS

Vote of Stockholders. — As a general rule, each stockholder in a corporation is bound by all acts adopted by a vote of a majority of the stockholders of the corporation, provided such acts are within the scope of the powers and authority conferred by the charter.

In *Dudley* v. *Kentucky High School*, 72 Ky. 576, a corporation was authorized to receive and hold for the benefit of a high school any land by gift, devise, or purchase. A stockholder brought action to restrain the corporation from purchasing certain real estate, claiming that it could not afford it and the result would be the bankruptcy of the corporation. Held, that the action could not be maintained, as the majority of the stockholders had voted for the purchase. Every stockholder contracts that the will of the majority shall govern in all matters coming within the limits of the act of incorporation.

But the majority can not bind the minority by any acts outside of the powers conferred by the charter.

In *Barton* v. *Enterprise Loan Association*, 114 Ind. 226, it was provided in the articles of association of the company that it shall continue in operation eight years, unless it shall sooner have sufficient funds to pay its debts and redeem its stock. A resolution was passed by a majority of the stockholders dissolving the association before the time limit, and it was held that without the consent of all the stockholders and with unredeemed stock outstanding, such a resolution is of no effect.

In some cases, the management of the corporation is vested in the directors, and then the authority vested in the stockholders is the election of the directors. The directors alone are authorized to act in the management of the business. The right to make by-laws is generally in the majority of the stockholders, although in some cases that power is by charter vested in the directors.

Notice of Meeting. — Notice of the time and place of the stockholders' meeting must be given to each stockholder unless it is definitely designated by the charter or by-laws. Each stockholder is usually entitled to one vote for each share of stock owned by him, although at common law each stockholder had but one vote without regard to the number of shares of stock he owned. At common law the right to vote could be exercised only in person, but now the right to vote by proxy (that is by power of attorney) is generally conferred by statute. The proxy or authority to vote is in the form of a written power of attorney, and is revocable at the pleasure of the person executing it.

Directors. — As stated above, the active management of the corporate business is usually vested in a board of directors selected by a majority of the stockholders. The directors act by a majority vote. The powers and duties of the directors and other officers are generally fully defined in the by-laws.

6. RIGHTS OF CREDITORS OF CORPORATIONS

In General. — The creditors of a corporation generally have the same rights and remedies against the corporation and its property that they would have against a natural person. They may obtain a judgment against it and issue an execution against its property, or adopt the other remedies that they would have against an individual. Aside from the rights of creditors to proceed against the property belonging to the corporation, there are cases in which the creditor may also look to the stockholder, notwithstanding the general rule that a stockholder is not individually liable for the debts of the corporation.

Liability of Stockholders. — The first of these cases is where the stockholder is indebted to the corporation on his stock, and the payment of the amount is necessary to pay the creditors. It is held that a stockholder must contribute the full amount of his subscription for stock if the amount is needed by the creditors. This amount is a part of the capital stock of the company, and the capital is held by the courts to be in the nature of a trust fund for the payment of the corporate debts.

In *Payne* v. *Bullard*, 23 Miss. 88, it was held that where a person subscribes for a certain number of shares of bank stock and does everything necessary in order to secure his right to the stock, but does not fully pay for it, he can not afterwards by an agreement with the bank diminish the number of his shares so as to affect the creditors of the bank. Stock subscribed to a bank is in the nature of a trust fund for the payment of its liabilities.

Hatch v. *Dana*, 101 U.S. 205, held, that creditors of a corporation who have exhausted their remedy against the corporation can, in order to satisfy their judgment, proceed against a stockholder to enforce his liability to the company for the amount remaining due upon his subscription for stock.

The stockholder is also liable to the creditors of the corporation if any part of the capital stock has been unlawfully distributed or paid out to him, either directly or indirectly, leaving creditors unpaid. This may be accomplished by distributing funds as dividends when there are no surplus profits, or in other ways, but however accomplished, the stockholder may be compelled to refund for the benefit of the creditors the amount so received.

In *Bartlett* v. *Drew*, 57 N.Y. 587, defendant was a stockholder in the New Jersey Steam Navigation Co. Three boats of the company were sold for a gross sum of $15,000, which amount was divided among the stockholders. This action was brought by a creditor of the company to reach the amount so received by defendant. Held, that plaintiff could maintain an action to reach whatever defendant had so received. It is immaterial whether he got it by fair agreement or by a wrongful act, the creditors have a right to be paid first out of the assets of the company.

The statutes, which in some of the states have imposed additional liabilities upon the stockholders, vary greatly. Some make the stockholder liable for all debts until the whole capital stock is paid in. Others make him liable for a sum equal to the amount of stock held by him in addition to the amount yet due on his stock, and so on, many different provisions being found in the different states.

McDonnell v. *Alabama Gold Life Insurance Co.*, 85 Ala. 401, held, that by statute in that state a stockholder in a life insurance company was liable for the debts of the company, not only for the amount of his unpaid subscription for stock, but also for an additional sum equal to the amount of his stock.

QUESTIONS ON CORPORATIONS

1. Define corporation.
2. The New York Supply Co. was a corporation which owned a piece of real property that was sold by the officers of the corporation, the deed being signed personally by all of the stockholders in their individual names. Was the conveyance good?
3. Webster owes the Standard Novelty Works, a corporation, $500.

Three persons own all the stock of the corporation. They in their individual names sue Webster for the amount. Can they succeed?

4. Distinguish between public and private corporations. Give an illustration of each.

5. Define stock corporations; non-stock corporations.

6. Name the five powers and attributes of nearly all private stock corporations.

7. What is meant by perpetual or continuous succession?

8. Is the power to hold real estate necessary to a corporation's existence? Is the power to use a seal necessary?

9. When is the right to make by-laws in a corporation necessary? Are they commonly employed?

10. In what two different ways are corporations created by the government? Which is the most frequently employed?

11. Has a corporation any powers except such as are conferred upon it by its charter?

12. The Georgia Railroad Co. has authority by its charter to maintain a railroad between the towns of A and B. It buys boats and seeks to establish a boat system on one of the rivers running into the town of B. Has it that authority?

13. What powers has a corporation aside from those expressly granted?

14. The American Dry Goods Co. is incorporated for the purpose of buying and selling dry goods. In the course of its business the company borrows $1000 and gives its note therefor. Has it this authority?

15. The above-named company owns a store and land where it conducts business. It places a mortgage upon this property for the purpose of raising $5000. Has it the right?

16. The above corporation forms a partnership with one Greene in an adjoining town for the purpose of conducting a branch dry goods store. Has the company the authority?

17. What would the act of the company in the above case be termed?

18. In question 14 one of the clerks of the company is guilty of fraud in making a sale to a customer. Is the company liable?

19. Name four ways in which a corporation may be dissolved.

20. Can the stockholders of a corporation dissolve it by mutual consent?

21. Can the state dissolve a corporation without the consent of the stockholders? If so, how?

22. The Southern Tobacco Co , a corporation, entered into a combination with twenty other manufacturers of tobacco for the purpose of forming a tobacco trust and combining all of their business under one management. An action is brought to dissolve the Southern Tobacco Co. Can it be done?

23. How is membership in a corporation acquired?

24. Is the possession of a certificate of stock necessary to membership in a corporation?

25. A is a stockholder in a corporation. He learns that the profits for the past year have been about 10 per cent on the amount of capital stock, but no dividends have been declared. He therefore sues the corporation for an amount equal to 10 per cent on his stock. Can he recover? If 'not, what remedy has he against the corporation?

26. In the above case suppose A sells his stock to B on January 1, and stipulates that all profits upon said stock up to that time shall belong to A. On July 1 an annual dividend of 10 per cent is declared. A claims one half of it; can he recover?

27. What is preferred stock?

28. How are shares of stock transferred?

29. What power has a majority of the stockholders of a corporation?

30. How is the stockholders' meeting called, and how many votes has each stockholder?

31. A, B, and C are stockholders in the Standard Glass Co. Only 50 per cent of their capital stock has been paid in. The corporation fails and the creditors sue A, B, and C personally for the amount of their stock not yet paid. Can they recover?

32. If in the above case after the corporation was practically bankrupt certain of the assets had been sold and the proceeds distributed among A, B, and C, could the creditors recover this amount as well as the amount unpaid on their stock?

INSURANCE

1. IN GENERAL

Insurance Companies. — Certain events or catastrophies may happen which, although by no means frequent in the experience of the average man, are of so much importance and may entail upon him such severe loss that he seeks a mode of protection. The impending loss may be the destruction of one's property by fire, flood, or cyclone; or it may be the loss of one's earning capacity, by accident to his person; or the loss to his family, by reason of his death.

For the purpose of affording protection against these calamities there exist many large corporations known as insurance companies, which engage in the business of assuming such risks for a certain compensation known as a premium. These premiums, although comparatively small, being contributed by the many, form a large fund, out of which the losses to the few are indemnified.

Definition. — Insurance is defined as a contract whereby for a stipulated consideration one party undertakes to compensate the other for loss on a particular subject for a specified peril. The party agreeing to make the compensation is called the insurer, or the underwriter, the other party to the contract being the insured. The written contract is called the policy, and the event insured against, the risk.

Every state has an insurance official, whose duty it is to regulate and inspect the different insurance companies doing business in his state and to see that they are solvent and that their affairs are properly conducted.

2. FIRE INSURANCE

Insurable Interest. — The insured must have an insurable interest in the risk or property insured. This means that he must have an interest of such a nature that the fire insured against would directly injure him.   If the person had no interest in the property upon which he obtained insurance, the only object would be a mere speculation, and the contract would not be upheld in law.

Riggs v. *Insurance Co.*, 125 N.Y. 7, was a case in which a stockholder in a steamship company had one of the boats of the corporation insured in his favor, and the question was whether or not he had an insurable interest in the property of the company of which he was a stockholder.   It was held by the court that he had such an interest.   The stockholder in a corporation has no legal title to the assets of the corporation, but he has an equitable right of a pecuniary nature which may be prejudiced by the destruction of the property belonging to the corporation, as a loss of the property would affect the dividends distributed by the company and would also lessen the assets which would be distributed among the stockholders upon the dissolution of the company.

This interest may be an existing interest; as, for example, the absolute ownership, or a life interest, or a right by mortgage or lien.   Or it may be only an interest in expected profits or goods, as a shipowner's right to insure goods upon which he has a claim for freight.

In *National Filtering Oil Co.* v. *Citizens Insurance Co.*, 106 N.Y. 535, plaintiff had an agreement with Ellis & Co., by virtue of which Ellis & Co. were to pay plaintiff royalties for the use of plaintiff's patents, which royalties were guaranteed to amount to $250 per month.   Plaintiff insured the plant of Ellis & Co., the agreement of the insurance company in the policy being that in case the buildings occupied by Ellis & Co. should be damaged by fire, so as to cause a diminution in said royalties, defendant would pay the amount of such diminution during the repairs of said premises.   Held, that plaintiff had an insurable interest in this property.

The owner of property does not lose his insurable interest by mortgaging, leasing, or giving an executory contract to sell it, as more than one person can have an insurable interest in the property.   For example, A owns a house and lot, and leases it to B, mortgages it to C, and gives D an executory contract of sale.   Each one of these four parties has an insurable interest in the house.

Davis v. *Insurance Co.*, 10 Allen (Mass.) 113, held, that the omission to state in an application for insurance on a building that a written agreement had been given by the applicant to convey the building to a third party in consideration of a certain sum of money being paid within a fixed time, does not affect the right to recover the full amount of insurance.

Divided Interest. — Each person having an insurable interest in the house could not recover the full value of the house in case of fire, but merely the value of his interest. The owner can recover the market value at the time of the loss, and the mortgagee can recover the value of the house up to the amount of his mortgage.

In *Kernochan* v. *Insurance Co.*, 5 Duer (N.Y.) 1, it was held that the mortgagee's insurable interest in the mortgaged property corresponded in amount to the debt secured, and, in the event of total loss, he can recover the whole sum insured, provided it does not exceed the sum due upon the mortgage. This recovery can not be defeated by showing that the property, notwithstanding the loss, is still ample security for the mortgaged debt.

Form of Contract. — The contract of insurance is usually in writing, although it may be oral, unless expressly required by statute to be written. The forms adopted by the various companies are much alike and generally set forth in detail all of the agreements between the parties.

This contract requires a meeting of the minds of the parties, and certain terms must be definitely settled upon, viz.: The property insured, the risk insured against, the rate of premium and the term of duration of the insurance.

In *Goddard* v. *Insurance Co.*, 108 Mass. 56, defendant insured a building as a machine shop against fire. The representation that it was such was made by an insurance broker without the knowledge or consent of plaintiff. It was in fact used as an organ factory. The risk on an organ factory was greater than it would have been on a machine shop, and it was held that the policy was void, as the minds of the parties never met on the subject-matter of the contract.

Description. — The policy must contain a description of the property insured. This is generally set forth briefly and gives the nature of the building or article. It also gives the title or interest of the insured in the same, that is, whether he is the owner, mortgagee, bailee, etc. The risk insured against must also be agreed upon. The property may be insured against fire, flood, tornado, or some other unforeseen casualty.

Oral Contract. — The contract is binding and in force as soon as the agreement is completed, although the written policy may not have been actually delivered, nor in fact ever have been issued.

Fish v. *Cottenet*, 44 N.Y. 538, held, that if an agreement for insurance is made with an agent authorized to bind the company, but through the negligence of the agent the application is not received in time to be acted on by the company before the loss occurs, the company is liable.

In *Ellis* v. *Insurance Co.*, 50 N.Y. 402, plaintiff applied to an insurance agent for insurance upon a quantity of cotton. The amount and the premium were settled upon and the agent agreed to insure as requested. It was left with the agent to select the companies in which he would insure, and he decided to place $6100 with defendant, entering it upon his books, and crediting defendant with the amount of the premium which was forwarded to defendant before the loss. Held, that this constituted a contract to issue a policy for the amount so placed and was binding on defendant.

Effect of Fraud. — A contract of insurance is one requiring good faith between the parties, and the party seeking insurance is bound to disclose any circumstance that will affect the risk. Any fraudulent dealing is fatal to the rights of the party responsible for it. Any concealment of a material fact inquired into by the insurer will, if made intentionally by the insured, avoid the policy. Still neither party is bound to volunteer information regarding matters of which the other has knowledge or of which in the exercise of ordinary care he ought to have knowledge. But the insured must not withhold information which would affect the judgment of the insurer.

In *Armenia Insurance Co.* v. *Paul*, 91 Pa. St. 520, one of the questions in the application for insurance was, "What is the distance, occupation, and material of all buildings within 150 feet?" No answer was made to this question and the company sought to avoid the policy on that ground. Held, that they might have refused to issue the policy or have sought further information, but that by issuing it they waived the answer to this question.

Representation. — A representation in connection with this subject is said to be a statement of fact made at the time of, or before the contract relating to, the proposed adventure, and upon the good faith of which the contract is made. A material misrepresentation of fact, whether innocent or fraudulent, avoids the contract.

In *Armour* v. *Insurance Co.*, 90 N.Y. 450, defendant issued a policy of insurance upon plaintiff's warehouse, by the terms of which losses should be apportioned between the different policies on the building, and it also stated that any misrepresentation whatever would avoid the policy. Plaintiff's agent, who applied for the policy, stated through mistake that there was already $200,000 insurance on the building, when there was in fact but $30,000. Held, that the misrepresentation was material, and the plaintiff could not recover on the policy.

Warranty. — A warranty is a statement of fact or promise of performance relating to the subject of insurance or to the risk, inserted in the policy itself or expressly made a part of it, which, if not literally true or strictly complied with, will avoid the contract. It differs from a representation, which, as we have seen, is a collateral inducement outside of the contract and need be only substantially complied with, whereas the warranty must be contained in the policy and must be strictly performed.

In *Wood* v. *Insurance Co.*, 13 Conn. 533, it was held that any statement or description on the part of the insured on the face of the policy which relates to the risk is an express warranty, and such a warranty must be strictly complied with or the insurance is void.

If questions in the application are not answered or if the answers are incomplete but not false, there is no breach of warranty, provided the insurer accepts the application without objection.

Although the breach of warranty or misrepresentation of a material fact may not contribute to or cause the loss, nevertheless the policy is avoided, for the risk is different from that which the insurer undertook to assume.

In *Ripley* v. *Ætna Insurance Co.*, 30 N.Y. 136, at the time the insurance was obtained the question was asked whether there was a watchman in the buildings during the night. The insured answered, "There is a watchman nights." It appeared that by the custom at the mill no watchman was kept from 12 o'clock Saturday night until 12 o'clock Sunday night. The above answer was referred to and made a part of the policy. Held, that the answer was to be understood to mean that there was a watchman at the mill every night, and a failure to keep a watchman every night constituted a breach of the warranty and avoided the policy, without regard to whether it had anything to do with producing the loss.

3. FIRE INSURANCE POLICY

Uniformity. — Statutes have been passed in New York and in several other states adopting a standard form of fire insurance policy, the object being to establish a uniformity of contract and to avoid conflict between different companies insuring the same property.

Loss by Fire. — Insurance in the policy against loss by fire includes loss which is caused by the burning of the property insured or which is the result of fire in close proximity, the heat from which damages the property insured. It also includes the loss or damage by the water from the fire engines or from the exposure or theft of the goods during their removal to a place of safety at the time of a fire.

White v. *Insurance Co.*, 57 Me. 91, was a case in which it was held that the damage and expense caused by removing, with a reasonable degree of care suited to the occasion, insured goods from apparent immediate destruction by fire, are covered by a policy insuring the goods against "loss and damage by fire," although the building in which they were insured and from which they were removed was not, in fact, burned.

It includes loss by fire caused by lightning, but does not include loss caused by lightning unless a lightning clause is inserted; therefore it is customary to include such a clause.

In *Babcock* v. *Montgomery Insurance Co.*, 6 Barb. (N.Y.) 637, it was held that under a policy of insurance against loss or damage by fire, one of the conditions being that the insurer will be liable for "fire by lightning," the company is not liable for the destruction of the building by its being shattered and torn by lightning without its being burned. Unless the loss is the effect of actual ignition, the insurers are not liable.

If the fire is caused by the act of an incendiary, or by the acts of the insured while insane, or by the careless acts of a third person, the insurance company is liable.

Location. — The standard policy contains a statement of the location of the property insured, and if it is removed to another or different place without the consent of the insurer, the policy is no longer in effect. So if a party insures his household furniture while living on a certain street, and then moves to another street, the insurance ceases to be in force. The reason for this rule is plain, for the risk is likely to vary in different locations, and whether it does or not, the insurer has the right to know what risk he is assuming, as he may wish to decline placing any more insurance on property in the same building.

In *Lyons* v. *Insurance Co.*, 14 R. I. 109, a policy of insurance against fire was issued on furniture described as contained in a house on McMillen Street, Providence, R. I. The insured, without the knowledge of the insurer, moved the articles to a house on another street, in which they were burned. Held, that the insured could not recover. The statement of the location of the goods is a continuing warranty.

Bradbury v. *Insurance Co.*, 80 Me. 396, was a case in which plaintiff had a fire insurance policy on a "frame stable building," specifically described, and on his "carriages, sleighs, hacks, horses, harnesses, blankets, robes, and whips contained therein." It was held that this insurance does not cover damage by fire to the plaintiff's hack while in a repair shop one eighth of a mile away and on another street, without the knowledge and consent of the insurer, for the temporary purpose of being repaired.

Amount Recoverable. — The market or cash value of the property at the time of the fire is the amount that can be recovered of the insurance company if this sum does not exceed the amount of the policy. If the property is only partially destroyed, the amount that may be recovered is the difference in the value of the property before and after the fire. The insurer generally reserves the right to rebuild or repair, and in case he elects so to do, this takes the place of money damages.

Additional Insurance. — The standard policy of insurance contains a clause which provides that the policy shall be void in case the insured now has, or shall hereafter make or procure, any other contract of insurance, whether valid or not, on property covered in whole or in part by this policy, without an agreement indorsed or added thereon, allowing such additional insurance. The reason for this provision is that the companies do not wish to have the property insured for more than its value, and they also desire to know whether any other insurance is carried on the property, as in case of loss, if insured in several companies, each need contribute only its proportionate share.

Sanders v. *Cooper*, 115 N.Y. 279, held, that where one of the conditions of a policy declares it void in case of other insurance on the property insured, not indorsed on the policy or consented to in writing by the insurer, the fact that there was such other insurance outstanding, the existence of which was not communicated or known to the company, is a breach of a condition of the policy that renders it void.

Alienation Clause. — The standard policy also contains a clause known as the alienation clause, which renders the policy void if any change other than the death of the insured takes place in the interest, title, or possession of the subject insured (except change of occupants without increase of hazard), whether by legal process or judgment, or by the voluntary act of the insured. This section means any parting with or sale of the premises, and does not include the giving of a mortgage upon the insured premises.

Judge v. *Insurance Co.*, 132 Mass. 521, was a case in which the insurance policy contained practically the above clause. After the policy was issued, the insured gave a mortgage on the property covered by the policy, but the mortgagee had made no move to foreclose, in fact the mortgage was not yet due. Held, that the policy was not avoided.

Assignment. — A fire insurance policy is not assignable, and if assigned without the consent of the insurer it is void.

In *Lett* v. *Insurance Co.*, 125 N.Y. 82, defendant issued a policy of insurance on property owned by B, the loss being payable to A as mortgagee. B afterwards conveyed the property to C, who in turn conveyed it to plaintiff. At the time of the last conveyance, B executed to plaintiff an assignment of his interest in the policy, but the consent of defendant was not indorsed on the policy, although such an indorsement was a condition of its remaining in force. Held, that the policy was invalid because of the failure to obtain defendant's consent to the assignment.

If with the consent of the company the property insured as well as the policy is assigned, a new contract is formed which will not be affected by any act of the assignor.

Unoccupied Dwelling. — The standard form of policy also provides that if the property is a dwelling and remains vacant or unoccupied without the consent of the company for the period of 10 days the insurance is of no effect. This clause is held to be a reasonable restriction, as the insurer is entitled to know that the premises are receiving ordinary supervision. It means that the dwelling must have a tenant living in it.

In *Corrigan* v. *Insurance Co.*, 122 Mass. 298, the insurance policy provided that it should be void if the house insured should remain vacant or unoccupied for the space of 10 days without written notice to, and consent of, the company. Held, that if the house had not been used by some one as a dwelling place within 10 days of the date of the loss the policy would be void, the consent of the company not having been obtained. If the former tenant had moved his family into another house in which they slept and took their meals, the fact that he still retained the key and that some of the furniture was still in the house did not constitute an occupancy of the premises.

Factory Buildings. — There is a further provision rendering the policy void if the subject insured is a factory building and is operated after 10 o'clock at night or some other given hour, or is not operated for 10 consecutive days or some other specific length of time.

In the case of *Day* v. *Insurance Co.*, 70 Iowa 710, the policy of insurance on a flour mill contained the provision that if the mill were shut down or remained idle from any cause whatever for more than 20 days without notice to the company, the policy would be suspended from the expiration of that time until the mill resumed work. Held, that the stoppage of the mill for more than 20 days without the required notice suspended the policy, though the mill was stopped for necessary repairs to the mill or race.

Renewals. — The policy is often renewed by a short form of receipt which obviates the necessity of a new policy. This renewal, which may be either in writing or by parol, in substance creates a new contract on the same terms and conditions as those agreed upon in the old policy.

Hay v. *Insurance Co.*, 77 N.Y. 235, held, that an agreement to renew a policy of fire insurance in the absence of evidence that any change was intended implies that the terms of the existing policy are to be continued.

Cancellation. — The standard form of policy contains a stipulation that the policy may be canceled at any time by the company, or at the request of the insured upon giving five days' notice of such cancellation. And in case of such cancellation the unearned premiums paid shall be returned to the insured.

Mortgaged Property. — When the property insured is mortgaged and it is desired that in case of fire the insurance shall be paid to the mortgagee to satisfy his claim, it is the custom to attach a mortgage clause which provides that the insurance shall be paid to the mortgagee named as his interest may appear.

Notice of Loss. — After a loss it is the duty of the insured to give immediate notice to the company. Under the standard form of policy this notice must be in writing. The damaged goods must be inventoried, and a proof of loss duly sworn to must be filed within sixty days.

Knickerbocker Insurance Co. v. *McGinnis*, 87 Ill. 70, was a case in which a policy of fire insurance required immediate notice to be given by the assured in case of a loss, and in the great Chicago fire on October 9, 1871, plaintiff's property was burned, notice of the loss being given November 13, 1871. It was held to have been given in sufficient time in view of the great derangement of all kinds of business caused by the fire.

Unless the notice is given as stated and the proof of loss filed within the specified time, no recovery can be had on the policy.

Pro Rata Clause. — The standard policy contains a *pro rata* clause, under which the insured can not recover more than the amount of his loss in the property insured, where there is more than one policy on the same property. Thus a man may have his house insured in three companies, as follows : in number one for $4000, in number two for $6000, and in number three for $2000. The house is damaged by fire to the amount of $6000. The insured can recover only this amount, and the companies will be compelled to pay their *pro rata* portions ; that is, number one will be required to pay $2000, number two $3000, and number three $1000. This rule does not apply to the case of several persons with different interests in the same property, but to the case of any insurer who, if he recovered the full amount on all policies, would be getting double insurance upon the loss.

4. LIFE INSURANCE

Definitions. — Another form of insurance becoming more general every year is life insurance. This kind of contract appears in an almost endless number of forms. It is in its simplest form an agreement upon the part of the insurer to pay a specific sum of money upon the death of a certain person, called the insured, to a specific person called the beneficiary. The consideration paid by the insured is called the premium, and is generally a certain amount payable annually or monthly. The agreement may take the form of what is termed an endowment insurance, whereby the insured, after paying the premium for a given number of years, will receive a certain sum of money, or if he dies before the expiration of the period, the amount of the policy will go to the beneficiary. The beneficiary, instead of being a specific person, may be the estate of the insured.

Insurable Interest. — In life insurance, as well as in other classes of insurance, the applicant for the policy must have an insurable interest in the life of the insured, otherwise the insurance would be a mere speculation upon the life or death of the person insured, placing a premium upon his death in favor of one who had no other interest in him. Every person has an insurable interest in his own life and also in the life of any person upon whom he depends either wholly or in part for education or support, and in the life of any person who is under a legal obligation to him for the payment of money. In short, a person may be said to have an insurable interest in the life of any one whose death would naturally cause him a pecuniary loss or disadvantage.

In *Bevin* v. *Life Insurance Co.*, 23 Conn. 244, plaintiff advanced to Barstow $300 and some articles of personal property, under an agreement that Barstow should go to California and labor there for at least one year, and then account to plaintiff for one half the profits. Plaintiff then insured Barstow's life with defendant for $1000. Held, that plaintiff had an insurable interest in Barstow's life and could recover the amount of the policy.

A partner has an insurable interest in the life of his copartner, and a creditor of the partnership in the life of each partner.

In the case of *Connecticut Mutual Life Insurance Co.* v. *Luchs*, 108 U.S. 498, A and B formed a partnership with a capital of $10,000, in which each was to contribute one half. A temporarily contributed B's half, and after B's failure to comply with his agreement he had B's life insured for $5000. Held, that A had an insurable interest in B's life to the amount which B should have contributed to the firm.

Morrell v. *Life Insurance Co.*, 10 Cush. (Mass.) 282, held, that a creditor of a firm has an insurable interest in the life of one of the partners thereof, although the other partner may be entirely able to pay the debt, and although the estate of the insured is perfectly solvent.

A woman has an insurable interest in the life of a prospective husband as well as an insurable interest in a husband's life, and a man has the same interest in the life of his wife. Mere relationship is not enough to give an insurable interest. There must be an element of dependency coupled with the relationship. A nephew has no insurable interest in the life of his uncle nor has one brother in the life of another.

Lewis v. *Insurance Co.*, 39 Conn. 100, held, that one brother did not, from the mere relationship, have an insurable interest in the life of another brother.

If the person taking out the policy has an insurable interest to support the policy at the time it is obtained, he may make it payable to any one, and it is generally held that he may subsequently assign it to any one whether such beneficiary or transferee has an insurable interest or not, unless it is apparent that the transaction is a mere cover for a wagering contract.

St. John v. *Life Insurance Co.*, 13 N.Y. 31, held, that a policy of life insurance is assignable and the assignee for value of such a policy is entitled, on the death of the party whose life is insured, to recover the full amount of the policy without reference to the amount of consideration paid by him for the assignment.

If the person taking out the insurance had an insurable interest at the time, the fact that the interest ceases does not affect the policy. Therefore if a man insures the life of his debtor and the debtor subsequently pays the debt, the policy may still be continued and enforced at the death of the party insured.

In the case in which the insured designates another person as beneficiary the right of such beneficiary as a general rule becomes vested at once and it can not be disturbed by assignment or in any other way without the consent of such beneficiary, unless the right to make a new appointment is reserved in the policy itself.

In the case of *Glanz* v. *Gloeckler*, 104 Ill. 573, it was held that when a father takes out a policy of insurance upon his own life in favor of an infant daughter, paying all of the premiums himself and retaining the policy, the contract is between the insurance company and the daughter, and upon the father's death the legal title to the policy vests in her and she is entitled to the possession of it.

Premiums. — The premiums on life insurance are graded according to the age of the risk. The person insured must undergo a physical examination, as only healthy persons are insured. The amounts of the premiums are determined by average results computed upon the length of life of a large number of persons carefully arranged and tabulated. These results so arranged are called "mortuary tables."

Effect of Concealment. — The contract of life insurance like that of fire insurance requires the exercise of good faith between the parties, but to avoid the policy the concealment of a material fact not made the subject of an express inquiry must be intentional.

In *Mallory* v. *Travelers Insurance Co.*, 47 N.Y. 52, the defendant company issued an accident policy of insurance on the life of A. Prior to the issuing of the policy, A had been a canvasser for defendant company and while so acting had been directed to be careful not to insure insane persons. Before the policy was issued A had been insane but had been discharged from a hospital cured. He did not disclose this fact, but said that there were no circumstances rendering him peculiarly liable to accident. Held, that no fraudulent concealment was shown and the policy was not void if the insured did not conceal any facts which in his own mind were material in making the application.

Misrepresentation. — A misrepresentation, if material, will avoid the policy. The same rules apply to misrepresentations in life insurance as in fire insurance, but warranties are statements of facts which are a part of the policy and must be strictly performed or the policy is avoided.

Cushman v. *Life Insurance Co.*, 63 N.Y. 404, was a case in which, by the terms of a life insurance policy, the statements made by the insured in his application were made a part of the contract, and it provided that if they were untrue the policy was avoided. The applicant stated that he had never been afflicted with a certain disease. It was shown that he had twice been ill with this disease before the policy was issued. Held, that the statement was a warranty and its breach avoided the policy.

Life insurance companies generally ask many questions in their applications and unless the application is expressly incorporated in and made a part of the policy, the answers to these questions are considered as representations and not as warranties. If they are so included, they must be strictly true.

Dwight v. *Germania Life Insurance Co.*, 103 N.Y. 341, was a case in which, in an application for insurance on his life, the applicant in answer to a question as to whether he was then or had been engaged in or connected with the manufacture or sale of intoxicating liquors answered, "No." By the terms of the policy the assured warranted the truth of his answers and it was stipulated that any substantial deviation from the truth in an answer would avoid the policy. It was shown that the insured had kept a hotel for three and one half years prior to the issuing of a policy, and while he had no bar he kept wine and liquors which he sold to his guests. Held, that the answer was false and the policy was avoided.

If the questions are not answered or are only partially answered, there is no misrepresentation or breach of warranty.

Phœnix Life Insurance Co. v. *Raddin*, 120 U.S. 183, was a case in which in the application this question was asked, "Has any application been made to this or any other company for insurance on the life of the party? If so, with what result?" To this inquiry there was no answer. Held, that the failure to disclose unsuccessful applications for additional insurance did not avoid the policy. The issuing of the policy without further inquiry was a waiver by the company of the right to inquire further.

Forms of Policies. — There is no standard form of life insurance policy, and the forms of the different companies vary materially. It is customary to have the policy provide that the application be made a part of the contract, thereby making the statements in the application express warranties. So a denial that one is affected with a disease avoids the policy if untrue. The application often inquires as to what other insurance is carried, and a deceptive statement on this point is fatal to the policy. So also a statement as to age is material and the answer must be correct.

In *Ætna Life Insurance Co.* v. *France*, 91 U.S. 510, the insured in his application agreed that if the answers made by him were untrue, the policy should be null and void. Held, that the insurance company was not liable if the statements were untrue. In this case the applicant's age was asked and he answered thirty, but it was shown he was from thirty-five to thirty-seven.

Payment. — If the policy contains a provision that the insurance ceases unless the premium is paid when due and that the policy is not to take effect until the first premium is actually paid, the condition must be strictly complied with or the policy fails. Prompt payment is essential.

In *Holly* v. *Life Insurance Co.*, 105 N.Y. 437, the policy upon plaintiff's life contained a provision that in case of non-payment of premium when due by the terms of the policy it should be forfeited. Held, that punctuality in the payment of premiums in the case of life insurance is of the very essence of the contract, and if a payment is not made when due, the company has a right to forfeit the policy if such is the contract.

Sickness or other inability to comply with the terms of payment offers no excuse. If the insurer accepts the payment of the premium after it is due, the breach will be waived.

Suicide. — If the policy contains no express stipulation to the contrary, the insurance company is liable on a policy if the party insured commits suicide, in case a third party is the beneficiary. If the insured is the beneficiary, the rule will be otherwise. The policy frequently contains a clause exempting the company from liability if the insured commits suicide within a certain time.

Fitch v. *Life Insurance Co.*, 59 N.Y. 557, was an action on a policy of life insurance taken out for the benefit of the wife and children of the insured. It contained no clause forfeiting it in case of death by suicide. The court held that the fact that the insured committed suicide would not defeat the policy. The parties interested were not bound by the acts of the deceased after the policy was issued, unless in violation of some condition thereof.

When the exemption does not expressly state that the company shall not be liable whether the insured be sane or insane, the suicide clause does not vitiate the policy if the suicide is committed while the person is insane. If the clause contains these words, it is vitiated in any event.

Bigelow v. *Life Insurance Co.*, 93 U.S. 284, was an action upon a life insurance policy, which provided that it should be null and void if the insured died by suicide, "sane or insane." The company pleaded that he died from a pistol wound, inflicted by his own hand, and that he intended inflicting such a wound to destroy his own life. Held, that the policy was avoided even though the deceased was of unsound mind and unconscious of his acts when he inflicted the wound.

Notice of Death. — In life insurance the company generally requires immediate notice of death and due proof that the person insured is dead.

5. MARINE INSURANCE

Definition. — Marine insurance is a contract by which the insurer agrees to indemnify the insured against certain perils or risks to which his ships, cargo, and profits may be exposed during a certain trip or during a specified time.

Insurable Interest. — The rules governing this class of insurance closely follow the laws of life insurance. The person procuring the policy must have an insurable interest in the property insured. The owner always has an insurable interest, even though the property has been chartered to a person who agrees to pay its value in case of loss. The charterer also has an insurable interest in the ship. Practically the same rules apply to the insurable interest here as in fire insurance.

Oliver v. *Greene*, 3 Mass. 133, held, that a part owner of a vessel who has chartered the remainder with a covenant to pay the value in case of loss may insure the whole vessel as his property.

Effect of Fraud. — The requirement of good faith between the parties is even greater in marine insurance than in any other branch of insurance. The reason for this is that the insured has every opportunity to know all of the facts and the insurer but limited opportunity to determine them. A concealment of a material fact either innocently or fraudulently avoids the contract.

In *Proudfoot* v. *Montefiore*, L.R. 2 Q. B. (Eng.) 511, plaintiff in Liverpool had an agent in Smyrna to buy madder for him and ship it. The agent shipped a cargo and advised plaintiff on January 12, sending the shipping documents on the 19th. On the 23d the ship sailed, but it was stranded and the cargo destroyed on the same day. The agent got word of the loss on the 24th, and on the 26th, the day that the next mail went to Liverpool, he wrote to plaintiff, informing him of the loss, but purposely abstained from telegraphing him in order that plaintiff might not be prevented from obtaining insurance. On the 31st, plaintiff, after receiving the letters of the 12th and 19th, but before receiving the letter of the 26th and without knowledge of the loss, obtained insurance. Held, that plaintiff could not recover, as the agent should have telegraphed.

A material fact was concealed in this case which rendered the policy void by reason of concealment and misrepresentation.

Misrepresentation. — So a material misrepresentation of a fact, whether innocently or fraudulently made, avoids the contract. The rule is even more strict here than in fire insurance.

Hodgson v. *Richardson*, 1 W. Black. (Eng.) 463, was an action on a policy of marine insurance obtained at and from Genoa. The load was put on at Leghorn, bound for Dublin, but the vessel put in at Genoa and had been there about five months before sailing. The defendants contended that the policy was vitiated because of the non-disclosure to the insurer that the vessel was not loaded at Genoa. Held, that the plaintiff could not recover. The concealment of the port of loading vitiated the policy.

Warranty. — A warranty, as in fire insurance, must be strictly performed. In marine insurance there are three implied warranties which are understood in every contract. They are in respect to seaworthiness, deviation, and legality.

Seaworthiness. — There is implied the warranty that the ship is seaworthy at the time of the commencement of the risk. A ship is seaworthy when reasonably fit to perform the services and encounter the ordinary perils incident to the voyage. This means that the ship shall be stanch, properly rigged, and provided with a competent master and a sufficient number of seamen.

In the case of *Thebaud* v. *Insurance Co.*, 52 Hun (N.Y.) 495, under a policy of marine insurance plaintiff insured with defendant the steamboat, *Dos Hermanos*, on a voyage from Philadelphia to Frontera, Mexico. The defense set up was that the boat was unseaworthy. It appeared that the boat was built simply for river navigation, and sank during the ocean voyage. Held, that it was not sufficient to show that the vessel was stanch and strong for river and smooth water navigation, but in order to comply with the implied warranty the plaintiff was obliged to show that everything that could be done to render the vessel fit for the voyage had been done. When the evidence is without dispute that the voyage was one for which the vessel was not fitted, and to the effect that no precautions were taken to provide for the perils which were to be encountered, the plaintiff can not recover.

Deviation. — The second implied warranty is that there shall be no voluntary deviation or departure from the course fixed by mercantile usage, for the voyage contemplated by the policy; and also that there shall be no unreasonable delay in commencing or making the voyage.

In the case of *Burgess* v. *Marine Insurance Co.*, 126 Mass. 70, a vessel was insured against perils of the seas, " At and from Plymouth to Banks, cod-fishing, and at and thence back to Plymouth." The premium was at a certain rate per month, and the policy was to end with the voyage. The vessel sailed with the usual quantity of bait, expecting, as usual, to catch more at the Banks. In previous years bait at that place had been plenty, but this year it was scarce; so, being unable to get a supply, the master went to the nearest port for bait, and then returned to the fishing grounds. The vessel was after-wards lost by the perils of the sea. Held, that, in the absence of evidence of usage to put into port for bait under such circumstances, the doing so was a deviation which discharged the insurer.

If no course has been fixed by mercantile usage, such a course must be pursued as would appear reasonably direct and advan-tageous to a master of ordinary skill. A deviation is justified when caused by circumstances over which neither the owner nor master had any control, as when forced from the course by stress of weather, a mutinous crew, etc.

Turner v. *Insurance Co.*, 25 Me. 515, held, that if the master of a vessel which has been insured, in departing from the usual course of the voyage from necessity, because of leaking of the vessel, acts in good faith and according to his best judgment, and has no other object than to conduct the vessel by the safest and shortest course to the port of destination, the insurance will not be forfeited.

Legality. — The third implied warranty is that the voyage shall be legal, both in its nature and in the manner in which it is prosecuted. Smuggling voyages and trading trips to an enemy's port are cases of illegal voyage.

Losses. — The loss may be total, in which case the whole insurance is ordinarily recoverable; or it may be partial, and then only a *pro rata* part can be recovered. When the loss is total, it may be an actual total loss or a constructive total loss. An actual total loss occurs when the subject insured wholly perishes, as when a vessel is so completely wrecked that it can not be repaired.

Carr v. *Insurance Co.*, 109 N.Y. 504, held, that when a policy of insurance upon a vessel is against " actual total loss only," if the vessel is afloat or it is practicable to put her afloat, or if she is capable of being repaired, at any expense, it is not such a total loss.

A constructive total loss occurs when the article insured is so far damaged or lost that it can not be reclaimed or repaired, except at a greater cost than its value. For example, a vessel may be sunk in shallow water, but the cost of raising it would be greater than it is worth.

Insurance Co. v. *Fogarty*, 19 Wall. (U.S.) 640, was a case in which a sugar-packing machine was insured, and no part was delivered capable of use. Held, to be a total loss, although more than half the pieces, in number and value, may have been delivered, and though they would have some value as old iron. To constitute a total loss, it is not necessary that there should be an absolute extinction or destruction of the thing insured, so that nothing of it can be delivered at the point of destination.

The rule adopted in some jurisdictions is, that if the property insured by a marine insurance policy is damaged to such an extent that its value is reduced one half or more; that is, if there is a one half loss or more, the person insured may abandon the property as a constructive total loss, and claim the full amount of insurance. Notice of the abandonment must be given the insurers so that they may take measures to claim the property and avail themselves of whatever may be saved.

6. CASUALTY INSURANCE

Definition. — Casualty insurance is an indemnity against loss resulting from bodily injury or the destruction of certain kinds of property. It may be accident insurance, which is an indemnity against personal injury by accident, or it may be one of the numerous classes of insurance that have sprung up within the past few years, granting indemnity against almost every conceivable form of catastrophe. Among these special forms of casualty insurance may be mentioned plate glass, boiler, tornado, employer's liability, fidelity, credit, and title insurance.

Accident Insurance. — Accident insurance is a branch of life insurance, the latter insuring against death by any cause, while the former insures against death or injury caused by accident. This class of insurance usually provides a certain payment in case of accidental death, a weekly indemnity for either perma-

nent or total disability by reason of accident, and a fixed sum
for such permanent injury as the loss of one or both of the
hands, feet, or eyes. An accident in this sense is an unforeseen
event which results in injury to one's person. Being thrown
from a wagon in a runaway and being struck by a falling
timber, etc., are accidental injuries.

In the case of the *North American Insurance Co.* v. *Burroughs*, 69 Pa. St.
43, the injuries were caused while the insured was pitching hay. The handle
of the fork slipped through his hands and struck him in the body, inflicting
an injury which caused inflammation resulting in his death. Held, that the
death was the result of an accident.

Fidelity & Casualty Co. v. *Johnson*, 72 Miss. 333, held, that death at the
hands of a mob by hanging is within the terms of a policy insuring against
" bodily injuries sustained through external, violent, and accidental means."

Unless the policy expressly excludes death by poisoning, the
accident policy is held to cover death due to the accidental
taking of poison.

Healey v. *Mutual Accident Association*, 133 Ill. 556, held, that death caused
by accidentally taking and drinking poison is a death produced by bodily injuries received through " external, violent, and accidental means," within the
meaning of a policy of insurance providing indemnity in case of death resulting through such causes. The death in such a case may be regarded as
received through violent means.

Employer's Liability Insurance. — Employer's liability insurance is a class of protection afforded to employers of men engaged in manufacturing or other business, against liability for
damages for personal injuries caused by the negligence of the
employer or his servants. The occasion for this class of insurance has arisen because of the fact that as soon as an employee
in a factory is killed by reason of some faulty machinery his
survivors sue the company for damages. The insurance company in which the employer has insured this risk defends the
case, and if the proprietor is defeated, the insurance company
pays the loss.

In *People's Ice Co.* v. *Employers' Liability Assurance Co.*, 161 Mass. 122,
plaintiff in his application for insurance represented that he was an ice dealer
and that the work carried on by his employees was cutting and handling ice.
The insurance was to cover an expenditure in wages of $5000 each year. The

plaintiff warranted his statements in the application to be true. Held, that injuries caused to employees by the fall of an ice house while in the process of construction by him, not in the season for cutting ice, were not within the policy.

Fidelity Insurance. — Fidelity or guaranty insurance is a contract by which an employer is insured against loss by the fraud or dishonesty of his employees. It is in fact a guarantee of the honesty of an employee. These insurance companies issue bonds guaranteeing the faithful performance of contracts as well, and in all cases in which bonds are required it is now the common practice to purchase them of a fidelity insurance company.

In *People* v. *Rose*, 174 Ill. 310, the court said that the business of guaranteeing the fidelity of persons holding public or private places of trust, and the performance by persons, firms, and corporations of contracts, bonds, and other undertakings, is guaranty insurance.

Credit Insurance. — Credit insurance protects merchants and tradesmen from loss through the insolvency or dishonesty of their customers. For a certain premium the insurance company guarantees the merchant against bad debts. The merchants must usually bear a certain small per cent, and all losses over that amount are paid by the insurance company.

In *Tebbets* v. *Mercantile Credit Guarantee Co.*, 73 Fed. Rep. (U.S.) 95, defendant in consideration of a premium paid, insured plaintiffs against losses in their business during the year 1893. The application, which was a part of the policy, stated the amount of their gross sales for the preceding 14 months and their total losses for that period. The defendant agreed to purchase of plaintiffs an amount, not to exceed $15,000, of uncollectable debts arising during 1893 in excess of one half of one per cent of their total gross sales and deliveries subject to certain conditions. The policy contained this provision, "The contract is issued on the basis that the yearly sales of the insured are between $1,800,000 and $2,500,000." Held, that this was not a stipulation that they would equal that amount, requiring that the one half of one per cent must be computed on at least $1,800,000, but that plaintiffs were entitled to receive their losses, not exceeding $15,000, in excess of one half of one per cent on their actual total sales.

Title Insurance. — Title insurance is a guaranty to the owner of real property that his title is clear. It is an insurance against defects in the title to the property insured, and in case of loss by reason of liens or incumbrances prior to the interest of the insured, the company indemnifies him.

Plate Glass Insurance. — Plate glass insurance is another branch of casualty insurance frequently employed. Many of the larger stores and offices have plate glass fronts representing a large investment, and to avoid the danger of loss the owners employ insurance companies to take the risk of the breaking of these windows. A certain premium is charged by the companies assuming this risk, the premium being based upon the cost price of the windows.

Elevator Insurance. — Elevator insurance consists of a contract which covers the risk incidental to the use of elevators, including both the damage to the elevators themselves and to persons or property that may be injured by the use of, or by accident occurring to, such elevators.

Steam Boiler Insurance. — Because of the frequent explosions occurring from the use of steam boilers the damage caused not only to the boilers themselves but to surrounding property is insured under this head. This insurance does not cover a loss by fire, even though it be caused by the explosion, but does cover the injury to persons or property from such cause.

QUESTIONS ON INSURANCE

1. Define insurance.

2. What is an insurable interest that is sufficient to uphold a fire insurance policy?

3. A owns a house and lot which is mortgaged to B for $1000. C has a lease of the property for one year, and D has agreed with A to purchase the property, A having given him a contract whereby he is to deed it to D as soon as D has paid $1000 on the purchase price. Which of the above parties have an insurable interest in the property?

4. Did A, the owner in the above case, lose his insurable interest in the house and lot when he mortgaged it to B? Did he lose his insurable interest when he gave the contract to D?

5. Must the contract of insurance be in writing? In such a contract what must be definitely agreed upon?

6. Moore goes to Emery, an insurance agent, and asks him to insure his house and lot for $5000, giving him a description of the property. Emery

agrees to insure it for one year and states that the premium will be $12. Emery has authority to bind the insurance company. Moore's house burns before the policy of insurance is delivered to him. Can he recover?

7. If, in the above case, Moore's house had been set on fire twice within one month previous to applying for the insurance, would the fact that this information was not imparted to Emery affect the contract?

8. A, upon applying to B, an insurance agent, for insurance upon a warehouse that he owns, is asked the distance of the warehouse from the railroad, as the insurance company will not insure such buildings within 30 feet of the track. A, believing his answer to be true, states that the warehouse is about 40 feet from the track, as the party from whom he has recently purchased the building stated that to be the distance of the building from the track. The building, in fact, was less than 25 feet from the track. Would this affect the policy?

9. Distinguish between concealment, misrepresentation, and warranty.

10. In which class would the statement in question 8 fall?

11. If an insurance application which is contained in the policy is left blank, does this affect the policy?

12. In a policy of insurance in which the application was attached to and made a part of the policy, the party obtaining the insurance had represented that the building insured was brick for the first two stories and frame the third story, when, in fact, the building was brick for only the first story and the remaining stories were frame. Did this avoid the policy?

13. What is meant when a standard form of fire insurance policy is spoken of?

14. A insured his household furniture located in the lower flat with other tenants occupying the same building above. Fire broke out in the upper floors and A's goods were damaged by smoke and water, but the fire did not reach him. Can A recover the damage under his fire insurance policy?

15. If, in the above case, A had moved his goods out to avoid their being ruined by water, and temporarily placed them across the street until a place could be found to store them, and about an hour after they were placed there a certain part of the goods was stolen, could the value of the stolen goods be recovered under the fire insurance policy?

16. If, in the above case, the remainder of the goods left in the street were damaged by rain which came immediately upon their being removed from the building, could this damage be recovered from the fire insurance policy?

17. If, in question 14, the fire had been caused by lightning and A's goods had been destroyed by the fire, could he have recovered, nothing having been said in the policy about lightning?

18. Evans insures his house and barn, and in the policy there is a condition that the insurer will be liable for fire by lightning. Lightning strikes his barn, tearing off the roof and greatly damaging it, but the barn does not catch fire. Can Evans recover the damage from the insurance company?

19. If, in the above case, Evans's barn had been set on fire by an incendiary, could he have recovered the damages from the insurance company?

20. If, in question 18, Evans, during a period of temporary insanity, set fire to the barn himself, could he recover from the insurance company?

21. A insures his household furniture while living in a certain house on Edmunds Street. Within a month after taking out such insurance, he moves about one block away to a house on Meigs Street. Both of the houses are frame dwellings, and there is apparently no difference in the risk. The policy contains a clause that if the property is removed without the consent of the insurer the policy is no longer of any effect. Shortly after moving, A's furniture burns. Can he recover of the company?

22. If A takes out a fire insurance policy of $1000 on a house worth $2000 and the house burns, what amount can he recover? If the insurance policy is for $3000 and the house is worth $2000, how much can he recover?

23. Levitt insures his house and then sells it. The policy of insurance contains the alienation clause. Shortly after selling the house it burns. Can Levitt recover under the policy?

24. If, in the above case, Levitt had mortgaged instead of sold his house, could he have recovered under the policy?

25. If, in question 23, Levitt upon selling the property had assigned the policy to the purchaser without obtaining the consent of the company, could the purchaser have recovered under the policy in case of fire?

26. Under the standard form of policy, what is required of the insured immediately after a loss?

27. Define life insurance. The insured. The beneficiary.

28. In life insurance, what constitutes an insurable interest?

29. Has a man an insurable interest in the life of his wife? In the life of his brother? In the life of his business partner? In the life of his debtor?

30. A takes out an insurance policy upon the life of B, his business partner, who owes him $10,000. After the policy has been running about two years, A and B dissolve partnership, and B pays A all that he owes him; but A continues the policy upon B's life. Is it valid?

31. A insures his own life in favor of B, his wife. After two years he obtains a divorce from her, then marries C, and, wishing to make her the beneficiary under his policy, seeks to change it. Can this be done?

32. In an application for a life insurance policy, A, the applicant, was asked if any of his brothers or sisters had died with consumption. No answer was given. A had, in fact, lost two brothers by this disease. The policy was issued. Would the concealment render it void?

33. Dwight applied to a life insurance company for a policy of insurance upon his life. He stated in answer to a question that he was engaged in running a grocery, while in fact he was a farmer. One occupation was not considered a greater risk than the other by the insurance company. Would this affect the policy?

34. If, in the preceding case, the answers of Dwight had been included in his policy and made a part of it, would the misstatement made by him affect the policy?

35. If a policy contains no stipulation to the contrary, is the insurance company liable when the insured party commits suicide and a third party is the beneficiary?

36. Is the insurance company liable if the estate of the insured is the beneficiary?

37. The insurance policy contains a stipulation that the company will not be liable if the insured commits suicide, and he dies from the effects of a revolver bullet fired by himself while insane. Is the company liable on the policy?

38. If the stipulation in the policy had been that the company shall not be liable if death is caused by suicide committed when either sane or insane, would the company have been liable in the above case?

39. Define marine insurance. Is the insured required to have an insurable interest in this class?

40. What is the effect of the concealment of a material fact innocently made in this class of insurance?

41. Richardson loads his vessel with merchandise at Albany, runs it down the Hudson River to New York, and there obtains a marine policy on the ship and cargo at and from New York to London. He did not state anything in reference to the loading at Albany. Would this affect the policy?

42. What are the three implied warranties in marine insurance?

43. Distinguish between actual total loss and constructive total loss.

44. What is casualty insurance ? Accident insurance?

45. Elliott took out an accident policy insuring him against " bodily injuries sustained through external violence and accidental means." He was killed by accidentally drinking poison. Was the company liable?

46. If Elliott had been struck by a timber blown from a building being erected, would the company have been liable?

47. What is employer's liability insurance?

48. What is fidelity or guaranty insurance?

49. Define credit insurance.

50. Define title insurance.

51. Define plate glass insurance.

52. Define elevator insurance.

53. Define steam boiler insurance.

REAL PROPERTY

1. IN GENERAL

Definition. — Real property or real estate is defined as including such things as are fixed, permanent, and immovable, comprising land and whatever is affixed to and issuing out of the land. It will therefore be seen that it includes not only the land itself, but buildings erected thereon, as well as trees growing therefrom and oils and minerals included within the land extending downward to the center of the earth and upward indefinitely.

Aiken v. *Benedict*, 39 Barb. (N.Y.) 400, was a case in which it was held that an action for damages would lie against one who erected a building upon the line of his own premises, so that the eaves or gutters projected over the land of his neighbor.

Standing water belongs to the owner of the soil, but the owner of the land has only the right to use and enjoy running waters, having the exclusive right to fish, sail, etc., in the waters over his land.

Ocean Grove v. *Asbury Park*, 40 N.J. Eq. 447, was a case in which the plaintiffs bored in their own land for water over 400 feet, and procured a flow of 50 gallons per minute. The defendants then sank a shaft 8 feet less in depth than plaintiffs, on land of a third party where they had permission to bore. This shaft was 500 feet from plaintiff's well, and a flow of 30 gallons per minute was obtained. As soon as this well started, plaintiff's flow decreased to 30 gallons per minute. The defendants proposed to sink other shafts still nearer to plaintiff's. Held, that they had a right so to do, and the court would not enjoin the defendants from either sinking other wells or from continuing to use this well.

In the case of navigable waters there is no such right, as the title to the soil under them is held by most of the authorities to belong to the state. In waters that are not navigable the owners of the land on each side, as a general rule, own to the center of the stream or lake.

Cooley v. *Golden*, 117 Mo. 33, held, that a grantee from the United States, of land in Missouri on the banks of a navigable river, such as the Missouri River, takes only to the water's edge and not to the middle of the stream. The owner of the bank is not the owner of an island which springs up in the river, no matter whether it be on one side or the other of the center of the stream.

Ice belongs to the owner of the land over which it forms, except when it is on navigable waters, in which case it belongs to the one first appropriating it.

State v. *Pottmeyer*, 33 Ind. 402, held, that when the water of a flowing stream, not navigable, freezes while in its natural channel, the ice attached to the soil constitutes a part of the land, and belongs to the owner of the bed of the stream, who has a right to remove it. A person who owns the land on one side and cuts the ice beyond the center of the stream is liable to the owner of the land lying under the ice which was taken.

In the case of *Wood* v. *Fowler*, 26 Kans. 682, it was held that the owner of the bank along the Kansas River, a navigable river, does not own to the center of the stream, neither does he own the ice which is formed on the stream adjacent to his land without first taking possession of it.

We have considered on pages 55 and 86 the cases in which trees, crops, and grass are a part of the realty, also the question as to when fixtures become realty and when they retain their character as personalty.

Corporeal and Incorporeal Real Property. — Corporeal real property includes the land itself and the buildings, trees, minerals, and other tangible appurtenances thereto. The examples of real property just discussed belong to this class. Incorporeal real property is an intangible right in the land which does not amount to the ownership of it. The principal illustration is an easement, which is defined as a right that the owner of one tract of land may exercise over the land of another. A right of way which a man has over the land of his neighbor for the purpose of reaching his own land is an easement. Lots in a city are sometimes sold with the covenant that the purchaser will not build within a given number of feet from the street. This creates an easement in favor of the seller. The easement may be granted perpetually or for a limited time.

In *Wolfe* v. *Frost*, 4 Sandf. Ch. (N.Y.) 72, it was held that an agreement between the owners of adjacent city lots that if one will build a dwelling upon his lot three feet back from the line of the street the other will set his buildings back the same distance when he builds, creates an easement in the party so building in the land of the other.

Peck v. *Conway*, 119 Mass. 546, was a case in which A, the owner of a large tract of land, conveyed a portion to B with the reservation in the deed " That no building is to be erected by the said B, his heirs, or assigns, upon the land herein conveyed." A retained the balance of the land as his homestead and later sold to C. B afterwards sold to D without making any mention of the reservation. Held, that the reservation created an easement in B's land and for the benefit of A's adjoining property, and it could be enforced by C against B's grantee.

2. ESTATE IN LAND

Definition. — The estate is the interest which one has in land. This interest may amount to absolute ownership or it may be only a temporary or conditional ownership. Under the early English law, what is called the feudal system was in force and the absolute title to all real property was in the king, all others holding under him as tenants. The king generally granted large tracts of land to his nobles or followers, who in return for the grant rendered him certain military service in the wars which were frequently occurring between the different nations in those times. Each follower of the king had his followers or servants to whom he rented the land, and who gave him a certain amount of their time as soldiers for the king. The estate of the tenant in the land was called " fee." This feudal system does not exist in the United States, but many of the terms and rules still used in real property law are derived from it.

Estate in Fee Simple. Eminent Domain. — Estate in fee simple is the nearest approach to complete and absolute ownership of real property. Excepting the right the state has to take his land for taxes or under the power of eminent domain, it can not be taken from him without his consent, except by creditors to pay his debts. It is an estate which exists for a man during his life, and if not disposed of by him descends to his heirs. When an estate of this nature exists in land, the owner can use the land as he chooses, provided he does not cause injury to others, and he may dispose of it or grant privileges in reference to it as he may desire. The land can be taken by the state, under the right of eminent domain, for public use only, as for a road, railway, etc., and in every case just and adequate compensation must be given the owner. This right is often delegated to corporations or private persons who perform some public function, as railroad companies, telegraph companies, etc.

Beekman v. *Saratoga Railroad Co.*, 3 Paige (N.Y.) 45, held that eminent domain remains in the government and it can resume the possession of private property not only when the safety but also when the interest or even the convenience of the state is concerned; as when the land is wanted for a road, canal, or other public improvement, but it can not be taken without just compensation to the owner.

Were it not for this right in the state the construction of a highway or a railroad might be prevented by the arbitrary acts of a single individual.

Life Estate. — The fee in all real property must rest in some one, but there may be carved out of it various lesser estates. The absolute owner has the right to do what he will with his land, therefore he may grant the use of it for life or for a term of years to another person. Estates ranking next to estates in fee are life estates. There are estates in land which are limited by the life of some human being. It is not necessary that the estate shall last during the life, but that an estate be created which may continue during that period. An estate to a woman during her widowhood is a life estate, although she may remarry and thus defeat it before her death.

In the case of *Warner* v. *Tanner*, 38 Ohio St. 118, Tanner and one Bartlett executed an instrument under seal by which Tanner leased to Bartlett two acres of land with use of water and the privilege of conducting it to a cheese house to be erected by Bartlett. Bartlett agreed to pay $30 per year for the premises while he should use them for the manufacture of cheese, and when the premises were no longer to be used for that purpose, they were to revert to Tanner, Bartlett having the privilege of removing all buildings and fixtures erected by him. Held, that the agreement created a life estate in Bartlett provided he continued to use the premises for the manufacture of cheese and paid the rent.

Tenant for Life. — The owner of the life estate, or the tenant for life, as he is called, unless restrained in the grant to him, may dispose of his interest in the land, or out of it may grant a less estate, as for a certain number of years, but he can grant to another no rights in the land that will extend beyond his life. The life tenant can recover nothing for the improvement which he makes on the property, and he is bound to make ordinary repairs at his own expense.

In *Hagan* v. *Varney*, 147 Ill. 281, it was held that a life tenant by placing permanent improvements upon the land, however much they may enhance the value of the estate, can not create a charge for the moneys thus expended against the party who takes the next estate or the remainder. Such improvements are deemed to have been made by the life tenant for his own benefit and enjoyment during the pendency of his own estate.

In *re Mary E. Steele*, 19 N.J. Eq. 120, it was held that a life tenant is bound to keep the premises in repair. If a new roof is needed, he must put it on, and if paint wears off, he must repaint.

The life tenant has the right to cut timber on the land for use as fuel and for the purpose of repairing the buildings and building fences.

Elliot v. *Smith*, 2 N.H. 430, was an action against defendant, a life tenant of certain premises, for cutting down and carrying away two oak trees. They were cut and sold for the purpose of paying for labor and material in building fences on the land. Held, that a tenant for life may cut trees for fuel, wood, and fencing, but can not sell wood to pay for fencing the land. To justify the cutting, the trees themselves must be used for these purposes.

A tenant for life must not commit waste, that is, cause or allow any permanent and material injury to the property that would affect the interest of the owner of the fee. The one who is entitled to the property after the estate for life has terminated has the right to have it come to him without being impaired by injury to any part of the premises.

In the case of *Proffitt* v. *Henderson*, 29 Mo. 325, David Proffitt, at his death, was seized of a certain tract of land, in which he devised to his wife a life use, and at her death the remainder went to his children. The widow conveyed her interest to defendant. This action was brought by the children against defendant for waste in cutting and carrying away timber worth $600. It was shown that the property was timber land and not valuable for anything else. Held, that the cutting of timber may be waste, although necessary to the profitable enjoyment of the land, and although the land is valuable for timber only. Waste is a lasting damage to the reversion, caused by the destruction by the tenant for life of such things on the land as are not included in its temporary profits.

The tenant may continue to work mines or take gravel from pits that have been previously worked, but if he opens new mines or quarries, he is guilty of waste.

Sayers v. *Hoskinson*, 110 Pa. St. 473, was an action for waste brought against life tenants for mining coal and quarrying limestone. It was shown that the quarries and mines were opened and had been worked before the life estate of defendants began. Held, that mines and quarries open at the beginning of a life estate may be worked by the life tenant even until they are exhausted, without rendering him liable in damages for waste.

Emblements. — Emblements are the annual products of the land which are the result of the tenant's labor, and which he is entitled to take away after his tenancy has ended. All grains and other products which are planted and cultivated by one having an interest of uncertain duration, may be removed by him if that interest terminates without his fault before they are harvested.

In *Harris* v. *Frink*, 49 N.Y. 24, it was held that when, under a parol contract for the sale of land, the vendee, with the consent of the vendor, in pursuance of the terms of the contract, enters into possession and puts in crops, the fact that the contract to sell is invalid does not affect the title of the vendee to the crops, and if the vendor refuses to perform the contract and ejects the vendee, the latter does not lose his title to the crops.

Therefore, the representative of a tenant for life is entitled to emblements, since the tenant's estate is of uncertain duration.

In *Bradley* v. *Bailey*, 56 Conn. 374, it was held that the executor of a tenant for life is entitled to crops sown during the tenant's lifetime but maturing after his death. It does not affect this right that the life tenant was rapidly failing in health and had reason to expect his early death when the land was sown.

If the life tenant terminates the estate by his own act, he can not claim emblements.

Debow v. *Colfax*, 10 N.J. L. 128, was a case in which a minister of a certain church was entitled to the possession of the parsonage land, and while in possession he sowed the land with grain. He sold the crop to B, before it was harvested and voluntarily ceased to be minister of that church, removing to another charge. Held, that B could not claim the grain. If a person has an estate in land, the duration of which is uncertain and may continue until the grain is ripe, he will, if he sowed the land, be permitted to reap the grain, although the estate is previously ended, unless the estate be terminated by the act of the tenant himself before the crop is harvested.

3. ESTATES BY MARRIAGE

Classification. — Estates by marriage may now be included under the three heads of Curtesy, Dower, and Homestead. Under the common law there existed an estate during coverture, or during marriage, but this has been practically abolished by statute in all of the states. The estate during coverture arose from the common law disability of a married woman to hold property; therefore the husband acquired an interest in all of the wife's real property, which gave him a right to the use and profits of it until the marriage was terminated by death or divorce. If the wife died first, her real property at once descended to her heirs, unless a child was born of their marriage, in which case the husband was entitled to curtesy.

Curtesy. — Curtesy is the estate for life of the husband in the real estate of his wife. Under the common law such an estate was created, when there existed a valid marriage, if the wife died before the husband and a child had been born which might have inherited the property. These conditions existing, the husband had a life estate for the remainder of his life in the real property of which the wife died possessed. It was not necessary that the child should live until the mother's death; if it lived but a moment after birth, it was sufficient to vest this estate in the husband. This estate by curtesy has been abolished by statute in some of the states, while in others it exists only in case the wife dies without disposing of her real property by will, this being the rule in New York State. In other states still the husband takes the same interest in the wife's estate as the wife takes in the husband's.

Breeding v. *Davis*, 77 Va. 639, held, that by the common law a husband and wife were jointly seized of her real property, and after a child was born the husband had an interest as a tenant by curtesy, by reason of which after the wife's death he has a life interest in said land. By the Virginia married women's act no interest in the wife's property vests in the husband during coverture. But, if a child is born and the husband survives the wife, he has an estate by curtesy of the land which she held in fee when she died and which she had not alienated during the coverture.

Dower. — Dower is the provision which the law makes for the support of a widow out of the lands of the husband. Under the common law it was a life interest in one third of the husband's realty. By statute in a few of the states this has been changed to a life interest in one half of his realty. In order to give rise to this estate, it is necessary that there be a legal marriage, that the husband own the land during some time after their marriage, and that the husband die before the wife. The husband may own the real property but an instant, still that will be sufficient to cause the wife's right of dower to attach. Therefore, if A buys a piece of land of B to-day and sells it to C to-morrow, the right of A's wife attaches. But this is not so if it is the same transaction, as, if A buys a farm and gives back a purchase money mortgage, the wife of A gets a dower interest in the farm subject to the mortgage.

In *King* v. *Stetson*, 11 Allen (Mass.) 407, it was held that if, at the same time that a deed of land is received, and as a part of the same transaction, the grantee mortgages the land to a third party for the purpose of procuring money to enable himself to obtain his deed, his seizin is only instantaneous, and the mortgage will bar his wife's dower, although she did not sign it.

Under her right of dower the wife has no vested interest until the husband dies. He may sell the land without her consent, and she will have no right in it until his death; but after that event, into whatever hands it comes the wife can claim her interest. Therefore, if one takes land from a married man, the wife must join in the conveyance in order to cut off her right of dower. But the wife can not release her dower interest to her husband nor to any one else except the person to whom the land is conveyed.

In *re Rausch*, 35 Minn. 291, we have a case in which Maria Rausch, by an instrument in writing which recited that, in consideration of the sum of $100 to her paid by her husband, Henry Rausch, and the further sum of $300 agreed to be paid to her by him in two years, she did " Remise, release, convey, and set over unto the said Henry Rausch " all her estate or claim to all real and personal property now owned or hereafter acquired by said Henry Rausch. She further agreed to make no claim on him or his heirs for any further interest in his property. At his death she applied for her dower interest. Held, that she could recover. A married woman can not so release to her husband her contingent interest in his real property as to exclude her, as his widow, from dower.

Statutes in many of the states have changed the law as to dower. In a few of the states the wife is not required to join in a conveyance with her husband, as she takes dower only in the property of which he dies possessed.

Homestead. — Homestead right is an exemption of certain property from sale for debts, generally the home and a certain number of acres of ground or land of a given value. Under the common law there was no such provision, but statutes have been passed in many of the states creating a homestead law. These statutes vary in the different states, and grant the exemption only to the head of a family or one upon whom there rests the duty to support dependent persons living with him. A husband and wife constitute such a family. (See Appendix, p. 359.)

Powers v. *Sample*, 72 Miss. 187, held, that an aged widower living with a married son in a house built and controlled by the son, though on the land of the father who receives no rent for it, but who contributes nothing to the support of the family beyond what is necessary for his own maintenance, and who is under no moral or legal duty to contribute to the support of the family, is neither a householder nor the head of a family, so is not entitled to homestead exemptions.

Marsh v. *Lazenby*, 41 Ga. 153, held, that an unmarried man whose indigent mother and sisters live with him and are supported by him is the head of a family in the sense in which the term is used by the state constitution, and is entitled to a homestead.

This homestead exemption is acquired by occupancy of the premises as a home. In some states there must be recorded a notice that the premises are claimed as a homestead.

Estate for years is an estate in real property less than a life estate. The tenant for years is called the lessee or tenant, and the owner, the lessor or landlord. This estate will be treated under the chapter on Landlord and Tenant.

Equitable Estates. — The estates which we have been discussing are termed legal estates. There also exist equitable estates; that is, the legal title may be in one party, while the equitable title is in another. Property may be conveyed to A to hold in trust, or as trustee, for the benefit and use of B. A is the legal owner, but holds the property only for the purpose of turning over the profits to B, who is the equitable owner. In this case, A is the trustee and B is the beneficiary.

Estates in Severalty and Joint Estates. — Estates are divided, according to the number of owners, into estates in severalty and joint estates, estates in severalty being those in which the ownership is in one person. Joint estates are those which are owned by two or more persons. The common classes of joint estates are joint tenancies and tenancies in common. The chief distinction between the two is, that in the case of a joint tenancy, upon the death of one of the joint tenants his interest vests in the survivor or survivors, while upon the death of a tenant in common his interest passes to his representatives. In the United States, all joint estates are presumed to be tenancies in common, unless it appears that there was a contrary intention.

4. SALE AND CONVEYANCE OF REAL ESTATE

Title. — The title to real property is the means by which the ownership is acquired and held. It is, in other words, the evidence which a person has of the right to the possession of property. It may be either by descent or purchase. The title by descent is acquired either by will or by the law of descent, controlling the disposition of the real property of a person dying without a will. Purchase includes all other means of acquiring the title to real property, whether by gift or for a valuable consideration.

Land Contract. — When the title is acquired by purchase, the transaction is the result of a contract or an agreement of one party to purchase or take the property upon the prescribed terms, and of the owner to sell and convey the particular property for the stated consideration. This agreement is often called a land contract, and is required by the fourth section of the statute of frauds to be in writing. It must be remembered that this contract does not convey the land, but agrees to convey at some future time. If the conveyance immediately follows the making of the agreement, the contract to convey is unnecessary, but in the passing of the title to real property much care is necessary to ascertain that the title to the person about to sell, or the grantor, is clear; that is, that no third party or parties have any claims on it. To ascertain that the title is clear, a search of the records in the public office where all deeds, mortgages, and other important documents are kept, is made, generally by a lawyer, or by some officer or company accustomed to perform such duties. When the results of this search are put in writing, the document shows all of the transactions affecting the particular piece of land, and is called an abstract of title. It requires some time to obtain this abstract of title and to perfect other arrangements for the conveyance of the property, and the land contract binds the parties to their agreement during this interval. Sometimes the purchaser has not the ready money to pay for the property, and in such a case this contract is given until he has paid a certain amount by installments, at which time a deed will be given him.

A land contract, used in New York State, is usually in some such form as the one shown on the two following pages. The acknowledgment which would be used with this contract, and which is generally used with real property conveyances, is similar to the form given on page 98.

If, in the above case, the purchaser had not had the money to pay down, the contract might have provided that he was to have possession upon the execution of the contract, and that he would pay $200 a year for five years, at the expiration of which time Drake would give him a deed, the balance of the purchase price being secured as provided in the above contract. This contract may assume a variety of forms, the object being to set forth the actual agreement of the parties.

Agreement, *made the* f i r s t *day of* September *in the year one thousand nine hundred* and five **Between**

Charles A. Drake, of Geneva, Ontario County, New York

party of the first part, and Edward Simmons, of Rochester, Monroe County, New York

party of the second part, in manner following: The said party of the first part, in consideration of the sum of

Two Thousand (2,000) *Dollars, to be fully paid as hereinafter mentioned, hereby agrees to sell unto the said party of the second part,* **All** that TRACT or PARCEL of LAND, situate in the City of Rochester, County of Monroe and State of New York, and more particularly distinguished as lot number twenty(20) as laid down on a map of Snyder & Stone's subdivision of a part of the Strong Tract on file in Monroe County Clerk's office in liber 5 of maps at page 83; said lot number twenty (20) being situate on the east side of Kenmore Street, and being thirty-three (33) feet in width, front and rear, and one hundred and fifty-nine (159) feet deep.

And the said *party of the second part hereby agrees to purchase said premises at the said consideration of*

Two Thousand (2,000) *Dollars, and to pay the same as follows.*

One Thousand (1,000) Dollars upon the execution of the conveyance to second party within thirty days from the date hereof and the balance two years thereafter secured by a mortgage on the above described premises for the sum of one thousand (1,000) Dollars.

And the said *party of the first part, on receiving such payment* and on the execution of the mortgage by the party of the second part *at the time and in the manner above mentioned, shall, at* his *own proper costs and expenses, execute, acknowledge and deliver, or cause to be executed, acknowledged and delivered to the said part* y *of the second part, or to* his *assigns. a proper deed containing a general warranty and the usual full covenants for the*

*conveying and assuring to   them the fee simple of the said premises,
free from all encumbrance;*

*which Deed shall conform to the requirements of the Real Property,
Law of the State of New York, relating to short forms of Deeds, as
far as the same is applicable thereto, which Deed shall be delivered on
the* first *day of* October *19* 5 *at* 10 *o'clock* A M, *at* the
Merchants National Bank, Rochester, New York. ————————

And it is Understood *that the stipulations aforesaid are to apply
to and bind the heirs, executors, administrators and assigns of the respective parties.*

In Witness whereof *the parties to these presents have hereunto set
their hands and seals the day and year first above written.*

Sealed and delivered in the presence of

J H Warner   Edward Simmons

Charles A Drake

5. DEEDS

Definition. — The conveyance of the title to the property may
be absolute, in which case it is made by deed, or conditional, in
which event it is made by mortgage.

A deed, in real property law, is defined as a written contract,
signed, sealed, and delivered, by means of which one party conveys real property to another. The two principal kinds of
deeds are warranty and quitclaim. The warranty deeds are
conveyances which, aside from granting the land, contain certain warrants or covenants concerning the title. A quitclaim deed
merely grants what interest the grantor has and nothing more.

A form of warranty deed used in New York State is shown
on the following page. (Acknowledgment in the same form as
that given on page 98.)

This Indenture, *made the* fifteenth ——— *day*

of September ——— *in the year nineteen hundred* and five ———————

Between Charles A. Drake, unmarried, of Geneva, Ontario County,

New York, party of the first part, and Edward Simmons, of

Rochester, Monroe County, New York, *party of the second part.*

Witnesseth, *That the said part* y *of the first part, in consideration of* the sum of

t w o   t h o u s a n d   (2,000) *dollars, lawful money*

of the United States, paid by the part y *of the second part, do*es *hereby grant and release*

unto the said part y *of the second part,* ——— his ——— *heirs and assigns for ever,*

All that Tract or Parcel of land situate in the City of Rochester,

County of Monroe, and State of New York, and more particularly

distinguished as lot number twenty (20), as laid down on a map

of Snyder & Stone's subdivision of a part of the Strong Tract

on file in Monroe County Clerk's Office in Liber 5 of Maps at

 page 83.   Said lot number twenty (20) is situate on the east

side of Kenmore Street, and is thirty-three (33) feet in width,

front and rear, and one hundred and fifty-nine (159) feet deep

Together *with the appurtenances and all the estate and rights of the part* y *of the first*

part in and to said premises.

To Have and to Hold *the above granted premises unto the said part* y *of the second part,*

his heirs *and assigns forever.*

And *the said* Charles A. Drake, ——————————————————

part y *of the first part, do*es *covenant with said part* v *of the second part as follows;*

First. *That the said* Charles A. Drake, ——————————————

part y *of the first part, i*s *seized of the said premises in fee simple and ha*s *good right to convey*

the same.

Second. *That the part* y *of the second part shall quietly enjoy the said premises.*

Third. *That the said premises are free from incumbrances.*

Fourth. *That the part* y *of the first part will execute or procure any further necessary*

assurance of the title to said premises.

Fifth. *That the said* Charles A. Drake, ——————————————

part y *of the first part, will forever warrant the title to said premises.*

In Witness Whereof, *the said part* y *of the first part ha*s *hereunto set* his

hand and *seal the day and year first above written.*

In presence of

B. T. Cox   *Charles A. Drake*   [seal]

Conditions. — All deeds must be in writing (or printing), and must have parties competent to contract. To constitute a valid deed, or conveyance of property, it is also requisite that there be (1) property to be conveyed, (2) words of conveyance, (3) description of the property, (4) a writing signed, and in some states sealed, by the grantor, (5) delivery and acceptance, (6) acknowledgment in some states, witnesses in others, and in still other states the instrument must be registered.

Property to be Conveyed. — The first condition is self-evident, as a valid deed can not be given unless there is real property to convey.

Words of Conveyance. — The deed must contain words of conveyance, called the granting clause, which consists of words sufficient to transfer the estate to the grantee. In the above deed the words, " Do hereby grant, sell, and convey," constitute this clause. The words " give, grant, bargain, and sell " are sometimes used, or again the phrase, " grant, bargain, sell, remise, release, convey, alien, and confirm."

Hummelman v. *Mounts*, 87 Ind. 178, held, that a writing as follows, " This indenture witnesseth, that I, Jacob Smith, warrant and defend unto Christena Smith, her heirs and assigns forever," certain real estate that was then described, the instrument being then signed, sealed, and acknowledged like a deed, was not effective as a conveyance, as it contained no granting clause, nor words signifying a grant.

The granting clause should contain the names of the parties, also the words defining the estate, as in the above deed, " unto the said party of the second part his heirs and assigns forever." By the clause used in this case an estate in fee is granted. Under the common law, if the word " heir " was omitted and the grant was to the grantee alone, only a life interest would be conveyed.

In *Adams* v. *Ross*, 30 N.J. L. 505, it was held that a grant to A for her natural life and at her death to her children, conveyed a life estate to A and then an estate to her children during their lives, but that they did not take it in fee, as the grant contained no words of inheritance.

Sedgwick v. *Laflin*, 10 Allen (Mass.) 430, held, that a grant to A and " his successors and assigns forever," conveyed only a life estate. The court said that it is a well-settled rule of the common law that the word " heirs " is necessary to create an estate of inheritance.

But this rule has been changed by statute in some of the states, and a conveyance showing an intent to grant a fee will be so construed.

The conveyance clause may contain exceptions; that is, there may be reserved something that would otherwise pass with the property conveyed. The exception, for instance, might be of a right of way over the land, or the right to mine coal or minerals. The exception must be stated and particularly described.

The habendum is that part of the conveying clause which begins with the words "To have and to hold." It designates the estate which is to pass. If it is repugnant to the granting or conveying clause, it is void, and if the conveying clause defines the estate granted, the habendum clause is not necessary, although it is usually employed.

Ratliffe v. *Marrs*, 87 Ky. 26, held, that where the granting clause grants an absolute estate to A, and the habendum recites that a life estate was given to A, remainder to B, A takes an absolute estate. When the granting clause and the habendum do not agree, the latter gives way to the granting clause.

Description. — The deed must contain a description of the property sufficient to identify it. The description may include references to maps, monuments, distances, or boundaries.

Travelers Insurance Co. v. *Yount*, 98 Ind. 454, held, that a creek is a monument which may be referred to as a boundary in a deed or mortgage.

The description often closes with the words, "with the privileges and appurtenances thereto belonging." But it is not considered that this clause adds anything to the deed. The appurtenances are such rights as watercourses, rights of way, rights to light and air, etc., and these are all included in the general grant, unless they are expressly reserved.

Signature and Seal. — At common law a seal was necessary to the legality of a deed, but in many states this requirement has been abolished. Between the parties themselves to a deed a consideration is not necessary to its validity, although it may in some cases be attacked by creditors of the grantor. A date is not strictly necessary to the validity of a deed, and when used may be placed in any part of the instrument. It is generally at the commencement or just before the signature at the end. A deed takes effect from the time of delivery, and the presumption is that the date of delivery is the date of the instrument.

It is usual for the deed to close with the testimonium clause, which recites, "In witness whereof the party of the first part has hereunto set his hand and seal the day and year first above written," and immediately thereafter the grantor signs his name. By the statute of frauds the deed is required to be signed. In some states the statutes require that the deed be subscribed, and in that case it must be signed at the end, otherwise it may be signed at any other place.

In *Devereux* v. *McMahon*, 108 N.C. 134, it was held that while the laws of North Carolina require all deeds conveying land to be signed by the maker, the signing is not necessarily required to be at the end of the deed. If the signature is in the body of the instrument, it is sufficient. Nor is it essential that the maker should actually sign his name. He may authorize another to do it in his presence, or he may affix his mark, which will have the same effect as his own writing.

Delivery and Acceptance. — A deed does not become operative until it is delivered and accepted ; that is, the instrument must pass out of the control of the grantor, but it must be his voluntary act, and if taken without his consent, as by theft, it is not a delivery.

In the case of *Fisher* v. *Hall*, 41 N.Y. 416, a conveyance of real property had been subscribed and sealed by the grantor and attested by witnesses under a clause stating that it had been sealed and delivered in their presence, but the grantee was not then present, and remained ignorant of the deed until long after the death of the grantor, who continually retained the deed in his possession until his death. It was held that such a conveyance did not pass title to the grantee, as there was no delivery to him. The court further held that it is not necessary for the grantee to be present at the signing of the deed, or that he should have actual possession of it, but if he does not receive the deed, it should be placed within the power of some third person for the grantee's use.

The instrument may be intrusted to a third person to be delivered to the grantee on the performance of some condition. This is termed a "delivery in escrow." To constitute a valid delivery in escrow there must be no power in the grantor to recall it.

James v. *Vanderheyden*, 1 Paige Ch. (N.Y.) 385, was a case in which a mortgage and a deed were delivered to a third person, to be kept by him during the pleasure of the parties and subject to their further order. Held, that the papers were not delivered in escrow, such delivery as in this case amounting to a mere depositary. To constitute a delivery in escrow the papers must be placed in the hands of a third person, who is to deliver to the grantee upon the happening of some event or the performance of some condition.

Not only must there be a delivery, but there must be an acceptance by the grantee, though acceptance will sometimes be presumed from the grantee having possession of the deed or from the beneficial character of the instrument.

Jackson v. *Phipps*, 12 Johns. (N.Y.) 418, held, that a delivery of a deed is not complete until it has been accepted by the grantee. The grantor agreed to give the grantee a deed of his farm as security for a debt, and upon returning home executed and acknowledged a deed as agreed, and left it in the clerk's office to be recorded. Neither the grantee nor any person in his behalf was present to receive it. Held, that this did not constitute a delivery and acceptance.

Acknowledgment. — Acknowledgment is necessary to entitle the instrument to be recorded in some states, and in other states it is necessary to give it validity. An acknowledgment consists in the grantor going before an officer designated by law and declaring the deed to be genuine, and that it is his voluntary act, the officer making a certificate to this effect. An ordinary form of acknowledgment is shown on page 98.

Blood v. *Blood*, 23 Pick. (Mass.) 80, held, that if a deed of land be recorded without having been acknowledged before a magistrate, the record is of no effect.

In some states one or more witnesses to a deed are required by statute in case there is no acknowledgment in order to entitle it to be recorded, while in other states they are necessary to give it validity.

Record. — The statutes in all of the states provide for the registration or recording in some public office of all deeds and other instruments affecting real property. Instruments so recorded are notice to the whole world that they exist, as every one can examine the records. Therefore the first instrument recorded has priority over another like instrument on the same property. But as between the parties themselves and all parties having actual notice, the instrument is in most of the states equally valid without recording. It is only against subsequent purchasers who buy in good faith that unrecorded instruments are of no effect.

Warranties. — As we have said, a deed may be a full warranty deed, as set forth on page 303, which contains the five covenants of title, or it may be a simple warranty deed containing only the covenant of quiet enjoyment and covenant warranting the title of the grantor. Upon a breach of a covenant the grantor is liable for damages. They are contracts by which the grantor warrants certain facts to the grantee.

Seizin. — In the full warranty deed above mentioned the first covenant is that of seizin and right to convey. This is a covenant that the grantor has possession of the property granted and has a right to convey it. He must have the very estate in quantity and quality which the deed purports to convey. This covenant is broken when the grantor is not the sole owner, or when the property is in the adverse possession of another, or when the land described does not exist, or there is a deficiency in the amount of land conveyed.

Bacon v. *Lincoln*, 4 Cush. (Mass.) 210, was an action for breach of covenant of seizin. The land conveyed was described as a tract of land in the county of Hamilton and state of New York, and known upon a map of township No. 38, filed in the office of the clerk of Montgomery County as No. 5. On the trial it was shown that there was no such map on file in the Montgomery County clerk's office, that township No. 38 had never been surveyed nor subdivided, and that no such lot as the one described in the deed existed. Held, that this constituted a breach of the covenant of seizin. The defendant covenanted that he was seized of the lot described in the deed, and if no such lot existed, the covenant was broken.

This covenant is often set forth in the deed in more elaborate form after the following manner : —

" The party of the first part does hereby covenant and agree that at the time of the ensealing and delivery of these presents he was the lawful owner and was well seized, in fee simple, of the premises above described, free and clear from all lien, right of dower or other incumbrances of every name and nature, legal or equitable, and that he has good right and full power to convey the same."

Quiet Enjoyment. — The second covenant is that of quiet enjoyment, and is to the effect that the grantee and his heirs and assigns shall not be legally disturbed in their quiet and peaceable possession of the premises, but that they shall possess it without suit, trouble, or eviction by the grantor or his heirs or assigns.

In *Underwood* v. *Birchard*, 47 Vt. 305, it was held that a covenant of quiet enjoyment relates to the grantor's right to convey the premises. It is a covenant that the grantee shall not be rightfully disturbed in his possession, and not that he shall not be disturbed at all. So where it appears that the grantee was kept out of possession by a party who had no right or claim, it is not a breach of the covenant.

Incumbrances. — Number three is a covenant against incumbrances, and warrants that there are no outstanding rights in third parties to the land conveyed. It is a covenant against both mortgages and easements in favor of third parties. It is broken by an outstanding mortgage, an unexpired lease, an easement, unpaid taxes, or judgments that are unsatisfied.

Clark v. *Fisher*, 54 Kans. 403, was an action brought for a breach of a covenant against incumbrances in a deed given by defendant. It seemed that one Dent was a tenant under a lease under which he was to give up possession to the grantor on thirty days' notice in case of sale, but Dent was to have the right to harvest sixty acres of wheat which he had sown. Held, that this right to gather a growing crop was an incumbrance, and the amount of damages which plaintiff could recover was the value of the crop, less the cost of harvesting and marketing. This case also held that an outstanding lease was an incumbrance. An incumbrance is defined as any right to or interest in the land which may exist in a third person to the diminution of the value of the land, but which does not prevent the passing of the fee by conveyance.

Hall v. *Dean*, 13 Johns. (N.Y.) 105, held, that a judgment against the grantor, outstanding at the time of the execution of a deed, is a breach of the covenant against incumbrance.

In *Hill* v. *Bacon*, 110 Mass. 387, it was held that taxes assessed to the grantor on the land conveyed, before the execution of the deed and which are not paid by the grantor, constitute a breach of the covenant against incumbrances.

Further Assurance. — The fourth covenant is one of further assurance, and is an agreement by the grantor to perform any acts that may be necessary to perfect the grantee's title, including the execution of such further instruments as may be required for this purpose.

In *Colby* v. *Osgood*, 29 Barb. (N.Y.) 339, it was held that the release of a mortgage is a further assurance, and an action may be brought for the breach of this covenant if the grantor refuses to clear the title to the premises by obtaining such a release, unless the property was expressly conveyed subject to the mortgage.

Warranty of Title. — The fifth and last covenant is the warranty of title, which is an assurance by the grantor that the grantee shall not be evicted from part or all of the premises by reason of a superior title in any one else. This covenant is broken by an eviction from any or all of the premises, the removal of fixtures by one having a right to do so, or the taking of the premises by one having a paramount title.

Norton v. *Jackson*, 5 Cal. 262, held, that eviction by process of law is required to enable one to maintain an action for breach of covenant of warranty.

Quitclaim Deed. — The quitclaim deed, mentioned on page 302, is drawn in New York State in the form shown on the following page.

The quitclaim deed contains none of the covenants of a warranty deed, and purports to grant only what interest the grantor has, if he has any. The quitclaim deed does not even aver that he has any title. If he has a defective title, the grantee has no claim on him. The words of conveyance differ from those in the warranty deed. This form of deed is used when the grantor has an interest in land, as one of several heirs or as a joint owner, and wishes to convey his share to another heir or to the other joint owner. It is also employed when a person having an easement or other minor estate in land wishes to transfer his estate to the owner in fee for the purpose of clearing the title.

Covenant against Grantor. — The covenant against the grantor is the only covenant used in a quitclaim deed. It is also sometimes used in a warranty deed, when the grantor is not willing

This Indenture, *made the* fifteenth ———— *day*

of — October ——— *in the year* 19 *hundred and* 5 ——————————

Between Charles Simmons and Sarah his wife, of Rochester, ———

Monroe County, New York, parties of the first part, and Thomas

B. Curtis, of the same place, party ———————————— *of the second part,*

Witnesseth, *That the said part*ies*of the first part, in consideration of* the sum of
two thousand (2,000) ———————————— *dollars, lawful money*
of the United States, paid by the party of the second part, do hereby remise, release and
*quit-claim unto the said part*y *of the second part* his *heirs and assigns forever,*

All that Tract or Parcel of Land, situate in the town of

Lansing, County of Tompkins, and State of New York, being a part

of lot number forty-nine (49) in said town, and bounded and de-

scribed as follows, to wit: - Beginning at the southeast

corner of land owned by John T. Reynolds and running thence

north one hundred and twenty-six and one half (126 1/2) rods;

thence east to the east line of said lot number forty-nine (49);

thence south to land owned by Chauncey R.Brown; thence west to

the northeast corner of land owned by Brown; thence south to

the center of the highway; and thence west to the place of be-

ginning, containing one hundred and three (103) acres of land,

more or less.

Together *with the appurtenances and all the estate and rights of the parti*es *of the first part*
in and to said premises.

To Have and to Hold *the above mentioned and described premises unto the said part*y
of the second part, ——— his ————— *heirs and assigns for ever.*

In Witness Whereof, *the said parti*es*of the first part* have *hereunto set* their
*hand*s*and seal*s*the day and year first above written.*

In Presence of
E.F. Beatty

Charles Simmons

Sarah Simmons

to warrant the title absolutely, but is willing to covenant that he has not himself done or permitted to be done anything that would injuriously affect the title to the premises. Such a deed is called a special warranty deed. The form of this covenant as used in New York State is as follows : "The said party of the first part covenants with said party of the second part that the party of the first part has not done or suffered anything whereby the said premises have been incumbered in any way whatever."

In *Buckner* v. *Street*, 15 Fed. Rep. (U.S.) 365, it was held that a deed with a special warranty against all persons claiming by, through, or under the grantor, can not be extended to a general covenant of warranty against all persons.

6. MORTGAGES

Definition. — A mortgage is a conveyance of land as security for a debt or some other obligation, subject to the condition that upon the payment of the debt or the performance of the obligation the conveyance becomes void. The debtor, or the person who gives the mortgage, is called the mortgagor and the creditor, or the person to whom it is given, is the mortgagee.

Equity of Redemption. — Under the common law the mortgage was strictly a conveyance, and the mortgagee held the legal title to the property. His title was subject to be defeated upon the payment of the debt secured, and in default of the payment his estate became absolute. This often led to hardship and injustice, for the value of the property might be greatly in excess of the mortgage debt. The courts of equity recognized this injustice and extended relief by giving the mortgagor the right to redeem the land by paying the debt with interest. This right was termed an "equity of redemption," and to cut off such right an action was brought in court giving the mortgagor a certain time in which to pay or else lose the right entirely.

Lien. — Now, in many of the states, the mortgage is looked upon as a lien which the mortgagee has in the mortgaged premises, the mortgagor still being the legal owner subject to the lien which the mortgagee holds upon the land as security for his debt.

In *Dutton* v. *Warschauer*, 21 Cal. 609, it was held that the doctrine respecting mortgages which prevails in the state of California is that a mortgage is a mere security operating upon the property as a lien or incumbrance only, and is not a conveyance vesting in the mortgagee any estate in the land.

Any Interest in Realty which is Subject to Sale may be Mortgaged. — A widow may mortgage her right of dower, or a mortgagee may mortgage his mortgage, and an heir may mortgage his undivided interest.

In the case of *Neligh* v. *Michenor*, 11 N.J. Eq. 539, A and B entered into a written contract, by which B bound himself to convey certain lands to A. Held, that A may mortgage his interest in the land under this contract. Everything that is the subject of a contract or that may be assigned, is capable of being mortgaged.

Form. — A mortgage is in substantially the same form as a deed, with the addition of the defeasance clause. This is a clause containing a statement that the conveyance is made conditional upon the payment of a specific amount, which amount being paid, the instrument is void. A mortgage is executed with all of the formality of, and in practically the same manner as, a deed. As a rule, when the mortgage is given to secure a debt, it is accompanied by a note or bond or other evidence of indebtedness, making the mortgagor personally liable, so that the mortgagee may look to him personally in case the mortgaged property is not sufficient to pay the debt. This is not necessary to the validity of the mortgage, as there may be a valid mortgage without any personal liability on the part of the mortgagor; for example, when the creditor's only right to payment is out of the mortgaged property.

Hodgdon v. *Shannon*, 44 N.H. 572, held, that the validity of a mortgage depends upon the genuineness of the debt described in the condition thereof. This debt need not exist in the form of a promissory note.

The ordinary form of a mortgage in New York State is shown on the two following pages. (Acknowledgment as on page 98.)

Defeasance Clause. — In the form of mortgage shown, the defeasance clause is that paragraph beginning with the words "Provided Always." No particular form is necessary for this clause. So long as it shows that the conveyance is made to

This Indenture, *made the* fifteenth *day*

of September *in the year nineteen hundred* and five

Between Edward Simmons, unmarried, of Rochester, Monroe County, New York, party of the first part, and Charles A. Drake, of Geneva, Ontario County, New York, ———— *party of the second part;*

Whereas *the said* Edward Simmons is ———— *justly indebted to the said part* y *of the second part, in the sum of* One Thousand (1,000) ———— *dollars, lawful money of the United States, secured to be paid by* — his ———— *certain bond or obligation bearing even date herewith, conditioned for the payment of the said sum of* One Thousand (1,000) ————

———— *dollars, on* ———— *the* fifteenth *day of* September,———— *nineteen hundred and* eight, ———— *and the interest thereon, to be computed from* the date hereof *at the rate of* six (6) *per centum per annum, and to be paid* semiannually,

It being thereby Expressly Agreed *that the whole of the said principal sum shall become due after default in the payment of interest, taxes or assessments, as hereinafter provided.*

Now this Indenture Witnesseth, *That the said part* y *of the first part, for the better securing the payment of the said sum of money mentioned in the condition of the said bond or obligation, with interest thereon, and also for and in consideration of one dollar, paid by the said part* y *of the second part, the receipt whereof is hereby acknowledged, do* es *hereby grant and release unto the said part* y *of the second part, and to* his heirs — *and assigns forever*

All that Tract or Parcel of Land, situate in the City of Rochester, County of Monroe, and State of New York, and more particularly distinguished as lot number twenty (20) as laid down on a map of Snyder & Stone's subdivision of a part of the Strong Tract on file in Monroe County Clerk's office, in Liber 5, of maps at page 83. Said lot number twenty (20) is situate on the east side of Kenmore Street, and is thirty-three (33) feet in width front and rear, and one hundred and fifty-nine (159) feet deep ————

Together *with the appurtenances and all the estate and rights of the part* y *of the first part in and to said premises*

To Have and to Hold *the above granted premises unto the said part* y *of the second part,* his heirs *or assigns forever.*

Provided Always, *that if* the said Edward Simmons, ——————————

—————————— *the said party of the first part,* his *heirs, executors or administrators, shall pay unto the said party of the second part,* his heirs *executors, administrators or assigns, the said sum of money mentioned in the condition of the said bond or obligation and the interest thereon, at the time and in the manner mentioned in the said condition, that then these presents and the estate hereby granted shall cease, determine, and be void.*

And *the said* Edward Simmons, ——————————

party of the first part, covenants with the party of the second part as follows:

First.—*That* the said Edward Simmons, ——————————
the party of the first part will pay the indebtedness as hereinbefore provided, and if default be made in the payment of any part thereof, the party of the second part shall have power to sell the premises therein described, according to law.

Second.—*That* the said Edward Simmons, ——————————
the party of the first part will keep the buildings on the said premises insured against loss by fire, for the benefit of the mortgagee.

Third.—*And it is hereby expressly agreed, that the whole of said principal sum shall become due, at the option of the said party of the second part, after default in the payment of interest for* thirty *days, or after default in the payment of any tax or assessment* for thirty days *after notice and demand.*

And *that the said party of the first part will execute any further necessary assurance of the title to the mortgaged premises, and will forever warrant said title.*

In Witness Whereof, *the said party of the first part, has hereunto set* his ——
hand and seal the day and year first above written.

In Presence of

J. H. Warner

Edward Simmons

secure the payment of a debt, it will constitute the conveyance a mortgage. And although on its face the instrument may be a deed, a court of equity will permit it to be shown that the agreement really was that the conveyance should be made as security for a debt and not absolutely; therefore when this is shown, although the instrument be a deed in form, it will be declared a mortgage, the defeasance clause in this case being made orally.

In the case of *Morrow* v. *Jones*, 41 Neb. 867, Jones gave Morrow a real estate mortgage to secure a loan of money, and after it matured Morrow brought an action to foreclose the mortgage and sold the property for a sum considerably less than the debt and costs. Before the sale was confirmed, Morrow wrote a letter to Jones, inclosing a deed of the property, in which Morrow was named as grantee, and made a proposition that if Jones would execute and return the deed, she could redeem the property at any time by paying the amount of the mortgage, costs, and interest. Jones accepted the proposition, executed the deed, and returned the same to Morrow, who immediately placed it upon record. Held, that the relation of mortgagor and mortgagee was not changed by the delivery of the deed on the terms upon which it was obtained, and that the deed was taken as further security for, and not as payment of, the mortgage debt. A deed of real estate, absolute in form, may be shown by parol to have been intended by the parties as security for a debt, and as between such parties it will be construed to be merely a mortgage.

Covenants. — The mortgage may or may not include one or more of the three covenants designated as first, second, and third in the foregoing mortgage. They are often inserted for the better security of the mortgagee. The first clause gives the mortgagee the right to sell the property, that is, to foreclose the mortgage upon default of the payment of any part of the principal as agreed, although the time for which the balance is to run has not yet expired. In this mortgage the whole amount is not payable until two years from the date of the instrument, but if the first payment is not made one year from that date, the mortgagee may foreclose the mortgage under this clause.

The second clause is known as the insurance clause, and is inserted when the mortgagee does not deem the land, aside from the buildings, ample security for the loan.

The third clause is called the interest, tax, and assessment clause, and compels the mortgagor to pay the interest, taxes, and all assessments levied against the property, and in case of default for a given number of days, the mortgagee may, if he choose, consider the whole amount of the debt due and proceed with the same remedies as though the time within which the debt was to have been paid had expired.

Bond. — As has been said, the debt is usually represented by a note or bond, by which the mortgagor personally obligates himself to pay the debt which the mortgage is given to secure. If notes are given, they are drawn in the usual form. If a bond is given, it is drawn in such form as to contain the same covenants as the mortgage. A bond to accompany the foregoing mortgage would be in the form shown on the following page. (Acknowledgment as on page 98.)

Assignment. — The mortgagee may desire to sell the mortgage or transfer it to another party. This he may do, as the interest

Know all Men by these Presents. That

I, Edward Simmons, of Rochester, Monroe County, New York, ——
party of the first part, am ————————————
—— *held and firmly bound unto* Charles A. Drake, of Geneva, Ontario
County, New York, party of the second part ———— *in the sum of*
T w o   t h o u s a n d   (2,000) ———————— *dollars,*
lawful money of the United States, to be paid to the said Charles A. Drake
or to his certain attorneys, heirs, *executors, administrators or assigns,*
For which Payment to be made I *bind* myself, my *heirs, executors*
and administrators jointly & severally *firmly by these presents.*
Sealed *with* my *seal Dated the* fifteenth *day of* — September ——
One Thousand Nine Hundred and Five

The Condition of the above Obligation is such, *that if the above*
bounden Edward Simmons, ———————————————

his *heirs, executors or administrators, shall pay unto the above named* Charles A. Drake,
his heirs, ————————————————————
—— *executors, administrators or assigns, the sum of* ———————
———— O n e   t h o u s a n d   (1,000) ————— *dollars,*
on *the* fifteenth *day of* September, ———— *which will be in the year*
nineteen hundred and eight, —— *and the interest thereon, to be computed from*
the date hereof ————————————————————
at and after the rate of six (6) *per cent, per annum, and to be paid* semiannually,
then the above obligation to be void, otherwise to remain in full force and virtue.
And it is Hereby Expressly Agreed, *that the whole of the said principal*
sum shall become due, at the option of said mortgagee, or obligee, after default in the payment
of interest for ———————————————————
thirty *days, or after default in the payment of any tax or assessment for* thirty
——days *after notice and demand.*

And *the said part* y *of the first part also covenant with the party of the second part,*
that the part y *of the first part will keep the buildings on the said premises described in the*
mortgage accompanying this Bond insured against loss by fire for the benefit of the mortgagee.

In Presence of
J H Warner   Edward Simmons

of the mortgagee in the property mortgaged is subject to sale as well as the interest in the property remaining in the mortgagor. The assignee takes the mortgage with all of the rights of the assignor, but no others. The mortgage can be assigned only by an instrument in writing and under seal.

In the case of *Warden* v. *Adams*, 15 Mass. 233, Adams delivered a mortgage to a third party for the purpose of having him draw an assignment thereof to Warden. Before this assignment was prepared, Adams assigned the mortgage by a written instrument to Hamilton, another creditor. Hamilton knew that the mortgage was in the third party's hands for the purpose of drawing an assignment to Warden. Held, that Hamilton was entitled to the mortgage. The delivery to the third party did not constitute an assignment. An assignment of a mortgage can be made only by a written instrument.

An ordinary form of assignment of a mortgage is shown on the following page.

Foreclosure. — The remedy of the mortgagee when the debt secured by the mortgage is not paid as agreed is to foreclose his lien. This is called foreclosure of the mortgage, and means the proceedings by which the mortgaged premises are applied to the payment of the mortgage debt, and by which the equity of redemption is barred or cut off. This remedy usually consists of an action in the courts from which a judgment is obtained, decreeing that the property be sold and the proceeds applied toward the payment of the mortgage debt. If anything remains after the costs of the proceedings and the mortgage debt are paid, it is turned over to the mortgagor. This action bars all rights of the mortgagor to the property and cuts off his equity of redemption. All parties interested in the property must be made parties to the action, so that they will have notice of the proceedings and can present their claims to the court if they desire. The statutes generally require that the property be advertised for sale in the papers for a certain length of time before the sale takes place. In case the property does not sell for enough to satisfy the debt, a personal judgment on the note or bond is taken for the balance, this being called a deficiency judgment.

Record. — Mortgages are required to be recorded in the same manner as deeds, in order to give notice to subsequent pur-

Know all Men by these Presents, That

I, Charles A. Drake, of Geneva, Ontario County, New York,

party ————————————————————————————

of the first part, in consideration of the sum of one dollar ——————
——————————————— *lawful money of the United States, to* me *in hand paid*
by Fred C. White, of the same place, party —————————————
*of the second part, at or before the ensealing and delivery of these presents, the receipt whereof
is hereby acknowledged, have granted, bargained, sold, assigned, transferred and set over, and
by these presents do grant, bargain, sell, assign, transfer and set over, unto the said party of the
second part, a certain Indenture of Mortgage, bearing date the* fifteenth day
of September ———— *in the year one thousand nine hundred and* five,
————————————————— *made by* Edward Simmons to Charles A.
Drake to secure the payment of the sum of one thousand dollars
($1,000.00); and interest from the date thereof, ——————————

and duly recorded in the office of the —— Clerk —— *of the* ——————— *County
of* Monroe ———— *on the* sixteenth __ *day of* September, 1905,
in ———————————————— *Liber* 523, *page* 271,

Together *with the bond or obligation therein described, and the money due and to grow due
thereon, with the interest.* **To have and to hold** *the same unto the said party of the
second part* his heirs ———— *and assigns for* his or their

own use ——————————————————————————

subject only to the proviso in the said Indenture of Mortgage mentioned:

And I *do hereby make, constitute and appoint the said party of the second part*
my *true and lawful attorney, irrevocable in* his own *name or otherwise, but at* his *proper
costs and charges, to have, use and take, all lawful ways and means for the recovery of the said
money and interest: and in case of payment to discharge the same as fully as* I *might or
could do if these presents were not made.*

In Witness whereof —— I —— *have hereunto set hand and seal the*
fourth *day of* January *in the year one thousand nine hundred* and
six.

Sealed and delivered in the presence of *Charles A. Drake*

B. T. Cox

chasers of the property. If not so recorded, they are in most states valid as between the original parties, but not against persons who have purchased in ignorance of the existence of the mortgage. But in some states the statutes require the mortgage to be recorded in order to render it valid.

Discharge. — If the mortgage is paid according to its terms when it becomes due, it is discharged; or payment after it is due, but before an action is brought to foreclose, discharges the mortgage. In order to cancel the mortgage on the records, a formal discharge is executed and filed; otherwise the mortgage, although paid, would still appear by the records to stand against the property.

The mortgage which we have discussed would be discharged in the following form : —

STATE OF NEW YORK,
    County of Ontario } ss.

I, Fred C. White, of Geneva, Ontario County, New York, assignee of the mortgage hereinafter described,

Do hereby Certify, *That a certain Indenture of Mortgage, bearing date the* fifteenth ———— *day of* September , *one thousand* nine *hundred and* five , *made and executed by* Edward Simmons *to* Charles A. Drake, and thereafter and on, or about the fourth day of January, 1906, by an instrument in writing duly assigned to me ———————————————————————— *and recorded in the office of the* clerk of the ———— *County of* Monroe *in* ———————————— *Liber* 523 *of Mortgages, page* 271 , *on the* 16th *day of* September *in the year* 1905 ————————————— ———————————————— *is paid* ————————

And I do hereby consent that the same be discharged of Record.

    Dated the first *day of* February, *19*06.
In presence of

George LeBar   Fred C White

Second Mortgage. — The mortgagor may place a second or subsequent mortgage on the property. Unless it is otherwise stipulated, the mortgages take priority according to their date; that is, the second mortgagee gets nothing until the first is paid in full. But in case the first mortgage is not recorded and the second mortgagee has no notice of it, the second mortgage will, if recorded, have priority.

Any mortgagee may foreclose his mortgage when it is past due or the mortgagor is in default, but he can not affect the interest of a prior mortgagee by such proceeding, although he may cut off any subsequent mortgagee. By foreclosing his mortgage, therefore, the holder of a first mortgage will bar the second mortgage, and if the property sells for only enough to pay the first mortgage, the second mortgagee will lose. Of course if the property sells for more than enough to pay the first mortgage, the balance will be applied on the second mortgage. If the second mortgagee forecloses, he must sell **the** property subject to the lien of the first mortgage.

7. LANDLORD AND TENANT

Estates for Years. — We have discussed freehold estates and estates for life. But estates in real property may be created for a shorter definite period. These are called estates for years. The grantor is known as the lessor or landlord, and the grantee the lessee or tenant. The contract creating an estate for years is a lease.

Leases. — By the statute of frauds in most states the lease must be in writing, if for a longer time than one year. Generally, if for one year or less it may be made orally, and this is true even though the term is to commence at a date in the future. In a few states leases can be made for only a limited number of years, while in others a lease for more than a certain number of years must be recorded.

Toupin v. *Peabody*, 162 Mass. 473, was a case in which a lease for a term of 5 years contained a provision that the lessee was to have the privilege of renewing the lease upon the same terms for a further period of 5 years. Held, that it was a lease for more than 7 years under the meaning of the statute, which provided that all leases for over 7 years are invalid as against all but the parties to them and persons having actual notice of their existence. Therefore, so far as it purported to give the grantee the privilege of renewing, it was invalid as against a purchaser of the premises without actual notice of the lease, it never having been recorded.

On the following page is a common form of lease.

Covenants. — Aside from the above provisions, any further agreement between the parties may be incorporated in the writing. A lease is but a contract, and the full agreement of the parties should be set forth. Frequently the following covenant is inserted: "The party of the second part hereby covenants not to sublet said premises, or any portion thereof, without the written consent of said party of the first part;" or the following: "It is further mutually covenanted and agreed that, in case the buildings or tenements on said premises shall be destroyed or so injured by fire as to become untenantable, then this lease shall become thereby terminated, if said second party shall so elect; and in such case, he shall vacate said premises and give immediate written notice thereof to said landlord, in which case rent shall be due and payable up to and at the time of such destruction or injury."

Term. — The term of the lease is the time for which it is to run. In the following lease, it is two years. If the tenant has been in possession under a lease for one or more years, and he retains possession without executing a new lease, he is presumed, in the absence of some agreement, to be a tenant from year to year, which means that his term after the expiration of the lease is one year, and if he remains in possession after the next year he is a tenant for another year.

In *Haynes* v. *Aldrich*, 133 N.Y. 287, defendant leased certain premises for a year, the term expiring May 1. Before the expiration of the time, defendant informed plaintiff that she did not wish to renew her lease for another year. May 1 was a holiday, and possession was retained until May 4, the excuse given being the difficulty to get trucks to move defendant, also that on the 3d of May one of the boarders was ill. On the afternoon of the 4th of May the keys were tendered plaintiff and refused. Held, that the plaintiff was entitled to consider the lease renewed for another year. It was in the option of the landlord so to regard it or to accept the surrender of the premises.

A Lease,

Made and executed Between   William E. Weaver ——————————
of the   City —— of ———— Buffalo ————————, New York, of the first part,
and ——————————— Lyman Collins ——————————————

of the   City —— of —— Rochester ————————; New York, of the second part,
this   fifth ———— day of ——— November ——— in the year One thousand nine hundred
and   five.

In Consideration of the rents and covenants hereinafter expressed, the said party of the
first part *has* **Demised and Leased**, and does hereby demise and lease to the said *party*   of the
second part.———————————————————— the following premises, viz:

The house, barn and lot known as number 406 South Street in
said City of Rochester. ——————————————————

with the privileges and appurtenances, for and during the term of — two years ————
——————————— from the —— first —— day of —— December —————— 190 5
which term will end ——— November 30, 1907. ——————————
And the said *party*   of the second part *covenant*s that   *he*   will pay to the party of the first part,
for the use of said premises, the   monthly —— rent of —— Forty ——————————
Dollars ($ 40.00   ), to be paid   monthly in advance on the first day
of each and every month during said term. ——————————

And Provided, said *party* y   of the second part shall fail to pay said rent, or any part thereof,
when it becomes due——————————————————————————
———————————————————————— it is agreed that said party
of the first part may sue for the same, or re-enter said premises, or resort to any legal remedy.

The *party* y of the   first   part *agree*s to pay all ———————————taxes to be assessed
on said premises during said term ————————————————————

The *party* y   of the second part *covenant*s that at the expiration of said term   *he*   will surrender
up said premises to the party of the first part in as good condition as now, necessary wear and
damage by the elements excepted —————————————————————

Witness the hands and seals of the said parties the day and year first above written.

William E. Weaver.   [L. S.]
Lyman Collins   [L. S.]

Express and Implied Covenants. — The covenants contained in a lease are either expressed or implied. The implied covenants exist whether they are mentioned or not; the express covenants must be included in the express conditions of the lease, and may be many or few.

The implied covenants, on the part of the lessor, are those regarding quiet enjoyment and the payment of taxes. The usual words of grant in a lease are "demise and lease," or "grant and demise," these words being said to import a covenant of quiet enjoyment. This covenant is broken when the tenant is evicted by some one who has a paramount title.

Duncklee v. *Webber*, 151 Mass. 408, was an action for breach of an implied covenant of quiet enjoyment of a written lease for one year. Within the time the property was sold under a mortgage; and the plaintiff, upon receiving notice to quit, followed by threats of ejectment, moved away. Held, that plaintiff could recover.

The landlord also impliedly covenants that he will pay all taxes assessed against the premises during the term. There is no implied covenant on the part of the lessor, or landlord, that the premises are in a tenantable condition.

Reeves v. *McComeskey*, 168 Pa. St. 571, held, that no implied covenant that the landlord warrants the leased premises to be tenantable, or that he undertakes to keep them so, arises out of the relation of landlord and tenant; and in the absence of a provision in a lease that the lessor shall make repairs, it is no defense to an action for rent that the premises are not in a tenantable condition.

Lucas v. *Coulter*, 104 Ind. 81, was an action for rent of a store leased to defendant. The defense was, that the store was rented for the manufacturing and selling of musical instruments, and that it was so imperfectly and defectively constructed that rain and sand came through the roof and ceiling, causing damage to the instruments. Held, that in the letting of a store, room, or house, there is no implied warranty that it is, or shall continue to be, fit for the purpose for which it is let. The tenant must determine for himself the safety and fitness of the premises.

On the part of the lessee, or tenant, there is an implied covenant that he shall pay the rent stipulated for; and, although no sum is specified in the lease, the tenant must pay a reasonable rent, unless it appears that it was the intention of the parties that none was to be paid.

The lessee also impliedly covenants to repair, and if the leased premises consist of a farm, it is implied that he is to cultivate it in a husbandlike manner. The covenant to repair is not to rebuild when the property is burned down, but, as it is said, to keep it "wind and water tight," that is, to keep the roof from leaking and the siding tight. The premises must be kept in repair, except for ordinary wear and tear.

Turner v. *Townsend*, 42 Neb. 376, was a case in which the tenant sued the landlord for the value of a front window in the leased store. The window had been broken by a storm during the tenancy and replaced by the tenant, the landlord having refused to put in a new one. Held, that he could not recover. The landlord is not bound either to repair leased premises himself or to pay for the repairs made by his tenant unless he has expressly contracted to make the repairs.

Auworth v. *Johnson*, 5 C. & P. (Eng.) 239, held, that a tenant of a house from year to year is bound only to keep it wind and water tight.

Rights and Liabilities under a Lease. — Aside from the covenants in a lease there are certain rights and liabilities which arise from the relation of landlord and tenant. In the absence of an agreement to the contrary the tenant is entitled to the exclusive possession of the premises. He is liable for waste and is estopped from denying his landlord's title, that is, the tenant can not for any purpose claim that the premises do not belong to his landlord.

Gray v. *Johnson*, 14 N.H. 414, held, that if a tenant recognizes the title of his landlord by accepting a lease or by paying the rent, he will be estopped during the term of his tenancy from disputing it, although the want of title may appear from the landlord's own testimony.

Hamilton v. *Pittock*, 158 Pa. St. 457, held, that a lessee of an oil lease who takes a second lease of the same premises from a person claiming adversely to the original lessor, can not refuse to pay the rent under the second lease on the ground that the lessor in the first lease had the better title to the land.

As we have seen in the case of a life tenant on page 295, the tenant is entitled to emblements when his estate is cut off by some contingency without his fault.

In the case of *Gray* v. *Worst*, 129 Mo. 122, Shoemaker owned some land, of which he gave a deed in trust to Toms to secure a loan. Shoemaker afterwards leased the land to defendant for a year and defendant paid the rent in full. Before defendant had harvested his crops Toms foreclosed his claim and sold the property to plaintiff. Plaintiff at once claimed the crops as owner of the land, but defendant as lessee gathered them before leaving. In this action for the value of the crops it was held that the lessee was entitled to them and plaintiff could not recover.

The landlord is under no obligation to repair unless the lease expressly binds him to such duty. And he is entitled to the fixtures annexed to and made a part of the realty. The questions as to when the fixtures may be removed by the tenant, and when they may be claimed by the landlord, have been discussed in the chapter on Sales.

Assigning or Subletting of Lease. — Unless the tenant is restrained by an express covenant against subletting or assigning, he may assign or sublet his lease without the consent of the landlord. If the interest granted by the lessee is for a shorter time or for rights inferior to those granted in his own lease, it is a sublease.

In *Collins* v. *Hasbrouck*, 56 N.Y. 157, it was held that where a lessee executes an instrument conveying the whole of his unexpired term, but reserving rent at a rate and time of payment different from those in the original lease, and a right of reëntry on non-payment of rent and the breach of other conditions, and also providing for a surrender of the premises to him at the expiration of the time, the instrument is a sublease and not an assignment.

And in the case of a sublease the subtenant is not liable for rent to the original lessor, but only to the original lessee.

Trustees v. *Clough*, 8 N.H. 22, held, that he to whom the lessee sublets for but a part of the term is only a subtenant and not an assignee of the term. Such subtenant is not liable to the original lessor for the rent.

If the interest conveyed by the tenant is his whole interest in the lease, it is an assignment of the lease, and the assignee is liable to the original lessor for rent. In the case of an assignment of the lease the landlord may look to either the original lessee or to the assignee of the lease for the rent. The assignee takes all of the interest of the original tenant and is bound to pay rent, to repair and to use the property in any special way provided for in the lease. But these obligations of the assignee of the lease do not in any way release the original lessee from his obligations to his lessor.

In the case of *Sanders* v. *Partridge*, 108 Mass. 556, the lessees of real estate granted to them for ten years by a written lease, delivered the lease to defendant with the indorsement by which they assigned to him all their "right, title, and interest in and to the within lease." Neither the lessee nor the defendant personally occupied the premises, but after the assignment the rents were turned over to defendant. Held, that the landlord can maintain an action against the defendant for the rent.

Eviction. — At the expiration of the lease the landlord is entitled to the possession of the premises, and if the tenant does not surrender them, the landlord may institute proceedings to evict him. The statutes in the different states provide the procedure by which the tenant holding over after his lease has expired may be evicted on short notice. This is termed "summary proceedings." This form of procedure is also provided by statute for the eviction of the tenant when he does not pay his rent. The landlord who wishes to evict a tenant by summary proceedings obtains a process from some court which is served upon the tenant, and if it is found by the court when the case comes up for a hearing that the landlord is entitled to the possession of the premises, the court empowers one of its officers to evict the tenant from the premises.

Where the tenancy is not for any fixed period, but is a tenancy from year to year or month to month, it can not be terminated by either party except by notice. Under the common law a tenancy from year to year could be terminated by notice six months before the expiration of the period, and in the case of a tenancy for a shorter period, as from month to month, by a notice equal to the length of the period.

In *Steffens* v. *Earl*, 40 N.J. L. 128, it was held that in monthly tenancies a month's notice to quit is sufficient, but the notice must be to quit at the end of one of the monthly periods.

Until this notice has been given, the landlord can not evict the tenant, and until the tenant has given a like notice to the landlord, he is liable to be held for the rent unless the landlord accepts his surrender of the premises. The statutes in the different states have in many instances changed the common law rule and a shorter notice is rendered sufficient.

QUESTIONS ON REAL PROPERTY

1. Define real estate.

2. Is a dwelling house real estate?

3. Who owns the bed of a stream which is not navigable?

4. A has a farm upon which there is a pond one half mile in diameter. Has A the right to prohibit people from fishing and rowing upon this pond?

5. A's farm has a small river running through it. Has A the exclusive right to fish on the part running through his property?

6. In the above case, if the river had been a navigable stream, what exclusive rights would A have had?

7. In questions 4 and 5 to whom would ice, freezing on the water mentioned, belong? In question 6 to whom would the ice belong?

8. Define corporeal real property. Incorporeal real property. Easement. Give an illustration of each.

9. Define an estate in fee simple.

10. What is the right of eminent domain?

11. Wilson owns the absolute title in a farm. He dies leaving his widow the use of it during the remainder of her life. She leases it to Johnson for one year. What estate in the land did Wilson have? What estate did his widow receive after his death? What estate did Johnson have?

12. In the above case could Wilson's widow grant to any one an estate in the land that would exist beyond her own life? Could she grant an estate in the land that would last as long as she lived?

13. Had Wilson's widow the right to cut timber on the farm for the purpose of repairing the buildings? For use as fuel? To sell for lumber? To use in manufacturing wagons?

14. Explain what is meant when it is said that a life tenant must not commit waste.

15. In question 11 suppose there was a coal mine on Wilson's farm which he had been working during his life. Can his widow continue to work it under her life estate? Can she open it and work it if it had existed on the farm but had never been worked?

16. If Wilson's widow should sow a field of wheat on the farm and then die before it was harvested, would the wheat belong to her estate, or to the person to whom Wilson had left the farm after his widow's death?

17. Name and define the three estates by marriage.

18. What conditions are necessary in order that the husband shall have an interest as a tenant by curtesy in his wife's real property?

19. If, in question 11, Wilson had not left any will, what would the interest which the widow would have taken in his land be called? What interest in it would she have obtained under the common law?

20. A, a married man, buys a farm for $5000, and gives back a purchase money mortgage for $4000, paying the balance of $1000 in cash. A's widow

does not join in the mortgage. Upon A's death will his widow have dower in the whole farm, or will the mortgage which she did not sign come in ahead of it?

21. If, in the above case, the mortgage given by A had not been a purchase money mortgage, but had been given some years after A had purchased the farm and his wife had not joined in it, in what part of the land would the widow have taken dower?

22. What are homestead rights? Did they exist at common law?

23. Property is conveyed to A to hold in trust for B, a minor child, until he shall become of age, the use and benefit of the property to go to B. What estate in the land has A? What estate has B?

24. Distinguish between joint tenancies and tenancies in common.

25. What do we call an agreement to convey land?

26. What is a deed, and what are the two principal classes of deeds?

27. Name six requisites of a valid deed of conveyance.

28. What is the granting clause? Is it necessary to a valid deed?

29. What is the habendum clause in a deed, and with what words does it begin?

30. A gave a deed to B. In the granting clause it recited that an absolute conveyance was given to B. In the habendum it recited that B had a title in fee subject to a life estate in C. What estate did B get under the deed?

31. Is a date necessary to the validity of a deed? From what time does a deed take effect?

32. Fisher draws a deed of a house and lot, naming his grandson as grantee. He places the deed in his safe, and after two years dies. The deed is found and the grandson claims the property under it. Can he recover the property?

33. If, upon drawing the deed, Fisher had given it to his banker to hold until his death to deliver to the grandson at that time, could the grandson hold the land? What kind of delivery to the banker would this have been?

34. What is the acknowledgment?

35. Is the deed valid as between the parties when it is not recorded? Is it valid as to third parties who had no notice of it and who acquired rights to the land after it was given?

36. What is the covenant of seizin, and when is it broken?

37. What is the covenant of quiet enjoyment?

38. A sold a farm to B, and in the deed there was a covenant of quiet enjoyment. After B obtained possession, C, a third party, claimed title to the farm and brought an action against B to recover it. In this case C was defeated, as the court decided he had no claim whatever. Was A's covenant of quiet enjoyment broken? If C had recovered in his action, would the covenant of quiet enjoyment have been broken?

39. What is the covenant against incumbrances?

40. If, in question 38, A's deed had contained a covenant against incumbrances and there had existed a judgment on record against A, which was a

lien upon the property, would the covenant have been broken? If there had been unpaid taxes against the property, would the covenant have been broken?

41. What is the covenant of further assurance?

42. What is the covenant of warranty of title?

43. If A's deed to B, in question 38, had contained a warranty of title, and after B had possession D had gone upon the land and removed a building which he had erected temporarily and which he had the right under an agreement to remove, would the covenant have been broken?

44. Does a quitclaim deed contain any of the covenants of a warranty deed?

45. What covenant is sometimes used in a quitclaim deed?

46. What is a mortgage?

47. Under the common law, was it the mortgagor or the mortgagee that had the legal title to the mortgaged property?

48. In most of the American states which party has the legal title to the property?

49. What is the defeasance clause in a mortgage?

50. What three covenants are often included in a mortgage? Are they necessary to the validity of a mortgage?

51. Why is a note or bond generally given with the mortgage?

52. Can a mortgagee assign his interest in a mortgage? Can it be assigned orally?

53. What is the remedy of the mortgagee when the debt secured by the mortgage is not paid as agreed?

54. Is an unrecorded mortgage valid as between the original parties? Is it valid as to third parties who have acquired subsequent interests in the land?

55. Can the mortgagor place more than one mortgage upon the same piece of property? If so, which mortgage has the preference?

56. Must a lease of land for more than one year be in writing?

57. A rents a house and lot of B for one year at the annual rental of $200. At the end of the year nothing is said and he remains for another year, paying his rent. After remaining in the house for two months of the third year A vacates it. B claims the rent for the whole year. Can he recover?

58. What are the two implied covenants on the part of the lessor?

59. Is there an implied covenant on the part of the lessor that the premises are in a tenantable condition? Is there an implied covenant on the part of the lessee that he will pay rent? If the rent is not specified in the lease, how much will he be required to pay?

60. If there is no covenant to that effect in the lease, is there an implied covenant on the part of the landlord to repair during the term of the lease?

61. Is there an implied covenant on the part of the lessee or tenant to repair during the term of the lease?

62. Does the covenant to repair require the rebuilding of the premises if they are burned down?

63. Hamilton leases a house and lot of Turner. He does not pay his rent and Turner sues him. Hamilton claims that Turner is not the owner of the property, and it develops upon the trial that a third party has a paramount title. Can Hamilton defeat Turner's suit for rent in this way?

64. A leases his farm to B for one year. C, a mortgagee, forecloses a mortgage on the farm against A and sells it to D, who takes possession and ousts B before he has an opportunity of harvesting his crops. To whom do the crops belong, D or B?

65. If there is no restriction in the lease, can the tenant assign his rights?

66. Emery leases a building for one year and then leases all but one room to Boland for the whole length of his term. Which does this constitute, an assignment or a subletting?

67. In the above case the owner of the building sues Boland for the rent. Can he recover?

68. If, in question 66, Emery had rented the entire building for the full term of his lease to Boland without any restrictions, what would it have constituted, an assignment or a subletting?

69. In question 68 the landlord sues Boland for the rent. Can he recover?

70. If the tenant's lease of the property is for a definite time, how may the landlord evict him at the end of his term, provided he does not voluntarily surrender the property?

71. If the tenant is holding from year to year, how must the landlord proceed in order to terminate the tenancy?

COURTS AND THEIR JURISDICTION

Courts. — We have dealt with law as defining the rights and limitations of individuals in their dealings with one another; but these rights must often prove of little value in protecting the individual in his property and personal relations unless a means of enforcing them is provided. For this purpose the Constitution of the United States has established a system of Courts.

Jurisdiction. — The jurisdiction of a court is defined as the power to hear and determine a cause. The courts of a particular class are empowered to hear only a certain line of causes or disputes; while another line of cases, involving different amounts or arising between different parties or being of a different nature, will be determined by entirely different courts. It is essential in all cases that the particular court before which a question is brought for determination shall have jurisdiction, for if it has not, its decision is of no effect, and may be set aside at any time.

Jurisdiction of Subject-matter. — The jurisdiction of a court must be both of the subject-matter and of the person. Jurisdiction of the subject-matter means the power of the court regarding the subject or thing in dispute. Thus, in an action concerning the title to a particular piece of land in Monroe County, New York, if the case were brought in the county court of Erie County, New York, this court would have no jurisdiction of the question of the title to land outside of Erie County, therefore, there would be a lack of jurisdiction of the subject-matter. Again, the justice courts in New York have no power to determine questions affecting the title to real property, and, therefore, the above case could not be determined by a justice court, as such court has no jurisdiction of the subject-matter.

Jurisdiction of the Person. — Jurisdiction of the person, or of the party, against whom an action or cause is brought, is necessary, or the decision will have no effect as against such person or party. For example, a court of the state of Michigan can determine only matters of its own subjects. It can not therefore compel a resident of another state to obey its commands unless it obtains jurisdiction of the person while within the state of Michigan. Jurisdiction of the person is generally acquired by the service of a notice or command upon the party, which notice is generally called a summons and will be treated of later.

Classification of Courts. — The courts of the United States and of the different states may be arranged under several classifications, which we will consider in the following order: —

Courts of Original Jurisdiction.

Courts of Appellate Jurisdiction.

Courts of both Original and Appellate Jurisdiction.

Courts of Record.

Courts Not of Record.

Civil Courts $\begin{cases} \text{Law} \\ \text{Equity.} \end{cases}$

Criminal Courts.

Courts of General Jurisdiction.

Courts of Limited or Special Jurisdiction.

Courts of Original Jurisdiction. — Courts of Original Jurisdiction are those courts that have authority to hear and determine questions when they are first presented for judicial determination or decision. They are the courts that hear both sides of the dispute and render their decision therefrom.

Courts of Appellate Jurisdiction. — A Court of Appellate Jurisdiction has no power to hear a case when it first arises. It can only review the decision of a lower court when such decision is brought before it for determination. The taking of a case from a lower court to a higher one is called an appeal.

Original and Appellate Jurisdiction. — There are other courts that have in some cases original and in others appellate jurisdiction; that is, they have jurisdiction to hear appeals from some lower court or courts, and they can also try certain cases in the capacity of courts of original jurisdiction.

Courts of Record and Not of Record. — Courts are known as Courts of Record and Courts Not of Record. Courts of record are, as their name implies, those which are required by law to keep a record of their proceedings, this record being kept on file in some safe place for future reference. Courts Not of Record, on the other hand, have no record of their proceedings preserved.

Civil and Criminal Courts. — Courts are either Civil or Criminal. Civil courts hear cases in which the rights and liabilities of individuals towards each other are in dispute. A civil action is one which seeks the establishment, recovery, or redress of private rights, while a criminal action has for its purpose the protection of the community against those whose acts would endanger it. Criminal courts are those which administer criminal law and hear and determine criminal actions.

Common Law and Equity Courts. — Civil Courts may be either Common Law Courts or Equity Courts. The distinction between the common law court and the equity or chancery court was in former times well defined, a different set of judges presiding over, and an entirely different system prevailing in, each court. But the line of distinction is in most jurisdictions less pronounced now than formerly, and in New York State and many of the other states the same judge presides in both a common law and an equity court; at one term of court hearing common law cases and at another equity cases.

General and Special Jurisdiction. — Courts of General Jurisdiction are those in which it is assumed, unless the contrary is shown, that they have jurisdiction to hear the cases before them. In such a court the fact that it has jurisdiction does not have to be expressly pleaded or proved, while in the case of a court of inferior or special jurisdiction, the jurisdiction of the court over the case in question is not presumed, but must be especially set out in the pleadings.

Federal Courts. — The courts of the United States are called Federal courts and are empowered to hear cases arising under the United States Constitution, laws, and treaties. The Constitution provides that the judicial power of the United States shall be vested in one Supreme Court and in such inferior courts as Congress may from time to time establish. In pursuance of this authority, Congress has established, in addition to the Supreme Court, several inferior courts which are known as the Circuit Court and the District Court.

The Federal courts have jurisdiction only in those cases in which it is expressly conferred upon them by the Constitution, and by Congress under the power granted to it by the Constitution. This jurisdiction extends to all cases arising under the United States Constitution, the laws of the United States and treaties made under their authority, and all cases affecting ambassadors, public ministers, and consuls; to all cases of admiralty and marine law, which includes all things done upon and relating to the seas and all transactions in connection with commerce and navigation and to damages for injuries upon the high seas and the navigable lakes and rivers of the United States. They also have jurisdiction of controversies in which the United States is a party, and of cases between two or more states, between a state and citizens of another state, between citizens of different states, between citizens of the same state claiming land under the grant of a different state, and between a state or its citizens and foreign states, citizens, or subjects.

District Court. — The United States is divided into districts each comprising one state or less. Each of the following constitutes one district: Colorado, Connecticut, Delaware, Idaho Indiana, Kansas, Maine, Maryland, Massachusetts, Minnesota, Montana, Nebraska, Nevada, New Hampshire, New Jersey, North Dakota, Oregon, Rhode Island, South Carolina, South Dakota, Utah, Vermont, and Wyoming.

The following states contain two districts each: Arkansas, California, Florida, Georgia, Iowa, Kentucky, Louisiana, Michigan, Mississippi, Missouri, North Carolina, Oklahoma, Virginia, Washington, West Virginia, and Wisconsin; and the following, three districts: Alabama, Illinois, Pennsylvania, and Tennessee; while New York, Ohio, and Texas are each divided into four.

A judge is appointed to preside in each district. The district judge receives a salary of $6000 per year.

The district court has jurisdiction of all crimes and offenses cognizable under the authority of the United States and committed within the particular district or upon the high seas, except where the punishment is death; all causes of action arising under the postal and bankruptcy laws; all cases of admiralty and marine questions, and many other cases.

For the relief of the court, and the convenience of the parties in each district, a number of referees in bankruptcy are appointed. These referees hear the cases and report to the district judge, who grants or refuses the final discharge.

Circuit Court. — The United States is divided into nine circuits as follows: —

First Circuit: Maine, Massachusetts, New Hampshire, and Rhode Island.

Second: Connecticut, New York, and Vermont.

Third: Delaware, New Jersey, and Pennsylvania.

Fourth: Maryland, North Carolina, South Carolina, Virginia, and West Virginia.

Fifth: Alabama, Florida, Georgia, Louisiana, Mississippi, and Texas.

Sixth: Kentucky, Michigan, Ohio, and Tennessee.

Seventh: Illinois, Indiana, and Wisconsin.

Eighth: Arkansas, Colorado, Iowa, Kansas, Minnesota, Missouri, Nebraska, New Mexico, North Dakota, Oklahoma, South Dakota, Utah, and Wyoming.

Ninth: Alaska, Arizona, California, Idaho, Montana, Nevada, Oregon, and Washington.

The chief justice and the associate justices of the Supreme Court are allotted to the circuits, in which they may sit as circuit justices. Two or more circuit judges are also appointed for each circuit, and they have the same power in the court as the Supreme Court justice allotted to the circuit. The circuit court judge receives a salary of $7000 per year. In the first and fourth circuits there are two circuit judges, in the second and eighth four, and in each of the other circuits three.

A circuit court may be held by the Supreme Court justice of the circuit, by a circuit judge of the circuit, or by one of the district judges of the district.

The circuit court has original jurisdiction of cases in equity or common law where the amount in dispute exceeds $2000 and the question arises under the United States Constitution, laws, or treaties; also in controversies in which the United States is a party, and in disputes between citizens of different states. It also has jurisdiction when the amount involved exceeds the sum of $2000 and the controversy arises between citizens of the same state over a claim for land granted by a different state. Its jurisdiction includes all crimes arising under the authority of the United States, having concurrent jurisdiction with the district court of the crimes within its jurisdiction, and it has jurisdiction of patent and copyright cases and of questions concerning Indian lands.

Circuit Court of Appeals. — The circuit court as well as the district court has only original jurisdiction, all appeals from either court being taken to the circuit court of appeals, which consists of three judges, the presence of at least two being necessary to constitute a quorum. The Supreme Court judge assigned to the circuit and the district judges within the circuit are competent to sit as judges of the circuit court of appeals. This court has appellate jurisdiction only and hears appeals from both the circuit and the district courts. It hears all appeals from these courts except in a few special cases, which will be mentioned later, where appeals are taken directly to the Supreme Court of the United States.

Supreme Court. — The Supreme Court consists of the chief justice and eight associate justices. The chief justice receives a salary of $13,000 and the associate justices $12,500 per year.

This court has both original and appellate jurisdiction, its original jurisdiction extending over all proceedings brought against ambassadors, public ministers, consuls, and their families, and over all controversies of a civil nature in which a state is a party.

It has appellate jurisdiction to hear appeals from the district or circuit courts in all cases where the jurisdiction of the court is in question, cases of conviction of a capital crime, cases that involve the construction or application of the United States Constitution, and cases in which the constitutionality or validity of any law of the United States or any treaty made under it is drawn into question, also a few other important questions. Of the less important cases the determination of the circuit court of appeals is final, but in the more important matters and those in which a large amount is involved an appeal may be taken from that court to the Supreme Court.

State Courts. — While the federal or United States courts above enumerated deal only with certain specific cases over which they are given jurisdiction by the Constitution, the great mass of questions not specifically placed within the jurisdiction of these federal courts is within the jurisdiction of the state courts.

Justice Court. — The systems of courts in the different states differ somewhat, but in the more important features are essentially the same, the lowest court being the Justice Court, presided over by the justice of the peace. In New York State this is a town office, the justice being elected by the people every four years. It is a court not of record, and has original jurisdiction only. It hears both civil and criminal cases and is of limited or special jurisdiction.

In the larger cities there are two modifications of this court, one branch hearing civil cases and being known as the Municipal or City Court, and the other branch dealing with the criminal cases and known as the Police or Magistrate's Court.

The jurisdiction of the justice court is over the minor or more trivial cases, and includes the punishment of petty offenses which it is not thought necessary to bring before the higher courts. In civil cases it has jurisdiction when the amount involved does not exceed $200. It has no jurisdiction when the title to real property is involved. In its criminal branch it has exclusive jurisdiction of certain prescribed misdemeanors, such as petit larceny, assault in the third degree, malicious mischief, etc.

By way of definition of the term "misdemeanor" it may be said that crimes are classified as felonies and misdemeanors. A felony is a crime punishable by either death or imprisonment in a state's prison. All other crimes are misdemeanors.

County Court. — In New York and many other states, the court next in importance is the County Court. The jurisdiction of this court is limited to the county, and the judge is known as the county judge. It is a court of record, having jurisdiction of both civil and criminal cases, and having both original and appellate jurisdiction. Its jurisdiction is special or limited, being confined exclusively to those cases in which jurisdiction is expressly conferred upon it.

In civil matters it has jurisdiction to foreclose a lien or mortgage on real property when the mortgage does not exceed $1000 and the realty is within the county. It has jurisdiction in an action in which a judgment for a sum of money only is demanded, the amount not to exceed $2000, and the defendant or defendants reside within the county. It also has jurisdiction of the care and custody of the property of incompetent persons, such as lunatics, habitual drunkards, etc. In criminal cases it has jurisdiction over all crimes committed within the county and not punishable with death, except the minor criminal cases over which the justice court has exclusive jurisdiction.

The county court has appellate jurisdiction to hear appeals from the justice court in certain cases.

Surrogate's Court. — This court, or as it is known in some states, the Probate Court, has to deal with the settlement of the estates of deceased persons, the probating of wills, and the protection of minor children, and with all matters pertaining to the disposition of the property of deceased persons.

Circuit Court or Supreme Court. — In some states this court is called the District Court, and in others the Court of Common Pleas. In New York State it is called the Supreme Court, which name may be somewhat misleading, for instead of being the highest court, as its name would seem to indicate, it is a court of original jurisdiction. It is a court of record and has general jurisdiction. In this state it is properly divided into these branches: Trial Term, Equity Term, Special Term, and Appellate Division.   For the purposes of this court the state is divided into eight districts, in each of which there are a number of judges elected by the people.   For the purposes of the appellate division of the supreme court the state is divided into four departments.

Trial Term is a term of this court which convenes for the purpose of trying both civil and criminal cases.   It may convene with or without a jury.

Equity Term convenes for the purpose of trying equity cases.

Special Term.   In special term one judge sits without a jury for the purpose of hearing arguments and granting motions having principally to do with the practice of the court.

Appellate Division.   This court is composed of five judges in each department, except in the department which includes New York City, where there are seven.   It has appellate jurisdiction to hear appeals of both civil and criminal cases from the county, surrogate's, and supreme courts.

Court of Appeals. — The court of last resort in the state of New York is known by the above title, but in the majority of the states this court is known as the Supreme Court.   It has exclusively appellate jurisdiction.   In New York State it is composed of one chief judge and six associate judges.   This court never hears the evidence in a case, but merely hears appeals from the appellate division of the supreme court.   Not all cases can be taken before this court, the decision of the appellate division of the supreme court being final in many of them.

It reviews questions of fact in a case only when the judgment is death.   In all other cases it reviews questions of law.

Court of Claims. — From the fact that a state is supreme and can not be sued by its citizens, there arises a demand for some tribunal to hear and determine claims against the state, or on the part of the state against the citizen.   To meet this necessity a State Board of Claims has been established, consisting of three commissioners appointed by the governor.   This court convenes at various stated times, and hears and determines any of these claims which may be brought before it.

Reference. — A Referee is a person appointed by the court to hear the evidence in a case and to report thereon to the court. It is customary for the court to grant a reference when the case requires the examination of a long account. In some other cases a reference may be had either upon motion of the parties or in the discretion of the judge.

A case involving a long account is tried before a referee because of the difficulty the jurors would have in carrying in their minds the numerous items involved therein and the great delay to which the court would be subjected on account of the expenditure of time required to hear cases of this character. A referee hears the case in the same manner as a judge, and has the same power to preserve order and grant adjournments.

QUESTIONS ON COURTS

1. For what purpose are courts established?
2. What is the jurisdiction of a court?
3. What is the effect of a decision of a court not having jurisdiction of the question?
4. Name and define the two different classes of jurisdiction.
5. Name the different classifications of the courts of the United States and of the several states.
6. What is a court of original jurisdiction? Of appellate jurisdiction?
7. Define courts of record; courts not of record.
8. Define civil and criminal courts; common law and equity.
9. Distinguish between the courts of general jurisdiction and those of special jurisdiction.
10. How are the courts of the United States established, and over what questions have they jurisdiction?
11. Name the different United States courts, and describe each.
12. What is the lowest state court? Describe it, and state its jurisdiction.
13. Describe the county court and its jurisdiction.
14. Describe the surrogate's court and its jurisdiction.
15. Describe the circuit or supreme court and its jurisdiction.
16. Name and describe the four branches of the supreme or circuit court in the state of New York.
17. Mention and describe the highest state court and its jurisdiction.
18. What is the court of claims, and over what questions does it have jurisdiction?
19. How is a referee appointed and in what cases?

PLEADING AND PRACTICE

WE have learned that a system of courts is established in each state as well as in the United States. To enable the courts to conduct their business in an orderly manner, certain rules of practice are prescribed which must be observed by those desiring relief in these courts.

Action. — When a person desires the relief afforded by the courts, he institutes an action or suit. An action is defined as the legal and formal demand of one's rights made upon another person or party and insisted upon in a court of justice.

Parties. — In an action at law it is necessary that there be two or more parties. The party who brings the action is known as the plaintiff, and the one against whom it is brought, as the defendant. In a criminal action the plaintiff is the state or the people of the state, and the defendant is the one accused of the crime. The same person can not be both plaintiff and defendant. A party in all civil cases must be competent to contract; but when incompetent, as in the case of an infant or lunatic, he may bring suit through a person appointed for that purpose and known as a guardian.

Summons. — An action is commenced by the service of a notice upon the defendant, this notice being called a summons. The summons is in some jurisdictions issued by the judge or clerk of the court, while in other jurisdictions it may be issued by the attorney for the plaintiff.

In New York State if George Elliott of Buffalo, New York, should bring an action in the Supreme Court against Charles Phillips of the same place the summons would read as follows : —

SUPREME COURT, COUNTY OF ERIE

GEORGE ELLIOTT, Plaintiff,

v.

CHARLES PHILLIPS, Defendant.

TO THE ABOVE-NAMED DEFENDANT:

You are hereby summoned to answer the complaint in this action, and to serve a copy of your answer on the plaintiff's attorney within twenty days after the service of this summons, exclusive of the day of service; and, in case of your failure to appear or answer, judgment will be taken against you by default for the relief demanded in the complaint.

Trial desired in the county of Erie.

Dated this 10th day of February, 1904.

HERMAN J. WESTWOOD,

Attorney for plaintiff.

794 Ellicott Square,

Buffalo, New York.

This summons must be served personally upon the defendant, either by a sheriff or a constable, or by a person of suitable age. The laws expressly provide in a few cases that the summons may be served upon the defendant by advertising it in a newspaper, but this is only in case the defendant is not within the state, or if within the state he can not be located.

Pleadings. — After an action or suit has been commenced by the service of a summons, the parties must serve their pleadings within a certain prescribed time. These pleadings are the formal allegations of the parties by which both plaintiff and defendant present to the court and to each other their respective versions of the question in dispute.

Complaint. — The complaint, which is the first pleading in a case, and is in some states called the petition or declaration, consists of a statement of the cause of action which the plaintiff sets forth as his reason for seeking the aid of the court against the defendant. Under the old common law the forms of pleadings were very technical, but under the modern form of procedure they are required only to set forth the facts in a clear and concise manner. The complaint is commonly served with the summons, but may be served later. After the complaint has been served upon the defendant or filed with the court, as the rules of the particular court may require, it is then necessary for the defendant within a certain number of ·days (usually twenty) to file or serve a statement of the reasons why he should not comply with the demands of the plaintiff. If such a statement is not filed, the plaintiff is given judgment against the defendant by default. The pleading which is filed by the defendant may be either an answer or a demurrer.

Answer. — The answer, or plea as it is sometimes called, is a statement in concise form of the defendant's defense to the matters set up in the complaint. The answer may deny the claim of the plaintiff, or it may admit it and set up other facts by way of counterclaim or set-off.

To illustrate, the plaintiff may sue for $100, which he alleges in his complaint the defendant owes him for the purchase price of a horse sold by plaintiff to defendant. The defendant in his answer may allege that he did not purchase the horse, but merely took it to keep for its use, and this would be a denial. Again, he may admit purchasing the horse for $100, but allege that he worked for defendant three months at $50 per month, and that his wages had not been paid, and ask that this be an offset against the price of the horse, and that he, the defendant, be given a judgment for the balance of $50. This defense constitutes a counterclaim or set-off.

Reply. — When a counterclaim is alleged, new facts are brought up and it is necessary for the plaintiff, if he wishes to deny them, to make a reply, or replication, which is really the plaintiff's reply or answer to the new facts set forth by the defendant.

Demurrer. — The defendant may consider that the facts set up in the plaintiff's complaint, even if true, do not constitute a sufficient case in law against him, and for this reason it does not require that a defense be interposed, therefore he demurs to the plaintiff's complaint. By demurring he in effect says, admitting that all the plaintiff sets forth in his complaint is true, still he is not entitled to recover. The question on the demurrer must be argued before the judge, and if the demurrer is sustained, the plaintiff must correct or amend his complaint or he fails in his action. If the demurrer is overruled, the defendant must answer or the case will go against him. A demurrer may also be interposed to an answer or a reply in the same manner as to the complaint.

Trial. — After the pleadings are served the case comes to trial. A trial is held before the court, consisting of the judge alone in some cases and in others of a judge and a jury. A jury is a body of men, usually twelve, who are brought together to hear a case and sworn to decide the same according to the evidence brought before them.

Questions of Law or of Fact. — Questions which give rise to a trial may be questions of law or questions of fact. In the former the facts of the case are admitted, and the question to be decided is the application of the law to these facts. This is a question for the court and is tried without a jury. A question of fact arises when the testimony of the witnesses differs and the true state of facts remains to be determined. Questions of fact are generally tried before a jury. Every criminal case may be tried before a jury if the defendant demands a jury trial. In most cases an equity cause is tried before the judge without a jury. All cases involving simply a question of law are tried before a judge without a jury. It may be said that the law is to be decided by the judge, and the facts by the jury. The jurors are sworn to determine the case according to the evidence, and the question arises as to what constitutes the evidence.

Evidence. — We find that the evidence consists of the testimony of persons who know something about the facts and are sworn to tell the truth. These persons are known as witnesses. Written documents and papers pertaining to the case are also admitted as evidence.

Subpœna. — In order to procure the attendance of the witnesses at the trial of a case the court issues an order, called a subpœna, commanding them to appear at a certain time to give evidence in the case, and in default of their appearance they are subject to a fine for contempt of court. Refusal to testify when called as a witness is also contempt of court.

Deposition. — When a necessary witness is outside of the state, or, in the justice court, outside of the county or an adjoining county, it is not within the power of the court to compel his attendance, therefore statutes have been passed allowing his testimony to be taken in a certain prescribed way before a notary public or other officer, who reduces the testimony to writing and returns it to the court. The opposing party must have notice of the time and place of the taking of the deposition and also an opportunity to question the witness.

Lawyers. — The case for both the plaintiff and the defendant is conducted by officers of the court known as lawyers. The lawyer prepares the pleadings for his side of the case, presents the case to the court, and questions the witnesses.

Verdict. — After the jury has heard the witnesses for plaintiff and defendant, it weighs the evidence on both sides of the question and arrives at a decision as to the party in the right. This decision is called the verdict. In order to render a verdict the jurors must all agree. If, after a reasonable time, they have failed to agree, they are dismissed, and a new trial is held before another jury.

Judgment. — The verdict of a jury is but a determination of the facts of a case. It is for the judge to give the judgment, which is the official decision of the court upon the respective rights and claims of the parties to the action. Thus in a suit for damages against a railway company for running over plaintiff's horse, the jury might find that the plaintiff ought to recover $100 from the defendant, and bring in its verdict to that effect. Upon this verdict the judge decrees that the defendant shall pay this amount to the plaintiff and so gives the judgment of the court to the plaintiff for $100 dollars and costs. The costs are an allowance given to the successful party to compensate him for his expenses in conducting the case. In a criminal matter the jury finds the defendant guilty, and the judge pronounces the penalty or punishment.

Execution. — After the judgment of the court has been rendered, the party against whom the damages are adjudged may not voluntarily pay them. In such an event, the law provides a method of procedure called an execution, which is a command issued by the court to one of its officers, either a sheriff, constable, or marshal, authorizing and requiring him to collect the amount named as damages, and if not paid to take certain property of the person against whom the judgment is given, sell it, and apply the proceeds upon the judgment.

Levy and Sale. — The taking of the property under the authority of the execution is called a levy. The property after being levied upon is advertised by the officer and sold at public sale to the highest bidder.

Exemption. — The sheriff or officer can levy upon any property owned by the judgment debtor except certain articles which he is allowed by law to claim as exempt from execution and sale. The exemptions differ in the different states and are generally more liberal to a married man or one who supports a family than to a single man. The exemptions ordinarily consist of clothing, household articles of a certain value, etc., and are set forth in detail in the Appendix at page 359.

New Trial. — After the judgment has been given, the unsuccessful party may within a certain time move for a new trial, either for the reason that he has discovered some new evidence, or because of some error of the judge in the first trial. If the judge can be convinced that, during the trial, he has made a material error or that the defeated party really has discovered new evidence that is material to his case, the judge may, at his discretion, order a new trial. If a new trial is denied, the defeated party has no recourse but to pay the judgment or take an appeal.

Appeal. — The party dissatisfied with the judgment of the trial court may take an appeal to a higher court by fulfilling certain prescribed conditions, which in most cases consist in giving an undertaking to pay the costs if the decision of the trial court is affirmed.

The appeal is generally on questions of law alone, the decision of the trial court on questions of fact being final. The appellate court hears the arguments of the lawyers on each side, and it may then affirm the decision of the trial court, or it may reverse it and send the case back for a new trial.

When the case has been taken to the highest appellate court to which a case of its kind can be carried, and this last court affirms the judgment of the trial court, the case is finally determined.

Supplementary Proceedings. — In case the sheriff or other officer intrusted with the execution is unable to collect the money or find property sufficient to satisfy it, he may return the execution with his certificate that it is unsatisfied. The party who obtained the judgment, and who is called the judgment creditor, may then apply to the judge for an order to examine the judgment debtor in reference to his property. This order of the judge requires the judgment debtor to appear before a referee appointed by the court and answer questions which may be asked him in reference to his property. The referee also has power to subpœna other witnesses and to adjourn the proceedings from time to time. When the examination is completed the referee reports the evidence to the judge who appointed him, and if it is found that the judgment debtor has any property which is not exempt, he is ordered to turn it over to the proper officer.

Replevin. — This is an action brought to recover the possession of certain articles of personal property which have been wrongfully taken, or, if rightfully taken, are being wrongfully withheld. By giving a bond, the plaintiff can have the property taken from the defendant and held in the custody of an officer until the action is determined. In this action their right to the possession of the goods is the question in dispute.

Attachment. — In certain cases the court will issue a writ of attachment, which is an order to the sheriff or other officers to seize certain property of the defendant and hold it as security for any judgment which may be obtained. This writ is used principally against absconding, concealed, or fraudulent debtors. It is used also when the defendant does not reside within the state, but the goods attached are within it. In such a case the court gets jurisdiction of the property, which it may dispose of to satisfy a judgment thereafter obtained in the action.

Garnishment. — In some states there is a provision in the law by which a person owing money to the defendant may be brought into the suit and ordered not to pay the money over to the defendant, and he may also be ordered to pay it into court. This procedure is frequently employed when the third party owes wages to the defendant, as by garnishment proceedings he will be compelled to pay over a part of the wages to the court, or retain it to apply on any judgment the plaintiff may obtain.

QUESTIONS ON PLEADING AND PRACTICE

1. Define an action.
2. How many parties must there be to an action ?
3. Name the parties in an action.
4. What is a summons and how must it be served ?
5. What are the pleadings in an action ?
6. What is the first pleading served by the plaintiff ?
7. What is the first pleading served by the defendant ?
8. What is a reply ?
9. What is a demurrer ?
10. If the demurrer is sustained, what effect does it have on the action ?
11. If the defendant's demurrer to the plaintiff's complaint is overruled, what step must the defendant then take ?
12. Before whom is a trial held ?
13. Before whom is a question of law tried ?
14. Before whom is a question of fact tried ?
15. Before whom is a criminal case tried ?   An equity case ?
16. Define witnesses.
17. What is a subpœna, and what is its purpose ?
18. What is a deposition, and when is it allowed ?
19. What is a lawyer ?
20. What is the verdict in a case ?   The judgment ?
21. Define execution, levy, and sale.
22. What are exemptions ?
23. When and how may a new trial be had ?
24. What is an appeal, and upon what questions is it taken ?
25. Describe Supplementary Proceedings.
26. What is a Replevin Action ?
27. Define Attachment.
28. Define Garnishment.

APPENDIX

LIMITATION OF ACTIONS

THE following table will show in a general way the number of years that must elapse before a claim will be barred by the statute of limitations in the different states and territories. Many of the states recognize classifications and subdivisions which it is not practicable to include here, but a general idea of the time limit can be obtained from these columns.

STATE	OPEN ACCOUNT	WRITTEN INSTRUMENT	SEALED INSTRUMENT	JUDGMENT
Alabama	3	6	10	20
Alaska	6	6	10	10
Arizona	4	4	4	4
Arkansas	3	5	5	10
California	4	4	4	5
Colorado	6	6	6	20
Connecticut	6	6	17	No limit
Delaware	3	6	20	20
District of Columbia . .	3	3	12	12
Florida	3	5	20	20
Georgia	4	6	20	7
Hawaiian Islands . . .	6	6	6	20
Idaho	4	5	5	6
Illinois	5	10	10	20
Indiana	6	(10)(20)	10	20
Iowa	5	10	10	20
Kansas	3	5	5	5
Kentucky	5	15	15	15

State	Open Account	Written Instrument	Sealed Instrument	Judgment
Louisiana	3	5	10	10
Maine	6	6	20	20
Maryland	3	3	12	12
Massachusetts . . .	6	6	20	20
Michigan	6	6	10	10
Minnesota	6	6	6	10
Mississippi	3	6	6	7
Missouri	5	10	10	10
Montana	5	8	8	10
Nebraska	4	5	5	5
Nevada	4	6	6	6
New Hampshire . . .	6	6	20	20
New Jersey	6	6	16	20
New Mexico	4	6	6	7
New York	6	6	20	20
North Carolina . . .	3	3	10	10
North Dakota	6	6	10	10
Ohio	6	15	15	21
Oklahoma	3	5	5	5
Oregon	6	6	10	10
Pennsylvania	6	6	20	20
Rhode Island	6	6	20	20
South Carolina . . .	6	6	(20)(6)	20
South Dakota	6	6	20	(20)(10)
Tennessee	6	6	6	10
Texas	(2)(4)	4	4	10
Utah	4	6	6	8
Vermont	6	6	8	(6)(8)
Virginia	(3)(5)	5	10	(10)(20)
Washington	3	6	6	6
West Virginia . . .	5	10	10	10
Wisconsin	6	6	20	20
Wyoming	8	10	10	10

INTEREST TABLE

The following is a summary of the legal rates of interest prescribed by statute in the different states and territories, with the maximum rates allowed by special contract between the parties, and the penalties imposed for the taking of usury.

STATE	LEGAL RATE	MAXIMUM RATE	PENALTY FOR USURY
Alabama	8	8	All interest forfeited.
Alaska	8	12	Forfeiture of interest and costs.
Arizona	6	12	All interest over 12 per cent forfeited and also sum equal to such excess.
Arkansas	8	10	Principal and interest forfeited.
California	7	No limit	No penalty.
Colorado	8	No limit	No penalty.
Connecticut . . .	6	6	Interest over 6 per cent forfeited, but if paid it cannot be recovered.
Delaware	6	6	Forfeiture of a sum equal to the money lent.
District of Columbia	6	(6) (10)	All interest forfeited.
Florida . . .	8	10	All interest forfeited. If usurious interest is paid, double the amount may be recovered.
Georgia	7	8	Interest over 8 per cent forfeited.
Hawaiian Islands .	(6)(8)	12	Interest over 12 per cent forfeited.
Idaho	7	12	Forfeiture of 10 per cent of principal.
Illinois	5	7	All interest forfeited.
Indiana	6	8	Interest over 6 per cent forfeited.
Iowa	6	8	All interest and 8 per cent of principal forfeited.
Kansas	6	10	Interest over 10 per cent and also amount equal to such excess forfeited.
Kentucky	6	6	Interest over 6 per cent forfeited.
Louisiana	5	8	All interest forfeited.
Maine	6	No limit	No penalty.
Maryland	6	6	Forfeiture of all except real value of principal and also 6 per cent of such value.

State	Legal Rate	Maximum Rate	Penalty for Usury
Massachusetts . .	6	No limit	No penalty.
Michigan	5	7	All interest forfeited.
Minnesota . . .	6	10	Principal and interest forfeited.
Mississippi . . .	6	10	All interest forfeited.
Missouri	6	8	Interest over 8 per cent forfeited.
Montana	8	No limit	No penalty.
Nebraska	7	10	All interest forfeited.
Nevada	7	No limit	No penalty.
New Hampshire .	6	6	Forfeiture of three times the amount of the excess charged.
New Jersey . . .	6	6	All interest and costs forfeited.
New Mexico . . .	6	12	Forfeiture of double the interest and also a fine.
New York . . .	6	6	Principal and interest forfeited.
North Carolina . .	6	6	All interest forfeited.
North Dakota . .	7	12	All interest forfeited.
Ohio	6	8	Interest over 8 per cent forfeited.
Oklahoma . . .	6	10	All interest forfeited.
Oregon	6	10	Principal and interest forfeited.
Pennsylvania . .	6	6	Interest over 6 per cent forfeited.
Rhode Island . .	6	30	Contract is void.
South Carolina . .	7	8	All interest forfeited.
South Dakota . .	7	12	All interest forfeited.
Tennessee . . .	6	6	Interest over 6 per cent forfeited and a fine.
Texas	6	10	All interest forfeited.
Utah	8	12	Interest over 12 per cent forfeited and a fine.
Vermont	6	6	Interest over 6 per cent forfeited.
Virginia	6	6	All interest forfeited.
Washington . . .	6	12	All interest and equal amount from principal forfeited.
West Virginia . .	6	6	Interest over 6 per cent forfeited.
Wisconsin . . .	6	10	All interest forfeited.
Wyoming	8	12	All interest and costs forfeited.

DAYS OF GRACE

The following table shows the states and territories in which days of grace are still allowed on negotiable instruments. If allowed on paper payable at sight, the fact is designated in the first column; if on demand paper, in the second; and if on paper payable a certain time after date, in the third column.

STATE	SIGHT	DEMAND	TIME
Alabama	No	No	No
Alaska	No	No	Yes
Arizona	No	No	No
Arkansas	Yes	Yes	Yes
California	No	No	No
Colorado	No	No	No
Connecticut	No	No	No
Delaware	No	No	No
District of Columbia	No	No	No
Florida	No	No	No
Georgia	No	No	No
Hawaiian Islands	No	No	No
Idaho	No	No	No
Illinois	No	No	No
Indiana	No	No	No
Iowa	No	No	No
Kansas	No	No	No
Kentucky	No	No	No
Louisiana	No	No	No
Maine	Yes	No	No
Maryland	No	No	No
Massachusetts	Yes	No	No
Michigan	Yes	No	Yes
Minnesota	Yes	No	No
Mississippi	Yes	Yes	Yes
Missouri	No	No	No
Montana	No	No	No

State	Sight	Demand	Time
Nebraska	No	No	No
Nevada	No	No	No
New Hampshire	No	No	No
New Jersey	No	No	No
New Mexico	No	No	No
New York	No	No	No
North Carolina	No	No	No
North Dakota	No	No	No
Ohio	No	No	No
Oklahoma	No	No	No
Oregon	No	No	No
Pennsylvania	No	No	No
Rhode Island	Yes	No	No
South Carolina	Yes	No	No
South Dakota	Yes	Yes	Yes
Tennessee	No	No	No
Texas	Yes	Yes	Yes
Utah	No	No	No
Vermont	No	No	No
Virginia	No	No	No
Washington	No	No	No
West Virginia	No	No	No
Wisconsin	No	No	No
Wyoming	No	No	No

STATUTE OF FRAUDS — MARRIED WOMEN

The following tables show the amounts to which the Sale of Goods Act in the Statute of Frauds applies in the different states; also the condition of the statutes in the different states and territories that give married women the right to contract in their own name.

STATE	Statute of Frauds. Sale of goods, wares, and merchandise, to the value of $....., must be in writing, etc.	May a married woman become a trader, and carry on business in her own name, and sue and be sued as if single ?
Alabama.	Not in force.	Yes, but cannot sell or mortgage her real estate without the consent and joinder of her husband and cannot be surety for her husband, directly or indirectly.
Alaska.	$50.	Yes, if abandoned by her husband.
Arizona.	Not in force.	Yes.
Arkansas.	$30.	Yes.
California.	$200.	Yes, if she obtains a permit from the court.
Colorado.	$50.	Yes.
Connecticut.	$50.	Yes.
Delaware.	Not in force.	Yes.
District of Columbia.	$50.	Yes.
Florida.	Any amount.	Yes, if she obtains a permit from the court.
Georgia.	$50.	Yes, but she cannot bind herself by contract of suretyship, nor assume her husband's debts, nor sell property to him except by court order.
Hawaii.	$100.	Yes, on filing a certificate with the Treasurer of the Territory.
Idaho.	$200.	Yes.
Illinois.	Not in force.	Yes, except that she cannot form a partnership without her husband's consent.

STATE.	Statute of Frauds. Sale of goods, wares, and merchandise, to the value of $....., must be in writing, etc.	May a married woman become a trader and carry on business in her own name, and sue and be sued as if single ?
Indiana.	$50.	Yes, but she cannot sell or mortgage real estate without the joinder of her husband, nor can she be surety for any one.
Iowa.	Any value.	Yes.
Kansas.	Not in force.	Yes.
Kentucky.	Not in force.	Yes.
Louisiana.	Not in force.	Yes, if she carries on a separate trade.
Maine.	$30.	Yes.
Maryland.	Not in force.	Yes.
Massachusetts.	$500.	Yes, but she must file a married woman's certificate.
Michigan.	$50.	Yes, but she cannot be surety for nor partner of her husband.
Minnesota.	$50.	Yes, but she cannot convey the homestead without joinder of her husband, nor contract with him as to the real estate of either party.
Mississippi.	$50.	Yes.
Missouri.	$30.	Yes.
Montana.	$200.	Yes, on giving public notice, filing a petition and oath, and receiving the judgment of the court.
Nebraska.	$50.	Yes.
Nevada.	$50.	Yes, when declared a sole trader by order of court.
New Hampshire.	$33.	Yes, but she cannot become surety for her husband.
New Jersey.	$30.	Yes, but she cannot be surety for any one, nor encumber her real estate without joinder of her husband.
New Mexico.	Not in force.	Yes, but she cannot convey or mortgage real estate without joinder of her husband.

STATE	Statute of Frauds. Sale of goods, wares, and merchandise, to the value of $....., must be in writing, etc.	May a married woman become a trader and carry on business in her own name, and sue and be sued as if single ?
New York.	$50.	Yes.
North Carolina.	Not in force.	Yes, if registered as a trader with consent of her husband.
North Dakota.	$50.	Yes.
Ohio.	$2500.	Yes.
Oklahoma.	$50.	Yes.
Oregon.	$50.	Yes.
Pennsylvania.	Not in force.	Yes, but she cannot become surety, indorsor or guarantor.
Rhode Island.	$500.	Yes.
South Carolina.	$50.	Yes.
South Dakota.	$50.	Yes.
Tennessee.	Not in force.	Yes.
Texas.	Not in force.	The wife's separate property and the community property are subject to the management of the husband.
Utah.	$200.	Yes.
Vermont.	$40.	Yes, but she cannot convey or mortgage real estate without joinder of her husband, nor can she become surety for her husband, nor can she become surety for any one, except by mortgage made as stated.
Virginia.	Not in force.	Yes.
Washington.	$50.	Yes.
West Virginia.	Not in force.	Yes, if she lives separate and apart from her husband.
Wisconsin.	$50.	Yes, if her husband deserts or neglects or refuses to support her and her children.
Wyoming.	$50.	Yes.

EXEMPTION LAWS

In most of the states there exists a homestead law which exempts certain real property from liability of attachment by the creditors of the owner. Certain personal property is also exempt, and in most cases wages are exempt for a specified period. The following is approximately the law in the several states and territories : —

ALABAMA. — Homestead consisting of 80 acres in the country or any lot in a city or town, with improvements, not exceeding $2000 in value. Personal property to the value of $1000.

ALASKA. — Homestead, not exceeding 160 acres in the country or one quarter acre in a city or town, and not exceeding $2500 in value. Specified articles of personal property to the value of about $1000 and wages for sixty days if necessary for the support of the family.

ARIZONA. — Homestead, where claimant actually resides, to the value of $2500. Personal property to the value of $500. One half of wages for thirty days.

ARKANSAS. — Homestead in the country not exceeding 160 acres to the value of $2500, but not less than 80 acres regardless of value ; in a city, not exceeding one acre to the value of $2500, but not less than one quarter acre. Personal property, consisting of wearing apparel and other property to the value of $500 for the head of a family or $200 for a single person. Wages for sixty days if debtor has no other property and they are less than the amount allowed.

CALIFORNIA. — Homestead to the value of $5000. Certain specified articles of personal property not to exceed $1000. Wages for thirty days if necessary to support family, but one half of wages is liable for debt contracted for necessaries.

COLORADO. — Homestead actually occupied by family to the value of $2000. Certain specified articles of personal property. Sixty per cent of wages over $5 per week due the head of a family.

CONNECTICUT. — Homestead actually occupied to the value of $1000, if claim is recorded. Certain specified articles of personal property. Wages to the amount of $50.

DELAWARE. — No homestead exemption, and each county has a special law as to exemption of personal property.

DISTRICT OF COLUMBIA. — Specified articles of personal property. To the head of a family, wages for two months not exceeding $200.

FLORIDA. — Homestead consisting of 160 acres in country or one half acre in town, with improvements. Personal property to the value of $1000 for the head of a family residing in the state, and all wages.

GEORGIA. — By the constitution every head of a family, infirm person, etc., may claim an exemption of real or personal property or both to the value of $1600, which must be set apart. This exemption may be waived, except as to wearing apparel and certain necessaries to the value of $300. By the statutes the head of a family in the country may hold exempt 50 acres of land and 5 acres additional for each child under sixteen years old, and a dwelling to the value of $200. In any city an exemption of $500 is allowed. Specified articles of personal property and all laborer's wages are exempt. Either exemption may be claimed but not both.

HAWAII. — One half acre of land actually cultivated for family use and a building lot and house to the value of $250. Specified articles of personal property and one half of wages.

IDAHO. — Homestead to the value of $5000 for a married man or $1000 for a single man if declaration is filed. Specified articles of personal property and wages for thirty days if necessary for support.

ILLINOIS. — Homestead to the value of $1000. Personal property to the value of $400 for married persons or $100 for single persons. Wages to the amount of $15 per week for the head of a family.

INDIANA. — Real or personal property to the value of $600 for resident householders or married women. Wages of householders not exceeding $25 at one time.

IOWA. — Homestead of one half acre in town or 40 acres in country, not less than $500 in value. Specified articles of personal property, burial lot of one acre or less. Wages for ninety days.

KANSAS. — Homestead occupied by the family of the owner of one acre in town or 160 acres in country. Specified articles of personal property. Wages for three months when necessary for support of family.

KENTUCKY. — Homestead of a debtor, who is a bona fide householder, with a family resident in Kentucky, living on the land, to the value of $1000. Specified articles of personal property. Ninety per cent of wages up to $75 per month and $67.50 from all higher wages.

LOUISIANA. — Homestead of 160 acres, rural or urban, bona fide occupied and including implements, animals, etc., to the value of $2000. Specified articles of personal property and all laborer's wages.

MAINE. — Homestead to the value of $500 if recorded, and a cemetery lot. Specified articles of personal property. Wages to the amount of $20, except that only $10 is exempt in a suit for necessaries.

MARYLAND. — Wearing apparel, books or tools and $100 worth of personal property besides. Wages to the amount of $100.

MASSACHUSETTS. — Homestead to the value of $800 if recorded. Specified articles of personal property. Wages to the amount of $20, except that only $10 is exempt in a suit for necessaries.

MICHIGAN. — Homestead of 40 acres and a house in country, or house and lot in city, to the value of $1500. Specified articles of personal property not less than $500 in value. Wages to the amount of $30 to a householder, or $15 to others.

MINNESOTA. — Homestead, actually occupied, of 80 acres in country, one half acre in an incorporated village of less than 5000 inhabitants or one quarter acre in a town of more than 5000 inhabitants. Specified articles of personal property. Wages for thirty days to the amount of $25.

MISSISSIPPI. — Homestead to a householder, 160 acres in extent, to the value of $2000 in the country (or $3000 if a homestead declaration is filed) or $3000 in town. Personal property consisting of specified articles in the country or any articles to the value of $250 in town. Wages amounting to $50 per month.

MISSOURI. — Homestead consisting of 160 acres to the value of $1500 in the country; 5 acres to the value of $1500 in places of less than 10,000 inhabitants; 30 square rods to the value of $1500 in places having from 10,000 to 40,000 inhabitants; and 18 square rods to the value of $3000 in places having more than 40,000 inhabitants. Specified articles of personal property, or any personal property not exceeding $300 in value. Ninety per cent of wages due to the head of a family.

MONTANA. — Homestead of 160 acres in country or one quarter acre in town to the value of $2500. Specified articles of personal property for the head of a family. Wages for thirty days if necessary for support of the family, but only one half of such wages exempt on a claim for necessaries furnished.

NEBRASKA. — Homestead of 160 acres in country or two lots in town to the value of $2000. Personal property to the value of $500 if the debtor has no real estate. Wages for sixty days.

NEVADA. — Homestead to the value of $5000. Specified articles of personal property. Wages for one month to the amount of $50.

NEW HAMPSHIRE. — Homestead to the value of $500 and a cemetery lot. Certain specified articles of personal property and wages to the amount of $20 except as against debts for necessaries.

NEW JERSEY. — Homestead to the value of $1000 if advertised and recorded. Personal property to the amount of $200, wearing apparel and all wages.

NEW MEXICO. — Homestead to the value of $1000. Specified articles of personal property and, to the head of a family owning no homestead, any property real or personal in addition to that specified, to the amount of $500. Wages for sixty days if necessary for support of the family.

NEW YORK. — Homestead to the value of $1000 if notice is recorded. Certain specified articles of personal property to the head of a family and, in addition, personal property to the value of $250, except for the purchase price. Wages for sixty days if necessary for support of the family.

NORTH CAROLINA. — Homestead to the value of $1000. Personal property to the value of $500. Wages for sixty days if necessary for support of the family.

NORTH DAKOTA. — Homestead of 160 acres in country or two acres in town to the value of $5000. Specified articles of personal property for the head of a family and in addition certain kinds of personal property to the value of $500.

OHIO. — Homestead to the value of $1000. Specified articles of personal property. Wages for three months, except that ten per cent of all wages is liable for necessaries.

OKLAHOMA. — To the head of a family, a homestead to the value of $5000 (in town must contain from one quarter acre to one acre); specified articles of personal property, a cemetery lot and wages for ninety days. To one not the head of a family, less personal property, a cemetery lot and current wages.

OREGON. — Homestead of from 20 acres to 160 acres in country and from one lot to one block in town to the value of $1500. Specified articles of personal property. Wages for thirty days to the amount of $75 when necessary for support.

PENNSYLVANIA. — Real or personal property to the value of $300 and all wages.

RHODE ISLAND. — A burial lot, a pew in church, specified articles of personal property and wages to the amount of $10, except as against debts for necessaries.

SOUTH CAROLINA. — Homestead to the value of $1000. Personal property to the value of $500 to the head of a family or $300 to one not the head of a family.

SOUTH DAKOTA. — Homestead of 160 acres in country or one acre in town to the value of $5000. Burial lot, pew in church, specified articles of personal property and besides personal property to the value of $750 to the head of a family or $300 to one not the head of a family. Wages for sixty days if necessary for support of the family.

TENNESSEE. — Homestead to the value of $1000. Specified articles of personal property. Wages to the amount of $36 for a person drawing $40 per month or less.

TEXAS. — Homestead of 200 acres in country or one city lot in town to the value of $5000. Specified articles of personal property, or if they do not exist in kind, other articles to the value of $500. Current wages for personal services.

UTAH. — Homestead to the value of $1500 and in addition $500 for wife and $250 for each other member of the family. Specified articles of personal property. One half of wages for thirty days, if necessary for support, but not less than $30 per month.

VERMONT. — Homestead to the value of $500. Specified articles of personal property. Certain wages are exempt.

VIRGINIA. — Homestead of real or personal property to be selected by the debtor to the value of $2000 and in addition certain specified articles of personal property. One month's wages to a householder, to the amount of $50.

WASHINGTON. — Homestead to the value of $2000. Specified articles of personal property. Wages to the amount of $100, but only a small amount of wages exempt on a claim for necessaries furnished.

WEST VIRGINIA. — Homestead to the value of $1000, if duly recorded. Personal property, including wages, to the amount of $200.

WISCONSIN. — Homestead of 40 acres in country or one quarter acre in town to the value of $5000. Specified articles of personal property. Wages for three months, not exceeding $60 per month.

WYOMING. — Homestead of 160 acres in country or a house and lot or lots in town to the value of $1500. To the head of a family, wearing apparel and specified articles of personal property to the value of $500. To a single man, wearing apparel and tools, books, etc., to the value of $300. One half of wages for sixty days if necessary for support of the family.

CHATTEL MORTGAGES

The following paragraphs give the principal statutory provisions as to chattel mortgages in the different states and territories.

ALABAMA. — Must be recorded in the office of the probate judge in the country where the mortgagor resides and also in the county where the property is located, unless immediately removed to the county of the mortgagor's residence. If the property is moved to another county before the lien is satisfied the mortgage must be recorded in that county within three months. There is no provision for renewal of the mortgage.

ALASKA. — Must be filed with the Commissioner. Becomes void as against creditors after one year, unless renewed by the mortgagee, who must file an affidavit within thirty days before the expiration of the year, showing his interest in the mortgage. Subsequent renewals may be made in the same way.

ARIZONA. — Must be filed in the office of the county recorder of the county where the property is and of the county where the mortgagor resides. If the property is moved it must be again recorded. Must state the residences of mortgagor and mortgagee, sum secured, rate of interest and place and date of payment, and must be accompanied by an affidavit that it is given in good faith. Is invalid on a stock of goods daily exposed to sale and in possession of the owner.

ARKANSAS. — Must be filed or recorded in the county where the mortgagor resides, or if he is a non-resident, in the county where the property is.

CALIFORNIA. — Valid only on certain specified property. Must be accompanied by an affidavit that it is given in good faith, must be duly acknowledged and must be recorded in the office of the county recorder of the county where the mortgagor resides and of the county where the property is or may be removed. There is no provision for renewal.

COLORADO. — Under $300 and for a period of not more than six months may be filed and not recorded. In other cases must be recorded in the office of the recorder of the county where the property is. Remains valid for two years if for $2500 or less; for five years if for more than $2500 and less than $20,000; and for ten years if for more than $20,000. May be extended for two years by filing an affidavit of the mortgagee, within thirty days after expiration, showing the amount unpaid.

CONNECTICUT. — Valid as to certain specified articles only. Must be duly acknowledged and recorded in the town clerk's office of the town where the property is. No provision for renewal.

DELAWARE. — Must be recorded in the office of the recorder where the property is, and within ten days after it was acknowledged. The mortgage is then valid for five years, and may be renewed.

DISTRICT OF COLUMBIA. — Chattel mortgages are seldom made, but deeds of trust are used instead. Must be recorded in the office of the recorder of deeds within ten days after execution. No provision for renewal.

FLORIDA. — Must be recorded within ninety days after execution in the office of the clerk of the circuit court where the property is. Need not be renewed.

GEORGIA. — Must be recorded in the office of the clerk of the superior court where the mortgagor resides, or if he is a non-resident, where the property is. Need not be renewed.

HAWAII. — Must be recorded in the office of the registrar of conveyances at Honolulu.

IDAHO. — Must be recorded in the office of the county recorder of the county where the property is, and must be accompanied by an affidavit that it was given in good faith and not to hinder, delay, or defraud creditors. If the property is removed to another county the mortgage must be again recorded within ten days. No provision for renewal.

ILLINOIS. — Must be recorded in the office of the recorder of the county where the mortgagor resides, or if he is a non-resident, where the property is located. Is valid for three years, or until the earlier maturity of the debt, and may be renewed for one year by filing an affidavit within thirty days before expiration showing the amount remaining unpaid.

INDIANA. — Must be recorded within ten days after execution in the office of the recorder of the county where the mortgagor resides, or if he is a non-resident of the county where the property is. No provision for renewal.

IOWA. — Must be recorded in the office of the recorder of the county where the mortgagor resides. The wife must join in a mortgage on exempt property, except a mortgage for the purchase price. No renewal is necessary.

KANSAS. — Must be filed with the register of deeds of the county where the property is, and of the county where the mortgagor resides, if within the state. Is valid for two years from date of filing. May be renewed within thirty days before expiration by filing an affidavit of mortgagee showing the amount remaining unpaid. The wife must join in a mortgage on exempt property.

KENTUCKY. — Must be recorded in the office of the clerk of the county where the property is. Is valid for five years. No renewal is necessary.

LOUISIANA. — There are no statutory provisions as to chattel mortgages in Louisiana.

MAINE. — Must be recorded in the office of the town clerk where the mortgagor resides, or if he is a non-resident, in the county where the property is. No renewal is necessary.

MARYLAND. — Must be recorded within twenty days in the city or county where the mortgagor resides, or if he is a non-resident, where the property is, and must be accompanied by an affidavit that the consideration is true and bona fide, and also an affidavit that the mortgagor has not paid the tax. No provision for renewal.

MASSACHUSETTS. — Must be recorded within fifteen days in the office of the town clerk where the mortgagor resides, or if he is a non-resident, where the property is. Need not be renewed.

MICHIGAN. — Must be recorded in the office of the city or town clerk where the property is, and also where the mortgagor resides. Is valid for one year, and may be renewed within thirty days preceding expiration by filing an affidavit of the mortgagor showing the amount remaining unpaid.

MINNESOTA. — Must be filed in the office of the city, town, or village clerk where the mortgagor resides, or if he is a non-resident, where the property is. Is valid for six years, or for two years after the earlier maturity of the debt. No renewal is necessary. The wife must join in a mortgage of household articles.

MISSISSIPPI. — Must be recorded with the chancery clerk of the county where the property is. If the property is removed to another county it must be re-recorded within one year. When the remedy to enforce the mortgage has been barred by the statute of limitations, it may be revived by a statement on the record of the mortgage that the mortgage has been extended, which statement must be made within six months after expiration of the term.

MISSOURI. — Must be filed or recorded in the office of the recorder of deeds of the county where the mortgagor resides, or if he is a non-resident, of the county where the property is. Is valid for five years if filed and for the life of the debt if recorded.

MONTANA. — Must be filed in the office of the county clerk of the county where the mortgagor resides, or if he is a non-resident, of the county where the property is, and must be accompanied by an affidavit that it was given in good faith. Is valid for one year, or the earlier maturity of the debt, and may be renewed within sixty days after expiration by filing an affidavit of the mortgagee showing the amount remaining unpaid.

NEBRASKA. — Must be filed in the office of the county clerk of the county where the mortgagor resides, or if he is a non-resident, of the county where the property is. Remains in force for five years. No provision as to renewal.

NEVADA. — Must be recorded in the office of the recorder where the mortgagor resides and where the property is located, and must be accompanied by an affidavit that it was given in good faith. Is not valid for less than $100. No provision as to renewal.

NEW HAMPSHIRE. — Must be recorded in the office of the town clerk where the mortgagor resides, or if he is a non-resident, where the property is located, and must be accompanied by an affidavit that it was given in good faith. No provision for renewal.

NEW JERSEY. — Must be recorded in the office of the county clerk or register of deeds of the county where the property is. No renewal is necessary.

NEW MEXICO. — Must be filed or recorded in the office of the probate clerk of the county where the property is. Is valid for one year and may be renewed within thirty days before expiration by filing an affidavit of the mortgagee, showing the amount unpaid.

NEW YORK. — Must be filed with the register, county clerk or town clerk of the place where the mortgagor resides, or if he is a non-resident, of the place where the property is. Remains valid for one year, and may be renewed within thirty days before expiration by filing an affidavit of the mortgagee showing the amount remaining unpaid.

NORTH CAROLINA. — Must be recorded in the office of the register of deeds of the county where the mortgagor resides, or if he is a non-resident, of the county where the property is. No renewal is necessary.

NORTH DAKOTA. — Must be recorded in the office of the register of deeds where the property is. Remains valid for three years, and may be renewed within ninety days before expiration by filing an affidavit of the mortgagee showing the amount remaining unpaid.

OHIO. — Must be filed in the office of the county recorder of the county where the mortgagor resides, or if he is a non-resident, of the county where the property is. Is valid for three years, and may be renewed within thirty days before expiration by filing a true copy of the mortgage and a statement of the interest of the mortgagee.

OKLAHOMA. — Must be filed in the office of the register of deeds of the county where the property is, and if removed to another county must be re-filed. Is valid for three years and may be removed within thirty days before expiration by filing a copy of the mortgage and a statement of the amount due.

OREGON. — Must be filed or recorded in the office of the recorder or county clerk of the county where the property is. If removed to another county it must be re-recorded within thirty days. Need not be renewed.

PENNSYLVANIA. — Must be recorded in the office of the recorder of deeds of the county where the property is. Is valid only on certain specified property and for not less than $500. Is valid for three months only, but if the mortgagee files an affidavit within three months, showing the amount unpaid, it is valid for one year after the maturity of the debt.

RHODE ISLAND. — Must be recorded within five days after execution in the office of the the town clerk or recorder of deeds where the mortgagor resides, or if he is a non-resident, where the property is. No provision for renewal.

SOUTH CAROLINA. — Must be recorded within ten days in the office of the clerk of the court of common pleas or of the register of mesne conveyances of the county where the mortgagor resides, or if he is a non-resident, of the county where the property is. No provision for renewal.

SOUTH DAKOTA. — Must be filed in the office of the register of deeds of the county where the property is. It is valid for three years and may be renewed by an affidavit of the mortgagor, filed within thirty days preceding expiration, showing the amount remaining unpaid.

TENNESSEE. — Must be registered in the office of the register of deeds of the county where the mortgagor resides, or if he is a non-resident, of the county where the property is. Is valid for six years. No provision for renewal.

TEXAS. — Must be filed in the office of the county clerk of the county where the mortgagor resides, or if he is a non-resident, of the county where the property is. It is valid for six years, and may be renewed by filing an affidavit of the mortgagee, within three months before expiration, showing that the debt is not paid and the amount remaining unpaid.

UTAH. — Must be recorded in the office of the recorder of the county where the mortgagor resides, or if he is a non-resident, of the county where the property is. Remains in force for one year and may be renewed by filing an affidavit of the mortgagee, within thirty days after expiration, showing the amount remaining unpaid. Is not valid after five years.

VERMONT. — Must be recorded in the office of the city or town clerk where the mortgagor resides, or if he is a non-resident, where the property is. Need not be renewed.

VIRGINIA. — Must be recorded in the office of the county or city clerk where the property is. No provision for renewal.

WASHINGTON. — Must be filed within ten days in the office of the county auditor of the county where the property is, and must be accompanied by an affidavit that it is given in good faith. Remains valid until the mortgage is due, and may be renewed for one year at a time by filing an affidavit of the mortgagee, within two years after expiration, showing the amount remaining unpaid.

WEST VIRGINIA. — Must be recorded in the office of the clerk of the county court where the property is. If removed to another county it must be re-recorded within three months. No renewal is necessary.

WISCONSIN. — Must be filed in the office of the clerk of the city, town or village where the mortgagor resides, or if he is a non-resident, where the property is. Remains valid for two years and may be renewed by filing an affidavit of the mortgagee, within thirty days before expiration, showing the amount remaining unpaid.

WYOMING. — Must be recorded in the office of the county clerk of the county where the property is. Remains valid for the term of the mortgage and six months thereafter, and may be extended for one year at a time by filing an affidavit of the mortgagee, within six months after expiration, setting forth his claim.

GLOSSARY

Abandonment: In marine insurance, the giving up of property partly destroyed to the insurer, the owner's purpose being to claim the full amount of insurance.

Abrogate: To repeal; to annul or destroy; to abolish entirely.

Acceptance: In mercantile law (1) the act by which the person upon whom a bill of exchange or other order is drawn engages to pay it. (2) The bill after it has been accepted.

Acceptance for Honor: Acceptance for the protection of the drawer, by a person other than the drawee.

Acceptor: One upon whom a bill of exchange is drawn and who agrees to pay it at maturity.

Accommodation Indorser: One who indorses commercial paper without consideration, in order that another may raise money upon it.

Accommodation Paper: Commercial paper for which no consideration passed between the original parties.

Accord and Satisfaction: The settlement of a dispute or the satisfaction of a claim by an executed agreement between the parties, giving the aggrieved party something different in amount or value from the thing claimed.

Acknowledgment: The act by which a party who has executed an instrument declares or acknowledges it before a competent officer to be his or her act or deed.

Action: The formal means of recovering one's rights in a court of justice — a suit at law.

Act of God: Any accident resulting from a physical cause which is irresistible, such as lightning, tempest, etc.

Adjudication: The act of a court in giving judgment in a suit or controversy.

Administrator: One who is appointed to take charge of the property or estate of a person who died without having made a will.

Affidavit: A statement in writing, signed by the person making it, and sworn to by him before an officer authorized to take oaths.

Agency: The relation existing between two parties by which one is authorized to do certain acts for the other with a third party or parties.

Agent: A person who acts for another called his principal.

Age of Consent: The age at which infants are capable of entering into a valid contract of marriage.

Alias: A Latin word meaning otherwise or hitherto.

Alien: One who was born out of the jurisdiction of the country of his residence, and, never having been naturalized into it, owes allegiance to the sovereign of another country.

Alienate: To convey the title to property.

Alien Enemy: An alien who is the subject of a hostile power.

Alimony: An allowance made to a wife by order of the court, out of her husband's estate or income, during a suit for divorce or separation or at its termination, for her support for life or for a shorter period.

Annulment: The act of making void.

Ante-dated: Dated at a time earlier than the actual date.

Appraise: To set a price or value upon.

Appurtenance: In a deed or lease, anything that will go with the land, as a right of way, or a yard which has always been used with it.

Arbitration: The investigation and determination of a cause or matter in controversy, by an unofficial person or persons mutually chosen by the contending parties.

Articles of Copartnership: The written agreement by which a copartnership is formed.

Assent: Act of agreeing to anything; consent.

Assets: Property available for the payment of debts.

Assign: To make over; to transfer to another.

Assignee: (1) The person to whom a failing debtor transfers all of his remaining property, for the purpose of having it distributed among his creditors. (2) One to whom anything is assigned.

Assignment: (1) A transfer of his property to an assignee by a failing debtor. (2) A transfer by one person to another of any property, personal or real.

Assignor: One who assigns property.

Attachment: The seizure of property by legal process, for the purpose of bringing the same into the custody of the law.

Attestation: The act of witnessing an instrument in writing, and subscribing one's name to it as a witness.

Attorney in Fact: An agent appointed by power of attorney.

Award: The decision of arbitrators.

Bailee: One to whom the goods of another are delivered for a certain purpose.

Bailment: The delivery of goods to another in trust for a certain purpose, the goods to be returned after the object of their delivery has been accomplished.

Bailor: One who delivers goods to another under a contract of bailment.

Bank Note: A promissory note payable at a bank.

Bankrupt: One who has done some act which renders him liable to be proceeded against by his creditors under the bankruptcy law.

Bankruptcy: The condition of one who has been declared by a court of bankruptcy to be a bankrupt.

Barter: To trade by exchange of goods, in distinction from trading by the use of money.

Beneficiary: (1) In life insurance, the person to whom a policy is made payable. (2) The person for whose benefit another holds the legal title to real estate.

Beyond Seas: Denotes absence from the country, and is generally held to mean absence from the particular state.

Bill of Exchange: A direction in writing by the person who signs it ordering the one to whom it is addressed to pay a third person a definite sum of money at a specified time.

Bill of Lading: A document delivered by a carrier to one sending goods by him, acknowledging that they have been received by him for transportation to a certain place. It is both a receipt and a contract.

Bill of Sale: An agreement in writing by which one person sells his interest in personal property to another.

Blank Indorsement: The indorsement of a negotiable instrument by merely writing the name of the indorser without mentioning the name of any person to whom it is to be paid.

Bona Fide: In good faith. Openly and without deceit or fraud.

Bond: A written and sealed instrument by which one party agrees to pay to another a certain amount of money or to perform a certain act.

Breach: In the law of contracts, the violation of an agreement or obligation.

By-laws: The private laws or regulations made by a corporation for its own government.

Capital Stock: The fund or property as a whole, contributed or supposed to have been contributed to a corporation at its organization as its property.

Caveat Emptor: Latin phrase meaning "Let the buyer beware," and applying to a case in which the thing sold is before the buyer and he examines it.

Certificate of Deposit: A certificate issued by a bank or banker, showing that a certain sum of money has been deposited there, payable to a certain person or to his order or to the bearer.

Certificate of Stock: A certificate given by the proper officers of a corporation, showing that a certain person owns a certain number of shares of the capital stock.

Certified Check: A check drawn by a depositor on a bank and accepted by the bank as valid. After certification the amount of the check is taken from the depositor's account and set aside to meet the check.

Cestui que Trust: One for whose benefit property is held by a trustee.

Charter: (1) A special act of legislature creating a particular corporation. (2) A formal instrument by which a government grants special rights or privileges to a particular person or persons. (3) To hire or let a vessel or part of it.

Charter Party: The written instrument by which the owner of a vessel lets it, or a part of it, to another.

Chattel: An article of personal property.

Chattel Mortgage: A conditional sale of personal property, which is to become void if a certain thing happens. Chiefly used as a security for the payment of money.

Check: A written order for money drawn upon a bank or banker and payable immediately.

Chose in Action: A thing of which one has not the possession, but only a right to demand by action at law.

Chose in Possession: Personal property of which one has the actual possession.

Civil Law: The system of law of ancient Rome. Also used in distinction from criminal law.

Client: A person who employs an attorney to act for him in any legal business.

Collateral Security: A separate obligation given to guarantee the performance of another contract.

Common Carrier: One who, as a business, undertakes for hire to transport from place to place passengers or goods of all who choose to employ him.

Common Law: The old law of England that derives its force from long usage and custom.

Compromise: An agreement between a debtor and his creditors, by which they consent to accept a certain proportion of the amounts claimed and discharge him from the remainder.

Concurrent: Existing together.

Condition Precedent: A modifying clause of an agreement requiring some act to be performed by one person before another is liable, or in order to make him liable.

Condition Subsequent: A part of an agreement relating to a future event, upon the happening of which the obligation is no longer binding upon one of the parties to a contract.

Consanguinity: Relation by blood.

Consideration: The reason or inducement in a contract upon which the parties consent to be bound.

Consignee: One to whom merchandise given to a carrier by another person for transportation is directed.

Consignor: One who gives merchandise to a carrier for transportation to another.

Copartnership: Same as partnership.

Copyright: The exclusive privilege, secured from a government, of printing, publishing, and selling copies of writings or drawings.

Corporation: A collection of individuals united by authority of law into one body under a special name, with the capacity of perpetual succession and of acting in many respects as an individual.

Counter-claim: Same as set-off.

Covenant: Any promise contained in a sealed instrument.

Coverture: The legal state and condition of a married woman.

Crime: A wrong which the government takes notice of, as injurious to the public, and for the commission of which it inflicts a punishment.

Curtesy: The estate a man has in the lands of his wife upon her death, in case a living child has been born to them during their marriage.

Damages: Compensation in money to be paid by one person to another for an injury inflicted by the one upon the other.

Days of Grace: Days (usually three) allowed by custom for the payment of bills and notes beyond the day specified for payment on the face of them.

Decree: The judgment or decision of a court of equity.

Deed: A written agreement signed, sealed, and delivered by which one person conveys lands to another.

De Facto: In fact, actually.

Default: Omission; neglect or failure.

Defendant: The party against whom an action or suit is brought.

Demand: The request for payment of a claim.

Demise: A conveyance of an estate in real property for life or for years.

Deponent: One who makes oath as to the truth of a written statement.

Deposit: A bailment or delivery of goods to be kept and returned without recompense.

Deviation: In the law of marine insurance, a voluntary departure without necessity from the regular course of the specific voyage insured.

Devise: To grant by will.

Disability: Want of qualification; incapacity to do a legal act.

Disaffirmance: The annulling or canceling of a voidable contract.

Discount: (1) To take interest in advance. (2) A deduction from a price asked, or from an account, debt, or demand.

Dishonor: The non-payment of negotiable paper when it is due.

Divorce: The separation of husband and wife by decree of the courts.

Domicile: The place where a man has his permanent home, and to which he intends to return if absent.

Dower: The right of a widow to the use or ownership of some portion of the real estate owned by her husband.

Draft: Same as bill of exchange.

Drawee: The person upon whom a bill of exchange is drawn, and who is directed to make the payment.

Drawer: The person who draws or makes a bill of exchange.

Duress: Personal restraint or compulsion.

Easement: The right in the owner of one piece of land to use the land of another for a particular purpose.

Emblements: Growing crops of any kind produced by expense and labor.

Eminent Domain: The right of the sovereign power to take private property for public purposes.

Enact : To make a law, or to establish by law.

Entail : To limit the succession of real property; that is, to control the descent of real property after the death of the owner.

Equity of Redemption : The right which a mortgagor has to redeem his estate after the mortgage has become due.

Escheat : The reverting of land to the state upon the death of the owner without lawful heirs.

Escrow : A deed or bond delivered to a third party to be held and delivered to the grantee or creditor upon the performance of some condition.

Estate : An interest in property.

Estoppel : A rule of law which precludes a man from denying certain facts or conditions in consequence of his previous allegations or conduct or admissions.

Eviction : The dispossession of a person by process of law from land which he has previously held.

Executed Contract : One in which nothing remains to be done by either party.

Execution : (1) A written command issued to a sheriff or constable, after a judgment, directing him to enforce it. (2) The act of signing and sealing a legal instrument, or giving it the form required to make it a valid act.

Executor : A person named in a will to carry out its provisions.

Executory Contract : One in which something remains to be done on one or both sides.

Ex post Facto Law : A law which renders criminal an act done previously and which when done was innocent.

Extradition : The surrender by one government to another of a person charged with a crime.

Fee Simple : Full ownership in lands.

Firm : All the members of a partnership taken collectively.

Foreclosure : The process of cutting off the right or interest of the mortgagor and his assignees in mortgaged premises.

Forgery : The fraudulent making or altering of a written instrument.

Franchise : A privilege, or right, conferred upon individuals by grant from the government.

Fraud : Any cunning, deception, or artifice used to circumvent, cheat, or deceive another.

Freehold : An estate of inheritance or a life estate.

Freight : The compensation to be paid a carrier for the transportation of goods, or the goods themselves while being transported.

Good Will : Benefit arising from the fact that persons used to trading or doing business at a particular place will continue to do so ; it is a property subject to transfer.

Grant : To transfer by deed.

Guarantor : One who makes a guaranty.

Guaranty: A contract whereby one person engages to be answerable for the debt or default of another person.

Guardian: One who is entitled to the custody of the person or property of an infant or one not able to take care of himself, as an idiot or insane person.

Guest: A person received and entertained at an inn or hotel.

Idiot: One who never had reasoning power.

In Statu Quo: In the same state or condition as before.

Inchoate: Incipient; incomplete.

Incorporate: To form into a corporation.

Indemnity: Compensation for damage suffered or that which is given or promised to a person to prevent him from suffering damage.

Indorsee: One to whom an indorsement is made.

Indorsement: (1) A name, with or without other words, written on the back of negotiable paper. (2) The agreement implied in one's writing his name on the back of negotiable paper, to pay it if the principal debtor does not.

Indorsement in Blank: An indorsement in which the name of the indorsee is omitted.

Indorsement in Full: An indorsement to a definite person.

Indorsement without Recourse: An indorsement by which the indorser passes the title to the instrument, but does not assume the liability of an indorser.

Indorser: One who makes an indorsement on negotiable paper.

Infant: In law, one under the age of twenty-one years.

Insolvency: State of being unable to pay one's debts.

Insurable Interest: Such an interest in the thing insured that the person possessing it may be injured by the risk to which the thing insured is exposed.

Insurance: A contract of indemnity against loss from certain causes.

Insurer: The party agreeing to furnish insurance.

Intestate: One who dies without making a will.

Invalid: Of no legal force.

Issue: In real property law, all persons who have descended from a common ancestor.

Joint Stock Company: A species of partnership possessing some of the characteristics of corporations.

Joint Tenants: Two or more persons to whom land is conveyed by deed or devised by will, the survivor taking the whole interest.

Judgment: The final determination by a court of the rights of the parties in an action.

Jurat: The certificate at the end of an affidavit showing when and before whom it is sworn.

Jurisdiction: The legal authority of a court.

L.S.: An abbreviation of a Latin phrase, and means " the place of the seal." It now takes the place of a seal in some jurisdictions, or denotes where a seal is to be affixed.

Landlord: (1) One who owns and rents or leases lands or houses. (2) The keeper of an inn.

Law Merchant: The general body of usages in matters relative to commerce.

Lease: A contract by which one grants to another for a period the use of certain real estate.

Legacy: A gift by will; commonly applied to money or personal property.

Legal Tender: That kind of money which may legally be offered in payment of a debt.

Lessee: A person to whom a lease is made.

Letters of Administration: An instrument issued out of the court having jurisdiction, granting power to settle the estate of one dying without leaving a will.

Letters Testamentary: An instrument out of the court having jurisdiction, granting power to the person named as executor in a will to carry out the provisions of the will.

Lien: A right which one person has to retain the property of another by way of security for a debt or claim.

Liquidated Damages: The sum of money agreed by the parties to a contract in advance, to be paid in case of breach.

Litigation: A suit at law.

Lunatics: Persons who have lost their reason.

Mandamus: A writ issued by a superior court to an inferior court or to an officer, commanding something to be done.

Mandate: A bailment of personal property in which the bailee undertakes without compensation to do something for the bailor with the thing bailed. (The bailor is generally termed the mandator, and the bailee the mandatary.)

Maturity: The time at which commercial paper legally becomes due.

Merger: The absorption or extinguishment of one contract in another.

Minor: Same as infant.

Misrepresentation: A false and fraudulent statement made by a party to a contract, relative to a particular fact, with the knowledge that the statement is untrue.

Mortgage: A grant or conveyance of an estate or property to a creditor for the security of a debt, to become void on payment of such debt. The mortgagor is the one who gives the mortgage upon his property; the mortgagee the one to whom the mortgage is given.

Municipal Law: The rules prescribed by the supreme power in a nation or state.

Necessaries: Such things are as proper and essential for the sustenance of man.

Negotiable Paper: An instrument, as a bill or note, which may be transferred from one to another by indorsement or delivery.

Nominal Damages: Those given for the violation of a right from which no actual loss has resulted.

Non-suit: The name of a judgment given against a plaintiff when he is unable to prove his case.

Non-user: A failure to use rights and privileges.

Notary Public: A public officer whose principal function is to administer oaths and take acknowledgments.

Notice of Protest: A notice given by the holder of a bill or note to the drawer or indorser, that the bill has been protested for refusal of payment or acceptance.

Nuisance: Anything that unlawfully injures or damages a person in the enjoyment of life and property.

Oath: A pledge given by the person taking it that his promise is made under an immediate sense of his responsibility to God.

Offeree: One to whom an offer is made.

Offeror: One who makes an offer.

Open Policy: An insurance policy in which there is no valuation of the thing insured.

Oral Contract: A contract made by means of spoken words.

Ordinance: A rule, or order, or law. Usually applied to the acts or laws passed by the common council of a city.

Outlawed: A debt is said to be outlawed when it is barred by the statute of limitations.

Par: Equality of value. Bills of exchange and stocks are at par when they sell for their face value. They are above or below par when they are worth more or less than their face value.

Paramount Title: In real property law, denotes the superior or better title. The title which will prevail when a dispute as to ownership arises.

Parol Contract: Any agreement not under seal. It is often used as synonymous with oral contract.

Partnership: The relationship resulting from an agreement between two or more persons to place their money, effects, labor, and skill, or some or all of them, in some enterprise or business, and divide the profits and bear the losses in certain proportions.

Party Wall: A wall common to two adjoining estates.

Pawn: A sale of personal property on condition that it may be redeemed within a certain time.

Payee: The person to whom the payment of any kind of commercial paper is directed to be made.

Perjury: A willfully false statement by one who is lawfully sworn and required to tell the truth, made in a judicial proceeding and in relation to a matter that is material to the point in question.

Per Se: In itself.

Personal Property: Such things as are movable, and that may be taken by the owner wherever he goes.

Plaintiff: The person who brings a suit at law.

Pledge : A bailment of personal property to secure the payment of some debt or the fulfillment of some agreement.

Pledgee : The bailee of personal property under a pledge.

Pledgor : The bailor of personal property under a pledge.

Policy : The written contract of insurance.

Post-dated : Having a date subsequent to that at which the agreement is actually made.

Post-mortem : After death.

Power of Attorney : A written instrument under seal by which one party appoints another to act for him.

Premium : The consideration or price paid for insurance.

Presumption : An inference of the law, from certain facts, of the existence or truth of some other fact or proposition.

Probate : The act or process of proving a will.

Promisee : One to whom a promise is made.

Promisor : One who makes a promise.

Prima Facie : Literally, at the first appearance. Prima facie evidence is that which is sufficient to establish a fact unless it be rebutted or contradicted.

Principal : (1) A party for whom another is authorized to do certain acts with third parties. (2) A sum of money at interest.

Promissory Note : A written promise, signed by the party promising to pay a certain sum of money at a certain time to a person named, or to his order, or to the bearer.

Prosecute : To proceed against by legal measures.

Protest : A formal declaration in writing by a notary public of the demand and refusal to pay a note or bill.

Proxy : (1) One who represents another. (2) A writing by which one authorizes another to vote in his place.

Public Enemies : Those who belong to a nation at war with another.

Public Policy : The principles under which the freedom of contract or private dealing is restricted by law for the good of the community.

Quantum Meruit : As much as he deserves.

Quasi : As if; analogous to. (Quasi corporations are bodies like corporations, and yet are not strictly corporations.)

Quitclaim Deed : A form of deed in the nature of a release.

Ratification : Giving force to a contract which otherwise is not binding.

Real Estate : Same as real property.

Real Property : That which is fixed or immovable, and includes land and whatever is erected or growing on it, together with what is beneath or above the surface.

Realty : Same as real property.

Receiver : Usually a person appointed by a court to take and hold property in dispute, the property of an insolvent, or the property of a dissolved corporation.

Recoupment: A reduction or diminution of damages on account of a breach of warranty or defects in performance.

Release: An instrument in the general form of a deed that in distinct terms remits the claim to which it refers, and being under seal, although reciting only a nominal consideration, extinguishes the debt.

Remainder: An estate in real property to take effect after another's estate is terminated.

Remedy: The legal means employed to enforce a right or redress an injury.

Rent: Compensation for use of real property.

Replevin: An action to recover the possession of goods wrongfully taken and retained.

Rescission: The annulling or dissolution of contracts by mutual consent or by one party.

Residence: The place where a man makes his home, or where he has dwelt permanently for a considerable length of time.

Residuary Devisee: The person named in a will who is to take all the real property remaining after all of the other devises are paid.

Residuary Legatee: The person named in a will who has the residue of the personal property after the payment of the other legacies specifically mentioned in the will.

Revert: To fall again into the possession of the donor, or of the former proprietor.

Right of Survivorship: The right that the survivor or survivors have to take the interest of their deceased joint tenant, which in other cases would go to his heirs.

S.S.: Abbreviation for the Latin word " Scilicet," meaning to wit; that is, to say.

Sale: The transfer of the ownership in property for a price in money.

Satisfaction: Payment of a legal debt or demand; the discharging or canceling of a judgment or a mortgage, by paying the amount of it.

Seal: An impression upon any impressible substance, or a piece of paper pasted on with intent to make a seal of it.

Seaworthiness: The fitness of a vessel in all respects of materials, equipment, and construction for the service in which it is employed.

Set-off: A claim which one party has against another who has a claim against him; a counter-claim.

Severance: The removal of fixtures from the land.

Shipper: One who gives merchandise to another for transportation.

Simple Contract: A contract, either oral or written, which is not under seal.

Special Partner: One who invests capital in a partnership, and is liable for its debts only to the extent of his investment.

Specialty: A contract under seal.

Specific Performance: Performance of a contract according to its precise terms. It is frequently compelled by a court of equity.

Statute: An act of the legislature.

Statute of Frauds: An English statute, generally reënacted in this country, requiring certain contracts to be made in writing, designed to prevent fraud and perjury.

Statute of Limitations: A statute requiring an action to be commenced within a certain time after the demand has arisen. It limits the time to sue, hence its name.

Stock: Same as capital stock. It is also used to denote the shares into which the capital stock is divided.

Stockholder: The owner of one or more shares of the stock of a corporation.

Stoppage in Transitu: A stoppage by the seller of goods sold on credit before they reach their destination upon his learning of the buyer's insolvency.

Subagent: A person appointed by an agent to perform some duty relating to the agency.

Subcontract: A contract made by one who has agreed with a third party to perform labor or services, for the whole or part performance of that labor or service.

Subpœna: A writ commanding the attendance of a person in court.

Subrogation: The substitution of one person or thing in the place of another, particularly the substitution of one person in the place of another as a creditor, with a succession to the rights of the latter.

Suit: The prosecution of some claim or demand in a court of justice.

Summons: A writ directed to a sheriff or other officer, requiring him to notify the person named that an action has been commenced against him in the court from which the writ issues, and that he is required to appear upon a certain day and answer the complaint in such action.

Surety: One who has agreed with another to make himself responsible for the debt, default, or misconduct of a third party. Similar to guarantor.

Tenant: One to whom another has granted for a period the use of certain real estate.

Tender: An offer of a sum of money in satisfaction of a debt or claim, by producing and offering the amount to the creditor and declaring a willingness to pay it.

Testator: A person who makes a will.

Tort: A private wrong or injury, other than that arising from the breach of a contract, for which damages can be collected.

Trade-mark: The symbol, emblem, or mark which a manufacturer puts upon the goods he manufactures.

Trespass: Any wrongful act of one person whereby another is injured.

Trustee: One who holds property for the benefit of another.

Uberrima Fides: The most perfect good faith.

Ultra Vires: The acts or proceedings of a corporation done beyond the scope of its powers.

Underwriter: Same as insurer.

Usury: Illegal interest.

Validity: Legal strength or force; the quality of being good in law.

Vendee: One to whom anything is sold; a purchaser; a buyer.

Vendor: A seller; the person who sells a thing.

Verbal: Parol, by word of mouth.

Verdict: The finding of a jury reported to the court.

Vested: Already in force.

Void: Of no force or effect.

Voidable: That may be avoided; not absolutely void.

Waiver: The abandonment of a right, or a refusal to accept it.

Ward: A minor under guardianship.

Warranty: An agreement to hold one's self responsible, if a certain thing does not turn out as represented.

Waste: Damage or destruction done or permitted to land or trees by a tenant.

Wharfinger: The owner of a wharf who maintains it for the purpose of receiving and shipping merchandise.

Will: An instrument by which a person disposes of his property, to take effect after his death.

Writ: A precept in writing issued from a court, either as the commencement of a suit or incidental to its progress, and requiring the performance of a certain act or giving authority to do it.

ABBREVIATIONS

Abb. N. C.	Abbott's New Cases.
Ala.	Alabama.
App. Div.	Appellate Division.
Ark.	Arkansas.
A. & E.	Adolphus & Ellis.
Barb.	Barbour.
Blatchf.	Blatchford.
B. & C.	Barnewell & Creswell.
Cal.	California.
Can.	Canada.
Ch. Div.	Chancery Division.
Conn.	Connecticut.
Cush.	Cushing.
C. & P.	Carrington & Payne.
Del.	Delaware.
Eng.	English.
Exch.	Exchequer.
Fed. Rep.	Federal Reporter.
Fla.	Florida.
Ga.	Georgia.
Harr.	Harrington.
Heisk.	Heiskell.
How.	Howard.
Humph.	Humphrey.
H. L. C.	House of Lords Cases.
Ill.	Illinois.
Ind.	Indiana.
Johns.	Johnson.
Kans.	Kansas.
Ky.	Kentucky.
La.	Louisiana.
La. An.	Louisiana Annual.
Ld. Raymond	Lord Raymond.
L. R. Q. B.	Law Reports, Queen's Bench.
L. T. N. S.	Law Times, New Series.
Mass.	Massachusetts.
Md.	Maryland.

Me.	Maine.
Met. or Metc.	Metcalf.
Mich.	Michigan.
Minn.	Minnesota.
Miss.	Mississippi.
Mo.	Missouri.
Mo. App.	Missouri Appeal.
M. & W.	Meeson & Welsby.
Neb.	Nebraska.
N.C.	North Carolina.
N.H.	New Hampshire.
N.J. Eq.	New Jersey Equity.
N.J. L.	New Jersey Law.
N.Y.	New York.
Ohio St.	Ohio State.
Ont.	Ontario.
Ore.	Oregon.
Pa.	Pennsylvania.
Pa. St.	Pennsylvania State.
Paige Ch.	Paige's Chancery.
Pick.	Pickering.
Q. B.	Queen's Bench.
Q. B. D.	Queen's Bench Division.
R.I.	Rhode Island.
Sandf. Ch.	Sandford's Chancery.
S.C.	South Carolina.
Tenn.	Tennessee.
Tex.	Texas.
Tex. Civ. App.	Texas Civil Appeal.
T. & C.	Thompson & Cook.
U.S.	United States.
Va.	Virginia.
Vt.	Vermont.
Wall.	Wallace.
Wend.	Wendell.
Wis.	Wisconsin.
W. Black.	Wm. Blackstone.
W. Va.	West Virginia.

INDEX

15885